The Family Dynamic

A CANADIAN PERSPECTIVE

The Family Dynamic

A CANADIAN PERSPECTIVE

MARGARET WARD
CAMBRIAN COLLEGE

Nelson Canada

International Thomson Publishing
The trademark ITP is used under licence

Published in 1994 by
Nelson Canada,
A Division of Thomson Canada Limited
1120 Birchmount Road
Scarborough, Ontario M1K 5G4

Canadian Cataloguing in Publication Data

Ward, Margaret, 1935–
The family dynamic : a Canadian perspective

Includes bibliographical references and index.
ISBN 0-17-603499-4

1. Family. 2. Family - Canada. I. Title.

HQ518.W3 1993 306.8 C93-095448-3

Acquisitions Editor Charlotte Forbes
Editorial Manager Nicole Gnutzman
Supervising Editor Linda Collins
Developmental Editor Heather Martin
Art Director Bruce Bond
Design Liz Nyman
Cover Illustration Susan Leopold

Printed and bound in Canada
BBM 96

CONTENTS

CHAPTER 9 *The Second Time Around*

PART 5 • MIDLIFE AND BEYOND

CHAPTER 10 *Middle Age and the Empty Nest*

CHAPTER 11 *Grey Power and the Sunset Years*

PART 6 • SOCIAL PROBLEMS IN THE FAMILY

CHAPTER 12 *The Family Beleaguered—When Problems Come*

PREFACE

This book has been written for people like my own students at Cambrian College. Most of them are interested in earning a diploma that will help them find employment in a human services field. They are concerned that all of their subjects relate in a practical way to their future employment goals. There are also a few each year who plan to move on to university and need a theoretical grounding.

I have not attempted to write an exhaustive study of Canadian families, but rather have tried to open up the subject and to present the variety in our family experiences. I have also introduced challenges and issues to stimulate thought and discussion about the current state and the future direction of families. The orientation of the book is practical and tries to show how the theory relates to the students' lives and their future work situations.

One reviewer referred to this work as a "smorgasbook," a term I consider a compliment. I have tried to spread out a sampling of the rich fare of information available on Canadian families in the hope that readers will be tempted to feast where they have tasted.

ACKNOWLEDGMENTS

It is a joy to be able to thank people publicly for their many private kindnesses. I offer my gratitude and thanks

- to my colleagues at Cambrian College for their continuing interest and encouragement;
- to Caroline Hallsworth and the other library staff at Cambrian for their good nature and invaluable assistance in tracking down resources and information;
- to my friends Barbara Tremitiere and Jack Crouch and my daughter Mary Ward, who refused to let me give up;
- to the staff at Nelson Canada, especially Jim Rosza, Dave Ward, Charlotte Forbes, Heather Martin, and Linda Collins, for their unfailing encouragement, patience, and generosity, even through the worst of times;
- to my colleagues who reviewed the manuscript at various stages: Franceen Blidner, Fanshawe College; Patricia Kaiser, New Brunswick Community College; Mahfooz Kanwar, Mount Royal College; Gordon W. Ralph, Central Regional College; Michiko Sakamoto-Senge, Camosun College; John Sangster, Centennial College; David Sernick, Seneca College; and Ronald J. Solinski, Lethbridge Community College; for their thoughtful responses;
- and finally to my students over the years, who have both infuriated and challenged me in ways impossible to catalogue through their questions, comments, and stories.

PART 1

The Family

CHAPTER 1

What Is a Family?

OBJECTIVES

- To introduce the concept of family and to review a variety of definitions.
- To consider theoretical views of the family, along with their strengths and weaknesses.
- To review ways researchers study families.

Dear Ann Landers: I am writing to you with a simple yet confusing question. Please bear with me.

My parents were divorced years ago. The divorce was final May 30, and my father was remarried June 5 of the same year. It was some time before I accepted his new wife, Donna. After they had been married for about two years, I was asked if I would mind sharing my birthday dinner with Donna's brother, Ron. I said it would be just fine. We had a joint birthday dinner on Dec. 13 and had a super time. Ron and I went together to my father's New Year's Eve party. By March we were madly in love, and we were married July 23. Ron is 10 years older than I, and Donna is about 10 years younger than my father.

Two years later Ron and I decided to have a baby. Now comes the tricky part. What is the relation between our new baby girl and Donna? Is she her grandma or her aunt? Donna prefers to be her aunt. What relation is my father to our child? Is he her grandpa or her uncle? Is my father still my father or is he my brother-in-law? Is Donna still Ron's sister or is she his mother-in-law? My father and I have the same in-laws. The only thing that seems quite clear is that my in-laws are the baby's grandparents any way you look at it. However, since they are also my father's wife's parents, doesn't that make them the baby's great-grandparents?

When I tell this story I get confused looks. There is no incest involved yet people think we are quite strange. Please help me sort this out before our baby can talk so we can explain to her who's who and what's what. Thanks for your help.

—*DaughterSister-in-law, Columbus, Ohio*

Dear Columbus: I don't know whether this requires an effort of the left brain or the right brain but you lost me right after your daughter was born.

Source: *The Sudbury Star*, 17 September 1991, p. B3.

What is a family? Almost all of us have been members of at least one family. We see families all around us, both in real life and in the media. We all know what families are, yet when we actually try to define "family," as the Ann Landers column shows, the task is not so simple after all. Do we include only the people who live in our household? Should we count all of our relatives? One of the difficulties in defining family is that we use the word for many different things—our ancestors, our parents and brothers and sisters, all of our relatives, and our spouses and children. One commonly used definition in North America is the "traditional" family; this includes father, mother, and their children.

What Is a Family?

Definitions of the family have changed according to time and place. For example, in England during the Middle Ages, the town-dwelling family was not a private unit of parents and children. Husband, wife, and children shared their living space and daily activities such as work, meals, and prayers with servants, apprentices, journeymen, and unmarried or widowed relatives. Nowadays we would tend to define such a grouping as a household rather than as a family (Statistics Canada, 1992).

In other social groups, the family has been based on one person married to several others of the opposite sex. The general term for this practice is *polygamy*. *Polygyny* refers to a man who has several wives, and is currently the practice in many Moslem countries. Polygyny was encouraged among the early Mormons in the United States, and is still reported occasionally by the popular press (e.g., Solomon, 1979). *Polyandry*, in which one woman may have several husbands (as described in the past among some of the Inuit), is a less common family form (Larson, 1976). While these practices may seem far removed to those raised in a society that upholds *monogamy* (marriage to only one person at a time) in its customs, religious beliefs, and laws, they do have some practical implications. For example, if a family consisting of one husband and several wives applies for immigration status in Canada, should they all be accorded marital status? If so, are these marriages considered legal in the new country as they were in the country of origin? If not, who is considered the sole wife, and what becomes of the "extras"? Is it fair to exclude polygamous individuals as potential immigrants?

Communal living, which exists in Canada among some groups, provides still another image of family. Acting on the basis of their religious beliefs, the Hutterites share financial resources, work assignments, and even meals on a community basis. Accommodation, furniture, and clothing are provided according to need. From about the age of three, children spend most of their days in school. They eat their meals in the communal dining hall, seated separately from their parents, according to their age and sex. The community takes precedence over the family unit. The Hutterites have met with prejudice in some areas where they have settled, partly because their communal farming methods were seen as unfair competition, and partly because their lifestyle was so different from that of their neighbours (R. Macdonald, 1985; Peter, 1976).

THE LEGAL FAMILY

In Canada, the term family differs according to who is defining it. There are a variety of legal definitions. The census, which occurs every five years, counts what it calls the census family (Statistics Canada, 1992). Family members are defined in a host of laws and regulations. For example, people cannot marry certain individuals, such as parents or brothers and sisters, because they are too closely related. Child-welfare laws define parents, and specify which relatives are close enough to be allowed to adopt a child without agency approval (Katarynych, 1991). Immigration law considers certain relatives to be close family members, and thus to be given preference in entering the country. Some municipal bylaws may define family for purposes of zoning. Government regulations determine family for such services as medical and family benefits and special visiting programs in penitentiaries (Correctional Service of Canada, 1982). In fact, everyone who works in a human services field must learn specific legal definitions of the family in the course of their work.

SOCIAL DEFINITIONS OF THE FAMILY

Various groups and social institutions also define the family. A number of churches have studied the family recently and, in the process, have had to state what they consider a family (e.g., Canadian Council of Catholic Bishops, 1980; United Church of Canada, 1989a). Hospital intensive-care units usually permit visits by immediate family members only. Schools accept permission and absence notes from parents only, unless they are informed otherwise.

Various ethnic groups may also regard family membership in different ways. For example, aboriginal peoples in Canada tend to have a very broad definition of family membership, and children are often cared for by relatives as a matter of course. If a social worker defines a family as consisting of parents and children only, then he or she may feel that some aboriginal parents are neglecting or even

SOME DEFINITIONS OF THE FAMILY

STATISTICS CANADA
Census family: Refers to a now-married couple (with or without never-married sons and/or daughters of either or both spouses), a couple living common-law (again with or without never-married sons and/or daughters of either or both partners), or a lone parent of any marital status, with at least one never-married son or daughter living in the same dwelling.

Source: Statistics Canada (1992). *1991 Census Dictionary.* Ottawa: Statistics Canada, p. 119.

UNITED CHURCH OF CANADA
By family we mean persons who are joined together by reason of mutual consent (marriage, social contract or covenant) or by birth or adoption/placement.

Source: United Church of Canada (1989). "A Definition of Family," *All Kinds of Families,* Fall, p. 14.

ZONING BYLAW, SUDBURY, ONTARIO
Family: One or more persons whether or not related by blood, marriage, adoption and including domestic servants or gratuitous guests who live together in one dwelling unit and maintain a common household as distinguished from a group of persons occupying a boarding house, rooming house, lodging house, club, hotel, fraternity, sorority or institutional building.

CORRECTIONAL SERVICE OF CANADA
The following family members are eligible to participate in the (private family visiting) program: wife, husband, common-law partners, children, parents, foster-parents, brothers, sisters, grandparents and, in special cases, in-laws.

Source: Correctional Service of Canada (1982). *Private Family Visiting Program.* Ottawa: Author.

abandoning their children, when these parents feel their offspring are safe within their caring family circle (M. Ward, 1984a).

Underlying many of the differences in the way people regard families are two basic concepts: the nuclear family and the extended family. The *nuclear family* is made up of married parents and their children. Nuclear families come in two forms, depending on our perspective: families of origin or orientation are those we are born into and raised in; families of procreation are those we form through marriage, and in which we raise our children. We can imagine society made up of interlocking sets of nuclear families with many individuals being members of two or more. This pattern only works neatly if all couples get married, have biological children, and never divorce. As it is, many families do not fit this description. Children may have more than one family of orientation. When parents divorce, their children may have two families to which they are connected, with one parent in each. Adopted children start out in one family, which they may or may not remember, and are raised in another. With the current trend toward making contact with birth parents, adoptees may resume membership in their birth families. Some adults have more than one procreative family. This occurs most often with single mothers who later marry and with individuals who remarry. Occasionally two families result when an individual enters an illegal bigamous relationship.

The second concept is the *extended family,* which encompasses the nuclear family and all other relatives. Once again, there is variation in what constitutes membership. Some people include more distantly related cousins, for example, than do others. In the past, most families that lived in small rural communities in Canada were related through marriage or descent. For these individuals, the entire community could be considered their extended family. In both nuclear and extended families, genetic or "blood" relationship is important, although other types of relationship, such as marriage or adoption, are recognized by most people.

PERSONAL DEFINITIONS

There are also quite personal definitions of the family. In many families, a close friend is counted as a member. Unmarried heterosexual couples or homosexual couples who live together may regard themselves as families, although legally they may be considered single individuals sharing accommodation. In other cases, where there has been a high level of conflict and where there is continuing bad feeling, a family may not consider one member as belonging, even though he or she is a legal member. This is especially true when parents have disowned a child or when a marital partner has disappeared but no divorce has occurred. Different family members may have separate ideas of who belongs, e.g., a child may include her divorced father, while her mother does not.

Thinking About Families

Just as there are many definitions of the family, so there are many theories about what makes families work and how they relate to society as a whole. Sociologists have used a number of approaches, either singly or in combination, to try to find some order and meaning to these questions. It is important to study theories because they help shape government policy, agency regulations, methods of therapy, and other ways society relates to families. Each approach tells us something of interest about families; each, however, also has limitations on how much it can explain. As we discuss theories, there are some questions we should keep in mind:

1. How does the theory account for both change and continuity in family patterns?
2. Does the theory show the way society and the family influence each other?
3. What does the theory say about relationships within the family?
4. How has the theory affected the policies and practices of government, social agencies, and others who deal with families?

How Does Society Influence Families?

Families do not exist in isolation—they are part of a vast network. Family members are part of the larger society in which they live through their membership and participation in the neighbourhood, schools, work, religious organizations, and social and recreational groups. The influence of society operates through social institutions, such as schools and religious groups; laws; political and economic factors; pressure from activist groups; and the mass media. Society provides expectations for behaviour. For example, family members are supposed to look after one another physically and emotionally, and are not supposed to harm one another. They are expected to socialize children to meet certain standards of behaviour. Society also limits family behaviour by means of laws such as those against violence, by the level of benefits provided through social assistance, and through stigma and labelling of those who do not conform to societal expectations.

The ecological theory looks at the relationship of family and society. According to James Garbarino (1982), families are part of interlocking systems that influence each other at four levels.

LEVEL 1—THE MICROSYSTEM

The *microsystem* consists of the small groups in which people interact face-to-face. For adults this might involve family, workplace, and organizations of which they are members. The microsystem most directly affects the quality of life through relationships with individuals, therefore its nature and quality are important. Each family member has a different microsystem; e.g., those of young children include whoever cares for them during the day. They may be cared for in their own homes by either of their parents or by someone else. They may be looked after in another home by a babysitter, who may or may not be approved by a licenced home-day-care agency. Others go to licenced day-care centres. Some spend part of the day in a nursery school (Park, 1991).

Figure 1.1

THE ECOLOGY OF HUMAN DEVELOPMENT

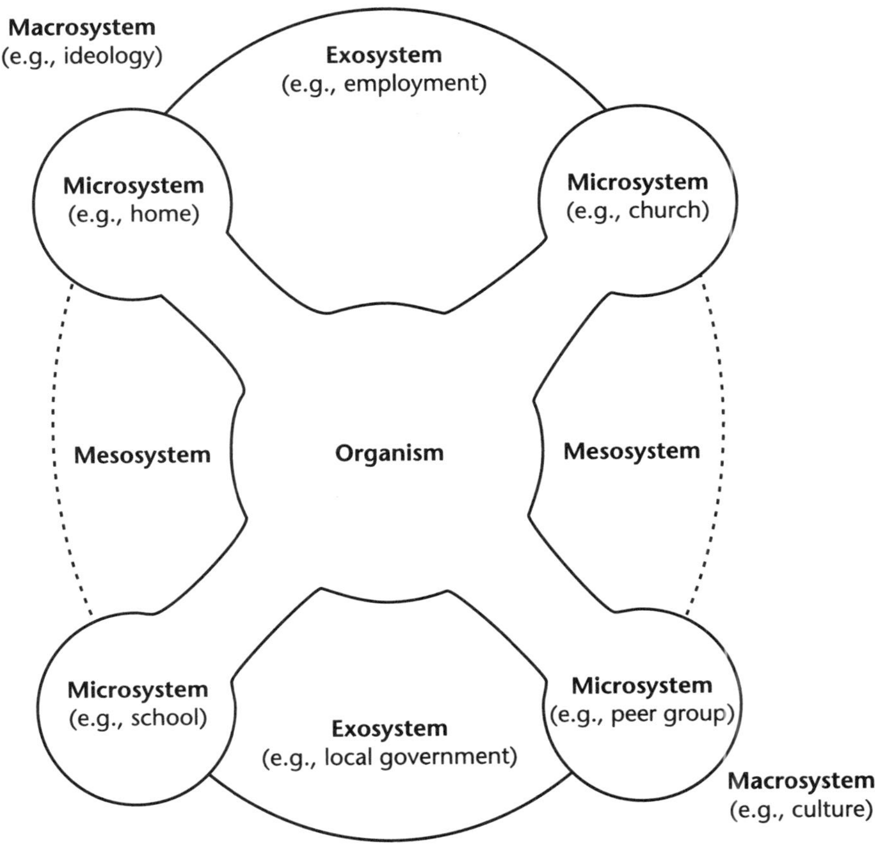

Source: James Garbarino (1982). *Children and Families in the Social Environment.* New York: Aldine, p. 26.

LEVEL 2—THE MESOSYSTEM

The *mesosystem* is made up of the relationships between two or more groups of which the individual is a member. A child's mesosystems would consist of the relationship between parents and the day-care centre, or between parents and the school, or between parents and the neighbourhood. The quality of the connections is important—whether they are weak or strong, negative or positive. For parents, the mesosystem might consist of the relationship between the family and the workplace.

LEVEL 3—THE EXOSYSTEM

The *exosystem* is a setting in which individuals do not take an active part, but which has an affect on them through the mesosystem or microsystem (Garbarino, 1982). For children, this could consist of expectations in the parent's workplace or decisions made by the school board. For parents, it might also involve the school board, which can affect family life by closing the school during a workday to allow for staff development, thus forcing parents to make special arrangements for the care of their children.

Many of the important decisions made by exosystems that affect the family are not even thought of as family-related (Garbarino, 1982). Some obviously are, such as funding provided day-care centres to permit subsidies for low-income families. In the workplace, fringe benefits are clearly family oriented; even these are affected, however, by the definitions of the family that are used. More companies are including long-term homosexual relationships for benefits purposes, although this is by no means universal. Other policies, both in the government and private sector, although not seen as "family" issues, also affect families. Governmental decisions such as the location of major highways can affect children's routes to school or travel time to the day-care centre or place of employment. Policies and assumptions in the workplace can also have an impact on family life. One of these is the assumption that if you are on the executive track, you will work long hours and "move to move up." The time demanded can interfere with family life, and relocating can disrupt natural support networks, such as the extended family.

Although the exosystem may seem to be made up of immovable institutions, individuals and groups have often been successful in changing it. For example, unions have affected working conditions; parent groups have prevented the closing of local schools; and many pressure groups working together have forced government to increase funding for day care.

LEVEL 4—THE MACROSYSTEM

The *macrosystem* consists of a society's ideology and culture. These basic shared beliefs and ways of doing things are the basis on which policy decisions are usually made (Garbarino, 1982). Most social policies are based on assumptions concerning the pattern of relationships between the sexes, such as the division of labour between males and females both inside and outside the family. It is also assumed that families have the chief responsibility for passing on to their children the values generally held by society (Lero & Kyle, 1991). Such policies tend to change in response to problems that arise out of changing economic or political situations; however, change is often slow.

EVALUATION OF THE ECOLOGICAL VIEW

Garbarino's theory better explains change that occurs in families than it does change that occurs in society as a whole. Although this theory does address family relationships in the microsystem, its real strength is in its explanation of how society and family interact. The awareness that a policy in one area may have quite unintentional effects on the family can be important if service is provided by more than one social agency.

Macro or Micro?

We can use Garbarino's diagram to help classify other theories, most of which concentrate on either the macrosystem or the microsystem. Macro theories principally study the values of a society and the way those values affect the family. These viewpoints include the structural-functional and conflict theories. Micro theories emphasize relationships within individual families. Among these are the symbolic-interaction, systems, and developmental theories. We will consider first the macro and then the micro theories of the family.

The Family as an Institution

The structural-functional theory views the family as an institution among other social institutions, such as the legal and educational systems. As such, it has a structure and function that both connect it with society as a whole and separate it from other institutions.

According to this view, the family has a number of important functions in society. First, it provides for the physical protection of its members. Usually this means that one or more family members must have a job or some source of income to support the family. Second, the family provides for the emotional well-being of its members. Third, it produces and shapes new individuals who will as adults be prepared to take their place in society. This shaping process is called *socialization* (Parsons & Bales, 1955).

A major contribution of the structural-functional theory is its development of the concepts of values and norms, and how they are passed on from one generation to the next. *Values* are social principles accepted by a society as a whole or by groups within that society. One example is the principle of one marriage for life. Many people do not have such a marriage, but may still hold it as their ideal, i.e., they value it. Values often vary among different groups in society. Some groups give drug dealers high status because they can make large amounts of money; others consider them to be dangerous parasites.

Ways of behaving that are typical of a certain group are called *norms*. Often social groups feel that norms are also values, i.e., that people ought to behave like most others if they are to be considered worthwhile members of society. At one time it was the norm for young women to be married by the time they were 19 or 20 years old. If a woman remained unmarried until she was 24 or 25 years old, she was considered to be an old maid, and people wondered what was the matter with her. In some groups nowadays, it is the norm for a young man to have had sexual experience with young women before he graduates from high school. If he does not have such experience, some of his peers may wonder if he is abnormal. In their eyes, if he does not behave like the others, i.e., if he does not follow the norm, then something is wrong with him. To such people no sexual experience whatsoever and homosexuality are both unacceptable. In groups that value individual freedom of choice, any of these forms of behaviour are seen as acceptable options.

More generally, the "proper" way of doing things in society, i.e., the basic knowledge of how to survive and how to take part in social life, is passed on to each generation through the process of socialization. Socialization can occur directly through teaching, e.g., in learning manners, or indirectly, through examples and unstated expectations of the people surrounding us. Most of us have formed ideas of how newlyweds, parents, or teachers "ought" to act. The cultural rules that tell us what, where, when, how, and why we should do something are referred to as *social scripts*. If people don't behave in the expected way, they leave themselves open to criticism or subtle pressure to conform.

According to structural-functionalists, the family is organized around three statuses: husband/father, wife/mother, and child. A *status* is a social position that carries a set of expectations concerning suitable behaviour, regardless of who fills the position. This behaviour is termed a *role* (Lundy & Warme, 1990). Structural-functionalists believe that role specialization increases the efficiency with which families function. In particular, they state, the husband/father is an instrumental (active or doing) specialist and the wife/mother is an expressive (emotional) specialist. Thus the man is responsible for economic support of the family members and the woman for their physical and emotional nurture (Parsons & Bales, 1955).

EVALUATION OF THE STRUCTURAL-FUNCTIONAL VIEW

The most important strength of the structural-functional theory is its explanations of how the family is related to other institutions and how it contributes to society as a whole. It also emphasizes family strengths, such as cooperation between members, rather than weaknesses (Porter, 1987). However, there are a number of difficulties with the structural-functional approach. Although this theory usually provides good explanations as to why society maintains values across generations, it is not as clear in explaining why families and society change. In fact, television programs may be quicker to recognize major changes in family patterns (Goldberg, 1990). The structural-functional theory often ignores topics such as family violence and sexual abuse, and sees delinquency and crime as social rather than as family problems (Porter, 1987).

ON THE FASTTRACK

Source: *The Toronto Star*, 2 May 1992, p. F8.

Another difficulty is that this view is not very tolerant of family differences. Anything that departs from the breadwinner-father and homemaker-mother raising their children is regarded as abnormal or defective in some way. Thus the majority of Canadian families would be labelled as inferior (Eichler, 1981; Porter, 1987).

Nevertheless, it is important for anyone involved in human service delivery to understand structural-functional theory. It has long been the basis for providing social services to families. If a man, woman, and children are living together, they are assumed to be a family. The father/husband is seen as responsible for supporting the family and the mother/wife is seen as responsible for the personal care of family members, especially child care. It is therefore often easier for a man to receive homemaking and other household help when there is no woman present in the home, and for a woman to receive financial support when there is no man present, than vice versa. This idea of the family has been responsible for "man in the house" rules, in which a woman could lose her social assistance benefits if a man was living with her. In all provinces welfare benefits used to be restricted to single mothers and their children. Single fathers were not eligible until the regulations were successfully challenged in the courts as being unconstitutional (Eichler, 1987).

In addition, the structural-functional view tends to assume that society has one set of norms and values. This is not true of a multicultural society such as Canada. Different groups have their own norms for choosing marriage partners, for deciding whether the new couple should live with relatives or by themselves, for the division of labour between husband and wife, and for many other aspects of family life (Nett, 1988). In fact, different ethnic and social groups fall along a continuum with nearly complete separation from the dominant society at one extreme, and assimilation (i.e., taking on the values and practices of the majority group) at the other extreme. Separation and assimilation can occur by choice or can be forced upon a particular group (Herberg, 1989). For example, the Hutterites, whom we have already discussed, have chosen to keep apart from mainstream society. On the other hand, during the construction of the Canadian Pacific Railway, Chinese labourers were not allowed to bring family members into Canada and were forced to live in ghettos (Nett, 1988). Immigrants may choose to take on the customs and values of the majority culture in Canada. For instance, East Indians may choose their own marriage partners instead of agreeing to arranged marriages. However, native children who attended residential schools were forced to speak English.

The Family as Centre for Conflict

As with structural-functionalism, conflict theories tend to view the family from the perspective of society. Instead of emphasizing the positive aspects of the relationship, however, they stress negative influences. Conflict theories are particularly concerned with power relationships. Marxism, for example, views the family as part of a system in which a few people exploit the majority, and reap the benefits of their labour. Political economists study the relationship between the system of property rights and power within a society (Cheal, 1989b). Currently the most influential of conflict-based theories is feminism. Although there are variations among them, feminist thinkers agree that family relations, and society as a whole, are based on the power and authority of men. As a result, women are limited in their choices and are denied opportunities to develop themselves (Duffy, 1988).

Feminist thinkers criticize structural-functionalism for supporting the patriarchal view of the family. They state that the political and social control men hold over women is tied to the belief that a man is naturally head of the family. Within the family, as in the wider society, men tend to have more power and control than women and tend to receive more benefits (Duffy, 1988). This is reflected, for example, in the imbalance in responsibility for household work when both spouses are employed (Luxton, 1986). Focusing power in the hands of one family member can also lead to abuse of that power, including the use of violence.

The values that support men in a power role are widespread in our society. The inequality between men and women begins in the socialization of earliest childhood. Boys are expected to be active and aggressive, and girls to be nurturing and sensitive to others. Often the differences that result from socialization are pointed to as "natural" differences between men and women; these then form the basis for further socialization. In adulthood, it is difficult for a woman to choose not to marry and have children. There is widespread acceptance of the idea that a woman can be fulfilled only as a wife and mother (Duffy, 1988). It is still viewed as somewhat unnatural for a woman to remain single and childless, and it may even be seen as a sign that she is inadequate because she is unable to attract a husband.

Feminists also point to higher levels of pay in traditionally male-dominated occupations such as mining, construction, law, and medicine. Traditional "female" occupations such as providing child care, preparing and serving food, and cleaning tend to be lower paid. Part of the original basis for lower pay was the notion that women's work merely provided luxuries for the family; it was the man's work that supported the family. Furthermore, women, rather than men, are expected to take time off work for child care. This, in turn, reduces their ability to advance their careers and makes them more dependent on men (Duffy, 1988).

EVALUATION OF CONFLICT THEORIES

Conflict theories, including feminism, explain why families and societies change—a result of shifts in the balance of power. They point to the way that values in society are passed from generation to generation, and how they affect family life. Conflict theories are not strong, however, in demonstrating how families contribute to society as a whole.

Feminist thought, in particular, has a continuing and growing impact. It is a driving force producing much current research on the family, by both men and women. One example already mentioned is the study of the difference in the amount of housework done by men and women (Luxton, 1986). Feminists have also supported equity in the workplace, including pay and promotion opportunities.

The Family as Interacting Members

In contrast to structural-functional and conflict theories, symbolic-interaction theorists use a micro approach to family relationships. They feel that the best way of understanding relations between family members is to examine the meanings each sees in other members' words and actions. Such meanings affect behaviour directly (Burgess & Locke, 1960). For example, one spouse may say to the other, "Why are you reading that book?" The partner might interpret the question to mean, "Why are you wasting your time?" or "Why did you choose that book and not another?" or something else again. The response will differ according to the meaning read into the question. Interpretations develop out of the history of interactions between family members. Behaviour and objects gain meaning, i.e., become symbols, through the process of interaction (Porter, 1987).

A major contribution of the symbolic-interaction theory is an expansion of role theory. In contrast to structural-functionalists who study roles from the viewpoint of society, symbolic-interactionists study roles from the viewpoint of the individual (Porter, 1987). Individuals develop a sense of self through the attitudes of others and through relationships with parents, peers, and other significant individuals. They also develop a sense of the roles they are expected to fulfill. As they interact with others, individuals are able to anticipate the behaviour of others, and can tailor their own to match. This ability to put oneself in another's place is called "role-taking." Role expectations come from past experiences. For example, husbands and wives may have different notions of how they should behave in marriage based on their experiences in their families of origin. As a result they may have problems because their role expectations clash. Role strain is a sense of discomfort or tension felt by one who has difficulty meeting role expectations. A stepparent who tries to fill the role of a birth parent experiences such strain.

EVALUATION OF THE SYMBOLIC-INTERACTION POSITION

One of the values of symbolic-interaction is the emphasis it places on the individual's responsibility in shaping his or her view of the world. Since it explains individual sameness and change, it has been used as a basis for family therapy. If a therapist can help family members change their interpretations of behaviour, then the quality of their interaction can be improved.

However, symbolic-interaction has been criticized for the micro view that is its main strength; it pays little attention to the impact of the wider society on family relationships. Thus it ignores factors such as laws, economics, social class, or values, and does not explain society-wide changes in families.

Fair Trade

According to exchange theory, much of family life can be viewed in terms of costs and benefits. Most of us have an idea of how much we are worth in terms of our abilities, personality, appearance, and even possessions. We expect to get the best return for what we provide in relationships at the least cost to ourselves. For example, if we feel we are reasonably attractive, we usually choose someone as a mate who is also good-looking, or we look for some other benefit, such as an exceptionally pleasant personality. We also go by the rule that when we receive favours, they must be repaid. Similarly, we expect favours we have given to be returned (Brinkerhoff & Lupri, 1989).

CRITIQUE OF EXCHANGE THEORY

Exchange theorists have helped us understand decision-making in families. For the most part, exchange theorists have focussed on husband-wife relationships. For instance, they have studied marital interaction as a bargaining process that occurs when one member wishes to change family rules (Cheal, 1989a). Power in families is not shared equally by the spouses; in many families, the husband has the advantage in education, income, prestige, social status, and even size. As a result, he has more resources with which he can bargain. In such situations, there is not equal exchange; rather, one spouse exerts power over the other (Brinkerhoff & Lupri, 1989).

The Family System

A third micro view of the family is the systems approach. This concept comes partly from structural-functional thought, which regards the family as an important part of the social system. It has also grown out of general systems theory, which originated in the field of engineering, but soon expanded into many other areas (Cheal, 1991).

A *system* contains a set of interrelated parts. Like all systems, anything that affects one part of the family will affect all parts (R. Hill, 1971). For example, if one parent loses his or her job, all family members have to make do with less money.

In the family system, there is a complementarity of roles. This means that if there is one social role such as parent, there must be the corresponding role of child. Similarly, it is impossible to be a husband without having a wife, or a sister or brother without having a sibling. Society expects certain patterns of behaviour from a person who fills a particular role. A parent is expected to be nurturing and self-sacrificing, while a child is expected to be loving and reasonably obedient. There can be difficulties if there is a misfit between the individual and the role, or if there is really no recognized role for a person. An example of the latter is the stepmother. The only roles available for her are either the mother or the stereotypical wicked stepmother, neither of which fits the reality of most family situations. When a situation like this occurs, people are described as experiencing role strain (R. Hill, 1971).

Families also contain *subsystems* (Minuchin, 1974), or smaller groupings of members within the family. The most common are the spouse (or marital), parent, and sibling subsystems. In large families, the sibling subsystem is often further subdivided into smaller groupings based on age, sex, and interest (Bossard, 1956). In families where there is a marked separation of sex roles, there may be clear male and female subsystems. In such cases, chores may be divided along sex lines, with the men and boys doing outside and maintenance work, and women and girls responsible for housekeeping and child care.

Some families do not have all of the groupings, e.g., some families have no marital subsystem because the parent is unmarried or has been separated or divorced. In many such families, however, both parents are still highly involved with their children and form the parental subsystem even though they do not live in the same household. Childless families have no parental subsystem, and one-child families have no sibling subsystem.

Systems and subsystems have *boundaries* (R. Hill, 1971), which mark who is a member and who is not. In our society, boundaries have to be open enough to allow interaction with the outside world. For example, most of us would have difficulty surviving physically without income from a job or some other source. Other sources of input include school, religious organizations, friends, and social organizations (Broderick & Smith, 1979). The same holds true for subsystems within the family. Children need to be able to interact with adults in order to receive adequate nurture and to have appropriate adult behaviour modelled for them.

According to therapists, families are usually healthiest when boundaries are clear. However, there must be contact and communication between subsystems. In some families, parents and children never seem to do anything together or share any part of life. Such families are referred to as "disengaged." In others, there is hardly any separation between parents and children; such families are described as "enmeshed." Both of these extremes are often considered unhealthy for the socialization of family members, and a happy medium seems to be the best (Minuchin, 1974). In some particularly troubled families, the boundary between the marital and child subsystems has broken down so severely that a child becomes a sexual partner of a parent.

Family-systems theorists are interested in what occurs between input from outside the system and output, i.e., what occurs between an influence coming from outside the family or subsystem and the response of its members to that influence. Often, families behave in completely different ways in the same situation, e.g., the loss of a job or a parent-adolescent argument. Carlfred Broderick and James Smith (1979) state that each family has its own rules for transforming input to output. Some rules are explicit, i.e., they are stated. Rules of this sort might cover curfews, who drives the family cars, and who shovels the driveway. Although other rules are implicit, or unstated, members are still expected to follow them. Such rules might govern how fights are settled or control other forms of family interaction (Minuchin, 1974).

There are several patterns by which families apply the rules in trying to solve problems, and these are related to feedback. One such pattern is the vicious cycle, in which the behaviour of one family member sparks a response from others that increases the original behaviour, which in turn intensifies the response. Family conflicts often escalate in this way to the point that the family breaks apart. Many families have available several responses that they have used in the past. If one does not work, they try another response that has worked before. If this still does not produce a solution, some families will fall into a vicious cycle or confusion and inertia. Others try out new forms of behaviour, such as asking advice from friends, reading books on the subject, or seeking out counselling. This last response is called *morphogenesis* (Broderick & Smith, 1979).

EVALUATION OF FAMILY-SYSTEMS THEORY

The main strength of family-systems theory is its ability to account for the impact of the behaviour of one individual on all members of the family. It also explains why behaviour continues in destructive patterns, even through generations. For these reasons, many therapists have used it as a basis for their work with families.

There have also been criticisms of this theory, however. First, the theory takes for granted that all members want the family to stay together; this is not always true. Second, the concentration on the family system as a whole overlooks the experience of individuals, especially women. This is particularly true in cases of wife assault. The systems theory assumes that destructive behaviour is the result of a vicious cycle. This explanation comes suspiciously close to blaming the victim for her own misfortune. Third, theorists often make little or no reference to important social factors, such as unemployment, that affect family life, even though systems theory is quite capable of including such influences (Cheal, 1991).

The Family Through Time

Looking at the family using one of the frameworks we have discussed is rather like looking at a snapshot that has frozen a moment in time. As we leaf through a photo album, we develop a different perspective on our families. Over the years, old faces change or disappear and new ones are added. Often the pictures mark special events—birthdays, weddings, graduations, visits, and trips. Some theorists take the "album" approach to studying the family rather than that of a single snapshot.

Developmentalists look at the entire life cycle of the family from its formation to its end. They divide the cycle into stages, the number varying according to the theorist. Stages in Duvall's framework are based on the age of the oldest child (Duvall & Miller, 1985). Later theorists such as McGoldrick do not link the stages as closely to child development (Carter & McGoldrick, 1988).

At each stage the family changes in predictable ways. Having a baby, for instance, calls on parents to accomplish certain *developmental tasks*. The idea of tasks was borrowed from child-development theory. According to Robert Havighurst, who helped popularize the concept during the 1950s, a developmental task is a task which an individual is expected by society to achieve at a particular stage in his or her development. Success in this task leads to happiness and success in later tasks; failure brings unhappiness, social disapproval, and difficulty completing later tasks (Havighurst, 1952). New parents, for instance, must adjust their family arrangements to meet the physical and emotional needs of the baby as well as their own. If they do not do so, say developmentalists, the family will often experience difficulties at later stages.

TWO DEVELOPMENTAL THEORIES

DUVALL'S EIGHT-STAGE FAMILY LIFE CYCLE

Stage 1 Married couples (without children)

2 Childbearing families (oldest child birth–30 months)

3 Families with preschool children (oldest child 2 1/2–6 years)

4 Families with schoolchildren (oldest child 6–13 years)

5 Families with teenagers (oldest child 13–20 years)

6 Families launching young adults (first child gone to last child's leaving home)

7 Middle-aged parents (empty nest to retirement)

8 Aging family members (retirement to death of both spouses)

Source: Evelyn Mills Duvall and Brent C. Miller (1985). *Marriage and Family Development*, 6th ed. New York: Harper & Row, p. 26.

McGOLDRICK'S SIX-STAGE FAMILY LIFE CYCLE

Stage 1 Leaving home: single young adults

2 The joining of families through marriage: The new couple

3 Families with young children

4 Families with adolescents

5 Launching children and moving on

6 Families in later life

Source: Betty Carter and Monica McGoldrick (1988). "Overview: The Changing Family Life Cycle: A Framework for Family Therapy." In Betty Carter and Monica McGoldrick, eds., *The Changing Family Life Cycle: A Framework for Family Therapy*, 2nd ed. New York: Gardner Press, p. 15.

The stages and tasks are related to the *social time clock*, i.e., to a socially approved timetable for certain life events. If individuals are significantly off schedule, they may experience difficulties. For example, our society is not geared to provide for adolescent mothers. They have not finished school and have difficulties supporting themselves financially. If they wish to continue their education, the system is usually not very supportive and flexible regarding child care and school attendance. Officialdom often assumes that adolescent mothers are not competent to care for their children (Miller, 1983); this is reflected in expressions such as "children raising children."

EVALUATION OF THE DEVELOPMENTAL THEORY

There have been a number of criticisms of developmental theories. First, they have been described as providing a form of lock-step that real families do not fit. For example, if stages are determined by the age of the oldest child, as with Duvall (Duvall & Miller, 1985), families with "caboose" babies or other large variations in age between oldest and youngest child do not really fit the category. Roy H. Rodgers tried to overcome this difficulty by taking into account the ages of both the oldest and youngest children, but produced an unwieldy system with twenty-four stages (Porter, 1987).

A second criticism is that such theories depend on the concept of the nuclear family. Early developmental theorists assumed that the family consisted of the husband/father, wife/mother, and children who were born at a suitable interval following their parents' marriage. Other types of families were considered defective in some way; e.g., a single-parent family was considered to be missing either the husband/father or wife/mother. Of course, many present-day families do not fit the two-parent-plus-children pattern. Originally, developmental theorists also treated men's and women's family experiences as being similar, although women's life experiences are actually more variable than men's (Cheal, 1991).

Developmental theorists are responding to changing family forms. McGoldrick, for example, has added four developmental stages for divorce, two for the post-divorce family (one each for the custodial and noncustodial parent), and three for remarriage (Carter & McGoldrick, 1988). Family life cycles of women as distinct from those of men have been described (McGoldrick, 1989). There have also been comparisons of different life patterns among women, ranging from those undertaking professional education to those who have their first child during adolescence prior to marriage (Fulmer, 1988). In spite of these attempts to include varied family forms and life patterns, developmental theory has not broken free of the nuclear-family model.

A third criticism is that developmental theory concentrates on the internal life of the family; thus it has little to say about the relationship between families and the rest of society.

In spite of its drawbacks, the developmental view does have advantages. It allows researchers to compare family life in different cultures, even those as similar as the United States and Canada. In the 1970s, for instance, Canadians delayed having children longer, had their children closer together in age, married off their last child earlier, and survived jointly longer than Americans. As a result, Canadians had longer marriages and a longer period together once their children were grown (Rodgers & Witney, 1981). Also, this perspective is fairly easy to relate to the stages in both child and adult development, such as those described by Erik Erikson (1982). Since it also provides a framework that is utilized in family therapy, developmental theory is useful for human service professionals (Carter & McGoldrick, 1988).

Researching the Family

Where do we get all of the information we have about families? Sociology, including family studies, uses many of the same methods of research as other social sciences.

One such method is the *survey*, which involves approaching people for information face-to-face, over the telephone, or by mail. The survey method has the advantage of getting answers from a large number of people; on the other hand, it is difficult to investigate a topic in any depth using this method (Sanders, 1974). One of the most important survey researchers is Statistics Canada. As well as conducting a census every five years, Statistics Canada investigates many areas of Canadian life on a continuing basis, e.g., it provides annual estimates of poverty in families. Many sociologists are also involved in survey research. In addition, magazines often publish the results of questionnaires completed by their readers. We must be careful about accepting the opinions they report as being typical of all Canadians because many of the publications circulate in the United States as well as Canada, and the opinions and experiences of Americans may be different from our own. Also, there is no way of knowing how well readers who fill out questionnaires represent all ages and classes of people. A problem with any kind

Table 1.1

FAMILIES AND FAMILY SIZE IN CANADA

Year	Total Families	Average Size
1971	5 053 165	3.7
1976	5 727 895	3.5
1981	6 324 975	3.3
1986	6 734 980	3.1
1991	7 356 170	3.1

Most common family size in 1991: 2 members

Source: Figures drawn from Statistics Canada (1992). *Families: Number, Type and Structure.* Ottawa: Statistics Canada (Catalogue 93-312), p. 6.

of research that involves self-reporting is that participants may knowingly or unknowingly distort the facts.

A second research method is the *interview,* which involves more detailed and lengthier face-to-face questioning than the survey method. Interviews are often too time-consuming and costly to involve huge numbers of subjects (Sanders, 1974). The interview method is often used when the researcher is looking for information that cannot easily be transformed into numbers. One such study concerned how children felt about the support and punishment by parents in one-parent, stepparent, and two-parent families (Amato, 1987). At times, interview research is used as a basis for questionnaires that can be given to a larger number of individuals.

Direct observations by researchers avoid the problems found in self-reporting. In one form, naturalistic observation, the researcher is detached from the people studied, and will try to watch and record normal activities as unobtrusively as possible. At times, audio- or video-recording equipment is used and is analyzed in the office or laboratory. For example, interactions between mothers and infants have been observed from the moment of birth (Macfarlane, 1977). In another form of observation, the investigator actually takes part in the activities of the subjects and reports on his or her experiences. This method is often used when researchers, more often anthropologists than sociologists, study different cultures. By living in the society, it is possible to observe small details that the outside observer might miss, and to understand the meanings of certain activities.

Some observations, such as the *experiment*, are more controlled. The experiment involves changing conditions deliberately, and observing any changes in behaviour that result. In some cases, researchers perform experiments to test out relationships, e.g., the interaction between young siblings was observed under controlled laboratory conditions (Lamb, 1978). In spite of the ability to control factors, experiments do have drawbacks. Since the research laboratory is not a natural family setting, the behaviour there may not be typical of the individual family members. It is also unethical to conduct experiments that may damage a person physically or emotionally. For example, it would be unethical to isolate a baby from its mother to learn the effects of maternal deprivation.

Researchers also look at the forms of communications used during the period they are studying (Sanders, 1974), e.g., historical material on the family often depends on both popular and scholarly reports. Sheila Kieran, in her book on family law in Ontario, quotes letters and diaries, in particular those from the first half of the 19th century (Kieran, 1986); these types of sources help bring to life what can be dry official documents. More recently, the Canadian Radio-television and Telecommunications Commission (CRTC) commissioned a study of men's and women's roles as portrayed on radio and television (CRTC, 1990).

Once the researchers have gathered data, they often perform statistical analyses. One of the most common is *correlation* (Sanders, 1974), which attempts to find a strong relationship between two or more factors or variables. (Correlations cannot, however, prove that one factor or event caused another.) For example, in a study of marital satisfaction, researchers found a correlation between life events such as the birth of a child or children leaving home and the level of satisfaction (Lupri & Frideres, 1981).

In comparing life stages or historical periods, it is important to keep in mind two different approaches to research. *Cross-sectional research* studies individuals of different ages and compares them in relation to the factor under investigation. A major problem with comparing attitudes (toward sexuality for example) among people of different age groups is that these are affected by different historical events and values; the differences in attitude may not be the result of age but of changing times. This is referred to as a *cohort effect*. The findings of Lupri and Frideres (1981) concerning marital satisfaction may be showing cohort influences rather than the effect of the life stage. Cohort influences can be overcome by *longitudinal research*, i.e., by following the same people over a long period of time. One difficulty with longitudinal studies is the many years before results are available. In the interval, subjects may lose interest or disappear. Sometimes, to get information faster and yet reduce cohort effects, a combination of cross-sectional and longitudinal studies are used (Baltes, Reese, & Nesselroade, 1979).

Whatever method of investigation is used, the results are affected by the theoretical approach to the family because it determines questions asked. If a structural-functionalist wished to study decision-making in the family, the question may be, "How is decision-making related to traditional roles?" A feminist, however, would ask, "How is decision-making related to power in the family?" A family-systems theorist might want to know the impact of decision-making on subsystems in the family, and a developmentalist how decision-making differs in the various stages.

The Approach of This Book

Much of this book will follow the developmental approach to the family. We will consider six phases of family life: mate selection, marriage, reproduction, parenthood, the middle years, and old age. Despite its drawbacks, the developmental view offers some benefits: it enables us to tie the events in family life to studies in human development, and it allows comparisons of present-day families with those of other times and places. We can also add insights from other theories where they will help our understanding.

In order to overcome some of the drawbacks of the developmental view, we will need to pay attention to common variations that occur in our society, such as single-parent families and stepfamilies. Some issues, such as family violence and poverty, affect all age groups, and these will be discussed separately. Finally, we will need to consider how governments and social institutions affect family life.

SUMMARY

DEFINING THE FAMILY. Families have been defined in different ways according to time and place. In Canada today, there are several legal definitions of family, as well as social and personal definitions. Two ideas of family common in North America are the nuclear family, consisting of parents and children, and the extended family, which includes other relatives.

THEORIES OF THE FAMILY. Sociologists have suggested a number of theories to explain what happens in families.

1. The ecological view regards families as part of interlocking systems that influence each other at four levels: the microsystem, made up of small groups with face-to-face interaction; the mesosystem, made up of relationships between two or more small groups; the exosystem, which affects families through the mesosystem or microsystem; and the macrosystem, or a society's culture and ideology.

2. The structural-functional theory views the family as an institution among other social institutions. Families fulfill important functions in society: caring for the physical and emotional well-being of its members, and producing and shaping new members for society. According to this view, much of behaviour is governed by the values and norms within a society; these are transmitted to new generations through the process called socialization. Families are organized around the statuses of husband/father, wife/mother, and child, who each have roles assigned by society.

3. Conflict theories are concerned with power relationships. One such theory is feminism, which points to the political and social control enjoyed by men. This control is supported by the view that men head the household, by the assumption that caring for a family is a woman's responsibility, and by the higher levels of men's earnings, compared with those of women.

4. Symbolic-interaction theories look at the meanings individuals see in others' words and actions. These meanings develop from the history of family members' interactions. Symbolic interactionists have contributed the concepts of role-taking, role expectations, and role strain.

5. Exchange theorists look at the costs and benefits of family life to its members. They have been especially concerned with how husbands and wives make decisions.

6. Systems theory regards a family as a set of interrelated parts in which anything that affects one part affects all. Families also contain subsystems, which are smaller groupings. Boundaries mark out who belongs to a family or its subsystems. Families operate according to rules. These are related to feedback and, in a new situation, may produce a vicious cycle, confusion, or formation of new rules.

7. The developmental view considers families from their formation to their end. At each stage of the family life cycle, members must accomplish developmental tasks. These are related to the needs of members and to social expectations. Although this perspective has drawbacks, it will form much of the basis for this book.

STUDYING THE FAMILY. Much of what we know about the family is gained through surveys and interviews. These depend on what people tell researchers about themselves. Some information comes from direct observation or from the study of documents. Cross-sectional research compares people of different ages at the same moment in time. Longitudinal studies follow the same individuals for a period of time.

KEY TERMS

boundary: an imaginary line marking who belongs to a system

cohort effect: characteristics or attitudes that result from the period of history in which people have lived

communal living: a group of people, who may or may not be related by birth or marriage, sharing financial resources and living arrangements

correlation: a mathematical method for showing whether a relationship exists between factors

cross-sectional research: a method of research that involves comparing individuals of different ages

developmental task: a task that an individual is expected to achieve at a particular stage in development

direct observation: a research method in which the researcher watches and records behaviour

exosystem: institutions and organizations in society in which individuals do not take an active part, but which affect them through the mesosystem or microsystem

experiment: a research method that involves changing conditions deliberately and observing any changes in behaviour that result

extended family: the nuclear family and all other relatives

interview: a research method in which the researcher asks questions face-to-face

longitudinal research: a research method in which the same individuals are studied for a period of time

macrosystem: society's culture and ideology

mesosystem: the relationships between two or more microsystems

microsystem: small groups in which people interact face-to-face

monogamy: marriage to one person at a time

morphogenesis: developing new forms of behaviour

norms: ways of behaving that are typical of a certain group

nuclear family: a family consisting of a husband, a wife, and their children

polyandry: marriage of a woman to more than one man

polygamy: marriage of one person to more than one person of the opposite sex

polygyny: marriage of a man to more than one woman

role: a function expected of a person who has a particular status

socialization: the passing on of the basic knowledge of how to survive in and take part in social life

social scripts: cultural rules that tell us what, where, when, how, and why we should do something

social time clock: socially approved timetable for certain life events

status: a social position that carries a set of expectations concerning suitable behaviour

subsystem: smaller groupings within a system

survey: a method of research that involves getting information from many individuals

system: a set of interacting parts

values: social principles that are accepted by society as a whole or by a group within that society

CLASS ASSIGNMENTS

Complete one or both of the following assignments, as directed by your instructor.

1. Select an occupation in which you are interested. Do some library research or interview someone who is familiar with that occupation. Try to learn how knowledge of the family is important in the occupation. You might consider definition, family history, and influences of the family on the individual.
2. Often, cultural differences can be observed in customs of religious festivals. Interview a friend, neighbour, acquaintance, or classmate about the religious event most important to his or her family. Find out what practices are followed, such as worship, family events, special foods, and other possible activities. Learn how these have affected the person's relationship with others of the same faith and with people of other faiths. Discover the values the individual sees in this event.

PERSONAL ASSIGNMENTS

These assignments are designed to help you gain insight into your own family experiences.

1. Think about your own family. What are some of the events that have occurred which might affect your ability, either positively or negatively, to provide service to others? Are there any individuals you might have difficulty helping? Why?
2. Make a list of the many roles that you fill (e.g., student, friend, son/daughter, employee, parent). What is expected of you in each role? Where do you foresee conflicts related to family life? Which roles hold priority for you? Why?

C H A P T E R 2

Being Different

O B J E C T I V E S

- To examine the differences in family experiences of males and females in our society.
- To examine the basis for discrimination against minority groups.
- To consider two responses on the part of minority groups to discrimination by the majority.
- To introduce some issues in which minorities are currently challenging the majority.
- To look at some of the implications of the movements for equal rights.

"Retard"—there are some words in the English language that can make you wince. For me, retard is one of those words. Actually it does more than make me wince, it infuriates me, causes me to see red, and after 32 years is finally making me speak out.

The biggest offenders of the word are of course kids; kids that as you grow up your mother keeps telling you that, "They don't really understand what they're saying, dear." But you know differently. These same kids grow into adolescence and become a bit more sophisticated. As they say it, they look at you, smirk and say, "I meant that in the sense of the dictionary definition of the word, of course." Of course they don't.

I have studied language, majoring in theatre in college. Words for me have a color, a texture, and flavor. Books are my favorite companions and if nothing else is available, I'm one of those people who will read the back of cereal boxes. I am also the twin to a young man born with Down's syndrome.

I am not 'remarkable' or 'wonderful', or feel myself particularly 'blessed'. Growing up, I can remember walking ten steps ahead of mother and brother and hoping no one noticed I was with them. I endured what I consider to have been a hellish childhood in rural Upstate New York, as the farmers' kids made my life miserable riding back and forth on the school bus with my brother. I choked with suppressed rage every time these same kids chanted, "Retard, retard". Before making new friends, I'd have to brief them before coming home, warning them that Brian was 'different'. I lost a few chances with boys along the way because of my brother.

I have grown up. And so has Brian. In an eighth grade English class, a teacher discussing Fate and Shakespeare bombarded me with, "What good are these kids, those of them that are born relatively mindless? What good are they?" I didn't have an answer then. It was years until I found one.

Retarded 'individuals', retarded 'citizens', retarded brothers are good simply because they are people just like you and me. They are the finest example of people living extraordinary lives in an ordinary way. They personify courage and loyalty and love. Because of Brian I have experienced unconditional love, probably the only time on earth I'll ever experience it. They make you try harder.

Don't use that word and don't let anyone misuse that word in your presence. If no one has told you before, let me tell you. The word is offensive. It rates right up there with 'nigger' and 'kike'. And like those words, they are symbols for something that isn't true; they are limiting words from limited minds.

Source: Barbara Hungerford (1990). "A Sibling's View," *Sibling Information Network Newsletter,* 7(2):5.

As we study the family life cycle, we must remain aware of the many differences that exist in families. Frequently discussions assume that the family involves being married, becoming parents, and living together. There are many families that do not fit this pattern. Some people never marry but live in family-like groupings such as religious orders. Others who choose not to marry or never find a marriage partner keep close ties with relatives or friends. Gay couples often find family-like support and acceptance among friends. Many gay men and lesbians are parents, sometimes because they married before "coming out", sometimes through artificial insemination or adoption. Other couples choose not to have children. Some two-career families are built around commuter couples who live in different cities.

Women and Men

Among the most important differences in family experiences is that between males and females. This affects both the nature of relationships and family experiences themselves.

In our society, men and women, boys and girls, are brought up to relate to one another in different ways. According to Carol Gilligan (1982), females tend to focus on relationships and connections between people. Males, on the other hand, are taught to value independence and self-direction. One area where these differences can be observed is in nonverbal communication. Judith A. Hall (1984) found that women are usually better at reading and sending nonverbal messages than men, especially those regarding emotions. Men are not as dependent on the immediate situation in their thinking. There are other differences. It is commonly accepted that males, in general, are more likely to take part in sexual acts without being in a love relationship, while women much more often become romantically attached first. That men are socialized to be independent and unemotional means that it is harder for them to become committed to a relationship, while women tend to try to keep the relationship together. Some of these differences between men and women are also seen in gay and lesbian unions. For example, gay relationships usually do not last as long as lesbian ones, and are more likely to include sexual encounters with individuals other than the partner (Glick, Clarkin, & Kessler, 1987).

As we shall discuss in more detail in later chapters, women's family experiences are often quite different from men's. According to one large cross-sectional study, couples with daughters are more likely to divorce than couples with sons (Morgan, Lye, & Condran, 1988). Women are more likely than men to be single parents, to live in poverty, to live alone, and to be widowed. On the other hand, men are more likely to be living with a partner, and are more likely to remarry if they are widowed or divorced. Women and girls experience physical and sexual abuse to a much higher degree than do men.

Is Being Different Acceptable?

In theory, we Canadians accept and even encourage differences. We point with pride to our federal Charter of Rights and Freedoms, provincial legislation recognizing the fundamental rights of all people, and our multicultural society, yet there are limits to what we view as socially acceptable.

According to Evelyn Kallen (1989), a minority is created by society. A *minority* is any social category that is seen by the majority in society as being incompetent and inferior, or abnormal and dangerous, i.e., it offends against the norms of society. The *majority* is the group in a society that is the largest in number or that holds the most power. The members of a minority group experience *discrimination* by the majority, and thus are denied political, economic, and social rights. As a result, members of this group become disadvantaged and stigmatized. A minority is not necessarily smaller than the majority; Kallen points out that blacks in South Africa fit the definition of a minority even though they far outnumber whites. So too women have been discriminated against through much of our history, e.g., when they have not been allowed to own property or to vote. In fact, many argue that women are still disadvantaged in respect to pay and opportunities for promotion. In much of Canada, social acceptability is based on white society and norms, and often on values that have come from our British rather than our French heritage.

We need to look at several aspects of majority/minority relationships if we are to understand their impact on families, e.g., discrimination based on majority values can profoundly affect the family life of minority-group members. Child-welfare workers who are members of the majority group may regard traditional child-rearing methods of some minority groups as poor parenting. In the chapter on socialization, we will discuss the way in which churches and educational and social-service organizations provided programs, often with the best of intentions, that worked to destroy family life and family ties among native peoples (P. Johnston, 1983; M. Ward, 1984a). One aspect of family that differs among cultures is the extent to which extended family members are considered part of the immediate family. Many misunderstandings about the caring and competence of parents have centred on just this difference. In the case of native families, many social workers felt that the custom of allowing grandparents or other relatives to care for children showed indifference and neglect on the part of the parents. As a result, they placed the children with families who followed the majority cultural practices. The parents, however, felt that they were behaving responsibly since their children were being looked after by caring family members (M. Ward, 1984a).

STIGMA

Members of minorities are often stigmatized by the majority. A *stigma* is any quality that is seen as offensive by society—anything that is considered wrong, crazy, disgusting, strange, or immoral, especially if it is labelled "unnatural." In the chapter opening, Barbara Hungerford describes attitudes toward her mentally challenged brother; these include the notion that such people should be put away in institutions and are not worth caring about.

Unfortunately, stigma has a way of spreading to other aspects of the individual (Higgins & Butler, 1982; Kallen, 1989); if one part is considered wrong, the whole person is considered faulty. For example, blind individuals may be spoken to loudly as if their hearing is also impaired. The caricature formed through this process is then used as a basis for justifying discrimination against a whole group of people. Physically challenged people, for example, have been considered unsuitable adopters since they are seen as being "impaired" as well in their ability to parent. The few who have successfully overcome this prejudice have proven themselves as competent as those parents with no obvious physical challenges.

Stigma can spread to others outside the minority group. If one associates too much with members of a minority group, one is regarded as being just like them. This is reflected in proverbs like "A man is known by the company he keeps." If a person works with an AIDS-awareness group, there is the sneaking suspicion that he or she might be homosexual.

INFERIOR OR DANGEROUS TOO?

Minority groups tend to be regarded as either inferior only or as both inferior and dangerous (Kallen, 1989). For example, much of the discussion over whether mentally challenged people should have children centres on the notion that their level of functioning makes them unsuitable parents (inferiority). Some argue, however, that allowing them to become parents will lower the intellectual level of the population as a whole, or will produce children who don't know how to behave properly in society (danger). The first attitude leads to attempts to deny parenthood to individuals "for their own good." The second tries to control their fertility, to permit sterilization without the consent of the individual "for the good of society."

If a particular characteristic is regarded as unnatural, it is considered particularly dangerous. One notable example is continuing prejudice against homosexual individuals. *Prejudice* is a negative attitude toward a minority group that is not based on fact. Over the years, homosexuals have suffered continuing harassment from both private citizens and members of the social work and legal professions (Kinsman, 1987). Homosexual parents, for example, have experienced many problems in gaining custody of their children; when they have managed to do so, generally it has been because they have shown themselves to be the far superior parent. Obtaining custody is particularly difficult for gay fathers (Gay Fathers of Toronto, 1981; Gross, 1986). Although research has shown that adult children of homosexuals generally have relationships with members of the opposite sex (Golombok, Spencer, & Rutter, 1983), there is continuing fear that the morals of these children will be corrupted so that they will follow their parent's "unnatural" lifestyle; this is especially true when the parent has a live-in lover.

VOLUNTARY OR INVOLUNTARY?

Minority groups are judged also on whether differences in behaviour or characteristics are voluntary or involuntary (Kallen, 1989). If they are judged to be voluntary, then presumably the individual has the ability to change the behaviour or quality. If no change occurs, the individual is presumed to have chosen minority status. The entire justice system works on this principle, i.e., there is the assumption that people have chosen to be criminals and therefore must suffer a penalty. Age is a factor in determining whether a behaviour or characteristic is voluntary. Children under a certain age—and this has changed over the centuries—are considered to have insufficient understanding to control their behaviour. Age of responsibility varies, of course, with activity; having dry pants or obeying a parent is expected at a much younger age than is the ability to care for a child.

The degree of stigma attached to a particular behaviour or status sometimes changes with time. For example, in the past, divorce was regarded as shameful, especially for women who chose to leave their husbands. Women had to prove adultery plus some other ground, such as cruelty, in order to win a divorce. Men had only to prove adultery. Financial support was available for women who were

A GAY FATHER WITH CUSTODY—INTERVIEW WITH A DAUGHTER

Briefly, what has it been like being raised by a gay father?
Being raised by a gay father has probably been different, but how different I cannot say as I have not experienced any other kind of lifestyle and thus can only go by what I've seen. I've grown up faster than most of my peers and I've seen and done a lot more, but I'm not sure if this is the result of my father's homosexuality or if it's just the way my father would have raised me anyway.

What kinds of problems has it created for you?
It would not have created many problems had my father and I lived by ourselves, unless, of course, he had had "friends" for short periods of time, which would have created some difficulties. In this regard his having a live-in lover has made things a little easier.

What are some of the disadvantages and some of the advantages?
Some of the disadvantages in having gay parents are trying to keep my mouth shut when some prejudiced person mouths off about homosexuals or, if they suspect there is a homosexual relationship at home, they crack a joke to see what kind of effect it has on me. Another problem is trying not to give "it" away, because if I did it could [put] us all through some torture. So one has to stay in the closet.

If you had the power to do anything, what aspect of your life to date would you change?
If I had the power to change any aspect I would alter the public's opinion. It is extremely hard to stay in the closet about homosexuality, whether it is one's parents, oneself, or one's friends.

Having a gay father is one thing, but having a gay stepfather is another. How has this gay coupling affected you? Specifically, what kinds of problems has it created for you?
It has affected me to the extent that I've had to share my father with someone other than my mother. Specifically, one of the problems that has arisen between us is that invariably one of us, at some time or another, feels left out, particularly the lover, who often feels that he does not belong or that we shun him for one reason or another.

Source: Gay Fathers of Toronto (1981). *Gay Fathers, Some of Their Stories, Experience and Advice.* Toronto: Author, p. 47.

abandoned but not for those who abandoned, regardless of the cruel or degrading circumstances of their marriage. Custody of children was generally granted to the father if his wife had left the family, unless the child was a baby dependent on mother's milk (Kieran, 1986; McKie et al., 1983). Now there are no distinctions made between men and women in assessing grounds for divorce, and financial support is determined by need rather than by fault. Although there is continuing social stigma against lone parenthood, as we shall see in a later chapter, it is not embodied in social policies to the same degree as in the past.

THE MAJORITY'S SENSE OF SUPERIORITY

Central to the discussion of minorities is the majority's sense of superiority—the notion that its way is the right way, and that any other is somehow wrong, or at best inferior. In part this is a power issue—changes in norms may threaten the majority's control over much of social life. Since many regard the family as the heart of society, they see any differences or changes in family patterns as a threat to society itself. In the past freer divorce laws were feared because it was felt that the family would be destroyed. We can see a similar fear expressed in statements on television or in newspapers that AIDS is God's judgment on homosexuality. The implication is that if we have sexual relations with the opposite sex within marriage (the traditional family), we are safe. Such a view, of course, ignores promiscuity and sex outside marriage. This sense of superiority and the fear that what we value most will be destroyed provokes the most violent forms of prejudice.

"Passing"—Accepting the View of the Majority

Due to discrimination, members of minority groups sometimes attempt to *pass* as a member of the majority group. Usually this involves accepting the stigma society places on the individual and trying to hide it in some way. In the 1950s, for example, one of the advantages claimed by adoption agencies over private adoptions was that they could give prospective parents a child that would resemble as closely as possible one they would have produced themselves. Matching of child to parents encourages what sociologist David Kirk calls "rejection of difference" (Kirk, 1984), i.e., it encourages parents to pass the child as their biological child and to pass themselves as fertile adults. In this way they avoid the stigma of infertility for themselves and of illegitimacy or abandonment for their child. Not telling a child he or she is adopted is a similar denial.

One problem with trying to pass is that it forces the individual to live a double life. This, by itself, causes a strain. Often, there will be uneasy moments as children or other relatives ask questions. Family members sense that this is a taboo subject. Such secrets can have long-lasting and quite unintentional effects on family relationships since they interfere with openness in family communication (Kirk, 1984; Pincus & Dare, 1978). In addition, there is the fear that the secret will be discovered; usually, there is someone who knows or suspects. Even if the family moves to another part of the world, there is always the possibility that someone who knows them will one day turn up. Thus there is a great deal of anxiety and role strain in the attempt to pass.

Challenges to the Majority

Another response to discrimination is that of challenging the majority. This has been the main thrust of equal-rights movements. In Canadian society today, there are several ongoing challenges to the traditional views of the family.

RACIAL AND ETHNIC MINORITIES

In the last twenty years, there has been a noticeable increase in visible minorities in the Canadian population. Before that time, there was a large aboriginal population, located mainly in the North, and defined pockets of other minorities, mainly Orientals and blacks. The latter were clustered in the Halifax area, where many who had fought on the British side during the American Revolution came to settle (Herberg, 1989). They were joined later by fugitive slaves who escaped from the United States. The two ends of the Underground Railway, as the escape network came to be called, were in Nova Scotia and southwestern Ontario.

The pattern of immigration to Canada has shifted dramatically over the last several years. Before 1967, immigration rules favoured those from Europe or countries of European heritage, such as the United States. Now nearly three-quarters of immigrants come from Africa, Asia, the Caribbean, and Latin America, and only one-quarter from Europe. The greatest pressure for change is being felt in large cities like Toronto, Montreal, Edmonton, Winnipeg, and Vancouver, which attract 95 percent of all visible-minority immigrants (Parekh, 1989).

There has been a growing demand for service agencies to develop policies that are sensitive to the cultural traditions of their clients. The need will probably increase, for a variety of reasons. The native population continues to be young, partly because the birth rate is higher than for the general population, partly because life expectancy is shorter (Maslove & Hawkes, 1989). Since most immigrants are young adults with children, they are concerned with government and agency policies regarding child care and education (D'Costa, 1987). Many go to small ethnic organizations for help rather than to mainstream agencies like children's aid societies or child-welfare departments that they fear do not respect the values of their group (Doyle & Visano, 1987). The Child and Family Services Act of Ontario recognizes the right of aboriginal peoples to be involved in planning for their children, both through the appointment of special officials and through the establishment of native agencies. In other provinces, agreements between native bands and provincial and federal governments have permitted formation of child-welfare and family-service agencies that are culturally sensitive. Immigrant groups do not have even this level of legal protection. They could, however,

Table 2.1

IMMIGRATION TO CANADA: 1968 AND 1988
10 LEADING SOURCE COUNTRIES

1968	1988 (Jan.-Sept.)
Great Britain	Hong Kong
U.S.A.	India
Italy	Great Britain
Germany	Philippines
Hong Kong	Poland
France	Vietnam
Austria	U.S.A.
Greece	Portugal
Portugal	Jamaica
Yugoslavia	Guyana

Source: Navin Parekh (1989). "Cultural and Racial Diversity in Canada: An Urgent Challenge," *Perception* 13(2):44. Updated from Barb Thomas and Charles Novogrodsky (1983). "Combatting Racism in the Workplace." Toronto: Cross Cultural Communication Centre.

be better served by developing closer ties between mainstream agencies and existing or new ethnic organizations.

CHANGING FAMILY FORMS

The "traditional" family model of breadwinner father, homemaker mother, and their two or three biological children persists as the basis for many practices. Government policy usually assumes that the household and family are the same, i.e., that man and woman living together are husband and wife, and that they are parents of children living with them. Thus people are responsible for supporting children in the household, whether or not they are the parents. Similarly, after the lapse of some specified time that varies according to province, the individuals are assumed to be married in common law and are responsible for each other (Eichler, 1987). On the contrary, if the couple is homosexual, they have major difficulties gaining recognition as a family.

Despite the best of intentions, some school practices discriminate against children from nontraditional families. Family trees, for instance, single out children from single-parent, stepparent, adoptive, or foster families. Who should be counted as parents? The issue becomes particularly troubling if family change has been recent, or if the child is attached to a substitute parent and wants that person included in the tree (M. Ward, 1980). Mother's Day and Father's Day cards may also highlight differences.

Changes in family patterns challenge accepted practices in many ways. The following are just a few examples:

1. The increasing number of working wives and mothers poses one such challenge. For example, sending home a child who is persistently late for school to get a note from a parent ignores the fact that often there is no parent home during the day. Similarly, appeals for parents to chaperone daytime school outings may receive little response. Young offenders are expected to appear in court with a parent; this means someone will have to take time off work, with a loss in pay they may not be able to afford.

2. Many children have a variety of parent figures. These include adoptive parents, foster parents, and stepparents, and individuals such as babysitters and day-care staff. The expectation that children live only with biological parents overlooks reality, and also tends to cloud the emotional effect some of the family differences may have on children. Not all parents fill traditional roles. For example, it was easier in the past for mothers to get child support and fathers to get child care help than vice versa. Now, however, most provinces will grant family-support payments to a single father staying home with young children (Eichler, 1987).

3. Medical advances and social changes have dramatically altered the options of those wishing to become parents. Advances in artificial techniques of reproduction and greater openness about using them are reflected in media stories about surrogate motherhood and open adoption. People today are less likely to pretend that they are a conventional family than in the past. There is still some resistance, however, to granting nontraditional methods the same status as biological reproduction. One mother of both biological and adopted children has been asked often, "Which ones are your own?" (meaning biological). Social workers are beginning to question the secrecy surrounding artificial insemination; they point out that individuals conceived by this method are usually denied knowledge of their genetic background. Adoptees have insisted that such knowledge is important to a healthy sense of identity (British Agencies for Adoption & Fostering, 1984).

4. Mentally and physically challenged members of the community are demanding the same rights as others. Within the school system, this

has emerged as *mainstreaming,* i.e., integrating children with exceptional needs into regular classrooms. Children with mental and physical challenges now live at home or in substitute homes within the community rather than in large institutions. As adults, they want jobs and normal family life, including marriage and children. Society has had to respond to the necessity of sex education for the disabled; no longer can it be assumed that those with mental and physical challenges are sexless beings (Poling, 1976). Society also needs to plan for the supports and services such individuals need to become the best possible parents.

MYTH: Disabled women are unable to fulfil the "natural-normal" functions of wives and mothers; **FALSE**.

FACTS: Women with disabilities are **not** all extraordinarily dependent on others. Disabled women point out that their individual personhood is ignored to the extent that they have been categorized, without exception, as being incapable of fulfilling the role of "mother." As a result, disabled women are not encouraged to have children. They may have to fight pressures from their families to have an abortion; or to keep the child once it is born. Some disabled women are engaged in a fight for reproductive rights which include the right to have a baby and the right to adopt children.

Source: *Focus on: Disabled Women,* fact sheet published by DisAbled Women's Network/Ontario.

5. Now that we have legislation granting certain rights to all Canadians, including members of minority groups, society needs to look again at families with homosexual partners. Some employers and insurance companies now do regard such couples as families. An issue that needs clarification, however, is when such couples are entitled to be considered family members. One possibility is using the same criteria as for a common-law marriage. At its General Council in 1992, the United Church of Canada debated the issue of allowing convenanting services for homosexual couples; the decision was left up to individual congregations (United Church of Canada, 1992). A related issue is the fitness of homosexuals to be parents. Some have resorted to artificial insemination to have children; others have had children before coming out, often in marriages where they tried to live a life that conformed to majority expectations. In child-custody cases, should homosexuals be presumed to be adequate parents until proven otherwise, like other parents seeking custody?

In the future, we can expect to see continuing pressure for the differences and rights of minority groups to be recognized under human-rights legislation. In response, however, the majority may feel endangered. If this occurs, we can expect a backlash against minorities and against rights movements to protect against what majority members feel is a threat to society. Indeed, there is evidence of this reaction in the formation of political parties and other organizations that emphasize the primacy of one race or ethnic group, or one model of the family. Unfortunately, there is a risk of violent confrontations between extremists on either side.

Differences and the Study of the Family

Why is it important for us to be aware of differences among families?

First, all of us are likely to be part of a minority at some point in our lives. It is important for us to understand that different does not equal inferior. Rather, we must realize that we have all been shaped by our past experiences. They help us develop our individual knowledge, strengths, vulnerabilities, and expectations as we go through life. Our experiences have also shaped how we perceive others, e.g., if we have been subjected to prejudice by a particular group, we may be suspicious of its members in the future. On the other hand, we may see others like us as being allies.

Second, we will all be affected by changes resulting from pressure for equal rights. New regulations may affect our eligibility to receive services. An expansion of services may mean a heavier tax burden. For those of us who work with people, new rules and policies may affect our working conditions. For example, the current pressure on police over alleged racial discrimination will probably result in changes in regulations concerning the use of force.

In much of the remainder of the book, we will be looking at the stages of the family life cycle. It is important for us to remember that many individuals and families do not go through the stages in a neat, orderly manner. Some take detours. Others vary the order in which they move through stages or miss some completely. This is part of the richness of human experience.

SUMMARY

MALE/FEMALE DIFFERENCES. Differences between males and females in our society are based mainly on differences in socialization. Females are encouraged to focus on relationships, and males on independence and self-direction. Family experiences of the two sexes also differ, with women and girls more likely to live in poor single-parent families.

MAJORITY/MINORITY RELATIONS. A minority is created by society. It is often seen as incompetent and inferior, or as abnormal and dangerous. Often minority groups are stigmatized by the majority. The negative attitude may spread to other characteristics of the individuals or to those who associate with them. Minority groups may be seen as inferior or dangerous, and either pitied or blamed. If they are considered to have voluntarily broken the norms of society, they suffer greater blame than if they are seen as unwilling victims. Often the minority-group members are considered in need of protection.

RESPONSES OF MINORITY GROUPS. Minorities can either try to pass, i.e., try to hide the conditions that cause stigma, or challenge the majority. Currently there are a number of challenges that call for a response from the government or various agencies. Some are the result of changes in the racial and ethnic mix of Canadians; others arise from changes in society that affect family forms: the increase in women employed outside the home, the fact that many children are raised by multiple parent figures, the advent of new reproductive technologies, and the pressure for equal rights for groups such as the disabled or homosexual partners. Regardless of our attitude, we will all be affected in some way by these changes.

KEY TERMS

discrimination: negative actions taken against a minority group

mainstreaming: integrating children with exceptional needs into regular classrooms

majority: the group in a society that is the largest in number or that has the most power

minority: any social category that offends against the norms of society

passing: trying to hide the fact that one is a member of a minority group

prejudice: a negative attitude toward a minority group that is not based on fact

stigma: any quality that is seen as offensive by the majority

CLASS ASSIGNMENTS

Complete one or both of the following assignments, as directed by your instructor.

1. For one week, track the topics discussed on one or two talk shows that often deal with family variations. What differences were featured? What appears to be the norm against which they are measured? Is this norm widely held by society? Explain.
2. Look at an occupation that involves working with people. What changes have occurred already and may occur in the future because of changes in families and/or the racial and ethnic makeup of your community?

PERSONAL ASSIGNMENTS

These assignments are designed to help you think about your own experience.

1. In what ways have people you know experienced difficulties because they did not fit regulations? How would you like to see these regulations changed? What effect do you think this change will have on the organization involved? Consider staffing, hours of operation, location, funding, and anything else you think is relevant.
2. List the areas in which you consider yourself part of a minority. Have you experienced any discrimination because of this? Explain. How might this experience help or hinder you as you interact with others?

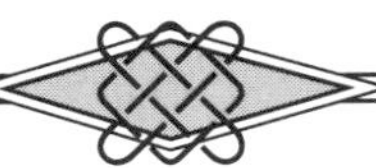

PART 2

Getting Together (or the merging of differences)

C H A P T E R 3

Getting Together

O B J E C T I V E S

- To point out variations in how families are formed.
- To locate mate selection in the family life cycle.
- To present two forms of mate selection—arranged and love matches—in social and historical perspective.
- To explain factors affecting present-day mate selection.
- To look at the lifestyle of the never-married.
- To outline some problem areas in relationships before marriage, and to describe methods of marriage preparation.

> As the king's son came up to the forest, the thorn branches burst into bloom and parted to let him pass. He climbed the tower stairs as the legend told him he should. Then he opened the door to the chamber where Briar Rose lay sleeping, still as lovely as the day she fell under the witch's spell. Immediately he loved her and gently kissed her. As soon as his lips touched hers, Briar Rose opened her eyes and smiled. As soon as the wedding festivities could be arranged, Briar Rose and her prince were married in royal splendour. The witch's curse was forgotten and they lived happily ever after.

In the story of Briar Rose we have all the essentials of romance—the beautiful princess who needs to be rescued, the handsome prince who rescues her, and above all something magical, including love at first sight and living happily ever after. This story and those of Snow White, Cinderella, and their sisters in spirit colour our imagination of love and courtship. In North American society, according to popular myth, man meets woman, they fall passionately in love and, after a suitable interval, fade into the misty shadows to the tune of The Wedding

THE BETTER HALF **by HARRIS**
Featuring HARRIET & STANLEY PARKER

"Back in college I kissed an enchanted prince. Then I married him and he turned into a frog."

Source: *The Toronto Star,* Saturday, 16 June, 1990.

March. Yet for many people, "happily ever after" is just an illusion. The reality is both more ordinary and more complex.

In our society, marriage is the norm, i.e., most people marry at some point during their lives. Society encourages marriage in a number of ways. Relatives and friends may ask, "When are you getting married?" or "Why aren't you married yet?" and may try to find you a suitable mate. There are also more subtle pressures, such as those found in advertising and popular culture. And, when most of the people you know are married, social life is organized around couples. If you are unattached, you may not fit in.

However, the greater acceptance of differences that we now see throughout society also affects marriage. Many people recognize that marriage may not meet a person's needs. Traditional marriage encourages women to put the needs of husband and children before their own. Men are encouraged to take on primary financial responsibility for wife and children. Even with the trend toward two-income families, parents find their activities limited both by the care that children need and by the cost of providing that care. If they remain single, both men and women are able to put their own needs first. For some, this is more important than the opportunity to form close family relationships (Conway, 1990; Papp, 1988).

There is also growing acceptance of relationships that do not include marriage. The number of people living together without marriage or before marriage (*cohabitation*) is increasing (Rothman, 1987). Individuals are becoming more open about homosexual relationships, and these are thus more visible (Weston, 1991). A person no longer has to be married to have children. Women can adopt a child, use artificial insemination, or find a man willing to father a child (Papp, 1988). Single men do not have as many options if they wish to raise a child, but a few adopt or raise a child they have fathered. These parents are invisible among those who become single parents through divorce.

Setting the Family Cycle Turning

In spite of these variations, mate selection, often referred to as *courtship*, is still the most common way of starting the family life cycle. Pairing may be heterosexual or, less frequently, homosexual. Both go through a process in which a partner is chosen with whom to share life. The next steps vary: some couples begin living together and never marry; others marry first; many begin with cohabitation and then move to formal marriage.

There are, of course, other ways of forming families. A common route is through single parenthood, either through adoption or, far more commonly, through birth. Either a mother or father may raise the child. In such cases, if courtship leading to marriage occurs at all, it is a later stage in the family cycle. Single parenthood is discussed in more detail in Chapter 7.

According to psychiatrist Erik Erikson (1963), the most important developmental task in young adulthood is the establishment of intimacy, in the sense of a close emotional relationship, with another. One of the key aspects to intimacy is the ability and freedom to disclose one's innermost self to another. This ability can be expressed in friendship, or in a sexual-romantic relationship with an individual of the same or opposite sex. In order to develop a sense of intimacy, it is important to know oneself and to be able to trust the other person not to inflict harm because one has been open (Roscoe, Cavanaugh, & Kennedy, 1988). In much of North American society, the development of a sense of intimacy is considered a prerequisite for marriage. Of course, not all intimate relationships, or even all formal engagements, lead to marriage.

A second developmental task is for a couple to establish the foundation for the marital relationship. There are so many shadings to a relationship that even the language we use cannot be exact. Communication, for example, can be verbal or nonverbal; it can carry information or emotional messages; it can be used to exert power or to be submissive. A trusting relationship may be one in which each partner's individuality is respected, or it may be one in which a submissive partner implicitly trusts a dominant partner to decide what is best for both. The pattern of relationships, if we follow symbolic-interaction thought, is established from even the earliest interchanges between partners. For example, when professionals counsel women who have been assaulted by their husbands, they often discover that the abusive relationship began during courtship. The same pattern holds true for other aspects, both good and bad, of a couple's relationship. The way a couple interacts while they are "going together" continues into the marriage.

In societies where couples do not have free choice of a partner, the basis of the relationship is also established before marriage. The shared experiences of the couple include the expectations of their families and of society at large. Personal aspects of their relationship, such as intimacy, may not develop until after marriage.

Mate Selection and Society

Despite the diversity in individual experiences, courtships can be divided into two basic streams—those decided upon by the couple, and those decided upon by the families of the couple. Both forms are closely tied to the values and traditions of the cultures that support them.

It is often easier to see the relationship between the couple and the macrosystem when we look outside our own culture. In the 17th century, for instance, differences among native peoples were tied to the conditions of their lives. The Ojibwa were migratory, and spent much of the year in small family groups made up of a man and his dependents. Contact with extended family members occurred for only short periods each year. Survival of the group depended on the man's ability to hunt and provide food for his family; thus men were the focus of Ojibwa society. However, without a woman's skills in preparing food, clothing, nets, and other necessities of life, a man's ability to hunt was limited. Women also had the mission of providing the next generation of hunters. The individual woman did not much matter, as long as the role was filled (Castellano, 1989). The importance of a woman's life-giving and nurturing function was supported by religion through identifying her with Mother Earth (B. Johnston, 1976). Women were obligated to marry. If they failed to do so, they were the objects of scorn and ridicule. Often first unions were arranged by relatives, yet women had the freedom to form a new relationship if the first proved unsatisfactory (Castellano, 1989).

Huron society, too, glorified men as hunters and protectors. Since males were often absent for long periods of time for hunting and trading, the relationship between a mother and her daughters was close. As in Ojibwa culture, women filled the nurturing roles. However, this agriculturally based society gave a much more prominent place to women because the land passed from a woman to her daughters. The family group consisted of a senior woman, her unmarried sons, her daughters and their husbands and children, who all lived together in a longhouse. Both men and women had considerable sexual freedom. Gradually, a couple developed a sense of commitment, but often the relationship did not become permanent until the birth of a child. Such unions tended to be stable, but either partner could dissolve them (Castellano, 1989). In Huron society, as in Ojibwa society, there is a strong relationship between the actual form of mate selection and the other systems within the society.

Some of the sexual freedom present among the traditional Ojibwa and Huron peoples has continued to the present. For example, many unions occur without legal marriage, a concept imposed on their societies by white culture. In fact, common-law unions have been encouraged by legislation, since until recently a woman lost her Indian status, and with it many economic resources, if she married a man without Indian status (Frideres, 1983). In this case, the customs based on traditional culture have been reinforced by an exosystem imposed upon the people.

More recently, the AIDS (Acquired Immune Deficiency Syndrome) epidemic is having some, though apparently only limited, effect on the sexual behaviour of young people. In a recent study of teenagers and college and university students, researchers at Queen's University in Kingston, Ontario, found that most young people were aware of AIDS and felt that they could avoid contracting the disease. Many had had more than one sexual partner by the time they were in their late teens and early twenties, but even with their knowledge of AIDS, about one-quarter of sexually active college students never used condoms. Among gay men, the number using condoms during anal sex increased from 2 percent to 50 percent in a period of two-and one-half years. Thus, in spite of the publicity around AIDS, many young people are not dramatically changing their sexual habits (King et al., 1988).

Similarly, in our society and others we will consider, there are close links among the macrosystem, or culture, and the exosystem, mesosystem, and microsystem. Although the discussion will not always point out the relationship in great detail, we need to be aware that it exists.

The Courtship Continuum

Usually arranged and self-chosen marriages are treated as if they are quite different. However, they lie along a continuum with completely arranged marriages at one end, and completely self-chosen ones at the other. Most fall somewhere in between, although they tend to be toward one side or the other. For instance, most individuals who choose their partners do take some account of their parents' feelings about their prospective partners. In arranged matches, the couple usually will not be forced to marry if either is opposed.

There is also a continuum for the idea of marriage as exchange and marriage as shared emotion. This is related but not identical to the arranged/free choice continuum. Arranged marriages tend to pay more attention to how each party will benefit from the union, while free choice tends to emphasize shared emotions, such as love and companionship. The latter is related more closely to symbolic interaction, as the couple create their own unique relationship.

In North America, most individuals are at the romantic love end of the scale (Goode, 1959). This is encouraged in many ways. We are socialized from childhood to fall in love. Adults tease children about their "girlfriends" or "boyfriends"; friends imagine how nice it would be for their children to some day fall in love. There is also the constant message of media and advertising—love is the mountaintop of experiences. Yet people tend to fall somewhere between the two extremes, often using both exchange values and emotional appeals to attract a mate. Several studies have found that men are more likely than women to show off their "material" assets, such as education, job, or car. Women tend to emphasize their physical appearance. Both, however, display sympathy, kindness, and helpfulness. They also use good manners and humour as methods of attracting one another (Buss, 1988).

Matchmaker, Matchmaker—Arranging Marriages

For centuries children were considered a family asset. They were expected to aid the family through their work or, especially in the case of wealthy or titled families, to help preserve or improve their social standing through marriage. In some societies, social class and family descent is very important. If love is allowed free play, social classes might be ignored. Such societies consider both love and the choice of a husband or wife too important to be left to mere children. Instead, marriages are arranged by parents and matchmakers. They may consider eligibility, similarity of background, horoscopes, financial and social position and, if the couple is fortunate, the personalities of the prospective bride and groom. Some lucky couples grow to love each other after marriage (Goode, 1959; Lee, 1975).

Arranged marriages were and continue to be considered unions of whole groups; thus the extended family is involved in the couple's relationship. In the case of European royalty, marriages arranged for political benefit affected their countries, since a wedding often sealed a treaty. Some couples, already married by proxy (with someone else saying vows for them), met for the first time at the borders of the groom's country. A number of these marriages were successful. Other pairs produced the necessary heir to the throne and then lived separately, and some, at least, engaged in extramarital affairs.

The present English royal family provides examples of tension between public and private marriages. On the one hand, the individuals are expected to select their own mates. Royal romances are considered fairy-tale material, with "happily ever after" the expected ending. On the other hand, members are limited in their choice if they expect to come to the throne—no divorced person or non-Protestant is an eligible partner; thus Edward VIII was forced to abdicate when he insisted on marrying a divorcee. There is also pressure for the new partner to understand the "royal business," all the ceremony and public appearances demanded of members of the royal family. When the couple experiences marital difficulties, as has occurred among present-day royalty, it becomes a matter for public concern and comment.

KEEPING LOVE UNDER CONTROL

Romantic love did exist in earlier times, right along with arranged marriages, but it was often considered a kind of madness (Goode, 1959). The famous lovers Romeo and Juliet came to disaster because they fell passionately in love instead of accepting marriages arranged by their parents. Since love was considered dangerous, it was controlled even before it struck.

Societies have used different methods to dampen love (Goode, 1959). One method is to marry off children before they reach puberty. Sometimes the child bride would be raised by her husband's family, and the marriage would be consummated at a suitable time. There could be strict rules outlining whom a person could marry. For example, the former caste system in Hindu India allowed marriage only to one at the same social level. This is referred to as *endogamy*, or marriage within the group. Standards of this kind may allow some choice of the actual marriage partner. Often parents seek approval of the young people before final plans are made and select another candidate if the first fails to please the prospective bride or groom. In some societies, girls and boys are not allowed to meet. This can happen only with wealthy families, who can afford to segregate the sexes. The zenana, or women's quarters, in some eastern countries are an example. In other societies, young people are chaperoned strictly by an elderly relative, or duenna, so that even if boy meets girl there might be fluttering eyelashes but no further interaction.

ARRANGED MARRIAGES IN CANADA

Immigrants to Canada bring the values of their societies to their new country. It is no surprise then that in New France, young people were encouraged by their wealthy landowner parents to marry not for love but for family and property (McKie, Prentice, & Reed, 1983). This also occurred in Upper Canada (Kieran, 1986). The government in France wished to make the society in New France a copy of French society. However, since there were few marriageable women in the colony, men formed longstanding relationships with native women. About one thousand French women, known as "Daughters of the King," were persuaded to sail to North America, for which they received a dowry and the essentials for starting farm life. Marriage became compulsory in New France, and those who refused to marry lost privileges. Prizes were offered to families with ten living children. These marriages were not arranged in the strict sense of the term, but there was relatively little choice available to prospective brides and grooms (Elkin, 1964).

In the early part of the 20th century, Sikh immigrants to British Columbia were not allowed to bring their wives and children with them. Given that there was a good deal of prejudice against them, unmarried men could not seek out white women for wives. Following changes in immigration laws in 1951, many Sikh men depended on relatives in the Punjab to arrange marriages for them; others advertised in East Indian newspapers (Ames & Inglis, 1976).

These customs are not confined to other times and other places. For example, relatives still advertise in newspapers published for East Indians living in North America, hoping to find spouses for the young people in their family. Usually an exchange of benefits is involved. In many cases, the bride or groom sees marriage as a route to immigration; in return they offer their ability to earn a living or to fit into North American society while keeping up religious and cultural traditions. Ethnic Indians see such marriages as a way of preserving their heritage (Bhargava, 1988).

Even when families do not actually arrange marriages, there can be extreme pressure on children of new Canadians to marry within their ethnic group. There is high potential for conflict when the young people want to follow customs they have learned in Canada instead. In some cases, young people come to social-service or mental-health agencies because they have become isolated from their families and social group; others may suffer physical or extreme emotional abuse as parents try to make them obey. There is often, however, a compromise between traditional ways and majority culture. Recently there have been reports in the media, for instance, of day-time dances organized for East-Indian teens in Toronto.

The Shift Toward Free Choice

There has been a gradual shift along the continuum in European-based society away from arranged marriages toward free choice. This has not been a smooth progression. Movement has occurred in parts of the population and not in others. There have also been rapid shifts in some attitudes, followed by a period of reaction. Many changes, including attitudes toward premarital sexual experience, reflect changing social conditions and even levels of scientific knowledge. Earlier practices still affect us today because some members of older generations find it hard to accept that values have changed since they were young.

EARLY YEARS OF SETTLEMENT

The conditions on the North American frontier were ideal for an emphasis on choosing one's own mate. Actual practices were related to three phases: the exploration of the wilderness, establishing new settlements, and the growth of larger towns and cities. Dates are hard to attach to the phases, since they occurred at different times in different places. For example, settlements were established earlier in the East than on the Prairies, and earlier near major waterways than in the hinterland.

In the exploration phase, and this would include early fur traders, survival depended on an individual's initiative and resourcefulness. Added to the harsh conditions was an extreme shortage of white women. Many men formed temporary or permanent unions with native women. These unions were often established on the basis of an exchange of goods for expertise in wilderness travel and survival (J.S.H. Brown, 1982). It is difficult to know what part, if any, romantic love played in such unions.

This phase was followed by a transitional period during which settlers moved into areas that had been explored and mapped by the traders and explorers. Although many travelled in extended family groups, many also left behind their relatives. The frontier saw an influx of unattached males since it provided opportunities for energetic and enterprising young men. In mate selection, practical matters were important. Was the prospective partner, male or female, strong and healthy? Was he or she a hard worker? Life in the remote parts to which they would be going was not easy. Both partners would have to put in long, hard labour to make their new farm productive. The choice of partners was limited, especially for men.

Yet it was also in the New World that romantic love came into its own. Many people came to the new colonies to escape tyranny and to express their freedom to worship as they chose. This individuality was also found in choice of marriage partners. Many unattached men came to North America to make their fortune, and they had few relatives nearby to influence their marriages. Even when families were present, young people had a good deal of freedom in selecting a mate. Their parents might, however, control when they married by either refusing or giving them land. Although everyone worked long hours, there were occasions to meet after church or at community events, such as barn raisings. The appropriate place for courting was the parlour, and often young couples would be left alone there to become acquainted (Rothman, 1987).

In this early period, values regarding sexuality were often contradictory. Men living among the native peoples often adopted their customs. In settled communities the attitude, at least officially, was much stricter. Many of the early European settlers of North America brought with them a puritan outlook—anything that is fun is probably sinful, especially sex. This attitude is reflected in the "marital standard" for sexual behaviour: sex is permissible only in marriage, and only to produce children (Reiss, 1960). One of the chief advocates of this stance has been the Roman Catholic Church.

Actual practices may have been more permissive. One custom, "bundling," has received a lot of attention, although it is difficult to tell how widespread it actually was. When a young man came to call on a young woman, in order to conserve precious firewood and yet allow them time to get to know each other, parents tucked them into bed together fully clothed. Bundling operated on the honour system. Records show, however, that premarital pregnancies, leading to hasty marriages, increased during the years bundling was practised (Rothman, 1987).

Life in cities also tended to encourage individuals to choose their own husbands or wives. As young people became less dependent on their parents for financial survival, they had more freedom of choice. On the family farm, which was worked by father and sons, parents had a relatively high level of control over marriages, whether or not they wished to exercise it, since they controlled their children's income. This is still true when a person works in a family business, especially in times when jobs are scarce. In the cities, where a greater variety of jobs was available, such control became weaker, and young people could please themselves more (McKie, Prentice, & Reed, 1983).

During the late 1800s, women were idealized as being pure and sexless, although this notion was not necessarily true (Reiss, 1960). At this time, there was an increase in pornographic material among men. They were also permitted much greater sexual freedom. This double standard has continued for a long period of time. Parents still tend to allow sons more freedom than daughters, and to see sexual activity among boys as "natural," while girls who have many sexual partners are regarded as "promiscuous."

Opinions based on faulty science were responsible for some restrictive ideas about sex. For example, around the turn of the century, many people believed that semen was a life force, and that men were weakened if they "spilled" too much. Red meat was blamed for inciting sexual passions. One Michigan doctor set up a spa where men could recuperate their strength. Since he wanted to provide a balanced diet that would not arouse sexual appetites, he invented a vegetable product that is still around today: Kellogg's Corn Flakes (Money, 1986). Although Kellogg's view might seem quaint to most people, some coaches still encourage athletes to avoid sex so that they will have the energy to win important contests.

A NEW CUSTOM—DATING

During the years before World War I, when a young man came calling on a young woman, his attentions were assumed to be serious. Courtship took place mainly at community activities and in the parents' home. World War I transformed Canadian society. In 1914, Canada was mainly a country of farms and small towns; by 1918, it had become an industrial nation. Society was forced to change. One of the changes was the invention of dating by young people. For the first time, single men and women would go out alone together without any particular intention of marrying each other. In most cases, the young man would pay the costs for the date. Willard Waller, who studied college dating practices in 1929, described them as a way of building status (Blood, 1955). For example, a university student who belonged to the best fraternity, came from a high-class family, and was extremely good-looking would raise the status of any girl he dated.

Later studies showed that the "rating and dating" system wasn't quite as simple as it seemed (Blood, 1955). It turned out that men and women became engaged to the same sort of people they had been dating—those who could provide them with the kind of life to which they were accustomed. For example, the daughter of a wealthy businessman would have been used to the best of everything; if she married someone with a similar background and similar resources, she would not have to change her lifestyle. At this time, it did not matter how high-class the woman was; she was given the same social standing as her husband. If the heiress had fallen in love with the son of the neighbourhood grocer, most of her friends and relatives would have looked down on her, if they even invited her to their homes. Nowadays, similarity in values and lifestyle still have an attraction when people look for permanent relationships.

Men and women apparently developed different attitudes toward dating. Men were socialized to emphasize sex, while women learned about love, romance, and marriage. According to one study, even though they were training for a profession, student nurses during the 1960s considered marriage as their first career, and nursing as something extra to be fit in around bearing and raising children. Most men who dated them believed that nursing students were easy sexual targets. The nurses, however, were looking for husbands (Skipper & Nass, 1966).

Dating serves four functions. As we have seen, it can add to a person's status if the date is the "right" person, such as the football hero. It can be a form of socialization, because it provides opportunity for members of both sexes to learn how to get along with each other. Dating is a form of recreation, engaged in just for fun. Finally, dating can be a part of courtship, with the purpose of marriage.

Power in relationships, including dating, has long interested researchers (Brinkerhoff & Lupri, 1989). If a man and a woman date each other for different reasons, their relationship may be in trouble. The person who has the least to lose in the relationship can usually control the relationship. For instance, in the case of the student nurses who were hoping for marriage, if the young men were dating them just for recreation, the nurses had much more to lose if the relationship ended, so the males were more likely to persuade the nurses to have sex than the nurses were to persuade the men to marry them (Skipper & Nass, 1966).

In societies that allowed individuals some choice in selecting a marriage partner, steady dating frequently became a part of courtship. It was often attractive to women since it combined love and permissible sex (Rothman, 1987). In the 1940s, however, "going steady" took a new turn—people far too young to be planning marriage started "going" with each other. Part of this custom came through a desire for social security. School proms required dates. If you didn't have someone you could rely on, you might be left sitting at home while all your friends were at the social event of the year. Dating and having to get used to being with a new person also caused a lot of insecurity. It felt much safer to date just one person who had made a commitment of sorts to you. As dating crept into the social life of younger teens, so did going steady (Herman, 1955).

BEYOND "GOING STEADY"

During the 1960s and 1970s, there was an increase in sexual experience among dating couples. Not surprisingly, studies conducted during the 1960s found that younger people had more permissive sexual attitudes than their parents. Many college students considered premarital sex acceptable for engaged couples, not as acceptable for people in love, and not very acceptable on a casual basis. In general, this attitude corresponds with what Ira Reiss (1960) calls "permissiveness with affection." By 1970, young English-Canadian and French-Canadian women still felt virginity until marriage was an ideal, although they might not practise it. Sex with love came second. English-Canadian men considered both about equal and French-Canadian men placed sex with love first. English-speaking women also reported much more sexual experience than had earlier generations (Hobart, 1984). A major shift in attitudes toward sexuality occurred in Canada for men between 1968 and 1971, and for women between 1971 and 1974 (Barrett, 1980). In general, attitudes became more egalitarian. The sex-for-fun standard, which had already been accepted for men, became more permissible for women (Rothman, 1987).

Currently there seems to be a change from the traditional dating pattern, in which a young man asks a girl out and pays the expenses of the entertainment, to a more egalitarian approach. One-on-one dating seems to be disappearing among teenagers (Murstein, 1980; Zarzour, 1987). They tend instead to move in clusters of friends with similar interests in fashion and music, and with similar values. In these groups, they can learn how to relate to members of the opposite sex in a safer environment than on the individual date. Eventually the young people pair off. Actual sexual activity appears related to the past experience of the woman. If she is sexually experienced, then the couple is more likely to have intercourse than if she is inexperienced. The past experience of men apparently has little relationship to the sexual practices of the couple (Herold, 1984).

It has become increasingly common for couples to move in together. There seem to be two forms of cohabitation, or living together. Most couples do not see this as a way of forming a family, and children are no part of their plan. If the woman should become pregnant, she would either have an abortion or the couple would get married. For these people, living together seems to be a form of courtship. Many, in fact, eventually have traditional weddings (Rothman, 1987). Some couples, however, do see children as having a place in their relationship, even if they are not married. This form of cohabitation is more like marriage than courtship. Predictions for the future see even more couples living together before marriage or without marriage.

There are signs that social attitudes are starting to swing towards more control regarding sexual behaviour. People are not advocating less sex, but they are promoting "safe sex" to avoid AIDS and other sexually transmitted diseases. There is little evidence, however, that young people's behaviour has been very much influenced by this trend. Rather, sexually transmitted diseases have

Table 3.1

NEVER-MARRIED MEN AND WOMEN, 1991

Age Groups	Male	Female
15–19 years	99.4%	98.5%
20–24	90.6	78.5
25–29	58.6	42.0
30–34	40.0	23.2
35–39	19.6	14.3
40–44	12.2	9.5
45–49	8.9	7.3
50–54	7.6	6.2
55–59	7.3	5.8
60–64	7.5	6.0
65 and over	7.2	7.8

Source: Based on figures from Statistics Canada (1992). *Age, Sex and Marital Status*. Ottawa: Statistics Canada, pp. 140–41 (Catalogue Number 93-310).

increased among both males and females. Only a few (14 percent) of sexually active college and university students report always using condoms (Page, 1989).

The changes in courtship, dating, and attitudes toward sexual behaviour that have occurred in this century are not purely historical. People now in their twenties worrying about "safe sex" may have parents who believed in sex during engagement, but not just for fun. Grandparents and great-grandparents grew up with still stricter values. Given that there has been such a large shift in attitudes, there is a high potential for misunderstanding and conflict among the generations.

Freedom of Choice?

Theoretically we can marry almost anyone we choose. We are, however, limited in many social and psychological ways.

Table 3.2

PERCENT EVER IN COMMON-LAW PARTNERSHIPS BY NUMBER, AGE GROUP, AND SEX, CANADA, 1984

Sex and age group	Currently in partnership	Ever in partnerships	Number		
			One	Two	Three or more
Male					
18–29	7.1	19.9	18.3	1.2	...
30–39	6.0	21.6	18.9	2.5	0.2*
40–49	3.2	10.3	9.2	...	...
50–64	2.9	6.4	5.9	...	–
All ages	5.2	15.6	14.1	1.3	0.2*
Female					
18–29	10.2	26.9	24.6	2.2	...
30–39	6.8	20.6	18.4	2.0	...
40–49	4.0	9.7	9.3	...	...
50–64	2.6	5.5	5.4	...	–
All ages	6.5	17.3	15.9	1.3	0.1*

... Due to a high standard error, these figures are not shown.

* These percentages represent very few cases and therefore may contain a high level of error.

Source: Thomas K. Burch (1985). *Family History Survey: Preliminary Findings*. Ottawa: Statistics Canada, August, p. 14 (Catalogue No. 99-955).

To begin with, there are legal limitations, e.g., we are limited to one marriage at a time. Some restrictions are based on the *incest taboo*, which appears in some form in every society, and which prohibits mating between people who are too closely related. Thus we are barred from marrying certain relatives, such as parents, grandparents, brothers, and sisters. Society does not, however, know exactly how to deal with the "irregular" relationships that occur in adoptive and stepfamilies. Biological siblings, even when adopted by different families and thus not legally related, are not allowed to marry. The situation of brothers and sisters by adoption is unclear. Stepsiblings are not legally related, but society frowns on marriages between them, especially if they have been raised together.

SIBLINGS RELATED BY ADOPTION WANT TO MARRY EACH OTHER

Dear Ann: My husband and I were not able to have children, so we decided to adopt. Our first was a healthy, beautiful boy. He was 22 months old when we got him. A year later we were lucky again: an adorable newborn baby girl. I taught them to be loving and considerate of one another. Our friends and relatives marvelled at how well they got along.

When "Nancy" was 5 she announced that she was going to marry her brother. We laughed and explained it just wasn't done. Now the children are in their 20s and I am a widow.

Last week, they came to me with the news that they want to be married. I was stunned. Both Nancy and her brother have dated other people a good bit and feel that the respect and deep feelings they have for one another are a far better basis for marriage than the head-over-heels glop that most people call "falling in love."

I appreciate the logic, but I can't help wondering if this would create problems for them and their children. I would be the sole grandparent. Wouldn't the youngsters be terribly confused having a grandmother who is both Dad's Mom and Mom's Mom?

Also would this be considered incest in the eyes of the law? Would they have trouble getting married?

—Bombshell

Dear Bombshell: It depends on where you live. Please suggest that they see both a lawyer and a counsellor before you hire a caterer.

(**Editor's note:** According to Raymond du Plessis, Q.C., law clerk and parliamentary council to the Senate, the most recent law concerning marriage came into force in 1991. Under the law, a brother and sister by adoption cannot marry each other. Neither can parents or grandparents marry their children or grandchildren by adoption. Other changes in the law clarified the situation for divorced people and closely related individuals. For example, a person can marry an ex-spouse's brother or sister. In addition, uncles and nieces, and aunts and nephews are permitted to marry each other.

Until the law was changed, a few individuals petitioned the Senate every year to pass a Private Member's bill so they could marry closely related individuals. The earlier law had its origins in the reign of Henry VIII. With only small changes, this law remained in place until the new Marriage Act took force.

Much as we might like to deny it, our families have both direct and indirect influence on our mate selection. Parents (and other relatives) can and do let young people know what they think of their choice of partner. Sometimes the approval or disapproval is openly stated; at other times it is communicated through the attitudes and nonverbal messages of relatives. Families may also introduce us to the people we eventually marry. When there are a number of brothers and sisters close in age, for example, one of the girls may fall in love with one of her brother's friends, or vice versa.

The influence of families can be more subtle. Our parents choose where the family lives; this in turn determines who our neighbours are, where we go to school, and the proximity of people our own age. Parents may influence whether we continue our education and where we do so, either through their direct influence or through factors such as income level.

We select our mates from a field of eligible people, who usually live in roughly the same geographical area. It is easier to get to know people who live nearby than those who live far away. In part because many immigrants live in *enclaves*, or groups within the larger society, they tend to marry people of the same ethnic origin. One of the great mixing places is the post-secondary institution. Here people with similar interests from a variety of places have an opportunity to socialize with one another. Sociologists have discovered that we are likely to marry those similar to ourselves in intelligence and education, in physical attractiveness and age, in religious and ethnic background, and in personal habits (Dumas & Peron, 1992; Epstein & Guttman, 1984). There is even a greater-than-average chance that we will choose someone with the same first initial (Kopelman & Lang, 1985). This tendency to marry someone similar to oneself is called *homogamy.*

Geographical and social factors outside our control also influence our selection of mate. Ask anyone who lives in a small community how much choice there is in finding a mate; they will tell you that there are only a few people of a suitable age. In the metropolitan areas of southern Canada, there are more options simply because there are so many people, and individuals can be more selective. When a city becomes too big, however, it may become difficult to find someone with similar values. That is one reason for the growing use of advertisements or dating services to locate a partner.

If there is an imbalance in the male/female ratio, one sex may have a much wider choice of partners. For example, the Northwest and Yukon Territories have had a reputation of being a happy hunting ground for marriage-minded women because there are more men there than women. Ottawa has long been a poor place for a woman to find a partner since government offices traditionally have been staffed by females. Until recently, immigrants have tended to be men, and have had trouble finding partners of the same ethnic group. When the first members of the baby-boom generation reached marrying age, women were at a disadvantage. Since men tend to marry women younger than themselves, there were fewer men a bit older than themselves from which the women could choose. However, as the last of the baby boomers matures, men are finding that they outnumber eligible younger women (Kettle, 1985).

The values we have learned from our families and from our friends and acquaintances also affect whom we marry (Epstein & Guttman, 1984). Most people prefer to marry someone from their own racial group. Racial differences are much more conspicuous than religious and ethnic differences. Prejudice, of course, plays a part in this preference. Since interracial marriages are relatively infrequent, the partners tend to be stared at when they are in public. Often individuals also choose someone of the same religious and ethnic origin. The larger the group in the area, the less likely people are to intermarry, since they have a wide choice among people of similar background and only a limited choice of people with different backgrounds. Some groups intermarry more often than others, e.g., Scandinavians marry non-Scandinavians more often than French marry non-French (Herberg, 1989). In part this is related to the proximity of eligible people of the same ethnic group; in part it is related to how much group values encourage young people to choose those like themselves.

The Disadvantaged in Romance

Some people have difficulty finding partners because they do not fit the accepted standards of eligibility that are promoted through popular fiction—whether in books, advertising, movies, or television. Desirable men and women are portrayed as young, slim, good-looking, and in control of their bodies and their lives. People who differ substantially from this stereotype may not even be able to establish an intimate relationship.

One such disadvantaged group has been referred to as "people of size." Especially when their weight exceeds 150 kilograms (unless, of course, they look like a football hero), they may be regarded as somewhat obscene, and as objects of curiosity and even ridicule, rather than as romantic partners.

Another group are those with visible physical differences such as a facial deformity or a crippling disorder requiring the use of a wheelchair. In addition to the disadvantage of physical difference, these individuals are too often seen as little more than their "disability" and thus as not being full participants in society. Since they are often regarded as only marginally employable, they have difficulty finding jobs that would allow them to support family life. Besides, they are not "supposed" to be interested in such activities as sex, marriage, or child rearing (Poling, 1976). Thus, in the competition for partners, such individuals are multiply disadvantaged. One young man with cerebral palsy has had sexual experiences with men more often than with women since, in his experience, his appearance does not seem to matter as much to men.

Figure 3.1

MALE ETHNIC ENDOGAMY RATES, 1931–81

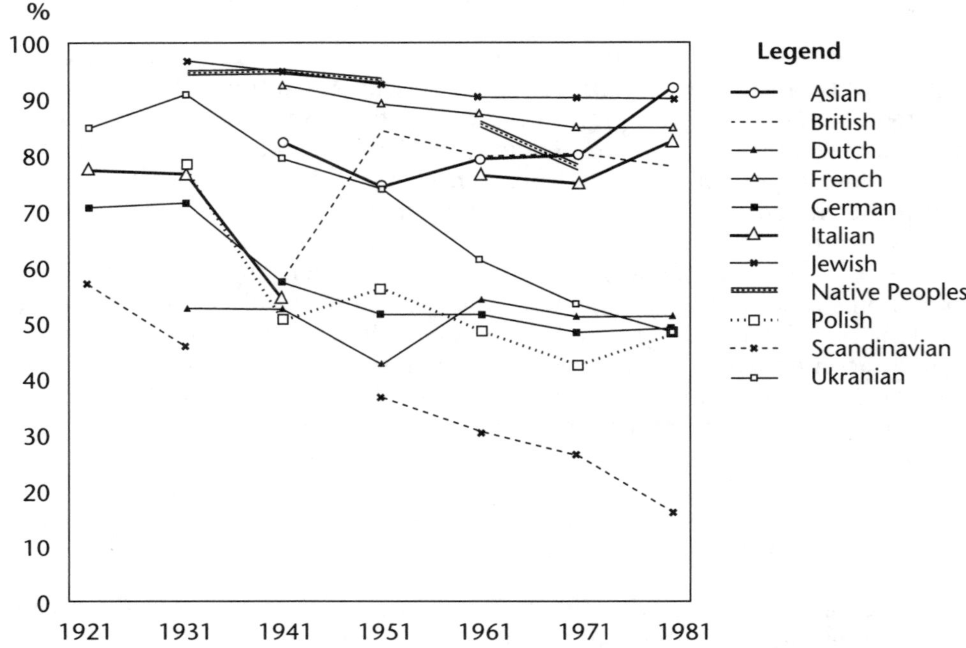

1981 data for joint rates, except for British, French, and Jewish.
Source: Edward N. Herberg (1989). *Ethnic Groups in Canada: Adaptations and Transitions*. Scarborough, Ont.: Nelson Canada, p. 188.

A third disadvantaged group are older people, especially older women. The chance of marrying for the first time drops off dramatically after a person reaches 30 years of age. There are a number of reasons for this. Since most people are married by their early-thirties, their choice of partners becomes more limited after that age. Often women who have devoted themselves to their careers are viewed as being aggressive and unfeminine and have to either overcome this stereotype or find someone who is not threatened by their success (Nagnur & Adams, 1987).

The number of eligible over-thirties is swelled by the growing number of people who are divorced (Price & Dana, 1987). They have problems getting back into the stream of searchers. The social networks of younger people are organized so that meeting eligible individuals is quite easy. Since most older people are married, social life has a couples basis, and meeting someone is more difficult.

Table 3.3

PROBABILITY OF MARRYING FOR NEVER-MARRIED MEN AND WOMEN, BY AGE, 1971, 1976, AND 1981

	Men			Women		
	1971	1976	1981	1971	1976	1981
At age			%			
15	95.3	92.7	89.1	95.1	92.8	89.7
20	94.9	92.3	88.2	93.3	90.8	88.1
25	88.1	85.2	81.7	79.6	77.8	75.0
30	70.6	68.7	63.8	58.3	57.3	52.2
35	51.0	50.4	44.1	37.2	39.4	33.4
40	36.3	35.5	29.1	27.0	25.8	21.5
45	25.4	24.9	20.0	17.6	17.2	13.9

Source: Dhruva Nagnur and Owen Adams (1987). "Tying the Knot: An Overview of Marriage Rates in Canada," *Canadian Social Trends*, Autumn, p. 5.

Women have the hardest time meeting eligible people. Men usually have more economic and social power than women, which makes up for their age. This fact is reflected in the popular notion that women grow old, but men become distinguished. Women, more than men, have custody of children after divorce. Many men do not wish to accept the economic disadvantage and emotional complication of a stepfamily. Some choose younger women without encumbrances, with whom they can renew a sense of their youthfulness. Women usually do not have this option because society looks down on the older woman-younger man relationship. In addition, men die younger than women; the older a woman becomes, therefore, the fewer the men.

The Never-Married

About 10 percent of the population never marry. Most of the information available regarding this group concerns women. There are a number of assumptions in our society about women and marriage. Wedlock is seen as a natural and necessary state if women are to reach their full development. Since women are supposed to be interested in relationships, it is assumed that they want to be married. If they are not, it is assumed that no one asked them, not that they chose to remain single. There is, therefore, a stigma attached to being an unmarried woman, which is reflected in expressions like "old maid" and "left on the shelf." Unmarried women are seen as both defective in personality and as leading tragic lives. The only group of unmarried women who are fully accepted are nuns (Hicks & Anderson, 1989; Wilson, 1990).

The truth is, however, that unmarried women tend to have a higher level of educational and professional success than their married sisters. In part this is because it is assumed that women will put their husband's and children's interests before their own; thus those who have not married are freed to concentrate on their own careers. Interestingly, they usually experience less anxiety than married women. Those who genuinely wish to be married, however, feel doubly disadvantaged: they are alone and they do not feel in control of their own fate (Hicks & Anderson, 1989). We must not assume, however, that unmarried means uncoupled. The unmarried may include both homosexual and heterosexual cohabiting couples. A number of these relationships are both longstanding and satisfying (Wilson, 1990).

The Love Ideal

In all of this discussion about factors involved in mate selection, we have not spoken about what most North Americans consider the most important aspect—love. How can we define romantic love? It is a strong emotional attachment between adolescents or adults. It is a mixture of sexual desire and tenderness, comradely affection and playfulness (Lee, 1975). Psychologists define the criteria for love as physical arousal, the presence (real or imagined) of someone to love, and the belief that you are in love.

THE ROAD TO ROMANTIC LOVE

The notion of romantic love developed in three stages, all related to the social situations of their times. The first two were played out against the reality of arranged marriages.

First came the tradition of courtly love that was developed by the troubadours in Provence, in what is now southern France, during the 12th century. Some of their ideas were drawn from Roman and Arabic traditions, but the feudal nobility gave courtly love its special flavour. At that time, many of the young knights who served a lord did not have the financial backing to be married, especially if they were younger sons. They diverted their sexual energy through adoration of the lady of the manor and through doing deeds to prove themselves worthy of love. This emotion was spiritual rather than sexual. Thus true love, they felt, was impossible within the arranged marriages of the time. Courtly love, therefore, served to contain the sexual desires of the many young single men and to safeguard the marital rights of the husbands (Beigel, 1951; Lee, 1975).

The second stage of romantic love emerged among the nobility in 17th- and 18th-century Europe. They also held the belief that love and marriage were incompatible, and that love was to be found only outside marriage. Unlike the courtly tradition, the nobility integrated love and sex. Gallant deeds and duels were rewarded not by admiration but by sexual favours. Some writers suggest that in this way the nobility compensated for some of the boredom of arranged marriages (Beigel, 1951). There is little record of the behaviour of the common folk of this time, but it is possible that they had more freedom to choose their own mates (Sarsby, 1983).

In the third stage, there was the same desire for a union of sex and love among the emerging middle class. Marriages were still arranged; and individuals had neither the time nor the money to engage in extramarital affairs, and their religious beliefs prohibited them. They compromised by allowing the love language of the courtly tradition to be used between engaged couples. Thus, for the first time, the notion of love was attached to an unmarried woman. During the Industrial Revolution, there was a growing emphasis on individuality. Young people began to demand the ability to choose their own mates. Since love had been associated with courtship, it was natural to use it as the basis for marriage (Beigel, 1951). It was this tradition that the earliest settlers from Europe brought with them to North America, where it has been combined with the emphasis on individual achievement.

THE WHEEL OF LOVE

How can we combine the evidence about homogamy in marriage with the ideal of romantic love?

Sociologist Ira Reiss (1980) described what he called the "Wheel of Love" (Figure 3.2). There are four processes through which all forms of love and friendship develop. The first is a feeling of rapport. When people feel comfortable with each other, they reveal aspects of themselves such as their experiences, hopes, desires, and fears. This second phase, self-revelation, can be broad, i.e., cover many areas of life, or it can be deep, i.e., expose more private feelings and ideas. Usually only close relationships involve depth of revelation; and these are more likely to involve sexual activity. The third phase is the development of mutual dependencies. Individuals begin to rely on each other to share ideas, jokes, and intimate feelings. Thus the fourth process, personal-need fulfilment, comes into play. Growing trust is also an important aspect of the developing relationship. This is a circular process. If needs are fulfilled, then there is a feeling of rapport, and the cycle is renewed (Adler & Towne, 1990, Reiss, 1980).

These four processes are related to the various factors involved in mate selection. If a couple has similar experiences and values, they are more likely to have rapport. Cultural background helps determine what each individual feels is proper to reveal. Some topics may be taboo. Certain types of sexual activity may be approved or discouraged. The needs of one partner may fit the strengths of the

Figure 3.2

THE WHEEL THEORY OF LOVE

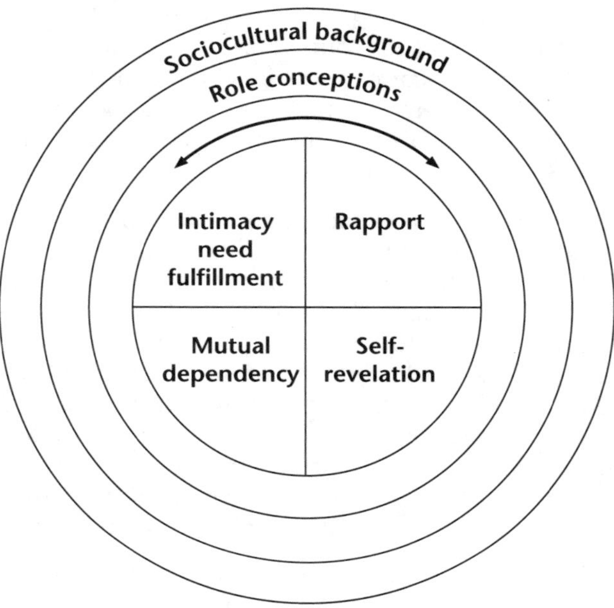

Source: Ira L. Reiss (1980). *Family Systems in America.* 3rd ed. New York: Holt, Rinehart and Winston, p. 129.

other and vice versa, in what is referred to as a complementarity of needs. Thus a woman who needs to look up to her mate will be most comfortable with a man who needs this type of relationship. Needs can be influenced by social values. In the preceding example, for instance, there are signs of a double standard.

Obstacles to Love Relationships—The Communication Gap

Many difficulties in intimate relationships are related to differences between men and women. For example, communication about feelings is more likely to occur nonverbally than verbally. In part, this occurs because our society does not encourage us to express our emotions verbally. As a result such communication is likely to be open to misunderstanding. As we saw in the last chapter, women are more skilled than men at interpreting nonverbal messages. Often we are afraid to reveal personal information or our innermost feelings to others, for a number of reasons. We may not want to risk being misunderstood or having our emotions used against us; we may also fear making others feel uncomfortable (Adler & Towne, 1990).

Individuals come to new relationships with expectations that are based in the past. They may have learned these in their families of origin or through relationships with friends or lovers. Some of the expectations can result in warped communication and crippling relationships. One example is the person who treats another as property. In other cases, one partner may see the other as someone from the past, such as a parent or previous lover. Others try to make the partner fit a fantasy ideal. During courtship people may deliberately present themselves as something they are not because they are afraid that no one will like the real person. In other relationships, one partner tries to absorb the other and allows no room for individuality, sometimes even telling outsiders the partner's "real" feelings (Sieburg, 1985).

The quality of a relationship during the process of mate selection and the communication on which it is based are important for the marriage that follows. Once they have been established, patterns of communication tend to endure and are difficult to change.

Thorns in the Relationship

Two problems that occur within marriage have their counterparts in premarital relationships—infidelity and violence. Both suggest a failure to achieve the kind of intimacy Erikson (1963) describes.

Infidelity breaks the trust and commitment that are expected in a love relationship. In dating relationships it can range all the way from flirting and kissing to sexual intercourse. Infidelity can also include emotional rather than physical involvement. The reasons given for infidelity in premarital relationships are similar to those for infidelity in marriage—dissatisfaction, revenge or jealousy, desire for variety, and sexual incompatibility. Adolescents who were studied also cited a sense of insecurity, immaturity, and lack of communication. One difference in premarital and marital infidelity is that people are more likely to consider ending a premarital relationship than a marriage because of infidelity, perhaps because they have not committed themselves as strongly to it (Roscoe, Cavanaugh, & Kennedy, 1988).

A more serious problem is premarital violence, which may be a reflection of power and conflict issues in society as a whole. It often results from the desire of one partner to exert power over the other. It may also be an expression of extreme jealousy and thus of a sense of insecurity in the relationship. The forms premarital violence take, are similar to those within marriage. The only exception is that date rape is reported more often than marital rape, perhaps because

When I was 17 I had a boyfriend who was abusive. I was abused many times over the two years I stayed with him. This was not a live-in arrangement; I was living at home at the time. I had a father, a mother, and four younger brothers aged 16, 15, 14, and 13. At first the abuse was "mild", as in slaps or being pushed or tripped by "accident" on the street. The remorse felt by him afterwards and the attention he gave me were enough to smooth things over. Of course, I told no one of the incidents. Gradually the abuse increased. Over the two years I received a fractured cheekbone, many bruises and scrapes, and I was made to feel that I was worthless. Despite this I stayed because a mutual friend, who had known him before he met me, told me that when his last girlfriend tried to leave, he tried to burn her family's house down. Of course, I knew nothing of this when I first met him. In retrospect, however, it probably wouldn't have made a difference because the initial attraction was too great. However, I was afraid to leave when I wanted to leave.

One day a friend of my brother saw my boyfriend kick me and trip me on a public street. He told my brother, then 16, who told my father. My father asked my boyfriend if he had done this. When my boyfriend said no, my father left it at that and went back to reading his paper. All those months I had suffered abuse to "protect" myself and my family and I felt as if my father couldn't or wouldn't help me. At that time I knew if things were to change, it would be up to me.

Finally I did leave the relationship and only after did I find out my brother, then 18, had been chumming around with my boyfriend, picking up other girls, and laughing at me and the situation. Even after I received the courage to leave, despite what could have happened to my family, my brother brought him home to our house. Again, I felt that nobody cared about how I felt; my parents allowed him in and my brother brought him home.

As to how it affected me, I felt my father had let me down and was a weakling. As for my brother, I decided he was a selfish, unfeeling, poor excuse for family, since up to then I felt we had been very good friends. I have never felt the same about him.

I thank God I had the wisdom and courage to wake up before it was too late.

sexual relations are regarded as the right of the husband or wife. Studies of dating violence show that both men and women use physical violence against the other. Both sexes, however, feel that men are usually the aggressors and women the victims. Since men are stronger physically, any couple violence is far more likely to result in the woman getting hurt. Women stay in these abusive relationships for a number of reasons—out of fear, to protect other members of their family, out of love for the abuser, or in the hope that the abuser will change (Burke, Stets, & Pirog-Good, 1988; Makepeace, 1986).

Get Ready, Get Set ...

Marriage preparation has taken different forms over the years. Two basic approaches reflect two different views of family life. The first, akin to the structural-functional theory, is an emphasis on traditional roles in marriage. In the past, men were trained to be breadwinners, often receiving their education outside the home. The physical care of both the household and family members was entrusted to the women. Traditionally women's education for marriage took place in the home; for generations, girls learned how to keep house from their mothers and other female relatives. If women expected to marry into a middle-class or wealthy family, they would probably also learn how to manage a servant or staff of servants. In a less-affluent family, they would learn to perform all the practical aspects of housekeeping and child care. Sex education was often limited, although many women learned about childbirth from helping others. It is difficult to know how much education concerning relationships took place, since this aspect was largely unrecorded.

In Canada, the government became involved in marriage preparation early in this century. In 1903 the Agricultural College in Guelph, Ontario, began what was popularly known as the "Diamond Ring Course." This one-year course was started by reformer Adelaide Hunter Hoodless, whose son had died from drinking unpasteurized milk. She got funding from the province to teach young farm wives subjects such as nutrition and health care (Kieran, 1986). Thus, in part, marriage preparation was regarded as a public health matter. Obviously, the emphasis was on the traditional role of woman as caregiver.

In more recent years, preparation has taken more of a symbolic-interactionist approach. As the divorce rate spiralled, religious organizations became alarmed at the number of marriage failures. They started to suggest, and eventually insist, that couples take part in marriage-preparation courses. The focus in these courses is not the physical care of the family, but rather the relationship between husband and wife. Couples may look at key issues such as communication skills, expectations they bring from families of origin, adjustments that need to occur during marriage, conflict management, sexuality, and financial management. Since many of these programs are offered by religious organizations, participants may also consider the religious perspective on marriage.

The rationale behind current marriage-preparation courses is that couples who have been helped to explore these areas will have more firmly based relationships. Thus organizers hope that marriages will endure rather than end in separation or divorce. Some leaders, however, state that many couples see these courses as a formality they need to go through in order to marry, and do not take the exercises too seriously; as a result they do not get the full benefit of the courses.

Briar Rose Revisited

We have come a long way from Briar Rose, the symbol of romantic love. Relationships between couples are far more complex than her story would have us believe. They involve the impact of our society and its values and norms. Families influence our choice. Relationships are a mix of our past history and our ability to communicate. They bring intimacy and conflict. For most couples, the relationship patterns that are developed during mate selection form the basis for the rest of family life.

SUMMARY

STARTING FAMILIES. Despite the growing variety in family types, most begin with mate selection. This is related to the developmental task of forming an intimate relationship, and builds a foundation for marriage.

MATE SELECTION AND SOCIETY. The forms mate selection take are closely related to the values and traditions of the societies of which they are part. This holds true for both aboriginal peoples and for white industrialized societies. Courtship practices fall along a continuum between arranged and self-chosen marriages, and another between those based on value exchange and shared emotion.

At one end of the scale are arranged marriages, which are planned by parents to link two families. Often strategies for controlling romantic love accompany such unions. In North America, there has been a shift toward choosing one's own mate. Although in the early years of settlement by European immigrants, choice was limited, choosing for oneself suited the individuality of many newcomers. Attitudes toward premarital sexuality were, at times, contradictory. Although official attitudes stressed sex only within marriage, practices may have been more permissive. A double standard, allowing men more freedom than women, was common. During the 1920s, the practice of casual dating emerged. It served the functions of status, socialization, recreation, and courtship. Since the 1960s, there has been greater sexual freedom, especially among young people, with an increase in premarital cohabitation.

We do not have complete freedom in mate selection. Laws, family influences, availability of potential partners, and the tendency toward homogamy all limit our choices. Some people, such as those with visible disabilities and older women, are at a particular disadvantage.

Often never-married women are regarded as objects of pity or contempt. Generally, however, they have a higher level of educational and professional achievement than married women.

THE LOVE IDEAL. The idea that romantic love is the basis for marriage developed gradually from the courtly love tradition celebrated by the court poets of the 12th century. The growth of love develops through a series of stages—rapport, self-revelation, mutual dependency, and personal-need fulfilment—that lead to greater levels of intimacy. This process has been referred to as the "Wheel of Love." The growth of intimacy and love is dependent on open communication. Problems in this area may arise because of difficulties in interpreting nonverbal messages and because of unrealistic expectations.

PROBLEMS DURING COURTSHIP. Problems that arise during the period of mate selection are similar to those in marriage. Infidelity may occur out of dissatisfaction, desire for variety, sexual incompatibility, or lack of communication. The causes of premarital violence are similar to those in marriage, except that date rape is reported more often than marital rape. Often violence is used to exert power over the partner.

MARRIAGE PREPARATION. There has been a move from the practical requirements of running a household to an emphasis on emotional and communication aspects of marriage. There has also been a shift from training in the home to sponsorship by religious organizations.

KEY TERMS

cohabitation: living together, usually referring to a couple with a sexual relationship

courtship: a process of mate selection

enclave: people of a minority culture who live as a group within the larger society

endogamy: marriage within one's social group

homogamy: the tendency to marry someone similar to oneself

incest taboo: social ban on marrying someone who is too closely related

CLASS ASSIGNMENTS

Complete one or both of the following assignments, as directed by your instructor.

1. Many people live together before marriage. Explain the advantages and disadvantages of this practice. Think about the relationship of the couple, family and community attitudes, as well as financial and legal factors. You may discover information through library research, through interviews with couples and experts, and possibly through TV talk shows.
2. In a group, plan and conduct a survey of students concerning their attitudes toward premarital sex. Be prepared to report the results and to discuss what factors might have affected the answers you received.

PERSONAL ASSIGNMENTS

These assignments are designed to help you think about your own family experiences and expectations.

1. Make a list of the qualities you would like in a partner. Which ones are most important? Explain.
2. Do you and your parents (and/or children) have the same attitudes about relations between men and women? How are they similar, and how do they differ? How do you handle differences of opinion about a boyfriend or girlfriend?

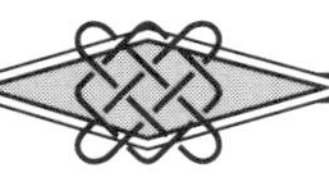

PART 3

Marriage and Children

CHAPTER 4

Wedding Bells ... and After

OBJECTIVES

- To present economic, legal, and historical aspects of marriage in Canada.
- To place marriage in the family life cycle.
- To examine the functions of marriage.
- To consider the roles of husband and wife in marriage.
- To look at the impact of two careers on marriage.
- To explore factors involved in marital happiness.

Today's the big day ... First, they'll do the traditional things: Walk down the aisle at 10:45 this morning, she in the conventional romantic gown, he in the traditional tux. Then they're going to party.

Everyone will hop aboard a boat, cruise around Toronto Islands, dance away the evening around the handmade ice sculptures. Bride and groom will make a grand entrance via helicopter and, for the grand finale, 200 helium-filled balloons equipped with tiny lights will soar into the night sky.

Then the newlyweds will return to life as usual in the home they've shared for the past 4 1/2 years.

Source: Kim Zarzour, *Toronto Star*, 1 August 1987, p. J1

Weddings are big business. Since many couples are marrying at an older age, there is more money available to spend on their weddings. One writer conservatively estimated in 1987 that a moderately priced wedding meant nearly $22 000 in business if you count the engagement ring, wedding gifts, and honeymoon, as well as the actual cost of the wedding itself (Maynard, 1987). Often families and friends spend much more, although not everyone uses a helicopter!

Society and Marriage

The wedding ceremony itself has a serious function. It is the public acknowledgment that a new family has been created legally. It is a ritual organized by the family itself and marks the change in status and roles among all family members (McGoldrick, 1988b).

Many of the customs surrounding the "standard Western wedding" are reminders of earlier practices. Does the father give the bride away? Does the groom give her a ring? Both of these are leftovers from arranged marriages where a daughter was considered a financial asset who could be purchased. The wedding ceremony still contains the traces of property transfer and the bride price. Does the bride wear white? This colour symbolizes virginity, which was valued in arranged marriages. Do we throw rice or its substitute, confetti? We are wishing the couple fertility. In the past, the production of children, especially an heir, was one of the reasons marriages were arranged (Nett, 1988).

In pioneer-era North America, things were different from today. Often weddings were much simpler, partly because of financial constraints. Many families were isolated, and marriages occurred whenever a travelling clergyman came by, often without much prior warning. In some cases, the minister or priest would marry the couple, and then baptize the first child, or two or three children.

Even when the engaged couple lived in a town or city and could plan a more elaborate ceremony, they might have little choice in church or clergyman. In Upper Canada (later to become Ontario), there was a further complication. Until 1797 only Anglican and Roman Catholic clergy could conduct legal marriages. Permission was later given to the clergy of several other denominations to perform weddings. Marriages performed by Methodists (and these included many of the circuit-riding clergy who visited remote communities) were not made legal until 1831. Over the years, many people were married in their own faith, although the marriages were not recognized by the government (Kieran, 1986).

Even the time of year weddings occur is related to social factors. In 1939, for example, there was a double peak in marriages during June and September. This phenomenon reflects the agricultural basis of Canadian society at the time. In June crops had been planted and there was a temporary slack in farm work; in September, the harvest was in. During this period, the number of marriages in Quebec was particularly low in March, because the Roman Catholic Church

Table 4.1

THE HIGH COST OF ROMANCE

As the average age of newlyweds increases, well-heeled brides are demanding all the trappings: nationwide, they spend $2 billion a year. Here's the tab for an average wedding.

Engagement ring	$	800
Bride's outfit (includes lingerie, shoes, veil)	$	1 040
Hairdresser for bride	$	60
Bride's going-away outfit	$	320
Three bridesmaids' outfits (including shoes, lingerie)	$	900
Two mothers' outfits	$	850
Six tuxes (groom, 2 fathers, 3 attendants)	$	700
Flowers (including church and table decorations, corsages, and boutonnieres)	$	700
Clergy's honorarium	$	75
Charge for use of church	$	200
Organist	$	50
Church custodian	$	35
Photographer	$	700
Two limousines	$	270
Disc jockey	$	200
Invitations (60)	$	200
Matches, napkins, placecards	$	100
Dinner for 120 @ $30 each	$	3 600
Wine (cheap)	$	300
Liquor	$	1 000
Bartender, ice, and mix	$	250
Sweet table	$	500
Cake	$	250
Car decorations	$	100
Wedding rings	$	400
Gifts for attendants	$	100
Gifts (60 @ $100)	$	6 000
Honeymoon	$	2 000
TOTAL	$	21 700

Source: Rona Maynard (1987). "Here Come the Brides," *Report on Business Magazine*, June, p. 30.

discouraged marriages during Lent. In 1985, weddings showed only one peak, during the summer. This was probably a reflection of vacation patterns in an industrial society (Dumas & Peron, 1992).

Economic and political factors are related to the age at which individuals marry for the first time. During the Great Depression, for example, marriages were delayed. In the early years of World War II, there was a spectacular increase in marriages of younger people. One explanation is that young men fearing conscription hurried to get married before they were sent overseas. During the prosperous times following the war, ages of both men and women marrying for the first time reached a low for the century. Now first marriages are once again occurring later in life. Two factors may be involved: poor economic times and an increase in couples living together before marriage (Dumas & Peron, 1992).

Figure 4.1

TOTAL FIRST MARRIAGE RATE AND UNEMPLOYMENT RATE AMONG MEN, AGED 20–24, CANADA, 1931–81

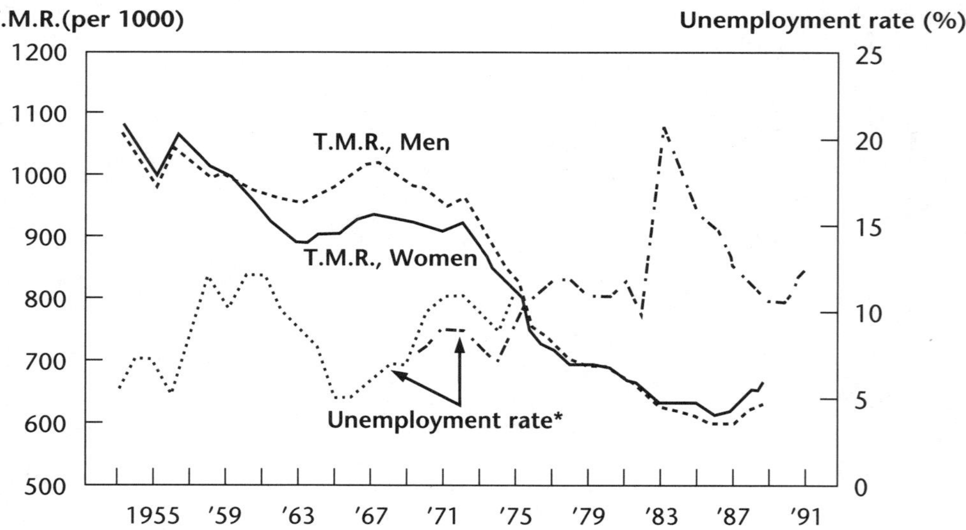

* This rate was calculated according to two different methods.
Source: Statistics Canada, "Vital Statistics and 1990 General Social Survey," In Jean Dumas and Yves Peron (1992). *Marriage and Conjugal Life in Canada: Current Demographic Analysis*. Ottawa: Statistics Canada, p. 76.

Law and Marriage

Since marriage is a legal contract, it is governed by law. There are rules about who can marry. For example, brothers and sisters cannot marry in Canada, although such marriages were popular among Egyptian royalty. Marriage to more than one person at a time is not allowed. A divorce or annulment is necessary before a married person can be married again. The law governs who may perform a legal marriage. It also states what happens to property if the marriage is dissolved through death or divorce.

A marriage brings with it both rights and duties. Each partner has the right to sexual access to the other; they have the right to be treated kindly and not to be abused; they have the right to expect faithfulness from their partner. A divorce can be granted if one partner refuses sex, if he or she has sexual relations with someone other than the spouse, or if he or she is cruel toward the other. There are laws against assault, which apply to spouses as much as to unrelated individuals. Both partners have the right to use family assets, although the individual who owns a car or cottage may sell it without the consent of the other. They have a right to the matrimonial home, which is usually treated in law as a special case. They have a responsibility to support each other and any children they might have. They also have the right to decide the kind of upbringing they want for their children, e.g., which schools they should attend and in which religious faith they should be raised.

Some couples draw up a *marriage contract*. This is a legal document that alters the effect of the law, usually as it applies to property. Some couples go so far as to include the number of children they will have and who will take out the garbage. One lawyer suggests that if couples need to include such details, their relationship may well be in trouble (Cochrane, 1991).

Most contracts are based on financial reasons when one partner (or both) wishes to opt out of the provisions of family law. It is difficult to talk about law and contracts in general terms, since legislation differs from province to province. In Ontario and most other provinces, legally married spouses have an equal share in the family home and in assets gained during the marriage. When an individual remarries, a contract may be used to protect the interests of the children from the first marriage, e.g., the new spouse may be barred from inheriting property, such as a house, that was acquired during the first marriage. In one case, a woman who had been in extreme poverty following a divorce saw the marriage contract as a sign of love from her second husband. Under the contract, her new husband has no legal right to the house she bought with her own money; thus she is assured that she will not lose financially as a result of her second marriage. When a wealthy spouse marries someone with little money, a contract may be drawn up limiting the share the poorer one can get if the marriage breaks up. Owners of businesses may draw up contracts excluding the business from the assets of the marriage because under equal-sharing rules, the spouse

HERMAN **by Jim Unger**

Source: *The Toronto Star,* 19 September, 1987.

would be entitled to half of the business if the marriage ends. This might jeopardize the business if there are several partners. A contract can avoid such difficulties. Though not common, a contract may also be drawn up by common-law spouses entitling the partners to a share of the other's assets. Depending on the province, a common-law partner may, after a specified period of time, gain the same right to support as a married spouse. This right does not extend to property, except in rare cases where he, or more commonly she, has shown that (s)he has contributed to the spouse's business (Cochrane, 1991).

A marriage contract can create problems. If the financial situation of one or both partners changes, it may impose an unfair settlement on the couple. For instance, both partners may be working when they marry. If they have a child and one spouse stays home to care for the child, then that person may not be in a good position to support himself or herself if they split up. It is also difficult to negotiate a contract, for example for business reasons, during the marriage since a contract means giving up financial rights (Cochrane, 1991).

Marriage in the Family Cycle

In the past, marriage was a major transition, which marked the fact that an individual had reached adulthood. With marriage came approved sexual relations, cohabitation, and parenthood. Marriage was closely related to the economic and social organization of society; e.g., in traditional native culture men and women had different roles based on sex and family status. The same is true of *patriarchal* cultures, where men work to support the family and women provide physical and emotional care for members. However, marriage is changing. It is no longer the official signal that an individual has adult status. In fact, as we saw in Chapter 3, marriages are being delayed until later in life, and individuals are not waiting for the ceremony in order to have sexual relations or to live together. The ability to support oneself financially has become a more common criterion of adulthood. Since more women are now in the work force, they are not necessarily dependent on men for support. Widely available contraceptives mean that parenthood can be postponed indefinitely (McGoldrick, 1988b).

Marriage involves a commitment to the new family system, which is separate from that of their families of origin (McGoldrick, 1988b). The couple needs to learn to depend first on each other for satisfaction of their needs. This task involves emotional separation from the family of origin, learning to accept the roles of husband and wife, and gaining a sense of identity as a family. Even couples who have lived together before marriage report that their relationship changes after marriage; many find this fact surprising. In fact, men and women often bring to marriage expectations learned in their families of origin that they did not have of the living-with relationship. They may for the first time have the security to act "natural." Each spouse brings a history of traditions and expectations. The couple must decide which of these they will keep, change, or drop altogether (McGoldrick, 1988b).

The wife and husband have individually been members of various microsystems—family of origin, friends, fellow employees. Now they must renegotiate as a couple their relationships with these groups. This may not have been done prior to marriage. Even if they have been living together, the partners may not have related to the extended families as a couple; each may have visited their family alone. Changes couples make in visiting patterns, in social activities such as a night out with same-sex friends, or in family rituals and traditions affect others. Some may become hurt or angry. Often the new marriage partner is the first new member of the extended family system in many years. The stress of change may lead the players, including the new couple, to see the situation in terms of villains and victims; thus there may be conflict with in-laws and friends. Some issues may be put on hold by the couple, e.g., they may not deal with sex-role related issues, such as the responsibility for child care, until they become parents (McGoldrick, 1988b).

Ethnic couples may face additional adjustment stresses, since the media, schools, and other institutions of the white majority society give off messages about what families should be (McGoldrick, 1988a). Minority groups may have different boundaries around the family than the majority, i.e., many Italian families place more emphasis on the extended family and less on the nuclear family. There may be conflict over the definition of sex roles. Immigrants from Moslem countries, for example, may expect more subservience from their women than is usual in English or French Canada. If women begin to accept new values, there

CULT MEN WITH MANY WIVES FACE NO CHARGES IN B.C.

Southamstar Network

CRESTON, B.C.—Leaders of a breakaway Mormon sect in British Columbia won't be hauled into court for having more than one spouse at a time, the provincial attorney-general has decided.

Attorney General Colin Gabelmann said polygamous cults are symptomatic of "a social problem" which needs to be attacked on various fronts, not just through the criminal law.

Moreover, the attorney-general's office believes the Criminal Code section outlawing polygamy is unconstitutional because it violates religious freedom guarantees, Crown counsel Herman Rohrmoser said. "Section 293 (of the code) is invalid and will not be enforced in B.C."

Constitutional experts decided after nine months of research that two leaders of the polygamous commune in Lister, near Creston in rural B.C., should not face charges.

"This decision is a legal one based on the fact that the present polygamy provision conflicts with the Charter of Rights and Freedoms," said Rohrmoser.

Police had recommended polygamy charges against:

- Palmer's father, Dalmin Oler, 60, who has five wives.
- Commune leader Winston Blackmore, who reportedly took his sixth wife, a 16-year-old, last September.

The commune is part of the 10,000-strong United Effort Order in North America, headed by Rulon Jeffs of Salt Lake City, Utah.

Jeffs welcomed the B.C. decision, but women who fled the commune say legalizing polygamy opens the way for more abuse.

He called B.C.'s ruling historic. "In the U.S. polygamy is still illegal but there have been no prosecutions in 37 years," he said.

In the past two years three men from the commune have been convicted of sexual abuse of wives and half sisters.

A woman who fled the commune vowed to fight for others trapped in polygamous marriages.

Debbie Palmer, 36, said she was outraged at the decision not to prosecute.

"It's legalizing all the abuse in such relationships," said Palmer, the mother of seven who fled a United Effort Order commune in the Kootenays in 1988.

Palmer was only 15 when she was paired up with a 57-year-old man—her step-grandfather who already had five wives. Most of his 31 children were older than Palmer.

Three years later, when the man died, she was matched to a 59-year-old man who kept her, another wife and eight children in two uninsulated rooms at the back of a store.

After two attempted suicides and a nervous breakdown Palmer persuaded the commune leaders to end the relationship.

Source: *The Toronto Star*, 13 June 1992, p. A10.

may be serious conflict between spouses. There are also different standards among cultures for the degree of emotional intimacy between spouses. In cultures where marriages are usually arranged, less intimacy may be expected than in white culture, with its emphasis on the self-sufficient nuclear family. Intermarriage may make adjustment more difficult for the couple, since they will have to reconcile the expectations brought from their separate cultures.

Why Marry?

Although fewer individuals in their twenties are marrying now than even ten years ago, most people will be married at some time during their lives; thus there must be some reason for its continuing popularity. Over the centuries, marriage has served a number of purposes, most of which are still background reasons for marrying.

STATUS

Marriages have been arranged for status reasons, both economic and social. Although this is usually not considered a purpose in most of modern North America, it does occur in many parts of the world. Arranged marriages need not be unhappy. Divorce rates are low among arranged marriages, perhaps because the partners do not expect the ecstasy of romantic love. Unlike those who marry for love, those in arranged marriages cannot be disappointed if love fades. The partners may have common interests, affection, and concern to make the marriage pleasant. Although most Canadians do not marry for money or position, they do consider whether their prospective partner earns enough money so that they can have the lifestyle they want, and if that person will fit into that lifestyle.

ECONOMICS

Marriage can ensure physical and economic survival. When homesteaders went west, both men and women had to put in long hours clearing stumps and breaking the soil; with luck, relatives and neighbours helped. After their children were born, the wife's responsibilities centred more on the small house they had built. Once the children were old enough, they helped out with farm chores. This pattern continued into this century in rural Canada. A study of a Quebec parish in the 1930s found that for a farm to be productive, the labour of all family members was required (Miner, 1939). In current Canadian family law, both partners have the duty to support each other financially, either by making money or by caring for the home and children (Wolfson, 1987).

Nowadays, marriage is not necessarily of financial benefit. Tax law actually may make it more practical for some couples to live together than to get married. Depending on income, a single parent may claim a greater Child Tax Credit than if he or she married (Birch & Matthews, 1990). On the other hand, marriage may make financial sense. Student grants and loans are usually awarded on the basis of parents' income. Upon marriage, couples declare only their income and may become eligible for much greater assistance. Government old-age-security pensions are given to individuals rather than to families. Because they can cut costs by sharing accommodation, a married couple is less likely to be poor than a single person.

SEX

Marriage is designed to regulate sexual behaviour. Usually marriage limits sexual relations to an exclusive partner (or in the case of polygamy, to one of a group of partners). This expectation is reflected in Canada in divorce law in which *adultery* is a ground for divorce. In the past, it was considered important that the bride be a virgin, and that she have sexual relations only with her husband. This demand ensured that land and titles were passed on to biological descendants of the husband only. It didn't matter, however, if he had sexual experience before and outside marriage. With improved contraception, however, childbearing can be separated from sexual activity. Although sexual access to the partner is presumed, it is not always present in marriage, e.g., when there is illness or when one or both partners do not choose to have sexual relations (for example, see Amiel, 1987). When this occurs, divorce may be granted on grounds of cruelty or marriage breakdown (Nett, 1988).

CHILDREN

Marriage is also designed to care for children. Since they need parents' care for so many years, the stability of the marriage relationship allows them to survive physically and to become socialized and productive members of society. Higher levels of female employment and family benefits have made it possible for single parents to raise children, although usually not in luxury.

IDENTITY

For women, in particular, marriage has, over the years, provided an identity. In the traditional family, the wife takes her husband's name. Since she has no paid occupation, she takes her status from her husband as well. During daily living the couple forms a family culture and world view that are unique. These aspects of the family identity also provide a sense of purpose and meaning for the individual.

LOVE AND SUPPORT

Finally, marriage serves to look after the emotional needs of the partners. Obviously this requirement arises from the idea of romantic love. No matter how wrong things are in the rest of the world, people expect their husband or wife to be loving, sympathetic, and encouraging. In marriage a person expects to find unfailing love and support (Lasch, 1979). As we can tell from the levels of marital violence and of divorce, however, not all partners are kind and loving. The unmarried can also have their emotional needs met by extended family members, friends, and lovers.

WHY MARRY?

Most of the functions traditionally considered part of marriage can be met in other ways. So why marry?

Most of us have been socialized to believe that marriage is the "natural" state for adults. There is also a good deal of pressure put on couples who are dating or living together to get married. Well-wishers, for example, want to see the couple happy, and marriage is considered a happy state. Often parents and grandparents see marriage as a desirable step toward parenthood, and they wish to be grandparents and great-grandparents. Once the majority of a particular age group, or cohort, are married, social life tends to be organized on a couples basis, therefore, there is further pressure for individuals to find mates.

The whole romantic view of love may also be involved in individual decisions to marry. For those who are having problems such as loneliness or difficulties with their family of origin, marriage may beckon as an instant cure (McGoldrick, 1988b). As we can see by the present high rate of divorce, such hopes are often dashed.

In spite of the pressures to marry, the marriage ideal has changed. It is no longer seen as the principal career for a woman, where she finds her greatest fulfilment, or as a financial partnership, with the roles of husband and wife clearly defined. It is no longer seen mainly as a setting in which to raise children. Rather, individuals come to marriage looking for self-fulfilment; marriage is an opportunity for emotional growth and satisfaction. Ideally, each partner is willing to work at making their relationship worthwhile. The result is a greater emphasis on equality and sharing (Papp, 1988; Schlesinger & Giblon, 1984).

Marriages Yesterday

The roles of husbands and wives are greatly influenced by the values and needs of society. To illustrate this, let us look at marriage in three different societies in the past.

OJIBWA

Before the establishment of reserves, the Ojibwa were nomadic. They travelled to food sources as the seasons changed. At certain times of the year, the entire band would gather food, but usually the Ojibwa lived as nuclear families. In the spring they visited maple groves to make syrup and sugar. Summer time was fishing time; large quantities were caught and dried for winter use. Wild fruits, berries, and roots were gathered and stored, and wild rice was collected. During the winter, they hunted moose, deer, and smaller game. Since they were always on the move, the Ojibwa stored their food in caches so that it would be available when and where it was needed.

There was a fairly distinct division of labour in Ojibwa culture. Men and boys hunted and fished. They were also responsible for battling unfriendly groups. Women and girls did the picking, gathering, and preserving of food. They made clothing and, of course, cared for young children. This division of labour made sense since women with children were not as mobile as unencumbered men.

Marriages were probably arranged. For women, especially, there was no option. Girls married soon after puberty, at about 14 or 15 years old, and men at 19 or 20.

The coming of European settlers drastically affected the lifestyle of native peoples. Women who formed liaisons with traders, for example, had access to tools, which made their lives easier. They also gained status as guides and interpreters. If they were abandoned by the settlers, they moved back into the native community, often with their original husbands. Once the reserve system was formed, native men found their traditional skills becoming less and less important. Women, however, were still involved with the care of their families, although the resources they had available did change (Brodribb, 1984; Castellano, 1989).

"VICTORIAN"

Nineteenth-century British and English-Canadian society seems far-removed from the hunting-fishing-gathering society of the Ojibwa. The differences are obvious. Victorian society was a money-based society in which families did not move around following the moose and deer. Instead they lived in houses and often accumulated elaborate furnishings that would be difficult to shift from one place to another. Men worked outside of the home to earn money or managed inherited wealth. The hunting and fishing they did was more likely to be for recreation than for survival. If the family was comfortable financially, the wife had servants to cook, clean, make clothing, and even raise children. Poor women did these jobs for those with money.

The money basis for society shaped the balance of power in the family. The husband controlled the money. The wife's dowry and any money she inherited were under her husband's control from the moment of marriage. He could gamble it away or refuse to allow her to spend any. His vow at marriage to endow her with all his worldly goods really worked in reverse.

In Upper Canada, women gained some property rights in 1859. From then on, a woman had rights to all property brought into the marriage or inherited after marriage, but she had no right to any money earned during the marriage. This meant that the husband who drank up all his own wealth could by law relieve her of any money she had earned. For the first time a woman could make a will, but she could leave her property to her husband and children only. In 1884, a married woman gained the right to all property she brought into the marriage, whether inherited or earned, and she could bequeath it to anyone she chose (Kieran, 1986).

Since the early 19th-century husband had a right to all the money in the family, and since he was considered "owner" of his wife and children, he had exclusive right to custody of their children if the couple separated. A woman in an unbearable marriage, where she was humiliated and beaten, for example, could leave only at the risk of extreme poverty and the complete loss of her children. Few women found freedom worth the price (Kieran, 1986).

RURAL QUEBEC

Like the Ojibwa and "Victorian" families, those in early 20th-century rural Quebec had a clear division between men's and women's roles (Miner, 1939). Men spent their time growing crops, raising large animals, and maintaining buildings and equipment. Women cared for the daily needs of family members; they cooked, sewed, cleaned, spun, and knit, and were responsible for the vegetable and flower gardens. Without modern appliances, tasks like dishwashing required a lot of time; it may have taken three women over an hour to do the dinner dishes for the ten to twenty people who sat down at meals. Women waited on the men, and often ate after they were finished.

The wife joined the husband's family. The son who would inherit the farm brought his wife to live with his parents. Although the marriage contract usually specified that both parties had an interest in any property, the husband was the administrator and could make whatever arrangements he wished, as long as he provided for his wife. Men managed family finances. Married women rarely had any way of earning much money (Miner, 1939).

The dress and social life of married people were governed by custom. Women wore dark-coloured dresses with long sleeves and long skirts. Married or financially independent men grew mustaches. They associated only with married people or with single individuals who were at least middle-aged (Miner, 1939).

Despite their differences, these three forms of society had in common their ability to meet the basic functions of families. Economically, the family was a unit that ensured survival of its members through differing roles for men and women. Exchange theorists point out that women traded their services in childbearing and household and family care for survival. Men provided food and protection, either physically or through money earned in the workplace. Status and power in these societies tended to be granted to men. As a result, women were exploited.

The "Modernization" of Marriage

Today couples look forward to a much more democratic marriage. The wife usually plans to keep working following marriage, since her pay is important in maintaining the couple's standard of living. In turn, husbands help more with the housework.

This change was gradual. Sociologists point to the effect of two world wars, in which women had to replace men in the factories and offices. After the war, most women returned to their traditional role, for the ideal of the breadwinner husband and homemaker wife and mother was still strong. One measure of the acceptance of the "traditional" family was the baby boom; it was as if the couples were making up for lost time, and more. This period has been called the "golden age of the nuclear family" (Cheal, 1991). Yet the principle that respectable women could work outside the home had been established.

Women who continued to work after marriage did so in order to help buy houses or new furniture. Once children were born, mothers stayed home, at least until the children were in school. Since women often worked part-time, their pay was seen as an extra, something to help buy luxuries; their real business was looking after the family. By the 1970s, income was not keeping pace with inflation. A wife's pay prevented the family's purchasing power from declining. In many cases, two incomes are now necessary for a family to survive economically. In 1986, 62 percent of marriages had incomes from both spouses; this figure had almost doubled since 1967. There was a further increase to 68.2 percent by 1992 (See Table 4.2). Younger families more often have two incomes. In 74 percent of dual-income households in 1986, the husband was under the age of 45 (Moore, 1989).

Table 4.2

MARRIED WOMEN IN TWO-EARNER FAMILIES, NOVEMBER 1992

	Percent
With children under 3 years	59.4
With youngest child aged 3–5 years	64.5
With youngest child aged 6–15 years	69.7
With no children under age 16	75.6
With no children under 16, one spouse aged 55 years or over	45.6
TOTAL	68.2

Note: These figures do not include women who were unemployed and looking for work.

Source: Statistics Canada (December 1992). *The Labour Force: November 1992*. Ottawa: Statistics Canada, No. 710001, Vol. 48, No. 11. (Calculations based on figures from p. B-22.)

In this shift from single-income to dual-income families, many have experienced conflicts around men's and women's roles in the family. Values and expectations about what their roles should be have not changed as fast as have families. Women traditionally have been the caregivers in our society. Often they are expected, and they themselves expect, to be responsible for the physical and emotional well-being of the family. Many women spend more hours per day working, in combined paid employment and family care, than do men or homemaker wives (Parliament, 1989). When the demands of paid work and family care conflict, women often feel in a bind. If they go to work, for instance, when a child is ill, no matter what quality of care they have arranged, they may feel guilty. If there is no one else to care for a sick family member, women are expected to stay home. This expectation is reflected in parental leave being granted to women only (although this practice is changing). On the other hand, if a woman stays home from work because she has a sick child, or to see the school principal, she feels guilty for slacking off on work responsibilities. A number of women experience burnout because they try to do everything.

Since men traditionally have not had to concern themselves with family-care responsibilities, some have difficulty viewing housekeeping chores as being masculine. Thus they feel demeaned if they do traditional "women's" work. On the other hand, they may well be aware of the overload their wives are suffering, and be concerned for their well-being. The norm appears to be undergoing change. There is evidence that suggests that men, especially younger ones, are now taking on more household responsibilities (Luxton, 1986).

Roles in Marriage

As might be expected, there is at present no one pattern of roles in marital couples. In fact, four have been described by sociologists.

CONVENTIONAL ROLES

The first, referred to as *conventional roles* (Nett, 1988), is based on the structural-functional notion that men and women have separate spheres of action, and that the home is the proper place for women, just as the labour force is for men. This pattern originated among the middle class in the 19th century. Since the man held the power base in the family, the woman gained her status from her husband. Such a view in an extreme form is represented by the expectation that a wife should be "barefoot, pregnant, and in the kitchen."

The conventional pattern has distinct advantages. The specialization in tasks allows the partners to become expert in particular areas. A particular strength is that it provides for care of children and home. Women also have the time and energy to provide the emotional support men need in order to cope with the work world (Armstrong & Armstrong, 1987). This division of labour fits with the organization of society, where paid employment tends to become more and more specialized. It also fits in with the socialization children receive in most families concerning sex roles—that girls and boys are expected to behave in different ways. Boys are supposed to be more interested in activity and in things, while girls are supposed to be more interested in people, human relationships, and ultimately in the family. For example, a study of television advertising published in 1985 showed that women were portrayed as involved with family members, child care, and home management much more frequently than were men. This trend was present in both English- and French-language advertising, although it was more pronounced in the former (Spears & Seydegart, 1985).

There are also disadvantages to the conventional model. The advantages are paid for financially, in a lower standard of living, since there is only one wage-earner. It is also very isolating for women, since housework tends to be done alone. In the past, in rural Quebec for example, the women of large families worked together to accomplish all the housework and there was ample opportunity for social interaction. Often wives are hungry for adult companionship, while their husbands want to relax after work without demands placed on them; thus there is potential for marital dissatisfaction and conflict (Armstrong and Armstrong, 1987). It may also be difficult for a woman to move from the work force to being a homemaker. She may miss the companionship on the job. Also, instead of having her own work identity, she now takes her status from her husband.

SHARED ROLES

More common now than conventional roles in marriage are *shared roles,* where both partners work and share household responsibilities (Nett, 1988). Since more women work, more are sharing the provider role. In the past, women were able to supplement family income in ways not available now, e.g., by selling produce or doing laundry. Modern appliances and city living make such options less feasible, although some women do care for others' children while the parents work, or do paid work at home, often at low wages (Armstrong & Armstrong, 1987). Now that women are sharing the provider role, men should be expected to do day-to-day chores. Instead, they tend to specialize in home repairs, garden work, and pet care—things that are not done routinely each day (see Table 4.3). Although women work full-time, there is still the general notion that men help with housework and women help with the provider role. We will look at the relationship between family and workplace more fully in Chapter 14.

DUAL-CAREER ROLES

A third pattern is *dual-career roles,* or marriage in which both partners are committed to their careers (Nett, 1988). This is sometimes difficult to distinguish from shared roles, because there is no clear dividing line. In addition, some women start working to help out financially, and what was originally just a job becomes a career. The difference is the priority set on the career. By definition, careers exclude interrupted or part-time work; so the proportion of women employed in

Table 4.3

TIME SPENT PER DAY ON SELECTED ACTIVITIES, BY EMPLOYMENT STATUS AND SEX, NOVEMBER 1986

	Employed men	Employed women	Women keeping house	Total population
		hours/minutes per day		
Work for pay	7:04	5:49	0:22	3:35
Family care:				
— housecleaning/meal preparation	0:53	1:53	3:44	1:45
— child care	0:15	0:27	1:03	0:25
— shopping	0:39	0:54	1:15	0:53
— total family care	**1:47**	**3:13**	**6:02**	**3:03**
Personal care:				
— sleeping	7:53	8:06	8:37	8:25
— eating	1:21	1:15	1:39	1:25
— washing/dressing	0:35	0:51	0:38	0:40
— other personal care	0:25	0:25	0:31	0:31
— total personal care	**10:14**	**10:37**	**11:25**	**11:01**
Leisure time:				
— media/communication				
— television/rented movies	2:08	1:31	2:29	2:20
— other media	0:05	0:06	0:09	0:08
— reading	0:22	0:19	0:26	0:27
— total media/communication	**2:35**	**1:56**	**3:04**	**2:55**
— socializing	0:59	1:05	1:17	1:08
— sports/hobbies	0:35	0:29	0:58	0:45
— organizational/voluntary/religious activities	0:10	0:16	0:22	0:15
— other leisure activities	0:25	0:22	0:20	0:24
— total leisure time	**4:44**	**4:08**	**6:01**	**5:27**
Education and other activities	0:11	0:13	0:10	0:54
Total	**24:00**	**24:00**	**24:00**	**24:00**

Source: Statistics Canada (1986). General Social Survey, November. In Joanne B. Parliament, "How Canadians Spend Their Day," *Canadian Social Trends*, Winter 1989, p. 24.

them is very small. Dual-career couples are more likely to share equally both household responsibilities and power, but this balance does not occur invariably. The arrangement may work very well until the couple has children, often later than other families because of the desire to get careers established. The presence of a child makes long workdays and business trips much harder to schedule. These couples may thus be faced with sacrificing one career, at least for a while, or purchasing household services and nanny care for children. They may also face difficulties such as the transfer of one partner, and not the other, and in deciding whose job has priority. Such decisions may be made on the basis of income earned or on the availability of jobs in the two fields (Sekaran, 1986).

REVERSE CONVENTIONAL ROLES

A fourth pattern, in which there is a breadwinner wife and a homemaker husband, is referred to as *reverse conventional roles* (Nett, 1988). This arrangement is often temporary. The man may be laid off, may want to experiment, may be recovering from illness, or may be someone who works at home, such as a writer or artist. Many report how rewarding it is to develop a close relationship with their children. In some ways this is deceptive, since the satisfied men usually have had the kind of work they could do at home, like writing. Men who have to stay at home unwillingly because of layoffs or unemployment often experience low self-esteem because they feel they have lost identity and power along with their jobs. Their wives may become frustrated over the husbands' failure to take on more household responsibilities. Yet the men often feel they cannot do housework well enough to satisfy their wives. Often, as a result of multiple stresses, there is an increase in family conflicts (Armstrong and Armstrong, 1987).

One Family, Two Incomes—The New Reality

The idea of marital roles has changed since the first half of the century. Most married women now work outside the home, even during a recession. In November 1992, for instance, 69 percent of married women aged 25 to 44 held jobs. This number does not include those who were job hunting at the time (Statistics Canada, 1992). Over half the mothers of preschoolers were employed, and the percentage increased proportionate to children's age (see Table 4.2). As a result of the number of two-income families, couples have new issues that they need to settle in their marriages.

ROLE CHOICE

Often circumstances rather than choice dictate family roles. According to Kathleen Gerson (1987), women follow four different life paths. The first group choose homemaking. These women tend to have a stable marriage and less exciting opportunities in the workplace. In contrast, a second group of women planned a traditional marriage, but ended up in the paid work force. They were more likely to be influenced by unstable relationships, economic problems, and job opportunities. A third group always wanted to have careers and were reluctant to become mothers and homemakers. Finally, some women planned to have careers, but circumstances prevented this. The paths chosen seem to depend on the stability of the marriage, on job opportunities, on the ability of a woman's partner to earn enough so that she can stay home, and on how rewarding she considers homemaking.

In each case, women are regarded as having made a choice about getting a job. Men, on the other hand, are not seen as having a choice, since they have been raised with the idea that men work outside the home. They are now expected to add household responsibilities to their traditional role.

ROLE OVERLOAD

Individuals must now fill more roles than was expected of them in the past, since there is no longer a clear-cut separation of men's and women's domains in family life. They need to juggle two careers, children, a marriage, and household responsibilities. This fact is especially reflected in two areas of life. First, the individual, family, and work worlds overlap, and one may interfere with the others. Often time for personal interests is sacrificed because of the time needed for work and family responsibilities. There are also differences according to sex. Men, more than women, allow work to intrude on family activities. Some bring work home. Others develop a camaraderie with men at work, and their social activities after work hours can cut into family time. Women, on the other hand, are more likely to let family responsibilities interfere with work (Halle, 1987; Sekaran, 1986; Skinner, 1983). Second, couples need to relieve the stress from role overload. Many use extra money to buy time-saving products such as permanent-press fabrics or microwaves, or they pay for household aids such as take-out food, house cleaning, or child care. Couples also reorganize household chores with men assuming more responsibility. Often, however, couples suffer guilt and frustration because they cannot fill traditional roles and must take on new ones. Often trying to balance the practical demands of the two-earner lifestyle leads to conflict between the partners (Hertz, 1987). Since there are now so many dual-earner couples, however, new role models are gradually being created (Hertz, 1987; Skinner, 1983).

ROLE-CYCLING PROBLEMS

One method of dealing with overload is to stagger work and family periods of stress. Just as families go through a life cycle, careers also have a cycle. The most stressful stages in the family cycle are often considered to be child rearing and adolescence. In the career cycle, getting established in a job or a promotion are the most demanding periods. Couples may set different priorities at different times of life. For example, some couples try to establish their careers before they have children in order to avoid having high levels of stress both at home and at work (Sekaran, 1986; Skinner, 1983). The theory may break down in practice, however. Once both partners are employed, it may be difficult for one to leave the work force because they may have accumulated debts and other obligations based on their higher income; e.g., they may have bought new appliances or an expensive car (Hertz, 1987).

BALANCING PARTNERS' CAREERS

In many occupations, individuals are expected to be single-minded if they are to gain promotion. People who choose to take time off to raise a child or to work part-time often are not considered to be serious about work. There can also be a conflict between careers. Some companies need an employee who is willing to relocate in order to be promoted; others require a person to stay in one place to get established. Some couples have commuter marriages, but such arrangements often make communication and sharing much more difficult. When one partner has to be away a great deal in his or her job, for instance a sales representative who is responsible for a large territory, there can be difficulties with communication and sharing. The same holds true for couples who work in different cities (Lang, 1988). If one spouse works long hours or is often out of town, it can be difficult for the other to have his or her own career, especially if they have young children (Fowlkes, 1987).

THE WORKING COUPLE AND THEIR SOCIAL NETWORK

Given the many demands on their time, dual-earner couples often spend relatively little time with friends and extended family. This places a greater demand on the nuclear family to meet all the social and emotional needs of its members. When social networks are limited, families may experience lower levels of social support, and thus may feel higher levels of stress. Support systems assume that give-and-take occurs. One person cannot expect to be helped all the time without helping in return (La Gaipa, 1981). If the relationship remains one-sided for too long, then the social support may be cut off. When this occurs, families may become isolated.

Married Happiness

There are problems measuring the success of marriage. What criteria do we use? Do we consider the number who stay married? Some researchers have done just that and have identified risk factors which are associated with higher levels of divorce (Peck & Manocherian, 1988); yet not all unhappy marriages end in divorce. Do we ask couples how satisfied they are? Researchers found that most people report being happily or fairly happily married. Do we look for signs of conflict? Couples who do not fight may be avoiding almost all interaction with each other. In spite of these research difficulties, it is possible to consider several aspects of happiness.

AGREEMENT BETWEEN HUSBAND AND WIFE

Generally we expect that couples who agree with each other are less likely to break up. Researchers have found that the more agreement there is between spouses, the greater the stability of the marriage. Disagreement in marriage is probably reduced by homogamy. If we marry someone with a similar cultural background, educational level, religion, and values, we are more likely to agree on major issues. Agreement also tends to be greatest when the couple has to coordinate their activities to look after the tasks around home and children (White, 1989).

CONFLICT IN MARRIAGE

As we might expect, verbal disagreements tend to be higher when the couple is having problems in their marriage. It is difficult to be sure, however, which is cause and which is effect (White, 1989). Are they having problems because they fight? Or are they fighting because they have basic problems in their relationship? Conflict occurs in every marriage—it is a sign that something in the relationship needs attention. What is important is the way the couple deals with conflict.

Individuals have different conflict styles. Some are nonassertive, i.e., they do not defend their own position but give in to the other person. Others go to the opposite extreme and use direct aggression or violence to force their opinions on their partners. Still others use indirect means of communication. Some appear to agree but manage to make things turn out wrong, a strategy called passive aggression. Others hint or use nonverbal messages, and expect to be understood. Those who are most successful in dealing with conflict are those who are assertive, i.e., they state clearly what they feel is right and are prepared to discuss the issue reasonably. In dealing with conflict, couples face the challenge of striking a balance between emphasizing their own individuality and togetherness. They need to understand as well that each of them can see the situation only from their own point of view. They also need to realize that there will always be differences between partners in how they deal with conflict (Adler & Towne, 1990; Cowan & Cowan, 1992).

SEX-ROLE DIFFERENCES AND HAPPINESS IN MARRIAGE

Sex-role identity appears to be associated with adjustment in marriage. *Masculine* persons of either sex tend to have high levels of drive and ambition. In the past these qualities have been associated with men, especially as they compete in the work force. *Feminine* people usually have a strong sense of responsibility and are concerned with interpersonal relationships. Again, the term relates to traditional sex roles. Both men and women have different blends of the two characteristics. They can be high in one, high in both, or low in both. Those who are either masculine or feminine have a range of qualities that they can bring to solve marital problems. An *androgynous* individual, one high in both characteristics, has even more to offer, while an undifferentiated individual low in both has the least to offer. Androgynous individuals rate highest in marital adjustment and undifferentiated individuals rate the lowest. The researchers explain this in terms of exchange theory, i.e., androgynous partners bring more resources to help solve problems than either masculine or feminine individuals. The undifferentiated bring the fewest (Baucom et al., 1990).

Researchers have also observed that a wife's response to her husband is an indicator of the health of the relationship. When the marriage is in trouble, wives almost always say something negative when they think that what their husbands have said is negative. Wives from untroubled marriages and husbands in general are more likely to say something positive that defuses the situation (Baucom et al., 1990).

COMMUNICATION AND MARITAL SATISFACTION

The quality of communication in a marriage is important, since it directly affects the way in which couples make decisions and solve problems. Couples with a high level of communication with each other are less likely to have problems and are more likely to have solved those they experience than couples with less communication. This is especially true concerning husband-wife relations and problems around child rearing (Petersen, 1969). For instance, couples who decide together to have children are more likely to remain happy with their marriages than those marriages in which the pregnancy was an accident or where the partners disagreed over having a child (Cowan & Cowan, 1992). Couples in two-career families, especially when one or both travel a great deal, also depend on frequent and clear communication to keep their marriages healthy (Lang, 1988).

Spending a long time talking, however, does not necessarily mean that a couple's communication is effective. When emotions such as anger get mixed up with factual messages, there may be a great deal of misunderstanding. Therefore it is important for a person to concentrate on what his or her spouse is saying, rather than planning his or her response. It is also important to think about how one's words will affect a partner's feelings (Lang, 1988; Cowan & Cowan, 1992).

Nonverbal communication may be more important than what a couple actually says. If a person can read his or her partner's nonverbal messages, the marital quality is probably high. This may be because he or she is aware of what their spouse is feeling, since nonverbal messages often communicate emotion more accurately than words (White, 1989).

MARRIED HAPPINESS THROUGH LIFE

The initial adjustment and commitment to the marriage does not last. This is true even of those who have worked out a good relationship with each other and with their extended families and circle of friends. People, families, and their situations change over the years. The marriage relationship must also change if the partners are to remain satisfied.

A number of sociologists have tracked marriage across the life span and report similar findings. For example, Lupri and Frideres (1981) studied married couples in Calgary. They found that levels of happiness were high early in the marriage, rose at the birth of the first child, then dropped to an all-time low when there were teenagers in the family. Gradually satisfaction with the marriage rose as the children left home and the couple were by themselves again. However, happiness never again quite reached the level experienced early in marriage. Another study suggested that parents got a respite between preschoolers and adolescents, when marital happiness rose slightly before dropping again (Walker, 1977).

There are a number of explanations given for this satisfaction curve. Marital happiness rises as the couple adjusts to living together. In one study, childless couples hoping to adopt gave each other more affection than couples with children, and more than they showed seven years after they had adopted a baby (Humphrey, 1975; Humphrey & Kirkwood, 1982).

The birth of the first child usually is experienced as a high, in many ways similar to a honeymoon. New parents, however, soon need to face the realities of day-to-day living with an infant. Family life changes with each addition of a child, whether through birth or adoption. Relationships become more complex as first-time parents make the transition to a threesome. If there is more than one child, then sibling relationships are also involved. Furthermore, one parent may be jealous of the baby's relationship with the other parent. The couple may become so tied up with the new daily tasks, especially if both are working outside the home, that they have less time to know what the partner is thinking and feeling. In fact, having children early in marriage is related to marriage breakdown (Murphy, 1984). This is probably because the couple have not yet consolidated their own relationship.

The demands the new child places on the parents can affect their relationship. There may be less time to spend as a couple because infant care consumes many hours. In the first months, sleep is often interrupted, so that parents do not get adequate rest. If both partners work, time demands are more extreme. They may be so tired that they either do not have the energy to spend on each other or they may become extremely irritable. If they do not take time to keep lines of communication open, then their intimacy, including their sexual relationship, may suffer. For example, couples report decreased sexual responsiveness in women for a year after the birth of the first child (Elliott & Watson, 1985). This may be related to fatigue and to less opportunity for sex because of the baby's demands. Sex without intimacy may be seen by the wife as a duty to be kept at a minimum, along with other demands on her time and energy. If that happens, the husband may feel that he isn't appreciated for all the effort he puts into helping around the house and supporting the family.

Children can have other effects on the marriage. There may also be conflicts over child rearing, especially if one parent is more permissive than the other. One babysitter, for instance, reported that a mother found it cute that her children tied her pantihose together to make a rope for lowering a basket up and down stairs, while the father forced the sitter, as well as the children, to eat two helpings of vegetables before any of them could have dessert. There may also be conflicts over division of labour in the house, especially if both partners work (Belsky, 1990).

The presence of children significantly influences decisions about jobs or careers, about where the family lives, as well as the nature of the husband-wife relationship. If, for instance, one of the children has serious medical problems, the parents may refuse job relocation to remain near an excellent children's hospital or near a trusted physician, even if such a choice limits the chance of promotion (Day et al., 1985). In less extreme circumstances, the family may think about the volume of traffic on the street and distance from the school when they are considering buying a new house or renting an apartment.

Highest levels of marital dissatisfaction are reported when children are teenagers (Lupri & Frideres, 1981). There are a number of possible explanations. Parents now have children who are keeping adult hours, so that privacy takes some planning. Teenagers, especially when parents disagree on how to deal with the challenges they present, can strain a marriage. Pubescent maturation among girls and early maturation among boys, for instance, are associated with more conflicts between adolescents and mothers, but not with fathers (Steinberg, 1987). Some families taking part in a study of marital stability in large adopting families reported that their marriages had been in danger of failing because of the stress placed on them by one or more very difficult children. For example, if a girl defied and challenged the mother and acted like a sweet innocent around the father, the parents often disagreed about the best way of handling her. In extreme cases, this disagreement resulted in such serious marital difficulties that the parents considered separation (Ward & Tremitiere, 1991). Financially, children may impose a strain if they go on to post-secondary education. At this time, a couple's parents may require more assistance if their health is failing; thus further strains are placed on the family. These have sometimes been called the "sandwich years" because couples are squeezed by both the older and younger generations.

Once children have left home, couples are probably in better financial health than they have been for many years. In these years, couples are required to adjust to living alone without children again. Frequently they must rebuild common interests. Yet, once the adjustment is made, husband and wife can develop a closeness that was lost when they had children at home; thus marital satisfaction increases.

WAYS TO KEEP YOUR MARRIAGE SATISFYING

- Touch your partner in an affectionate manner every day.
- Set aside some regular time daily to talk; be each other's best friend.
- Talk about sex and ways to make it satisfying to each of you. (This is one of the easiest topics to avoid, yet it can be one of the most important aspects of marriage.)
- Find some time to have fun together.
- Compliment or thank your partner for something he or she does at least every few days.
- Address issues directly and, where possible, without anger; in general, avoid shouting and strong criticism.
- Greet your partner affectionately each day.
- Do not minimize the consequences of occasional slapping in anger. While couples often minimize the seriousness of this physical act, it clearly has a negative impact.
- If you have children, make sure that you and your spouse have some time alone, apart from them, and that all of your attention and conversation do not focus on the children. Make plans to have romantic times.
- Try to have some pleasant contact with your own friends. (Frequent contact and conversation with friends are associated with marital satisfaction. No mate can provide everything for a partner.)
- Pay attention to your physical appearance. (Feeling good about your body is associated with general and marital happiness.)

Source: Daniel D. O'Leary, Ph.D., State University of New York at Stony Brook, quoted in Mary Ellen Schoonmaker (1988). "Marriage: The First Years," *Family Circle*, 1 September, p. 102.

Homosexual couples also go through periods of adjustment similar to that of heterosexual married couples, except that usually they do not have a marker event such as a wedding that announces their relationship to the world. Some churches do offer a covenanting service similar to a marriage ceremony, although it does not have any legal force. These couples also have additional adjustment difficulties because their union usually is not looked on kindly by society (McGoldrick, 1988b, 1988c).

There are a number of criticisms of the lifecycle view of marital satisfaction. Some of these are based on the fact that the surveys were conducted by asking people of different ages about their feelings, rather than following the same couples over the years. There may thus be differences in what different generations consider satisfaction. For example, older generations are shyer discussing sex with their partners than are younger couples. It may also be that more older couples report happiness than couples with children because those with unhappy marriages have separated or divorced, and more of the satisfied ones are still together.

Does Marriage Have a Future?

Some forecasters point to the rising rates of cohabitation and divorce, and the number of single parents, working mothers, and two-earner households, as indications that marriage is on the way out.

If we look at the figures, we can see that although the marriage rate appears to be down, this may be the effect of hard economic times. The same proportion of the population as in the past may eventually get married. We may be seeing a repeat of the pattern that occurred during the Great Depression. Three-quarters of those who have never married and are living common-law do get married. Just over half of these marry their first common-law partner. The high divorce rate does not necessarily mark the death of marriage itself. Many divorced persons, more usually younger individuals, remarry (Dumas & Peron, 1992).

Marriage appears to have changed, however, from a patriarchal, husband-led system to a more egalitarian partnership between husband and wife. Both wage-earning and home and child care are being shared by more couples. This trend has come about partly in response to hard economic times. In part, however, it reflects a movement in society to preserve the rights of minorities. It is impossible to tell what effect changing political and economic situations will have on marriage. What we can say is that in all likelihood it will continue to exist.

SUMMARY

MARRIAGE AND SOCIETY. Marriage is not merely a private event. It marks both the legal creation of a family and changes in social status and role. It has been influenced by social factors, such as the availability of clergy, and economic and political factors, such as the Great Depression and World War II. Laws govern whom we can marry and when we can dissolve a marriage. Marriage itself is a contract with implied rights and responsibilities. Formal marriage contracts can be drawn up to modify the financial provisions of family law.

MARRIAGE IN THE FAMILY CYCLE. In the past, marriage marked the transition to adult status; now the change is not so clear. It involves commitment to a new family system and accepting the roles of husband and wife. Couples must renegotiate their relationships with other microsystems of which they are members, such as their families of origin. The degree of separation varies with ethnic group. Over the years, marriage has served a number of functions. It can give both economic and social status, help physical and financial survival, provide a socially approved sexual relationship, and a setting in which children can be raised, and be a source of love and support. We are socialized to believe that marriage is the natural state for adults, and experience social pressure to be like others.

ROLES IN MARRIAGE. Historically, there has been a clear division between men's and women's roles. Among indigenous peoples, for example, men were hunters and protectors and women provided personal care for family members. Among the European settlers, men provided for the family's economic needs, either through wages or farming, and women cared for the household and children. The change to greater equality in roles has been gradual. Married women gradually formed a large part of the paid work force, especially since the 1970s when many families found two incomes necessary for economic survival. Families usually fall into one of four role patterns: conventional, shared, two-career, and reverse conventional. Both the conventional and reverse-conventional patterns have a clear division of roles between spouses, while shared and two-career role patterns do not make such a strong distinction. In many of these families, however, women are still expected to assume the major responsibility for family care.

MARRIAGE AND WORK. The majority of families are two-earner families. Women's choices to be homemakers or have careers depend on the stability of their marriages, on job opportunities, on the ability of their partners to earn enough to allow them to stay at home, and on the level of satisfaction they find in careers and homemaking. Men, however, are not seen as having a similar choice. With two earners, couples may experience the stress of role overload as they juggle jobs, children, marriage, and household responsibilities. Many find that work and family worlds interfere with each other. Some couples try to ensure that the most stressful periods of job and family do not occur simultaneously, i.e., they try to avoid having children as they get established in careers. There may also be difficulties in balancing the demands of both careers. Particular problems occur when one partner must travel, works long hours, or is transferred. Since dual-earner couples often have difficulty keeping up ties with friends and relatives, they may have low levels of social support.

MARRIED HAPPINESS. Several methods are used for measuring success in marriage, e.g., degree of agreement between husband and wife or positive and negative communication. Happiness appears greatest early in marriage, drops with the arrival of children, is at its lowest point when adolescents are in the house, and increases with the empty nest. Some reasons given for this pattern are the added stress of having more family members and the greater opportunities for disagreement.

KEY TERMS

adultery: the act of having sexual relations with someone other than your spouse

androgynous: an individual high in characteristics of both masculinity and femininity

conventional roles: a marriage with a homemaker wife and breadwinner husband

dual-career roles: a marriage in which both partners are committed to their careers

femininity: personality with a high level of responsibility and concern for interpersonal relationships

marriage contract: a legal agreement between a couple in which they agree to their rights and obligations during marriage or at its end

masculinity: personality with a high level of drive and ambition

patriarchal: social organization in which the man is dominant

reverse-conventional roles: a marriage with a breadwinner wife and homemaker husband

shared roles: a marriage in which both partners work and share household responsibilities

CLASS ASSIGNMENTS

Complete one or both of the following assignments, as directed by your instructor.

1. Select two television shows that present family life. What roles do men and women play? Do you think these roles are typical of society today? Explain.
2. Interview two individuals about the division of responsibilities, chores, and privileges in marriage. Do you feel that their answers are related to their age or cultural background? Why or why not? Compare your information with that gained by your classmates.

PERSONAL ASSIGNMENTS

These assignments are designed to help you think about your own family experiences.

1. Describe the kind of marriage *your* parents have, if indeed they are currently married. How has this affected your ideas about the role of husbands and wives in marriage? Why?
2. If you had a marriage contract or prenuptial agreement, what would you choose to include? Why? Would you want such a contract? Give your reasons.

C H A P T E R 5

Children – Yes or No?

OBJECTIVES

- To place the decision to have or not have children in the family life cycle.
- To look at the historical background of the choice to have children.
- To examine possible choices for those who do not want the children they conceive.
- To explore options available to those who are childless involuntarily.

Daddy and I wanted a little boy so much. We tried and tried, but we couldn't start a baby growing. Then we went to see Dr. Mason. He did lots of tests. He found Daddy didn't have the special seeds that make babies grow. We were very sad. So Dr. Mason borrowed seeds from another man. He put them inside Mommy in a special operation. Pretty soon Mommy and Daddy knew there was a baby growing. They were very happy. And you know what? That baby was you!

Does this scenario seem far-fetched? Not something we talk about, especially with children? We are much more comfortable with the more usual method of producing children, through sexual relations between a husband and wife. This has been the ordinary course of events for millennia. Often in the past, the first child was one of many. Sometimes the success of a marriage was calculated by the number of children a couple had, sometimes by the number of sons.

Enlarging the Family Circle

Having a child is a *marker event.* In present-day Canadian society, many of the negotiations of relationships that used to occur at marriage are postponed until the birth of the first child. This may be the first time that the parents have to take full responsibility for another person. In a conventional-role marriage husband and wife have clearly defined roles. When both partners are employed, however, the household and work responsibilities are shared. Once a child is born, husband-wife roles often need to be renegotiated to allow for the child's care (McGoldrick, 1988b). For young single parents, the transition may mean a shift from childhood to adulthood, from being looked after by parents to looking after a child.

THE SOCIAL SCRIPT

There is still a great deal of social pressure to have children, or to follow the *social script.* One of the pressures is the myth of motherhood. According to the myth, motherhood is an instinct that can fulfil a woman in a way no other experience can. Of course, much of the notion is true. Bearing and raising a child can provide satisfactions unlike any other life experience (Braverman, 1989). This notion is supported by society in many ways, e.g., women who choose not to have children are often considered anti-social or psychologically defective in some way. Their marriages are expected to be unsatisfying (Veevers, 1976). A study of teenagers' hopes for the future found that boys were not worried about possible conflicts between career and family roles; careers came first. Girls, however, wanted children, but felt they would have to do it all alone as wife, mother, and employee, whether or not they were married; they were worried about priorities already (Archer, 1985).

Another part of the myth is the importance of having a child of each sex for a well-rounded family. This expectation is similar to the structural-functional concept of four role types in families —adult male and female, and child male and female. Without all four, the family is felt to be incomplete. This belief accounts for a number of families who have a string of boys or girls before one of the other sex is finally born or adopted.

A minority of unmarried women in their thirties or forties hear their biological clock ticking and decide to have a child while they still can physically, even if they do not have a husband. Some seek out a temporary partner for the sole purpose of becoming pregnant; others resort to artificial insemination; still others adopt.

CHILDLESS THROUGH CHOICE

In view of the strength of social pressure to have children, why do some couples choose to remain childless?

First, they may fear that the husband-wife relationship will be damaged. Once the couple introduces another person into the family, they may not be able to remain as close as they wish. Women may also fear having to give up the equality they have established in their marriage relationships if there are children who require care. Second, there are occupational reasons. Some women do not wish to sacrifice a career to which they are dedicated. Having children may mean a conflict between family responsibilities and long hours, travel, or moves for work. Some individuals wish to keep their options open to change jobs to one that they will enjoy more but which will pay less. The financial commitment a child demands can remove this freedom. Third, some couples want to keep their options open for new experiences of all sorts. Some may look at parenthood as such an experience, but reject it because of the commitment involved. Finally, the voluntarily childless are more interested in learning about the world than teaching the young. Due to a growing acceptance of family differences, women choosing not to have children do not face as great a stigma now as in the past (Veevers, 1976).

The Shrinking Family

Although the pressure on couples to have children is almost as strong as ever, the size of the Canadian family has been shrinking. The change has not been constant. There have been periods in which the birth rate dropped, followed by increased levels of childbearing. Yet the birth rate for women born this century has shown a drop from almost four children to an estimated 2.5 children for those born in 1943 and completing childbearing in the 1980s (Dumas, 1987). Unless the situation changes dramatically, it appears that younger women will have still fewer children (Lachapelle, 1988).

In a rural economy, having many children made sense (Zelizer, 1985). The farm could be a true family business instead of having to rely on hired help. Daughters could help in the house with food preparation and preservation, making clothing and household linens, and caring for children. Horace Miner (1939) describes such a society in his book about St. Denis de Kamouraska.

Before the days of old-age pensions, family allowances, disability pensions, and welfare, the family provided almost the only social security system. If it failed, people were dependent on charity. Since many children died, it was important to have a large family so that two or three might survive to look after the parents when they were old or disabled. Feminists add that, until recently, women's economic survival depended on marriage. Men's power over women's sexuality and the resulting children were the price women paid for economic security.

Times have changed. The drop in family size has been especially marked in Quebec. In 1926, for example, the average number of children for a woman in Quebec was 4.3, for the rest of Canada, 3.0. By 1986, the rate had dropped to 1.4

Figure 5.1

HUSBAND-WIFE FAMILIES, BY NUMBER OF CHILDREN AT HOME, 1941–86[1]

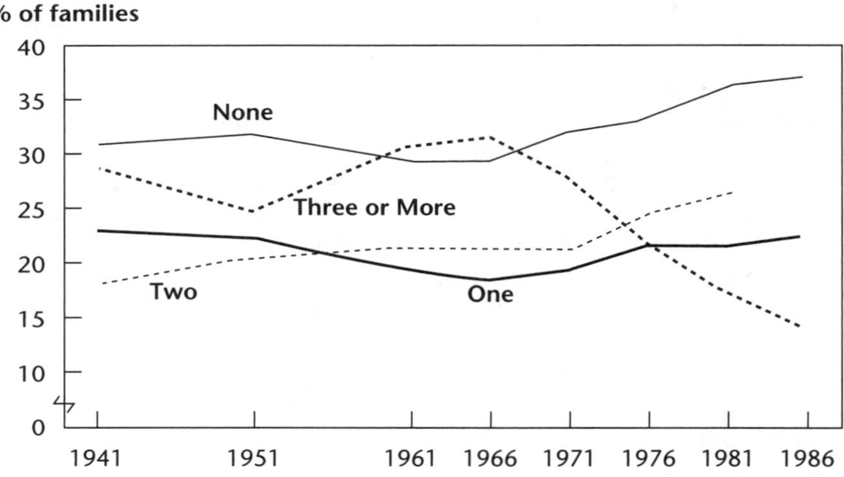

[1]Data for 1941–196 include only children under age 25.
Source: Statistics Canada, 1986 Census of Canada. In Mary Sue Devereux (1990). "Decline in the Number of Children," *Canadian Social Trends,* Autumn: 33.

in Quebec, and between 1.7 and 1.8 for the rest of Canada. In order to replace the current population, women need to have 2.1 children. Families with three or more children have decreased dramatically (Lachapelle, 1988). Now parents with more than three or four children are often greeted with questions like, "Are they all yours?"

The only exception to the general decrease in births is the increase in births to single mothers. The teenage pregnancy rate in Canada is 44 per 1000 (i.e., 44 of every thousand teenage girls becomes pregnant). The rate is about half that of the United States (Klein, 1986). One study of births in Gatineau, Quebec, found that out-of-wedlock births increased from 11.9 percent in 1976 to 27.1 percent in 1984, i.e., more than one-quarter of children were born out of wedlock. The change was mainly the result of an increase of births to never-married mothers. There were similar trends in the Quebec municipalities of Hull, Aylmer, and Maniwaki. This huge increase is, in part, a result of the number of common-law couples. The Quebec birth certificate did not include this as a category under marital status. In 1984, for example, 64 percent of young French-speaking couples living in the Mont-Royal Plateau in Montreal were unmarried; over a third of these had children (Mishra-Bouchez & Emond, 1987).

BABY BONUS PROGRAM WORKS AS QUEBEC BIRTH RATE INCREASES

QUEBEC CITY (CP) — The number of youngsters in Quebec rose to 1,620,000 last year, an increase of 6,000 over the figure for 1988, the annual report of the Quebec pension plan and family allowance board shows.

It was the first year-to-year increase since 1974, and indicates that the province's family birth incentive program, brought in two years ago, is working.

Quebec families get a $500 premium for the birth of a first child, $1,000 for a second and $4,500 for a third and all subsequent children.

In 1974, there were nearly two million people aged under 18 years in the province, according to payments made under family allowances. The number dropped in succeeding years to 1,614,000 by 1988 because of a declining birth rate, then an upward curve began.

The report indicates there was a 6 per cent increase in the birth rate last year. It also shows the number of retired people is increasing at 20 times the birth rate.

Source: *The Toronto Star*, 17 July 1990, p. A10.

A number of approaches to increasing the birth rate to replacement levels have been tried or suggested. For example, Quebec has offered incentive payments to parents with three or more children. Others suggest that encouraging immigration of young people who are of an age to have children will help shore up the sagging birth rate and offset the aging population of Canada (Samuel, 1990).

Why Is the Family Shrinking?

A number of factors have led to couples choosing to have smaller families, including medical advances, general economic trends, and various psychosocial reasons.

MEDICAL ADVANCES

Medical science has had two major effects on the birth rate. First, infant mortality has declined steadily in Canada since information on the subject was collected. Currently the rate is one of the best in the world, lower than the United States and most of Western Europe, with the exception of Sweden (Dumas, 1987).

As a result, it is no longer necessary to have a number of children to ensure the survival of two or three. Most children born today in Canada will live to adulthood, if there are no wars or major natural disasters. Second, contraceptives have become more effective since the birth-control pill became available in 1960.

CHANGES IN LAW

Until July 1, 1969, contraception was illegal in Canada. Under the 1892 Criminal Code, birth control was thought obscene and likely to corrupt morals. Since it was perfectly legal, however, to use contraceptive devices to prevent illness or to treat disorders, it was possible for those with sympathetic doctors to obtain contraceptives for birth-control purposes. The first family-planning clinics in Canada were operated illegally. Since they were established, the average age of women seeking advice on contraceptions has dropped from the mid-twenties to 16 and 17 (Sweet, 1989). The birth rate showed its sharpest drop following the legalization of birth control (Dumas, 1987). The availability of abortion, when a woman's life or health (including mental health) is in danger, also legalized in 1969, has made it possible to avoid having children after failure in birth control.

Religious groups, in particular, have taken positions concerning the morality of these methods of preventing births. The United Church of Canada, for example, states that family planning is a Christian duty since every child has the right to be wanted. However, the church condemns abortion as a method of birth control, although it may be used in situations like rape (United Church of Canada, 1989b). On the other hand, the Roman Catholic Church disapproves of artificial means of birth control, as being against the best of human nature, and completely opposes abortion because it destroys human life (Guimond, 1983). Part of the controversy surrounding abortion has been expressed in repeated demonstrations over the past years outside abortion clinics.

ECONOMIC TRENDS

The change from a resource-based economy to a manufacturing-based one has also had an impact on the birth rate. Family farms traditionally have depended on child labour. Children were also employed in other resource industries. In the mid-19th century, for example, boys as young as 8 years old worked in the coal mines of Nova Scotia and British Columbia. They were important both as a source of cheap labour and as contributors to family income (McIntosh, 1987/88). With time, a combination of cheap immigrant labour, better technology, and school-attendance laws made it difficult for children to participate in manufacturing. Increasing mechanization has further reduced the need for unskilled labour, both in food production and manufacturing. Thus children have become a financial liability instead of a resource.

The birth rate is also connected to national and global economics. During the Great Depression, families became smaller. The economic boom period following World War II saw an increase in the birth rate that lasted until the 1960s and produced the baby boom. The inflation and recession of the 1970s and 1980s, with the greater number of women in the work force, led to smaller families once again (Lachapelle, 1988). Part of this variation in fertility is related to the age at which women have their first child; in boom times it is earlier, and in bust times later. Since women have a limited number of years that they can bear children, the total number they have is related to the age at which they have the first child (Dumas, 1987).

The relationship between the economy and the birth rate, however, is far from simple. The recent drop in the birth rate is also connected to women's participation in the work force. Part of the phenomenon of working wives and mothers is related to the need of families to have two incomes, and to the growth of single-parent families. Since education is more important for employment than in the past, many individuals delay having children until they are through school and able to support them. Some career women delay having children until they are well into their thirties and have few childbearing years left.

Table 5.1

THE COST OF RAISING CHILDREN IN CANADA

Percentage of Gross Income Spent by Middle-Income[a] Families on Child-rearing Costs Including Housing and Child Care — Home-owners & Both Parents Employed

	Percentage of Gross Income		
Province or Region	**One-Child Family**	**Two-Child Family[b]**	**Three-Child Family[b]**
British Columbia	12%	20%	27%
Prairies	12%	20%	28%
Ontario	15%	24%	32%
Quebec	10%	19%	27%
Atlantic	14%	21%	29%

[a] Families with incomes of $30 000 to $45 000 per year in 1988.
[b] Averages include years prior to last child's birth when other children were present and years after older children left home.

Source: From Robin A. Douthitt and Joanne Fedyk (1990). *The Cost of Raising Children in Canada*. Toronto: Butterworths, Tables 11, 29, 47, 65, 83 (pages 101, 122, 143, 164, 185).

Children are expensive. Including housing and day care, families spend from 10 percent (Quebec) to 15 percent (Ontario) of their income for the first child (Douthitt & Fedyk, 1990). Costs vary among regions. For example, Ontario has higher prices for goods and services and a greater proportion of married women who work. Some of the variation between regions may be accounted for by different standards of what families feel they ought to provide for their children. The increased need to educate children for the technically demanding workplace also places demands on family income.

PSYCHOSOCIAL REASONS

A number of psychosocial reasons are offered in favour of small families. Some of the arguments are similar to those for having no children at all. Having large families places stresses on husband-wife relationships. The potential conflict and stress that arise from dealing with the complexity of relationships can threaten the marriage. As we have already seen, the child-rearing years in a marriage are the least happy.

Having many children too close together in age may also place a child at a disadvantage. Studies have shown that children in large families tend to have lower intelligence and possibly more emotional problems than children in small families (Insel & Lindgren, 1978). In addition, if resources must be spread among many family members, it is difficult to provide them with the same opportunities as children in small families.

Individuals who work with people all day may not want to come home to deal with more people. According to the literature on burnout, emotional exhaustion at work leads to irritability and inability to cope with family stresses (Maslach, 1982). One former high-school teacher explains that she changed occupations because she found it too stressful to deal with teenagers at work, and then go home to more teenagers.

Source: Lynn Johnston (1981). *I've Got the One-More-Washday Blues*. Kansas City: Andrews and McMeel, p. 9.

Unwanted Children

Many pregnancies are unwanted. This includes those of both single and married individuals. Basically, there are three options available to an expectant mother: not having the baby, giving the child to someone else to raise, or raising the child herself. Most of the discussion will be concerned with choices made by unmarried women because there is little information available about married women.

Until recently, unmarried women who became pregnant had to live with the shame of being labelled promiscuous. There were few choices available for so-called "fallen women." Life was difficult for both mother and child. Options were also limited. Unmarried parenthood was stigmatized. Abortion was illegal, costly, and often dangerous. Often adoption was offered as a form of rescue for both mother and child. The mother could keep her secret and the child did not have to bear the stigma of illegitimacy (Cole, 1984). Due to medical, legal, and social changes, women today have more choices.

NOT HAVING THE BABY

The first choice available is not having the baby, i.e., having an abortion. Like other aspects of reproduction, abortion has raised many questions. First, the morality of the procedure is related to the moment human life is presumed to begin. Is it at the moment of conception, the moment the child breathes on its own, or some point between these extremes? Second, whose life is to have priority — the woman who is alive now or the fetus that has the potential of living as an independent being? The answer to this is related to the first issue. Third, does a woman have the right to control her own reproductive system? This question has many related issues. Should an adolescent require her parents' consent before having an abortion? Should a wife have her husband's consent? A fourth area involves the timing of abortion. With medical advances in helping premature infants to survive, the time gap between the last date an abortion could be performed safely and the date at which a fetus could survive is becoming shorter. How late should an abortion be permitted? Should access be restricted to the first trimester when abortions are safer and do not raise the question of the potential survival of the child?

Some women are selective about which child they want to give birth to and raise. With greater sensitivity of prenatal diagnosis, it is possible to tell if a child will be born with a chromosomal or genetic disorder. For example, Down's Syndrome, a chromosomal disorder that results in low intelligence functioning can be diagnosed through *amniocentesis*, a procedure in which some of the fluid surrounding the fetus is drawn off through a large syringe and examined under the microscope. The list of disorders that can be diagnosed prenatally is growing. If an abnormality is found, parents have the option of aborting the fetus. This possibility raises serious questions. Is having a child with physical or mental challenges totally undesirable? Is the quality of life of these children inferior to that of others? What are the implications for other mentally or physically challenged people (Saxton, 1988)? Further complications arise since sex selection is also made possible through amniocentesis (Yoxen, 1986).

GIVING THE CHILD TO SOMEONE ELSE

In the 19th century, when children could be a financial asset, one option for children who were orphans or whose parents could not care for them was to be placed with *foster* families. In exchange for room and board and some education, the children were expected to assist in the foster household. Many children went from orphanages to these homes, often on farms where boys helped with farm work and girls helped indoors. Many more boys than girls were placed. Usually the families were not well-screened and unfortunate placements occurred. The story of *Anne of Green Gables* by Lucy Maud Montgomery (1908) is based on a mix-up that occurred when orphanage staff acted on a request sent through a third party. They did no checking up themselves and sent a girl rather than the boy Matthew and Marilla wanted to help with the farm work. Although Anne is a fictional character, there were many young people in Canada who went to work homes. A large group were sent from England to Canada. In many cases, the extent of the family check was a recommendation from the local clergyman. There was very little supervision once the children were in homes. The practice of fostering was praised for providing opportunities for young people who had no prospects in England. In reality, however, many children were exploited (Bagnell, 1980).

In such a society, infants were a liability. Abortion was expensive and required connections. Women could get only poor-paying jobs, and welfare was usually reserved for the "deserving poor." In New France during the 1700s, a number of women gave their illegitimate babies to native peoples to raise because they felt this was preferable to exposing them to the elements and allowing them to die (Moogk, 1982). Many children were abandoned. Foundling homes, which were set up to care for abandoned children, had mortality rates between 85 percent and 90 percent, partly because of problems with contagious diseases before immunization and the discovery of modern medicines, and partly because people did not understand the importance of attachment and stimulation to infant development and survival (Rooke & Schnell, 1983). In spite of this knowledge, there have been suggestions recently in the United States that one way of solving the crisis in finding *foster homes* is to once again set up orphanages for young children (Ford & Kroll, 1990).

Some women, often referred to as baby farmers, would take unwanted children for a fee and try to place them for adoption. Many of these children also died. This led to accusations that baby farmers killed the babies in their care so that they would be able to charge more fees for more babies (Zelizer, 1985). More recently, criticisms have been levelled at a maternity home in Nova Scotia for selling some babies and letting others die, the scandal of the so-called "butterbox babies" (Cahill, 1992).

By the turn of the century, foster homes were seen as the best substitute for the natural home. It involved an expensive commitment by the foster parents, since they did not receive any money for the care of the child. There was a gradual start of payments to foster parents for children who were hard to place —the very young, the sickly, and those with mental and physical challenges. Eventually, virtually all foster parents received boarding payments to help meet the costs of the children in their care.

Providing foster care until a child was grown used to be possible, but child-welfare laws now require early planning and/or periodic review of the child's status, with a view toward returning the child to biological parents or finding a permanent substitute family (Cruickshank, 1991). Adoption provides such a family. In *adoption,* legal rights and responsibilities are transferred from the birth parents to the adoptive parents. Given improved contraception and greater social acceptance of single mothers, fewer babies are now being placed for adoption. Those single mothers who keep their babies are more likely to come from situations where raising such a child is not stigmatized. In fact, some mothers experience considerable pressure from their peers to raise the child. They also tend to have a deep need for a close relationship, and a desire to demonstrate their love for the child's father or their ability to raise a child. Those who surrender a child for adoption are more likely to be students, less likely to come from single-parent homes, and less likely to have known the child's father for a long time (Cole, 1984; Kirsh, 1984).

Mothers who do make this choice are now offered various degrees of openness in adoption. Often they are able to select adoptive parents. Some agencies arrange actual meetings; others offer the mother descriptions of several suitable families and allow her to make a choice (McRoy, Grotevant, & White, 1988). Usually the decision to give up a child for adoption is extremely painful for the birth mother. Many experience a continuing sense of loss and desire for contact with the adoptee (Sachdev, 1989).

Many children are raised for part or all of their lives by members of the extended family. Although their biological parents may be unable or unwilling to care for them, they may be very much wanted by other relatives. This practice is more common among some ethnic groups than others, e.g., native peoples have customarily used the extended family for child care and informal adoption. In the past many native children, however, spent most of their formative years in residential schools away from families and culture. Recently native peoples have been taking control of child-welfare services for their own people (M. Ward, 1984a).

RAISING THE CHILD ONESELF

The number of people who resort to abortion, foster care, and adoption are relatively easy to discover since many are involved with hospitals and social-service agencies. The number who keep and raise unwanted children themselves is impossible to discover. There are several reasons for this. Any child born within a marriage is assumed to be wanted. In fact, married women do have abortions and do place their children with other families, but there is a stigma attached to those who do not raise their biological children. In addition, many children who were unplanned and initially unwanted eventually become much-loved children. Even calculating the number of unmarried mothers who raise their own children does not provide us with an accurate count. Some women in their thirties or forties who have no opportunity or no desire to marry choose to have a child rather than never experience the pleasures of motherhood. In these cases the child is very much wanted even though the mother is single.

A group virtually ignored are the unmarried fathers who wish to raise their children. Until 1970, they usually had no rights at all, and they often have problems gaining custody (Cole, 1984).

The unwanted child who is raised by a parent is at risk for physical or emotional abuse (Pagelow, 1984). One long-term study, conducted by Michael Bohman and Soren Sigvardsson (1980), of Danish children whose mothers initially chose to place them for adoption and then took them home, found that a similar group of children actually placed for adoption fared better than those who returned home. Those remaining in foster care were the most likely to be involved in alcohol abuse or criminal activity.

Single-parent families, who now make up a growing proportion of the population, are discussed in more detail in Chapter 7.

"Desperately Seeking Baby"

While some parents have children they don't want, others cannot have the children they do want. Infertility can pose a major crisis for a couple. Since our society has as a norm that married couples have children, infertile couples may have a sense of being defective, which reduces their overall sense of self-worth. The medical investigation of infertility is intrusive and often uncomfortable. The couple is asked intimate questions about their sexual activity. Sex may lose spontaneity as the couple plan intercourse when the woman is most likely to be fertile. If the treatment is successful, the woman may experience a very anxious pregnancy because she is afraid to believe she is really going to end up with a baby. If the treatment is unsuccessful, the couple mourn the loss of the children they will never have. Often the people around them may not be supportive, because they do not understand the severity of the loss. After all, no one has died. They just didn't exist. Sometimes the fertility-clinic staff may be disappointed and angry with couples who don't manage to achieve pregnancy. The couple is forced to rethink what parenthood really means to them. Should they plan a life without children or find some other way to become parents? (Mazor, 1979; Shapiro, 1986).

Usually women feel the lack of children more than men, because they have been socialized to believe that they only achieve full worth as human beings if they are mothers. Men see their own infertility as an assault on their manhood. Many experience a temporary impotence when they first learn that they are infertile. Many wives experience rage at their husbands. The balance of power in the family may change (Berger, 1980). Fertile partners may feel that if they were married to someone else, then they could have children; thus childlessness is part of the price of monogamy. The knowledge that the spouse might have children in another union further undermines the self-esteem of the infertile partner (Humphrey, 1986).

In the past, the only choices available to infertile couples were to find a child someone else did not want to raise or to remain childless. The options are wider now. They still include foster care and adoption; added to these, however, are the new reproductive technologies.

FOSTER CARE

In the past, families who wanted a child or more children sometimes would turn to foster care. Many children would enter care because of the death of a parent or dire poverty. They would remain in foster care until they reached adulthood; thus fostering involved providing a long-term home for a child. The foster family would receive support payments for the child, who often became a well-integrated member of the family. In the 1950s and 1960s during the baby boom in child-welfare services, many women who enjoyed babies could care for them for the first weeks or months of life until they were placed for adoption. For many people, this was a satisfactory way of increasing a family. One foster mother, for instance, stated that she and her husband could only afford to care for four children. Once their oldest was independent, they adopted a little girl they had fostered for five years. She was the last of a stream of infants and toddlers who had lived with them.

The trend in foster care, however, is now away from baby care and long-term placements. With advances in medical science so that children are unlikely to be orphaned, and with the improvement in benefits available for single parents, children are less likely to enter care because of their parents' deaths or extreme poverty. Instead, they are more likely to have behavioural problems or to be victims of abuse. Children entering care tend to be older than before, and to have many more emotional and physical problems. Foster parents are required to have special therapeutic and child-management skills as well as the ability to be a good parent (Steinhauer, 1991). Given the problems foster children can bring into the family, and given increased employment of mothers outside the home, foster families are in short supply. In 1988, because the situation was so troubled, Ontario foster parents threatened to go on strike (Kendrick, 1990).

Since foster care is seen as a temporary stop away from home, contact between the children and their birth parents is encouraged so that the move home will be smoother. It is therefore difficult for foster parents to feel that the child is theirs. There is also an emphasis on adoption planning for children who cannot return home. If they want the child to stay, foster parents may have to adopt him or her themselves.

ADOPTION

For many years, the comfort offered the childless was, "You can always adopt." Unlike foster care, adoption involves the legal transfer of the parent-child relationship to another set of parents.

But adoption was not always seen as a solution. In fact, adoption in North American society was regarded with suspicion. In the book, *Anne of Green Gables* (1908), Marilla was warned of the dangers of taking in an orphan. There was the fear that the child would inherit bad blood from his or her inadequate parents. At this time, it was considered safer to adopt a child who was somewhat older because you could better judge their character. In 1873, New Brunswick was the first Canadian province to pass adoption legislation, followed in 1896 by Nova Scotia. The remaining provinces passed adoption laws between 1920 and 1930 (J.A. MacDonald, 1984). Before that time birth and adoptive parents might sign an indenture of adoption; this document was not binding and the child could be returned to the biological parents at any time if he or she proved unsatisfactory to the adoptive parents. Frequently adoptions were informal without legal protections. Agencies were not involved in these placements. Often an unmarried mother wishing to find parents for her child would place an advertisement in the newspaper.

Beginning in the 1930s, adoption became more respectable. Agencies tried to place children like those the adopters might have had, matching them for race, religion, and hair and eye colour. Babies were at a premium; older children were rarely placed. During the 1950s, adoption specialists stated that it was in the children's best interests to completely sever ties with birth parents. By 1980 all but two provinces had passed laws declaring that adopted children became for all purposes the children of their adoptive parents (J.A. MacDonald, 1984).

Environment was felt to be more important than genetics for the development of children. There was also a growing realization that infants need a constant caregiver for the healthiest development. At first agencies tried to place "guaranteed" babies with "ideal" adopting couples; if there was some defect, the child could be returned. Soon, however, parents were forcing changes. Families might discover that their child had developed severe allergies or had other health problems. Since the parents had already come to love the child, they refused to return the child. Then agencies cautiously began placing children with minor correctable physical problems, then those with more severe difficulties. Now the definition of an adoptable child is one who is able to benefit from a permanent home (Reid, 1963).

As older children and more children with mental and physical challenges were placed, it became obvious that nice, childless middle-class parents sometimes had problems coping with their behaviour. One agency director stated, "We have weird kids, so we need weird parents." The notion of who would make suitable adoptive parents has changed. Blindness, paraplegia, or unmarried status are no longer complete barriers. Adoption subsidy may be provided to help parents adopting children with special needs (Lipman, 1984). Along with these trends, adoption was advocated as a way of reducing overpopulation. Couples were urged by many articles appearing in the popular press to have only two children to replace themselves and then adopt if they wanted a larger family (Cole, 1984).

While these developments took place, adoption was overtaken by the same factors that helped reduce family size — easy and legal contraception and legal abortion. In addition, unmarried parenthood became more acceptable as the numbers of separated and divorced parents grew. Suddenly in the late 1960s, the supply of adoptable babies dried up, just as adoption was reaching new heights of popularity (Cole, 1984). Now couples wanting to adopt a healthy white baby are in a position of extreme competition, with waiting periods of five years in some places. Due to reduced supply and increased government control, the temptation is high for desperate would-be parents to buy a baby in a black-market adoption, a highly illegal activity (Zelizer, 1985).

Our saga started quite innocently. We thought we needed another boy; we had three daughters and only one son. Adoption looked good. We were delighted with the one girl we had adopted as an infant, and were ready to try a boy a little younger than she was, perhaps aged 5 or 6. We submitted to the usual procedures for approval.

Mother's Day changed everything.

"Let's get them!" said our son as he opened the paper to see "Today's Child," a publication column presenting children needing adoption. Sure enough, there was our little boy, 4 1/2 years old. As a bonus, he would bring his four older brothers.

In about 2 months we were parents of six sons and three daughters, acquiring our first teenager, looking forward to a glorious year with eight teenagers, explaining three 7-year-olds, our lifestyle completely transformed.

Source: Margaret Ward (1978). "Full House: Adoption of a Large Sibling Group," *Child Welfare*, 57:233.

During the 1950s and 1960s, intercountry adoptions grew in popularity, especially in Ontario and British Columbia (Lipman, 1984). They led to the establishment of the Adoption Desk at Health and Welfare Canada in 1975. Individuals choose intercountry adoption partly because they want to be parents. Often babies are available from abroad. Many are also concerned about the welfare of children in danger because of war or extreme poverty. Some, however, see such adoptions as exploitation and imperialism, and fear the political difficulties (Cole, 1984). In practice, the situation is quite changeable. As some countries have banned foreign placements, others have become new sources of children.

Like foster care, adoption still carries a stigma. The blood tie in our society is seen as indissoluble and of a mystical nature. There are countless accounts of children placed for adoption as infants later finding their "real" parents. It is as if society considers the adoptive parents who have raised them as somehow unreal. There are beliefs present in society which devalue adoption, e.g., the biological tie is seen as important for the bonding of mother and child; therefore attachment in adoption is regarded as second best. Adopted children are also seen as second best because they have an unknown genetic heritage (Miall, 1987). This notion of adoption being second best has the effect of making some adoptive parents feel that they are not fully entitled to the child they are raising (M. Ward, 1979). As a result, they have problems in functioning like real parents in areas such as discipline. This emphasis on blood ties and genetic heritage also underlies the recent flood of adoptees seeking contact with their birth parents. Currently adoptive parents are fighting changes in the Unemployment Insurance Act which have reduced the leave available to adoptive parents, while increasing that granted biological parents.

Recently there has been a dropping off of all adoptions, of older children as well as of infants. In part, this trend parallels the number of children in care (Lipman, 1984). It is also a reaction to figures concerning adoption disruptions. In addition, theories of the importance of early attachments for the child have led to reluctance to sever birth ties (Steinhauer, 1991). Thus children can be left in foster care, moving from home to home, but retaining contact with a biological parent who cannot raise them.

Yet, in spite of the baby shortage, adoption still remains an alternative for individuals and couples desiring children.

THE NEW TECHNOLOGY

Some would-be parents dream of having a child who carries their own genes. Others do not qualify for adoption. These individuals may turn to high-tech methods of having children.

Artificial insemination. This new-old method has been around for many years. *Artificial insemination* (AI) involves placing the sperm from a donor inside the woman's vagina with a syringe so that she can become pregnant. This method is used when the husband is infertile. It has also been used to impregnate unmarried women who wish to have children. Since insemination is relatively simple, there are reports of do-it-yourself efforts. For example, in pre-AIDS days, lesbians wishing to have children have used sperm donated by gay men (Yoxen, 1986).

Usually the procedure is kept a secret and the husband's sterility need never become public knowledge. Stories like the one at the opening of the chapter are never told. In many areas of the world, the child conceived by AI is in legal limbo, not recognized automatically as the child of the marriage. The Ontario Law Reform Commission (1985), for example, recommends that these children be recognized as the legal children of the woman's husband. In a few instances in the United States, husbands have obtained divorces because their wives had a child they did not father.

Recently the need for secrecy has been challenged. Social workers point out that family secrets are bad for children. Telling children they are adopted, for instance, is related to better adjustment later in life. Those who find out accidentally report that they have been aware of some secret for some time, and their fantasies are worse than the reality. Other individuals are concerned that children may grow up without valuable genetic information (McWhinnie, 1984). Often there has been inadequate record-keeping so that when a child develops what might be an inherited disease, it is impossible to discover who the sperm donor was so that proper genetic studies may be done, or so that the donor could be warned about being a carrier of the disorder.

The possibility of using frozen sperm has multiplied the moral and legal questions. One question concerns the legal status of a child conceived using frozen sperm after the death of the donor husband. Is the child considered a product of the marriage? Another issue involves the ethics of trying to create a superior child. In California, the Repository for Germinal Choice operates a sperm bank using only high achievers as donors. Women must have an IQ of at least 130 to qualify as recipients. The expectations of parents that their children will be superior may result in child anxiety (Yoxen, 1986).

Surrogate mothers. When the wife cannot conceive or cannot carry a child to term, some couples turn to *surrogate mothers*. In this case, a fertile woman, usually for a fee, is impregnated with the husband's sperm and signs over the resulting baby at birth. Obviously there is not the same possibility for secrecy as in AI.

Surrogate motherhood has been ruled illegal in a few states, and surrogacy for pay is illegal in other places. Generally, however, these contracts are not covered by law. There is confusion about whether surrogacy contracts are legal. During 1987 and 1988, the case of Baby M, in which the surrogate mother wanted to keep the child, raised the question, "Who has a right to the child, the biological mother or the biological father?" In the Baby M case, the judge ruled that the contract was illegal, but gave custody to the father and his wife on the grounds that they could offer a better home to the baby than the birth mother. The latter was, however, granted visiting rights (Smyth, 1991).

Some people have questioned the morality of surrogate contracts. They point out that only well-off people can afford the huge fees involved. Will this make two social classes, the wealthy who buy surrogate services and the poor who provide them? Others feel that payment for pregnancy is baby-selling, or that payment for use of the body for pregnancy is just as much prostitution as payment for use of the body for sex. There are real concerns that the child may be unprotected. The Baby M case is one example of the uncertainty of custody of the child. If the father refuses to take the child, for example if it is physically challenged, who is legally responsible for child support? In one case, the father and his wife claimed only one of a set of twins — a girl — and refused to take the boy (*The Toronto Star*, 6 August, 1989).

In-vitro fertilization. This procedure became news with the birth in 1978 of Louise Brown in England, the first so-called "test-tube baby." It involves removing ripe eggs from the woman's body and fertilizing them with the man's sperm in the laboratory. Two or three embryos are then placed in the woman's uterus with the hope that one will be implanted and the couple will produce a baby. This procedure usually is used when the fallopian tubes leading from the woman's ovaries to her uterus are blocked. Unfortunately the success rate is only 25 percent to 30 percent. Sometimes embryos are frozen so that they can be thawed and implanted later if the first try is unsuccessful. There have been court cases over the use of frozen embryos. In one case, the parents both died before the embryos could be used (Yoxen, 1986). In another, the couple separated and fought for custody of the embryos, the woman wanting them implanted in her and the man wanting them preserved unused (Hepburn, 1989).

A variation is the "borrowed womb," where the embryo is implanted in a surrogate. One much-publicized case involved a mother giving birth to her daughter's and son-in-law's triplets (Levin, 1987). This procedure raises a whole new set of possibilities. For example, a child could have five parents: genetic mother, genetic father, gestating mother, rearing mother, and rearing father.

Instant Parenthood

In the past, before antibiotics were developed, many men and women died young. Stepfamilies were formed as widowed parents remarried. Nowadays such families more often follow divorce than death, with the complication that the children still have a living parent not in the household. With more unmarried parents and divorces than ever before, more people are becoming instant parents when they marry someone with children. The number can be expected to grow in the future.

Table 5.2

FAMILY HISTORY SURVEY
Parenting in Canada involves overwhelmingly one's biological children. The following figures are from 1984.

Have you ever raised?

	Natural child(ren)	Step child(ren)	Adopted child(ren)
MEN	60.3%	4.4%	2.6%
WOMEN	67.5%	2.1%	2.5%

Only a few stepparents adopt stepchildren:

STEPFATHERS 15.7% adopted their stepchildren

STEPMOTHERS 2.1% adopted their stepchildren

Source: From information presented in Thomas K. Burch (1985). *Family History Survey*. Ottawa, Statistics Canada, August, Tables 7, 10, pp. 17, 19.

Being a stepparent has its own particular problems. Although a fuller discussion occurs elsewhere in this book, a few points need to be made here. In some cases, the new partner does not particularly want the children, but is willing to take them for the sake of getting married. In other cases, while the stepparent is willing, the child is loyal to the birth parent and feels that he or she cannot love the stepparent. Stepparents are also hampered by their lack of legal authority over the child, while in some situations they are legally responsible for supporting the child and are considered parents in cases of sexual abuse. Thus society regards them as both parents and nonparents.

Some Issues

There are a number of issues that are common to various routes toward parenthood. This is true of adopted and foster children and children conceived by birth technologies, as well as stepfamilies and single-parent families.

The first question is how much right a person has to genetic information. Such information is denied in most cases of artificial insemination. It may also be denied to some children in single-parent families, step families, adoptive families, and foster families, depending on the will of the parents and the availability of information. For example, an unmarried mother may be unsure of the identity of the father of her child if she had sexual relations with more than one person. On the other hand, she may know his identity but may be unwilling to tell the child.

Second, does the individual have a right to have contact with the birth or genetic parent(s)? When divorce has occurred, contact is usually maintained through visiting, or more often nowadays through joint custody. Less often children whose parents never married have contact with the noncustodial parent, usually the father. At the moment, adoptees and birth parents have no legal right to contact one another. There is voluntary contact once the adopted individual is an adult through provincial adoption-reunion registries. For children in foster care, the situation varies. Some children may have frequent contact with biological parents, while others may have none at all. Since artificial insemination is usually kept secret, contact rarely if ever occurs. Indeed, donors usually do not wish even to be told if a pregnancy resulted from their semen donation (Nicholas & Tyler, 1983). In surrogate motherhood, there may be contact between the surrogate mother and the child. Although there have been some attempts to treat surrogate arrangements like simple adoption cases, this approach tends to break down because of the biological relationship of the father and child. Later contact is probably a matter for the surrogacy contract or the courts.

A third, and important issue, is protection for the child. There is some protection, but it is probably weakest in black-market adoption arrangements and in surrogacy contracts. In the former, there is no regulation as to the suitability of the adoptive parents, especially if they choose never to legalize the adoption. In the latter, most contracts do not spell out who has responsibility for the child should it be born with mental or physical challenges, or even of the wrong sex than desired.

A factor that affects all atypical families is that there is a lack of social script. Society still considers a married couple and their biological children as the norm. From early childhood we learn how biological mothers and fathers ought to act. Yet there are no norms for adoptive parents, foster parents, stepparents, and surrogate mothers. Since these relationships are not the standard ones, there are some areas where social expectations of families do not fit. Families may feel considerable discomfort that may interfere with their ability to parent the child. They may feel, in fact, that they are not entitled to be parents to the child.

Psychologically, members of these families have all suffered significant losses of some kind. Children have been separated from one or both genetic parents, even if this separation occurred before birth. Infertile parents have lost the ability to have their own biological child. Even fertile parents who have resorted to the new technologies have not been able to conceive the "normal" way, through sexual intercourse. All members of the family have some degree of pain and of a sense of being different with which they must come to terms.

The Future

Experts predict a continuing drop in the birth rate, as more women enter the work force. They also predict that more couples will have children than ever before because of the new birth technologies available to previously infertile couples. We cannot predict, however, what impact economic factors will have on family size, or the effects of possible wars and other disasters in the future, so any prediction is at best only an educated guess.

SUMMARY

ENLARGING THE FAMILY CIRCLE. Having a child is often regarded as the mark of adulthood. There is much pressure on couples to have children. Since motherhood is considered necessary for personal fulfilment, those who choose not to have children are stigmatized. In fact, these women often have higher levels of career achievement.

THE SHRINKING FAMILY. In the earlier rural economy in Canada, children provided labour for the family enterprise and social security for the elderly.

For a variety of reasons, the birth rate has dropped markedly in the last few decades. First, medical advances have reduced infant mortality and provided more effective contraceptives. Second, although there has been opposition on moral and religious grounds, both contraceptives and abortion have been legalized. Third, economic factors encourage smaller families. Child labour is not a part of manufacturing. Poor economic times and women's growing participation in the work force, as well as the cost of raising children, also foster smaller families. Finally, couples argue that large families may damage the marital relationship and have an adverse effect on child development.

UNWANTED CHILDREN. There are three basic approaches to the unwanted child. First, a woman may choose not to have the baby; i.e., she has an abortion. This choice has produced controversies on moral grounds. Second, a parent may give the child to someone else to raise. Often such a child is cared for within the extended family. During the 1800s, many children were placed in work homes, orphanages, and private homes. In time, foster care in which parents were given board payments for the child became more common. Adoption, which involves the permanent transfer of parental rights to other adults, became accepted during this century. A third choice is to raise the child oneself. There is stigma against married people who give up a child. Single-parent families have recently gained wider acceptance.

THE INVOLUNTARILY CHILDLESS. If a couple cannot have children, they may experience stress and loss of self-esteem, both because of their childlessness and because of the investigation and treatment of their infertility. They have several options if they wish to have children. Foster care is still possible, although now it is not usually intended as long-term care and the children are generally older and have more behavioural problems. If a couple wishes to adopt, they face a long wait for a baby; they may choose to parent an older child, one with physical or mental challenges, or one from another country. There is growing openness in adoption, which allows continuing contact with birth parents and the possibility of later contact with adult adoptees. Birth technologies, such as artificial insemination, in-vitro fertilization, and surrogate motherhood offer other choices, although some procedures have a low success rate, and all have been challenged on moral grounds.

ISSUES. All families in which children are not raised by both biological parents face a number of issues. Does an individual have the right to genetic information about and contact with biological parents? What legal protections are in place for children? What effect does the lack of social script have on these families? What significant losses have family members suffered?

KEY TERMS

adoption: the legal transfer of rights and responsibilities from one set of parents to another

amniocentesis: a procedure in which some of the fluid surrounding the fetus is drawn off and examined under a microscope

artificial insemination: the practice of using sperm from a donor to fertilize an egg

foster home: a home that provides temporary care for children

in-vitro fertilization: the technique of fertilizing a woman's eggs with her partner's sperm in a lab dish, and later placing the embryo(s) in her uterus

marker event: an event that signals a change in status

social script: cultural rule that tells us what, where, when, how, and why we should do something

surrogate mother: a woman who agrees to artificial insemination, usually for a fee, with a view to turning over the resulting child to the biological father and his wife

CLASS ASSIGNMENTS

Complete one or both of the following assignments, as directed by your instructor.

1. Discuss in small groups different options for dealing with an unwanted pregnancy. Design questions for a brief survey. Interview ten people each and compare your results. Were there any surprises?

2. For a month, keep a scrapbook of stories that appear in newspapers and/or magazines about having children. You may also wish to keep a log of news stories on radio or television. What were the main issues?

PERSONAL ASSIGNMENTS

These assignments are designed to help you think about your own family.

1. If you had your wish, how many children would you have? Why? Would your answer be affected by your marital status? Explain.
2. If for some reason you could not have a biological child, what options would you consider using? Why would you choose to use or not use particular methods of having children? If you would decide not to have a child, give your reasons.

C H A P T E R 6

Bringing Up Baby

O B J E C T I V E S

- ➢ To explain the place of socialization in the family life cycle.
- ➢ To consider the key role parents play in the socialization of children, both through their own involvement and through their control over children's environments.
- ➢ To look at the influence of other family members on the socialization of children.
- ➢ To examine the interplay of society and the family in the area of socialization.

The "pacifier" habit — the habit of sucking a rubber nipple — is an inexcusable piece of folly for which the mother or nurse is directly responsible. The habit when formed is most difficult to give up. The use of the "pacifier," thumb-sucking, finger-sucking, etc., make thick boggy lips, on account of the exercise to which the parts are subjected. They cause an outward bulging of the jaws, which is not conducive to personal attractiveness.

Source: Department of Public Health (1922). *The Care of the Infant and Young Child.* Toronto: Author, p. 30.

A pacifier is helpful for fretfulness or to prevent thumb-sucking ... A baby who has periods of mild irritability can often be entirely quieted by having a pacifier to suck. We don't know whether this is because the sucking soothes some vague discomfort or simply keeps the baby's mouth busy ... Most of the babies who use a pacifier freely for the first few months of life never become thumb suckers, even if they give up the pacifier at 3 or 4 months.

Source: Benjamin Spock and Michael B. Rothenberg (1985). *Dr. Spock's Baby and Child Care.* New York: Pocket Books, p. 286.

Over the years, there has been little change in the physical development of children. All newborn babies need care if they are to survive. Most children sit up before they stand, and stand before they walk. But society has changed in what it thinks is important, and in the kind of behaviour it expects of its members. The use (or nonuse) of a soother is just a minor example.

Socialization in the Life Cycle

Socialization is the term used for the process of passing on to new members a culture's ways of thinking and acting. It occurs mainly in childhood. By the time they are adults, people are expected to share the values and norms of society. However, the process does not stop in childhood. Individuals assuming a new role, such as parenthood, or entering a new group, such as a company, are also socialized to some degree (Lundy & Warme, 1990). As infants and children we learn rules for behaviour, e.g., that we mustn't bite little sister. As young people, we learn how to behave in school and college, and what is expected of us on the job. We learn to be married people and parents. We learn what behaviour is thought suitable for the middle-aged and elderly, for the separated or widowed. Socialization is, then, a cradle-to-grave process affecting us all.

This learning can occur through explicit instruction, but occurs most often through the assumptions by which parents and others treat children and adults, and through observation of other people's behaviour. Through learning, individuals develop a sense of their identity, status, and roles in society. They acquire the basic knowledge needed to survive physically in that society, and the skills needed to take part in social life. These differ from one society to another. To take a very simple example, the proper distance to stand from another person varies. In North America, it is farther than in Latin American countries. There people cannot talk comfortably with each other unless they are at about the distance that would be seen with either sexual or hostile feelings here (Edward T. Hall, 1973).

Socialization of children occurs first in families, beginning with one or both parents, and soon includes other close family members. The circle expands to include more distant relatives, babysitters, day-care personnel, other children, school, television, and many other aspects of society. In this chapter, we will look at family and other social influences on the development of children.

Most theories of the family look at how values and norms of a culture are passed on to new members of the society, i.e., they are concerned about how society reproduces itself. Predictably, some take a macro view. Structural-functional thinkers are interested in how transmission of cultural norms ensures the stability of both families and the society of which they are a part. On the other hand, conflict theorists and feminist thinkers look at the way inequities in society are maintained from one generation to the next. Others approach the topic from a micro perspective, i.e., they look at the way family relationships shape individual experiences. This occurs, according to symbolic-interactionists, in the day-to-day relationships of the individual members. Systems theorists point to the importance of the family subsystems and boundaries in shaping children.

The Socialization Smorgasbord

Socialization experiences are something like a buffet. You can eat only what is placed on the table, but you don't need to take everything. Thus the child is presented with a variety of experiences out of which he or she forms an individual identity and value system.

Socialization does not take place in a vacuum. The child participates actively in the process. The levels of physical maturation, intellectual development, and social experiences help determine whether a child can understand and perform a socially-approved behaviour (Elizabeth Hall, 1987). For example, toilet training depends on the ability of the child to understand what is expected, as well as on nerves and muscles sufficiently mature to control elimination. Similarly, if a child cannot "read" social cues, he or she cannot respond appropriately to them. This failure may be the result of a problem such as impaired vision or hearing or delayed intellectual development, or of a lack of familiarity with the particular cultural norms. The child's developmental stage also affects his or her ability to profit from experiences. In general, a child needs to move from a close relationship with one or two people to interaction with a widening social circle. The ability to profit from peer relations or school experiences will depend on the child's developmental stage (Table 6.1). Children also make choices about their behaviour. This fact helps explain why children from the same family can turn out to be so different.

What Are Children Worth?

How we socialize children reflects what we expect of their future. It also reflects the value we place on them. If we feel children are an economic resource for the family, then child labour makes sense, especially if the family needs the money to survive. If we value the closeness and love children can bring to parents, then we will emphasize the emotional development and sensitivity of the children. Over the years, family patterns have changed slowly and a variety of patterns continue to exist (Segalen, 1986).

PRE-INDUSTRIAL EUROPE

One idea that has become common is that in the past parents were uncaring. Children, especially those born outside of marriage, were often killed. Tight swaddling kept a baby warm, but it also restricted movement and kept the baby quiet, almost in a stupor so that it could be left alone for hours while the mother worked. Physical punishment was the norm (Frankel-Howard, 1989; Tower, 1989).

Table 6.1

CHILDREN'S DEVELOPMENTAL STAGES AND EXPANDING WORLD STAGES

Developmental Stages	Psychosocial Crises	Radius of Significant Relations
Infancy	Basic Trust vs. Basic Mistrust	Maternal Person
Early Childhood	Autonomy vs. Shame, Doubt	Parental Persons
Play Age	Initiative vs. Guilt	Basic Family
School Age	Industry vs. Inferiority	Neighbourhood, School
Adolescence	Identity vs. Identity Confusion	Peer Groups

Source: Adapted from Erik H. Erikson (1982). *The Life Cycle Completed*. New York: W.W. Norton, p. 32.

Yet there are signs that children were loved and treasured. Parents used folk medicines to help their babies through the first dangerous days. Those who lived were cared for according to their natural rhythms — fed, changed, and put in the cradle on demand. Once they were old enough, they were raised by both parents and grandparents, even if the generations lived separately. Grandparents made up for what the parents lacked in kindness. Children were a collective responsibility (Segalen, 1986).

Youth began usually at first communion and ended with marriage. In some ways this was a carefree period, since young men in particular associated with their peers with little parental supervision. Yet the young had responsibilities such as safeguarding social order, even if it meant spying on couples to make sure they behaved. They were also expected to help from an early age in the family business through such tasks as looking after farm animals such as geese, or winding spools of yarn for weaving. Through such responsibilities, young people were gradually trained to accept and support the values of their society (Segalen, 1986). In New France, many young people lived and worked away from home, for example as servants, apprentices, or students (Moogk, 1982).

THE 19TH CENTURY

During the 19th century, Europe underwent the Industrial Revolution. It was marked by the growth of the middle class, made up in part of factory owners and managers. There were different patterns of parent-child relationships among the middle class, rural farm people, and working-class people in the towns and cities.

The middle class. There was a growing sense among the middle class that children were a kind of resource, and that giving birth to many who never reached adulthood was wasteful. These families tended to have fewer children and to value them more. Hand-in-hand with a sense of the value of childhood was an extension of its length. Adolescence was recognized as a separate phase of life. Instead of being apprenticed at an early age, these children attended school; in England many boarding schools were opened. Education no longer took place in the heart of the family. With extended schooling, however, young people lost much of their earlier freedom to be with the peer group (Segalen, 1986).

This period was also marked by greater differences in the roles of the parents. The father was the head of the family and decided in principle on the education of the children. The mother looked after everyday relationships and the care of the children, and was helped by governesses and nurses. Boys were socialized to assume leadership roles. Girls, on the other hand, were closely supervised within the family (Segalen, 1986).

The farm family. In many ways, the farm family continued the old methods of childrearing, yet the growth of formal education affected the traditional manner of on-the-job training. Some families encouraged education as a way of escaping poverty through nonagricultural careers. In general, young men either remained on the family farm until they were married or left to work in towns, and became members of the working class (Gaffield, 1982; Segalen, 1986).

The working-class family. In France, working-class families that lived in towns and cities were affected by the unreliability of work and housing. They tended to live from hand-to-mouth. Having many children meant the opportunity for more income to help support the family. Since children were expected to make a financial contribution as soon as possible, adolescence did not exist for them (Segalen, 1986).

In Canada, children were also employed. In the mid-19th century, boys as young as 8 years old worked in coal mines in Nova Scotia and British Columbia, where they did boring jobs for low pay. The boys turned over their pay to their parents, as long as they were living at home. Once they were working, these boys were regarded as almost adult. There are reports of 11- and 12-year-olds getting drunk with adults (McIntosh, 1987/88). A report in 1882 found that many children aged 5 to 15 years old were still working in manufacturing, and some as young as 2 years old had been hired in the past (Kieran, 1986). These were not safe and easy jobs. One 12-year-old lost his arm and leg in a mill accident; his employer gave him $10 compensation and paid his hospital bill but not his doctor bill. Gradually fewer children were hired. Better technology, cheap immigrant labour, and compulsory school attendance combined to reduce paid child labour (Gaffield, 1982).

THE PRICELESS CHILD

Our century saw the arrival of the economically worthless but emotionally priceless child, who was expected to provide emotional satisfaction for the parents (Zelizer, 1985). Being a mother was seen as "the greatest duty allotted to womankind" (Department of Public Health, Toronto, 1922, p. 3). As medical science advanced, experts offered advice to mothers on how to raise healthy children. The idea that the scientific method could be applied to human behaviour produced experts on child rearing. Most of the experts' theories were based on observations of white middle-class children (Strong-Boag, 1982). In the past, women had sought advice from their mothers and other women experienced with children; now traditional methods were devalued by professionals who claimed to know better. They advocated rigid schedules and not too much cuddling so that the child would not become spoiled and would fit better into school routines. They felt that a rigid approach to discipline was the way to teach the child self-discipline.

This intrusion into family life by experts affected poor and minority families, especially those receiving welfare. Professionals would visit such families to ensure that funds went only to the deserving poor. If child-care methods did not conform to "scientific" standards, families were subjected to often unwanted advice. If they did not conform, they could lose their children. This still holds true in cases of child abuse and neglect as illustrated by the case of Gregory K, the American boy who sued his parents for "divorce" and won. The Dionne family and their quintuplets was one of the most-publicized cases of intrusion by professionals (Nihmey & Foxman, 1987). The children were made wards of the province, were separated from their parents, and were raised according to the best standards known to experts in Toronto. These were counter to all the traditions of the rural French-Canadian society to which the family belonged. Eventually the children were returned to the care of their parents, but there was a gulf between their early socialization and the values and customs to which they were now expected to conform. Much less publicized are the thousands of minority, especially aboriginal, children separated from their biological families in boarding schools and in foster and adoptive homes (P. Johnston, 1983; M. Ward, 1984a).

Childhood came to be regarded as a special time, and was increasingly differentiated from adulthood. This process led eventually to the development of specialized children's institutions. Children attended school regularly to help provide a much-needed skilled and educated labour force. Special recreational and medical facilities were created for children. The training school, a combination prison and educational facility, was established to teach out-of-control and criminal children socially approved behaviour. Children were given their own courts. Increasingly, children were segregated by age group. For example, the one-room school gave way to larger institutions with one or more rooms for each grade.

FLORIDA JUDGE GRANTS 12-YEAR-OLD DIVORCE FROM PARENTS

ORLANDO, Fla. (AP) — In a precedent-setting case, a Florida judge granted a 12-year-old boy's wish Friday to "divorce" the biological parents he said mistreated and abandoned him. Judge Thomas Kirk told Gregory Kingsley he could be adopted by his foster parents.

"Gregory, you're the son of Mr. and Mrs. Russ at this moment," Kirk said as the courtroom broke into applause.

Kirk said the boy's biological mother "lied consistently" during the legal battle initiated by Gregory to sever his family relationship.

"I believe by clear and convincing evidence, almost beyond a reasonable doubt in this case, that this child has been abandoned ... and neglected by Rachel Kingsley (his mother) and it is certainly in his best interests that her parental rights be terminated immediately."

Gregory took the witness stand Friday in his fight to "divorce" his parents and nervously recalled bouncing from his mother's home to foster homes until he finally "thought she forgot about me."

As his mother wept in the courtroom, Gregory recounted a joyless childhood full of uncertainty and abandonment. He said his mother was often out late drinking and kept marijuana in the house "in a brown box on a table in the living room."

Asked why he wanted to live permanently with his foster family, Gregory said: "I'm doing it for me, so I can be happy."

The brown-haired, pale boy gave one-word answers to many questions but also gave some insight to why he asked his foster father to adopt him.

He recalled years when he wouldn't hear from his mother, Rachel, even at Christmas.

He said his first memory was of his father leaving the family. He said he loves his foster parents but not his mother. The boy, who has been in and out of foster care most of his life, spoke of how his mother broke her promise.

"She promised she never would put me back in foster care again," Gregory said.

The boy said he prefers to be called Shawn, not Gregory.

"I hated the name Gregory."

Asked what he thinks about the other children in his foster family, he said: "I think of them as my real brothers and sisters."

The boy contends in his lawsuit his mother's abuse and neglect led him to seek legal freedom so he could be adopted by his foster parents — George and Lizabeth Russ, with whom he has lived for almost a year.

Some legal observers said the case could affect the ability of children to protect themselves from parental abuse or neglect.

Source: *The Sudbury Star*, 26 September 1992, p. B14.

Since it was recognized that children could not easily protect themselves, there was pressure on the government to protect children from exploitation by adults and mistreatment by parents.

Parents — The First Socializers

Parents are the single most powerful influence in the socialization of their children (Tesson, 1987). This is especially true during the early stages of development. They directly influence their children both by who they are and through day-to-day interaction. They also exert indirect control over a great deal of their children's environment. For example, by selecting the neighbourhood in which they live, they will affect who will form their children's peer group.

WHO ARE THE PARENTS?

The number, marital status, sex, sexual orientation, and age of parent figures helps shape children. The traditional husband-wife family, as we have seen, is becoming more the exception than the rule. With the increasing rates of both divorce and remarriage, there are increasing numbers of children growing up with one parent in the home, or with an unrelated parent figure. The majority of married women work for pay and may depend on others to care for their children. Thus more and more, the adults who care for children may not be their biological parents. A significant number of children have only one caregiver.

Children who grow up in two-parent families, one-parent families, and stepfamilies have different socializing experiences. Children in single-parent and stepparent families have, on the whole, more responsibilities than children who live with both biological parents (Amato, 1987). However, children in single-parent families also have more freedom than those in either stepparent or traditional nuclear families. Children who live with both parents are less susceptible to persuasion by peers to engage in antisocial behaviour. Some sociologists originally believed that this might be due to the fact that there were two adults to keep an eye on children. Studies of children in stepfamilies show, however, that they are as likely as those in one-parent families to give in to persuasion by peers (Steinberg, 1987). Girls living with divorced mothers, especially mothers who work outside the home, have less traditional attitudes about what men's and women's roles in society should be. However, the researchers feel that boys living with a female head of household are more likely than girls to reflect the opinions common in the outside world (Kiecolt & Acock, 1988). We will look at other factors in their development in later chapters.

Some families, notably those of lesbian couples, may have two female parent figures. One study of such families conducted in England found that their children differed little from those growing up with heterosexual single mothers. There was no evidence of higher levels of homosexuality among the children. Like other children growing up in single-parent and stepparent families, children in lesbian households have usually lived through the breakup of their biological family. For all these groups, the amount of conflict within the family seems more important to social adjustment than the number and sex of parent figures. If there is much conflict, the children have more problems than if there is little conflict (Golombok, Spencer, & Rutter, 1983).

More women are now having their first children after they are 30 years old. Others have "caboose" or "afterthought" children through middle-aged carelessness or as a child of a second marriage. How do these children feel about having older parents? One study learned that about half thought that it made no difference or was an advantage (Morris, 1987); the rest considered that it was a disadvantage. Some were embarrassed by their parents' appearance, especially when they were mistaken for their grandparents. Older parents were less likely to be involved in children's activities like playing ball. For some, the generation gap looked like an unbridgeable canyon. Many were afraid that their parents would die before they became independent. Some regretted not knowing their grandparents, who had died before their birth. Those children who were positive about having older parents felt that their parents could take more time to enjoy children and had more money for luxuries because they were established financially. Only children, especially those of older single parents, were especially lonely. Some late-born children may actually have much more adult attention than children in the family born earlier. One mother reports that her caboose son thought he had six parents, including his four older siblings. One day he asked why his oldest sister called their mother "Mom", and was shocked to discover that his mother was his sister's mother too. It is possible that with more women delaying childbearing, having older parents will not be regarded as so different in the future.

DAY-TO-DAY INTERACTION

The day-to-day treatment of children has long-term effects on the child's development. Diana Baumrind (1980) describes three types of parenting styles: authoritarian, permissive, and authoritative. *Authoritarian* parents are the drill-sergeant type. Children are expected to obey without question. These families are strong on obligations and responsibilities, but weak on recognizing children's individuality or their need to learn to make decisions for themselves. Children growing up in such families tend to become either submissive and unable to make decisions for themselves or to become defiant and rebellious. Adolescence will probably be a particularly difficult time for such families. *Permissive* parents are at the other end of the scale. They recognize children's individuality and their right to make decisions for themselves, but they fail to set limits or assign responsibilities and obligations. Children from these families may fail to recognize rights of others and may not develop self-discipline. As a result, they may live aimless and disappointing adult lives. Finally, *authoritative* parents take a middle position. They have high expectations of their children, but they are also aware of their children's needs and are willing to adjust demands to their interests and abilities.

Children from these families are often described as being competent, friendly, and achievers.

Another aspect of parent-child relationships is "goodness-of-fit." Stella Chess and Alexander Thomas (1987) describe children as having basic temperaments. If the child's temperament matches what parents expect, then there is goodness of fit between them. For example, a father who enjoys quiet activities such as reading and discussion of current events may have problems with a highly active son who finds it hard to sit still. A sports-minded father, however, will find such a child a much greater pleasure than a boy who is a bookworm. Thus the match between parent and child will affect the level of approval or disapproval the child experiences. In turn, self-concept and self-esteem will be affected.

FAMILY ROUTINES AND TRADITIONS

Socialization involves the most ordinary aspects of living. For example, one research project discovered that middle-class families use dinner time as an opportunity for teaching acceptable social behaviour, such as manners. Democratic values are, to some degree, also demonstrated. The whole family eats together, rather than in stages as in some cultures where women might serve the men first, and then eat whatever is left. Children and parents alike talk about their experiences during the day. Families that have extremely limited space, on the other hand, have to make other eating arrangements. These might include buffet-style meals or eating in shifts. Children growing up in these families will have quite a different view of proper mealtime behaviour (Dreyer & Dreyer, 1973).

Family story traditions also help shape children. The events that are remembered and retold often emphasize family values by emphasizing heroes or villains (Stone, 1988). Sometimes themes are repeated, e.g., one family told again and again the story about all the young men who ran away from home to make their fortunes in another country. This has given permission to youth in successive generations to move away from their family of origin, yet they keep their family identity because of the story traditions.

SOCIAL CLASS

Social class, as defined by the educational and occupational background of parents, has marked effects on the way they raise a child. Income of parents can affect the area in which a family lives. The school, recreational facilities, and peer groups are different from one part of a city to another, and from one part of a province to another. Income also determines, in part, how children are dressed and what activities they might take part in. For example, music lessons or competitive sports require lessons and/or expensive equipment as well as additional transportation costs. Clothing and activities can affect the peer group with which a child associates.

THE STRIFE OF BATH

Sometimes a source of consternation (at 7 a.m., who showers first?), occasionally grounds for an argument (should the seat remain up or down?), research has quantified what many have long suspected: too few bathrooms in a home may contribute to family stress.

Environmental designer Marjorie Inman distributed a series of questionnaires to 200 families in Indiana, asking them about the number of family members, rooms and bathrooms in their households, as well as their attitudes toward their living arrangements. Taking into account the size of each household (varying from two to nine members) and the available space (two to nine rooms, or more), Inman divided the families into two groups: those living in "crowded" spaces and those living in "adequate" spaces.

In the crowded household, having only a single bathroom could be a source of stress. Half of those families with only one bathroom reported stress from a lack of privacy. Only 14 percent of those with two or more bathrooms did so. Seven out of ten families with single baths said they felt stressed by the amount of living space, compared with 17 percent of those with two or more bathrooms.

Although a less acute problem, limited bathroom access may prove stressful to those living in the uncrowded homes, as well. Of those families with one bathroom, almost half reported stress from a lack of privacy (compared with 20 percent of those with two or more baths), and nearly 40 percent complained of limited living space (compared with 14 percent of those with more than one bathroom).

"This study is a clear indicator that having too few bathrooms in a household can be a major contributor to stress," Inman says. "We found that even an additional half bath [a toilet and sink without a shower or tub] can make an enormous difference." But Inman cautions against having too much of a good thing. "If a family has more than three bathrooms, they become a heavy chore to clean and keep stocked," she says, "and can cause a completely different kind of stress."

Inman is at the Environmental Design Center at Purdue University. Her research was sponsored by the Kohler Company in Kohler, Wis.

Source: Jeff Meer (1986). *Psychology Today,* May: 6.

Values and forms of interaction have been found to differ between middle-class and working-class families. Language patterns also differ. These may determine how well the child fits into the school system and thus how far he or she goes in school. Parents who have some independence on the job tend to encourage self-direction on the part of children. On the other hand, parents who must take orders at work tend to emphasize the importance of obeying rules. In fact, they are training their children for the kind of work experiences they themselves have had. These values will affect later initiative and job performance (Tesson, 1987).

FAMILIES AND GENDER-ROLE SOCIALIZATION

Children learn early what society expects of them as males and females. This process is referred to as *gender-role socialization*. Parents play a key role in this socialization. Boys tend to receive more attention from parents than girls, both negative, such as punishment, and probably also positive. When fathers interact with sons, they stress achievement and the cognitive aspects of what they are doing. With daughters, they emphasize interpersonal relations through encouragement and support. Boys are also more pressured than girls against behaviour felt to be inappropriate for their sex (Thacker, 1989).

The objects with which children are surrounded also affect their socialization. We need only take a quick look at home-decorating magazines to see girls' rooms in ruffles and pastels and boys' rooms with smooth surfaces and bright colours. Even this physical arrangement encourages females to be quieter and males to be more active. Girls' toys, such as dolls and sets of dishes, encourage caring and serving behaviours, while boys' toys are more active and complex, such as cars, and help develop such abilities as spatial relations. In addition, it is usually more acceptable for girls to play with toys that are designed for boys than vice versa. Children's books also tend to show boys and men in more active roles in which they shape their world, and girls and women in more passive roles at home or waiting to be rescued by a male (Thacker, 1989).

In these and other ways, girls are encouraged to conform to the stereotype that women are passive, dependent, and nurturing. Boys, on the other hand, are encouraged to be more independent, active, and aggressive (Thacker, 1989).

HOW DIFFERENT ARE ENGLISH CANADIANS AND FRENCH CANADIANS?

There have been few studies comparing the way English Canadians and French Canadians raise their children. One group of researchers did look at families of both cultural groups in Montreal (Taylor et al., 1978; Smith & Grenier, 1975), but their findings may not be typical of the rest of Canada. They discovered that the families were more alike than different. They did find that English-speaking Montrealers encouraged their children to be more independent in solving problems than did French-speaking Montrealers. Anglophones also tended to restrict their children's contact with friends and to treat their children more harshly. French Canadians encouraged in-group ties and tried to develop their children's reliance on the extended family. In general, the anglophone families were more traditional and authoritarian in their views than were the francophones. The authors wondered if these differences were the result of growing Quebec nationalism, which left anglophones feeling that they were a threatened minority. A group that fears it is losing its dominant position often becomes more conservative as its ideas are challenged. Since these studies are at least fifteen years old, they do not reflect fully the continuing nationalist and separatist movements in Quebec.

The Wider Family Circle

Parents have considerable control over the relationships of children with other family members. For example, parents decide how many children to have. They influence how often children see grandparents and other relatives. Of course, their control is greater for younger than for older children.

BROTHERS AND SISTERS — FRIENDS, FOES, AND TEACHERS

The *sibling* relationship is important to children because it is unique. Brothers and sisters are family members, but they do not have the kind of authority parents have over younger children, unless they are much older or the parents have failed in the caregiving role through neglect, illness, substance abuse, or some other physical or emotional absence. In many ways the sibling relationship is similar to the peer relationship in that it is more egalitarian than that between parents and children. There are, of course, wider age spans in sibling relationships than usually occur among friends. Yet unlike peer relationships, the sibling relationship is *ascribed,* i.e., it is given to a person and is not optional. For practical purposes, the sibling relationship can only be broken by death or by one or more children leaving the family and having no contact.

Birth-order effects. The number of siblings, their age, and their sex affect the socialization of a child (Clausen & Clausen, 1973). An only child, for example,

Source: Lynn Johnston (1981). *I've Got the One-More-Washday Blues.* Kansas City: Andrews and McMeel, p. 12.

does not have the same experiences in getting along with children as the middle child among nine brothers and sisters. Families with all boys are different from families with all girls or from those with a mix. One aspect of sibling relationships that has captured imaginations recently is the effect of birth order on personality development. For example, the eldest child is described as an achiever and, often, as bossy; the middle child as a hellion or mediator; and the youngest as a charmer (Leman, 1985). These characteristics result because the eldest associates more with adults and tries to win their approval, and by virtue of being bigger and stronger can often (but not always!) push the younger children around. The middle child is often ignored, even in the family photo album. In order to get attention, he or she will try to be different from the eldest. If, for example, the eldest follows parents' wishes, the middle one may be rebellious. The middle child also has to get along with both older and younger siblings; as a result the middle child learns bargaining skills to get what he or she wants from siblings. The youngest child is often the centre of attention, but is almost always the smallest and weakest during the formative years. The youngest child uses charm to get what he or she wants. If there are more than three children in the family, the roles may become quite specialized. Bossard (1975) identifies a variety of roles: the responsible one, the butterfly, the rebel, the princess, and sometimes the scapegoat. Since we usually feel comfortable in the roles we have grown up with, we try to repeat them in adult life. For example, the younger brother of sisters will probably be happier with an oldest sister of brothers. In their relationship, they will thus continue the familiar patterns (Toman, 1969).

Birth-order effects are not inevitable, e.g., a younger child may take over the role of an older one. This might occur in families where the older child is physically or mentally challenged. Personality is another factor. The eldest may be temperamentally unassertive and allow a younger sibling to be the leader.

Siblings as socializers. Older brothers and sisters help socialize younger ones in many ways. They act as role models. Many children have learned the use of makeup, how to smoke or drink, or how best to get around parents from brothers and sisters. Older siblings can introduce younger ones to the current games and rhymes of the schoolyard or playground. They teach skills. If they live in an isolated community in the bush, for example, children may learn to identify edible plants and animal tracks from older siblings. Older brothers and sisters can also provide support and advice in situations where parents do not have current know-how, for example, regarding appropriate ways of approaching a peer of the opposite sex or socially acceptable ways of behaving in a mixed group of children.

Role models are not always favourable. One study of juvenile offenders in the Ottawa area discovered that boys in all-male sibships are more likely to follow brothers in delinquency than those who also have sisters, since the first group do not have as wide a variety of models (Jones, Offord, & Abrams, 1980).

The early writings on sibling relationships tended to stress rivalry between brothers and sisters. This emphasis probably arose because first Freud and then psychiatrists such as John Bowlby emphasized the importance of the mother-child relationship to healthy child development. They and their followers saw siblings as competitors for a limited amount of parental attention. Yet even conflict has a positive side: given that sibling relationships are obligatory, brothers and sisters must learn how to resolve conflict issues (Bank & Kahn, 1982). For example, they need to know when to stand up for their rights and when to give in. Siblings learn the importance of social context: their behaviour may differ depending on whether a parent is present. Junior may hit little sister over the head to get a toy if mother is out of the room, but not when she is there. They also learn bargaining skills, for example, "If you let me use your stereo for a week, I won't tell Dad you came in drunk on Saturday morning."

Later investigators have pointed out that there is also great warmth and affection between brothers and sisters. The sibling relationship can be one of the most enduring in a person's life, e.g., elderly women who live with someone other than a husband are most likely to live with a sibling, usually a sister (Bank & Kahn, 1982). Siblings have a store of memories in common and have been socialized in similar ways.

Affection between brothers and sisters depends on access. This can be limited if the children are widely separated in age, because their interests are too different. Children from large families also comment that the younger ones do not really know the older ones, since they did not live in the same house for long. Access also depends on parents. If they feel it important that their children know and like each other, they will encourage such relationships.

Sometimes when parents abdicate authority, and the children have access to one another, siblings may develop extreme loyalty to one another (Bank & Kahn, 1982). Since the parental subsystem is not functioning, the children try to make up for the lack. One of the oldest may become a "parental" child, trying to fill a role for which he, or more often she, is unequipped. In such a case, the younger children are often parented inadequately and the parental child fails to achieve a normal adulthood. Once the younger children are no longer dependent on the older child, he or she may feel lost, unneeded, and depressed. Social workers often see these characteristics in brothers and sisters from neglected or abused families, or in children who have moved together from one foster home to another.

Family size. The number of brothers and sisters also affects development. Several studies show that children from large families tend to be at a disadvantage. Little attention has been paid to the effects of the style of living and the psychological stress from pressures on resources of parents' time, energy, and income. Yet lifestyle and parental stress level may have far-reaching effects on children's development. There tends to be a decline in I.Q. as the number of children in the family increases. This decline may be related to poverty rather than family size as such. Larger families have to spread income farther, and may not be able to provide food with sufficient protein and vitamin content for optimal brain development. They may also have to live in neighbourhoods where role models of achievers are limited. Younger children tend to have poorer language development, perhaps because they hear more child speech and less adult speech, or perhaps because the speech they hear in the neighbourhood is not the variety expected in school. As a result, these children tend to do less well in school and are less likely to continue to post-secondary education. Children in large families tend to have lower status jobs than their parents (Clausen & Clausen, 1973). All these factors are less extreme in families with higher incomes, where more resources are available for all needs, from better nutrition to extracurricular activities to higher education.

The physically or mentally challenged. Having a brother or sister with exceptionalities also affects socialization (Crocker, 1983). Children in such families may have to adjust to a change in the family rhythm as parents and other family members have to pay attention to the special needs of the exceptional child. Parents may be stretched thin by the demands of the exceptional child, and may not have the time and emotional resources necessary for the other children. Indeed brothers or sisters may be expected to help with child care, and may be asked to include the sibling in their social activities. Some youngsters feel they have to make up to their parents for what the sibling cannot achieve. Often parents impose a double standard on their children, expecting less from the exceptional child because of his or her limitations. Sometimes these standards are unreasonable, for example, expecting a higher standard of consideration from the "normal" child than from the one who is exceptional in some way. Shared stress can improve family communication and closeness. If, however, the stress is very great, the family can experience extreme tension, blocked communication, and possibly family breakdown.

The role of siblings in the socialization of children may be decreasing. Since families are becoming smaller, currently with an average of 1.8 children, this generation of children will have only one or two, if any, brothers or sisters to help socialize them. Some sociologists speculate that in the future peers may become more influential in socialization than they already are because they will fill some of the vacuum in sibling relationships (Tesson, 1987)

EXTENDED FAMILY MEMBERS

The extended family consists of relatives such as grandparents, aunts, uncles, and cousins. Families vary in the number of extended family members they keep contact with and in the amount of contact.

How important are relatives? According to some current theories, the extended family has been weakened by increased mobility. In fact, more children probably know their grandparents now than in earlier generations because of the increased life span. Many children grow up with a warm, continuing relationship with grandparents. Only a minority of families actually move very frequently, and even they tend to stay in contact with their relatives. From extended family members children learn how to get along with people of other generations. They also learn how elderly people should be treated by observing their own parents and grandparents.

Several studies of families have shown that extended families are strong in both rural and urban areas, and still act as support systems for members. Many families in rural Quebec, Montreal, and Hamilton reported that they had relatives living in the area and saw them at least once a week (Piddington, 1976; Pineo, 1976). Often relatives provide services, such as child care. This experience can be enriching for the child because often the older generation preserves the family stories and traditions. Some of these arrangements can, however, lead to conflict between parents and grandparents over rules, punishment, and spoiling the children. Usually such difficulties occur when boundaries between families and generations are not clear.

A particular point of contact between generations is maintaining rituals and traditions. Christenings, bar mitzvahs, birthdays, first communions, and many other events bring families together. If traditions are shared, they serve to underline the importance of tradition to the family. They both increase family solidarity and transmit family and cultural values.

Native families. Aboriginal cultures in Canada traditionally have assigned an important role to the extended family in child rearing. Even if grandparents or other relatives did not actively care for a child, they advised parents on the child's welfare.

White cultural practices have undermined the strengths of native families. In the late 1800s, many boarding schools were opened with the purpose of moving native children into white culture. Here they were punished for speaking their native languages and were expected to conform to a regimented life that was foreign to them. Brothers and sisters were separated; some grew up not even knowing one another. A whole generation grew up deprived of family experiences so that they had lost traditional ways of raising children without fully learning white ways (Graff, 1987; P. Johnston, 1983; M. Ward, 1984a). The disruption in parenting has been blamed, in part, for the problems many native families have later experienced.

Other factors affected the health of families. Not all reserves were able to support their populations. As game was depleted, traditional methods of providing for a family disappeared. Welfare dependency became the only way of survival for many families. Alcohol, which was introduced by white traders, became a way of temporarily escaping the hopeless situation. In turn, alcoholism increased the levels of violence among the people as evidenced in the high number of violent deaths (including accidents, murders, and suicides), and high levels of spousal and child abuse (J.A. Ward, 1988). Since white social workers did not understand the strengths of traditional native ways, many children were removed from healthy families and placed in foster or adoptive homes. In general, native homes were not used because the standards applied by social workers were appropriate for white middle-class families rather than for native families living on reserves. For example, standards such as the need for indoor plumbing and a telephone were clearly illogical for some communities. The loss of their children added to the despair of many native peoples.

The recent move toward native self-government has been accompanied by a growing self-respect. Many reserves have taken over administration of education and child-welfare services (P. Johnston, 1983). Many have also been combatting alcoholism, unemployment, and other social problems experienced by their people. Native children in many communities are now becoming involved in cultural activities, such as dancing and drumming. There is a growing pride in traditional native culture and spirituality.

Society at Large

Parents and other family members are not the only people who affect the socialization of the child. Society as a whole is involved, even in small details, such as the amount of noise families are allowed to make. As children move out of the home, parents do have some control over their environment. This control is, however, limited and grows less as children become older.

CHILD CARE

The choices parents make about child care for the time that they are at work affect a child's development. The atmosphere in a grandparent's home is different from that in homes where one woman may care for three or four children, and is different still from a babysitter coming into the child's home.

Even day-care centres vary. A study of licenced infant day-care centres in the United States found that children were treated differently in centres that looked after children of mainly low-income parents than those that served mainly middle-income parents. For example, workers in the centre serving low-income families gave infants and toddlers many commands, and treated boys and girls quite differently. In the centre serving mainly middle-income families, appeals were made for appropriate behaviour, rather than commands given, and boys and girls were treated in the same manner. In the first, children were being socialized into traditional male and female roles. In the second, the roles were more egalitarian. The plans to include a centre catering to high-income families in the study failed, since these parents usually used nannies or housekeepers (D.F. Miller, 1989).

RULING TOUGH ON PARENTS IN APARTMENTS

Was there a parent living in rental accommodation who didn't feel a chill on hearing that a couple was ordered out of their apartment by a Toronto judge last week because their baby cried?

District Court Judge Roger Conant gave Svetazor and Mira Lazarevic and their 22-month-old daughter Stefanie until April 30 to move out of their apartment after neighbors complained about the child crying when she was teething. (The couple plan to appeal and should be able to stay until the appeal is heard in Divisional Court, their lawyer says.)

In his decision Judge Conant was critical of Mira Lazarevic for refusing to do anything about the problem and ruled that it would be "unfair to the neighbors" not to evict the family.

It would have been helpful if the judge had made it clearer just what a mother is supposed to do when a child is teething. Did he have in mind handing the child over to the Children's Aid Society? Putting it up at the Ritz?

It would also have been instructive to have the judge's thoughts on just how this family, branded now as having a noisy child, will ever find alternative accommodation in a city where families are already treated by many landlords as if they had the plague, and where vacancies are so few that landlords can pick and choose their tenants.

By his decision, Judge Conant has claimed for Toronto, which was already showing signs of increasing hostility towards children, the title of the world's Hate Kids Capital as well as making us a laughing stock.

****

In all the legal jousting — and [Bruce] Porter [co-ordinator at the Centre for Equality Rights in Accommodation] says this case is by no means isolated —what's forgotten is the pressure put on families with small children. A parent dealing with a teething child is already under stress. How much worse is the pressure if that parent knows if the baby cries more the family may be out on the street!

Porter says of Conant's judgment: "It shows a total lack of understanding of the nature of parenting." He's absolutely right.

Source: Frank Jones, *The Toronto Star*, 3 April 1990, p. B3.

THE SCHOOL

Once a child has reached the age of 4 or 5 years, large blocks of his or her time are turned over to the school, which takes over much of the socialization process. At school children learn to interact with new authority figures and with children about their own age. They are introduced to many new ideas by the people with whom they interact. These may agree or conflict with the values they have already learned in the family.

The first years of formal education are important to children's sense of self-esteem. Many begin school feeling that they are worthwhile individuals. Studies have shown, however, that within a few years their self-esteem drops. In part, this is related to the amount of negative feedback children receive in school, in the form of criticism, comparison with other children, and poor marks. Children from low-income and minority-group families often do not have as much expected of them as children from middle-class families. Since youngsters are aware of differences in treatment, these expectations result in both lower achievement and lower self-esteem (Santrock, 1992).

In school children also learn about other families through their peers, through books and stories, and through teachers' attitudes. This learning can include family and gender roles. One class assignment that has been criticized by a number of parents is the family tree. This is all very well if children are members of a traditional nuclear family. It is difficult, however, to fit members of divorced, stepparent, and foster or adoptive families into a conventional family tree. In addition, some children may still be experiencing some of the trauma of separation, so that this assignment is very painful for them.

Schools and gender-role socialization. In the past, education was very strongly related to gender stereotypes. For example, industrial arts classes were for boys only and home economics classes for girls only. Boys traditionally have done better than girls in mathematics and science, and girls have done better than boys in language skills. Although there have been attempts made to desegregate subjects and encourage women to continue math and science into the higher grades, success has been somewhat limited.

Studies of schools have shown that role models in these subjects, such as science teachers, are primarily men. Science also tends to be taught to typical male interests, such as competitive sports (an example of earlier gender-role socialization). Some teachers still believe that girls are not as capable as boys of learning mathematics and science. A few also feel that these subjects are not related to the girls' futures as wives and mothers. Even some modern guidance counsellors tend to suggest to girls occupations that are typically filled by women, and to boys those filled by men; thus they help perpetuate gender-role stereotypes (Thacker, 1989).

Native children in school. The experience of many native children in school illustrates the interplay between home and school. As a result of their concern, education officials in Ontario commissioned a study looking into the causes of the high dropout rate of native students (Mackay & Myles, 1989). Although not the only factors involved, many of the reasons for dropouts were related to the home and its relationship to the macro system and exosystem.

First, schools demand knowledge and skills that some native children had not learned at home. Many dropouts had difficulty with English-language skills. Some had learned a nonstandard form of English at home. Others who came from remote areas spoke one of the native languages at home and used English as a second language. Other studies have shown that native children are at a disadvantage in school because of the emphasis on learning through words. Traditionally, native children have learned through watching rather than by following instructions. Thus their observational skills have been developed more than their verbal skills (Kaulback, 1984).

Second, teachers state that the children lack encouragement at home. They point to the high rate of school absence among the dropouts and their frequent failure to do homework. A number of home factors are noted, e.g., since many homes are small and may be crowded, students may lack a quiet study space at home. In addition, many parents have not gone very far in school and may not be familiar with the idea of homework. Native parents also tend to be less directive than non-native parents, and leave decisions about homework and school attendance up to their children.

Third, home problems and responsibilities may interfere with school attendance and achievement. Many students live in boarding homes in town to attend high school; in one area, those who came from a reserve with a high rate of alcoholism felt that they had the responsibility to go home, travelling over dangerous roads, when welfare cheques arrived. This was the only way they could ensure that the younger children in the family received enough food.

Fourth, school officials point to communication difficulties they experience with parents. For example, parents tend not to go to parent/teacher meetings. They can be difficult to contact because of distance or lack of telephones. When communication does take place, it is often unpleasant. School personnel contact parents when the student has done something wrong and tell them what should be done about the behaviour. Thus parents are often intimidated by the school system.

In this instance, we can see the impact on the child and family of the values of white society and the institutions of that society. As a result, the relationship of parents and school personnel is often difficult and full of misunderstanding and conflict.

PEERS

When children start school, peers begin to take on increased importance. Often parents think of the peer relationship as being negative and blame friends for being bad influences on their children. For example, children tend to try alcohol or drugs or become involved in delinquent behaviour when they are with their friends. Friends also influence children's desires as consumers — what the leader of a group has everyone wants, even if it conflicts with family standards.

Friendship, however, also has good aspects. Peers can make up for some of the negative experiences a child has at home. They also provide a dose of reality for the children who are the centre of their parents' lives. Before children start school, their view of reality is based on their family and immediate neighbourhood. They feel that everyone thinks of them as special in either a good or bad sense. Through friends, children come to recognize that instead of being unique they have interests and desires in common with others. They also come to understand that doing things together helps develop new ideas that one child could not create alone. The relationship is far more cooperative than that with parents and allows a different kind of development (Youniss, 1980). Children also measure themselves against others their own age in regard to physical appearance and abilities and intellectual performance. Thus they develop a sense of their capabilities.

Peers also help shape children's views of themselves in relation to society. Even very young children are described as popular, rejected by peers, or ignored by peers. These social statuses tend to continue year after year, partly because the children have learned particular forms of interaction and partly because they earn reputations. Even when they move from elementary to junior high or high school where they are not known, children often develop the same kinds of interactions with peers (Berndt, 1983; Coie & Dodge, 1983; Dodge et al., 1983; Ladd, 1983). The patterns of interaction children learn in their homes help form the basis for the attitude of peers. For example, a child who is encouraged by parents in shy behaviour may become one of the ignored children.

As children become older, the peer group assumes greater importance. Most adolescents, for example, rely more on friends than on parents. Yet the growing independence of young people from their parents does not begin in adolescence; rather it is a long process that starts early in life. It is the peer group that provides much of the opportunity for this gradual separation from the family of origin.

THE MEDIA

The media, especially television, are important socializing agents. Studies of commercials on television have found that visible minorities are rarely shown. Men, more than women, are presented as having high-status jobs. Commercials show women mainly in the home involved with children or household activities such as food preparation. English- and French-language television differ only in the number of times men are shown interacting with children, with French-speaking men more likely pictured with children (Spears & Seydegart, 1985). If one were to believe the commercials, most Canadian families are white, speak either English or French, and hold the conventional roles of wage-earner father and homemaker mother. Television programs do portray variations in family structure, although they rarely show problems of the immigrant family setting up their home in North America. Such shows are usually unrealistic, however, because the constraints of programming demand resolution of problems in half an hour or an hour. Life, of course, does not work that way. The exception to the instant solution is the daytime drama, whose characters are shown with continuing problems. Although daytime talk shows discuss many family variations, some of the situations presented are bizarre. Few programs present an ordinary, rather humdrum existence.

"When will the TV be back? I hate coming home to an empty house!"

Source: *The Single Parent*, December 1978, p. 11.

FAMILY TRENDS AND SOCIALIZATION

Given that society changes, every age group grows up in a different world. These age groups are called *cohorts.* Their family experiences are also different, e.g., individuals born during the Great Depression, like children born now, have fewer brothers and sisters and somewhat older parents. One cohort that has received a great deal of attention is the baby-boom generation. Their experiences in growing up differ markedly from those of both earlier and later cohorts.

John Kettle, in his book, *The Big Generation* (1980), describes eight factors which affected the socialization of this group. First, the country was in boom times, and the general affluence led people to expect that life would be easy. Second, there was a mushrooming of technology. Third, institutions were weakened, and there was a loss of respect for authority. Fourth, parents made Dr. Spock's book, *Baby and Child Care,* a best seller. His advice was much more permissive than that given in earlier years. An example is given at the beginning of this chapter concerning the use of soothers. Some parents, however, took his advice to the extreme, and provided very little structure for their children. Fifth, the effect of being born into a large family meant that more of the process of socialization was carried on by children, and that teamwork and social skills were emphasized. These children also experienced more family instability because of an increasing number of broken marriages. Sixth, this is the first generation that never knew what it was to live without television. Seventh, after World War II, there was a swift migration from farm to town, from town to city. Small towns tend to set and enforce standards more than do cities , but they are also much more supportive to families. Finally, advances in medicine meant that there was a rapid drop in infant and child mortality and a reduction of physical suffering.

As the big generation moved through the school system, they were subjected to more crowding and a greater number of young, hastily trained teachers. Added to the effect of numbers was the fact that more young people were staying in school longer, partly because they could not find jobs, and partly because the jobs that were available required a higher level of technical skill. A number of experimental plans were introduced to try to cope with the many more students who did not plan to go to university. It was for this generation that the community college system was developed.

According to Kettle (1980) the effect on many individuals in this cohort is that they tend to live by their feelings and tend to be suspicious of obligations. They tend to be concerned with personal development first and then with family happiness. Many have little loyalty except to themselves. The permissiveness with which many were raised did not train them in traditional values. There is also, according to Kettle, a greater potential for violence in this cohort, because they have not absorbed strong social controls, because they are experiencing frustration in finding employment, and because they have greater access to alcohol, drugs, and guns. There are problems with generalizations such as these; the baby-boom generation encompasses a large age group, and it is rash to equate people now in their forties with those in their twenties. In addition, such statements ignore the many variations in life experience.

The present trend to smaller families gives children experiences different from the large families of the baby-boom cohort. There is a narrower age range of people with whom the children relate on a regular basis. They do not have to learn to get along with other children as early as did the baby-boom generation. Since there are fewer children in the family, parents may have higher expectations of each child. In a large family, if one child is a disappointment, there is always another who might do well, an attitude that helps reduce pressure. Many more members of this cohort have the experience of living in single-parent families. The single-parent family, combined with periods of economic recession and the greater number of mothers in the work force, creates an entirely different environment for the current cohort of children.

Some Issues

There is growing concern about the amount of control over the socialization process that parents have given up or have lost. With both parents working, nonfamily socializers, including babysitters and day-care centres, influence children earlier than in the past. Children are also introduced earlier to the influence of peers, who are not chosen by their parents. There is some controversy over whether this lower level of control is neutral or harmful for children.

There is also less supervision of older children. Once they are beyond the age they require a babysitter by law, many are left to fend for themselves; these have been popularized as "latch-key kids." Some are without adult control for several hours between the end of the school day and parents' return from work. Some adolescents are also left unsupervised in their homes. There are concerns over the influence of television on such children and the opportunities allowed for experiments with drugs or for sexual activity.

Another concern is over the reduced interaction between parents and children when both parents work outside the home. Does this affect the attachment and emotional development of children? Research results have been mixed, with some studies showing that children who are in day care full-time during their first year experience insecure attachment, higher levels of aggression, and lower school performance. Other findings suggest that children suffer no ill effects. The results appear to depend on the quality of the care children receive (Santrock, 1992).

The recognition of physical and emotional abuse of children raises another issue. Should parenting education be compulsory? In the past, women have learned how to raise children from their mothers and other female relatives. Systems theorists point out that this practice results in the repetition of harmful patterns of interaction from one generation to the next. What an individual learns in his or her original family situation is often repeated in the family of procreation.

If parenting education is considered essential, who should be entrusted with it? Should it be a compulsory school subject? If individuals do not receive it, will child-protection agencies be allowed to step in to ensure that parents are adequately trained before they are allowed to raise their children?

Since socialization helps produce new members for society, it is a target for any group that feels that the family or society itself is threatened. As well, any who feel that the present society is unjust look for changes in the way children are raised. Thus, socialization provides a focus for conflicts over many social issues.

SUMMARY

SOCIALIZATION AND SOCIETY. Socialization is the passing on to new members of a culture's ways of thinking and acting. It is strongest in childhood, but takes place at each role or status change through life. Although all aspects of society are involved in socialization, the family plays a key role. Every society provides distinct socialization experiences. Each individual, however, remains free to accept or reject the values and norms of society. The roles people are expected to fill have changed over time. In pre-industrial Europe, children were involved at a young age in the family's livelihood. This pattern continued among rural families. In middle-class families following the Industrial Revolution, childhood was extended to allow more education. Children in working-class families, however, continued to work alongside parents, but in mines or factories rather than at home, until prevented by labour and school-attendance laws. In the 20th century, the child became a source of emotional satisfaction. A scientific approach to child rearing was stressed by child-development experts. Often this meant going against traditions of minority groups such as native peoples. As a result, many native families were damaged. Childhood came to be considered a special time, and services and institutions arose to meet its needs.

PARENTS AS SOCIALIZERS. Parents are the single most powerful influence on children. The number, marital status, sex, sexual orientation, and age of parent figures are important in shaping children's environments. Both parenting style (authoritarian, authoritative, or permissive) and goodness-of-fit between parents' expectations and the child's characteristics are important in day-to-day interaction. Families also affect the development of children through their routines and traditions, their educational and occupational levels, and cultural differences.

THE WIDER FAMILY. Other relatives also affect the socialization of children.

Siblings. Brothers and sisters affect socialization in many ways. The number, ages, and birth order influence development. Siblings also provide role models, teach about peer values and interaction, provide opportunities to practice solving conflicts, and provide affection and support. A sibling's exceptionalities can also affect the development of other children in the family.

Extended family. Extended family members can provide affection and teach the child family traditions. The extended family is important among aboriginal peoples, but has been damaged by the influence of white society.

SOCIETY AT LARGE. Children are also socialized by institutions and individuals who are not related to them. Babysitters and day-care personnel provide a variety of environments. In school, children learn social values about families and receive gender-role socialization, which help shape their self-concept and values. The high dropout rate among native students represents a mismatch between home and school experiences and responsibilities. Peers are both a source of individual development and of potential conflict with families. The media provide gender-role socialization and present popular ideas about families. Family trends also affect socialization, e.g., cohort size can affect opportunities and expectations about education and employment.

ISSUES. One concern is parents' shrinking control over the socialization of children, since both parents work outside the home in many families. Many also recognize problems arising from poor parenting and advocate compulsory education for parenting.

KEY TERMS

ascribed relationship: a relationship that belongs to a particular role rather than being a matter of choice

authoritarian: a parenting style that requires unquestioning obedience

authoritative: a parenting style that sets expectations for children, but adjusts them to the individual

cohort: a group of people, roughly the same age, living in the same historical time

gender role: what society expects of an individual as a male or female

permissive: a parenting style that allows children to make their own decisions without providing firm guidelines

sibling: brother or sister

socialization: the process of passing on to new members a culture's ways of thinking and acting

CLASS ASSIGNMENTS

Complete one or more of the following assignments, as directed by your instructor.

1. Some parents have difficulty letting go of their children. Discuss some of the reasons this might be so. What might be done to avoid this difficulty?
2. Look at five recent books written for preschool children that show family interaction in some way. What messages about family and gender roles are given? Do these messages reflect the reality of present-day family life?
3. Do you think there should be a law that requires people to take a parenting course before having children? What do you see as the advantages and disadvantages of such legislation?

PERSONAL ASSIGNMENTS

These questions are designed to help you look at your own family experience and its influence on your life.

1. How have brothers and sisters affected your socialization? Consider their age, sex, number, and personalities. If you have no siblings, what effect has this had on you? Why?
2. What family stories were you told? What messages did they give you? How did these affect your development?

CHAPTER 7

The Lone-Parent Family — The Future Majority?

OBJECTIVES

- To look at the place of single parenthood in the family life cycle.
- To consider variations in single parenthood.
- To examine the quality of life of single-parent families, including that of the children.
- To explore two special groups of single parents — the very young mother and the single father.

Joan is a public relations officer for a large corporation. She's the sole support for her 10-year-old son and has been since her husband walked out five years ago.

Joan says when her husband left, she took plenty of time to talk the situation over with her son. Even the very young benefit from an honest explanation of why Mommy or Daddy won't be living at home any more. It's important the child understands that he or she isn't the cause of the breakup.

Margaret was in her 30s and enjoying a successful career when she discovered she was pregnant. Marriage was out of the question. She considered abortion.

Then she began thinking about what it would be like to raise her own child. She talked it over with members of her family and with friends who encouraged her and promised to help with the baby.

Her daughter is now five. Margaret is very happy in her role as a working mother.

Source: Ontario Ministry of Community and Social Services (1987). *Single Parents: A Resource Guide*. Toronto, Queen's Printer for Ontario, pp. 6, 8.

As a whole, North American society expects adults in the family to come in pairs, one of each sex, husband and wife, mother and father. Single parents offend against what Dr. Ben Schlesinger (1990) calls the "Noah's ark syndrome": they don't come two by two.

In the past, sociologists, social workers, and other concerned individuals referred to "broken," "incomplete," or "atypical" families, as if something were missing or faulty (Hogan, Buehler, & Robinson, 1983). For example, Imber-Black (1989) tells of two male caseworkers who kept telling a single mother that her son needed a male role model without asking about her natural support systems. In fact, there was an uncle available and willing to be involved. Indeed, many individuals in society nowadays still feel there is an oddness to single-parent families. Some religious groups instil guilt if people do not follow a "traditional" pattern. Grandparents may feel that they went wrong somewhere in raising their child if he, or more usually she, is a single parent. Reactions may vary depending on whether the lone parent is considered a victim of circumstances or is blamed for the situation. "Innocent" victims usually do not experience as much stigma as people who are considered responsible for their situation. Thus a woman who left her husband may be seen as more to blame than a widow.

The single-parent family is the fastest-growing family type in Canada. From 1966 to 1986, the number of lone-parent families in Canada increased 130 percent, while the number of husband-wife families rose only 42 percent. Such families made up 13 percent of all Canadian families. This is a sex-related phenomenon. In 1991, nearly all (82 percent) of single parents were women. In 1986, 14 percent of children in Canada lived in one-parent homes (Moore, 1987). Since the census is a snapshot of society, these figures do not tell the whole story. Many families spend some time as one-parent families before, after, or between two-parent episodes.

There are several reasons for the trend toward single parenthood. There has been increased sexual activity among adolescents and young adults, but this has not been accompanied by a consistent use of contraceptives (Barrett, 1980; Page, 1989). Not all the members of the baby-boom generation have passed through child-rearing age and thus they are still swelling the numbers of single parents. Since the late 1960s, unmarried mothers have met less prejudice, although they are still subject to a certain amount of criticism. The growing number of divorces has increased their acceptance, because divorced and never-married single parents are virtually indistinguishable. Working mothers have become

Table 7.1

LONE-PARENT FAMILIES IN CANADA, 1991

	1986		1991	
	No.	**%**	**No.**	**%**
Male Parent	151 740	17.8	168 240	17.8
Female Parent	701 905	82.2	786 470	82.3
TOTAL	863 645	100.0	954 705	100.0

Source: Statistics Canada (1992). *Families: Number, Type and Structure.* Ottawa: Statistics Canada (Catalogue No. 93-312), p. 17.

commonplace, and family benefits are also more available to help them support their children; therefore there are many more unmarried mothers choosing to raise their children themselves. The divorce rate has also increased dramatically during the same period, partly as a result of changed legislation. Underlying all these factors is the waning of the emphasis on the traditional nuclear family and the growing acceptability of all family variations.

The Path of Single Parenthood

As we can see in the stories of Joan and Margaret, there is no one road for women to reach lone parenthood. At the 1986 census, most lone parents came from dissolved marriages, i.e., they were either separated (28 percent) or divorced (30 percent). Never-married parents made up 15 percent and widows 28 percent of the total (percentages do not equal 100 due to rounding). The proportions have altered dramatically since 1951. Then about two-thirds of female lone parents were widowed, 3 percent divorced, 29 percent separated, and one percent never-married (Moore, 1987). History and changes in law have helped produce these changes. The number of widows may have been so high in 1951 partly because many husbands and fathers of young children died during World War II. More recently, as we shall consider in more detail in the next chapter, divorces have increased following changes in the law in 1981 and 1986, making them both much easier to obtain and more acceptable.

The life patterns of never-married, divorced, and widowed female lone parents vary in a number of ways. Among other questions, the Family History Survey conducted by Statistics Canada in 1984 asked women if they had ever been single parents. The Survey also asked them how long they had been single parents and, if they were no longer single parents, how such parenting had ended (Burch, 1985; Moore, 1988). Differences in the life patterns of never-married, divorced, and widowed female lone parents include the age at which the individual became a single parent, the likelihood of marriage and remarriage, current life circumstances, and the impact of the life-cycle stage when single parenthood began. Many of these factors are interrelated.

Current living circumstances vary. The parent can live on her own, have a live-in friend, either male or female with or without a sexual relationship, live-in weekend friend, out-of-the-house heterosexual or homosexual relationship, or live with her mother and/or father (Schlesinger, 1990).

HOW LONG DOES IT LAST?

Several patterns occur in the length of lone parenthood and in the way in which it ends. These are related to both the age at which a woman becomes a single parent, and the way in which she becomes a single parent. According to research findings, those who had children out of wedlock began parenting alone at the youngest age (see Table 7.2). They also spent the shortest time as lone parents, and were most likely to have married or entered a common-law relationship. Lone parenthood for separated or divorced mothers began later because most had been in a marriage relationship for some time. It lasted longer and was less likely to end because mothers had entered a new union. The remainder had given up custody of the children or the children had become independent. Widows were the oldest when they became single parents. They remained lone parents the longest, and were least likely to remarry. These findings are predictable since in our society, younger women are far more likely to find husbands or partners than older women. A few women, more commonly those who had a child before marrying, had more than one period as a lone parent (Moore, 1988).

Table 7.2

AVERAGE DURATION OF ENDED AND CONTINUING LONE-PARENT EPISODES OF WOMEN AGED 18–65, BY ORIGINATING EVENT, 1984

Originating event	Episode ended		Episode continuing		Total	
	Average duration (years)	Number of women (000s)	Average duration (years)	Number of women (000s)	Average duration (years)	Number of women (000s)
Out-of-wedlock birth	3.5	384	8.9	77	4.4	460
Separation/divorce	5.3	394	6.0	303	5.6	697
Widowhood	5.2	113	8.8	127	7.5	239
Total	4.6	890	7.1	506	5.5	1396

Source: Statistics Canada. Housing, Family and Social Statistics Division, Family History Survey, 1984. In Maureen Moore (1988). "Female Lone Parenthood: The Duration of Episodes," *Canadian Social Trends*, Autumn, p. 42.

SINGLE PARENTHOOD AND THE LIFE CYCLE

Differences in women's experiences are related to life-cycle issues. Let's first look at those women who became pregnant outside of marriage. Unless they were previously married, they have missed a family stage, according to traditionalists, i.e., they have not formed a new family through marriage before having a child. Age is also extremely important to the experience of single parenthood. Pregnancy during adolescence comes at a point where most young women are struggling with the issues of independence from their family of origin. They often do not have realistic plans for future employment or, if they do, they have not completed the necessary education or training. The later pregnancy occurs, the more likely a woman is to have completed her education and to have become established in a career, and the more likely she is to be able to support herself and her child above the level of poverty. For males, many of the same factors are true. Those who are younger are less likely to be able to contribute in a meaningful way financially and socially to the rearing of their children.

The age factor also affects older women. They may feel, as Margaret did at the beginning of this chapter, that they are not likely to find a husband before they are past childbearing age. Some seek out a man to father a child or make use of artificial insemination. In this case, pregnancy is not accidental, but is the result of a woman's wish to include parenthood in her experience.

The divorced and widowed both must deal with the pain and anger that surrounds the end of marriage. The parent's age is a significant factor in the single-parenting experience. Did the breakup or death occur within two to three years of marriage, or as part of the midlife reassessment? What were their roles within the marriage? Long-term homemakers may not have the job skills necessary to support themselves at the level the family had enjoyed. Divorced couples share family assets (Cochrane, 1991). However, early in the family life cycle there may be more debts than assets. Widows have a greater chance than divorced women of being financially stable, partly because they do not share resources with an ex-spouse, partly because generally the family has had more time to acquire assets.

The situation for the formerly married is complicated by the age of the child at the time single parenthood begins. The impact of single parenthood will be completely different at different ages: a new baby, a school-aged child, a teenager, or a young person on the brink of leaving home. Since children's needs and developmental tasks are different at different stages, they will make different emotional and financial demands on their parents (Peck & Manocherian, 1988).

Are Children in Lone-Parent Families at Risk?

There are a number of stereotypes about children who grow up in lone-parent families. They are generally regarded as likely to turn out to be problem children who are emotionally disturbed or delinquent. One of the reasons given for this notion is that they have a missing role model, usually the father (Imber-Black, 1989). As a result of this misconception, children are thought to suffer in their social development. Boys, it is felt, do not learn appropriately masculine forms of behaviour and girls do not learn healthy ways of interacting with men. In fact Schlesinger (1990) suggests that the term "one-parent family" is misleading. Most children do have contact with the parent they do not live with. As we shall see in Chapter 8, there is also a growing tendency for separating parents to request *joint custody* of their children. Of course some children do have an absent parent, but most of these have a suitable role model to fill the gap.

Studies do show that children from single-parent families are somewhat more likely than those from traditional families to have psychological problems and poor results in school. Yet researchers found that the financial and social hardship of single-parent families, rather than the number of parents, accounted for the differences (Blum, Boyle, & Offord, 1988). Michael Rutter (1972), a British psychiatrist, also suggests that what causes problems for these children is not separation from a parent as such, but the family conflict or prolonged illness that led up to family breakup or death. In fact, only a third of Calgary single parents reported discipline problems with their children (City of Calgary, 1985). (See Table 7.3.) Given that there are no comparison figures available, it is impossible to tell, however, if single parents experience more problems than parents in husband-wife families.

If single parents live with their parents or depend on them for babysitting, there may be disagreements over how children should be raised. Discipline is a particular problem area. It is difficult to know, however, just what people mean by discipline. Does it refer to instant obedience to adult requests? Does it include what, when, and how much a child should eat (including snacks and treats)? If the mother complains too much, she may be afraid of losing her home or her child care. Another kind of difficulty arises when the child is used as a weapon in the parent-grandparent relationship. In one case, an unmarried mother who lived with her parents expected her mother to provide unlimited child care and laundry services. If her mother complained about her lack of responsibility or about how often she went out, she threatened to move out and cut off any contact between grandmother and adored grandchild.

These problems are symptoms of boundary and role confusion. Ordinarily the individual has established an adult identity separate from her family of origin before becoming a parent. When three generations live together, there may be confusion about who should fill parent and child roles, since responsibilities may not be clearly divided between generations. Is the single mother an adult or a child? Since she has not separated from her parents, she is filling the role of a child in the family. However, her motherhood marks her as an adult. Should the grandparents act as parents to the grandchild? If so, what position does the mother hold?

Table 7.3

PROBLEMS RESPONDENTS HAVE RAISING CHILDREN

PROBLEMS	N	% of sample*
No problems	54	16
Lack of a father/mother role model	102	30
Discipline problems	109	33
Tired of having all responsibility for child care	123	37
Difficulty arranging child care for social outings	72	21
Difficulty arranging child care when child is ill	82	24
Lack of time	15	4
Emotional stress	17	5
Financial constraints	37	11
Inadequate child care	9	3
Other	15	4

*Percentages total to more than 100 because respondents gave up to three responses.

Source: City of Calgary, Social Services Department (1985). *A Profile and Needs Assessment of Calgary's Single Parents*. Calgary: Social Services Department, p. 55.

The Quality of Life

Since there are so many single-parent families and so many children are involved, it is important to look at their lifestyle. Many of the details that follow about the life of female single parents are drawn from a comprehensive survey and needs assessment of single parents carried out by the Calgary Social Services Department (City of Calgary, 1985). Conversations with single parents in college have confirmed and expanded the Calgary findings.

SOCIAL LIFE

What kind of social life does a single parent have? According to social-services agency staff, many parents lack emotional support and social activities. Most Calgary single parents, on the other hand, reported adequate contact with others, although one-third of single parents report being lonely. Half the parents were involved in leisure activities at least once a week. When asked what

CUSTODY OF DAD **© 1987 Barry Maguire**

Source: *The Single Parent*, March/April 1992, p. 28.

problems they encountered regarding leisure activities, they cited lack of money as significant. This is easy to understand if you add up the costs: food, movie admission, fees and supplies for evening courses, babysitting, transportation. Some found that timing was inconvenient. There can be scheduling conflicts with a job or with the need of children to have a parent home after school. Some single parents had problems finding babysitters. Others were so busy with jobs and caring for children that they found they had no time for anything else (City of Calgary, 1985).

Social support can be separated into two areas: how supportive society is as a whole and the immediate sources of help. Most single parents in Calgary reported that they had informal support networks made up of friends, parents, and brothers and sisters who provided emotional support, financial help or advice, child care, and assistance if mother or child were sick. A few single parents could not count on friends or relatives to help them out at all. Some members of their networks were so critical or demanding that they added to the parent's stress level (Hogan, Buehler, & Robinson, 1983). Parents with poor support systems may not have the resources to cope with emergencies or long-term stress. As a result, they may become clients of social-service agencies in order to get the kind of back-up that informal networks provide for other single parents.

In the second chapter, we looked at some of the problems minority groups face. Single parents meet with some of these same problems. Often criticism is greater if the individual is considered to be responsible for his or her circumstances. Never-married mothers are seen as more responsible for their situation than abandoned wives or widows. For example, one grocery-store cashier cashed a government cheque for a young woman. She complained to her next customer, another young mother, about unmarried parents getting taxpayers' money. Even worse in her eyes was the fact that the mother had not had the good taste to choose a white man; the child's father was obviously black.

Victims who are perceived as playing no part in their own misfortune usually do not experience such *stigma*. In the past, the one-parent family that needed financial aid was seen as having personal rather than economic problems, i.e., the poverty came about because of what they did or did not do. Therefore it was felt that such families needed skilled professional social-work investigation and supervision. The original legislation establishing *Mothers' Allowance* made only widows and deserted wives eligible (Guest, 1985; Kieran, 1986).

SINGLE PARENTS AND ECONOMIC SURVIVAL

Female lone parents are at risk of living in poverty. In Calgary, for example, a needs assessment of single parents found that more than one-third were living at or below the *poverty line*. This was especially true for those below the age of 35; 68 percent were living below the poverty line. Older single parents were more likely to be employed, and their children were old enough to contribute financially to their own costs (City of Calgary, 1985).

Female-headed lone-parent families in Canada are more likely to receive Family Benefits or Welfare than husband-wife families with children. On the average, their income is less than half that of husband-wife families. As a result, they must spend a greater percentage of their income on necessities. Few can

Figure 7.1

SOURCES OF INCOME OF FEMALE-HEADED LONE-PARENT FAMILIES AND HUSBAND-WIFE FAMILIES WITH CHILDREN, 1985

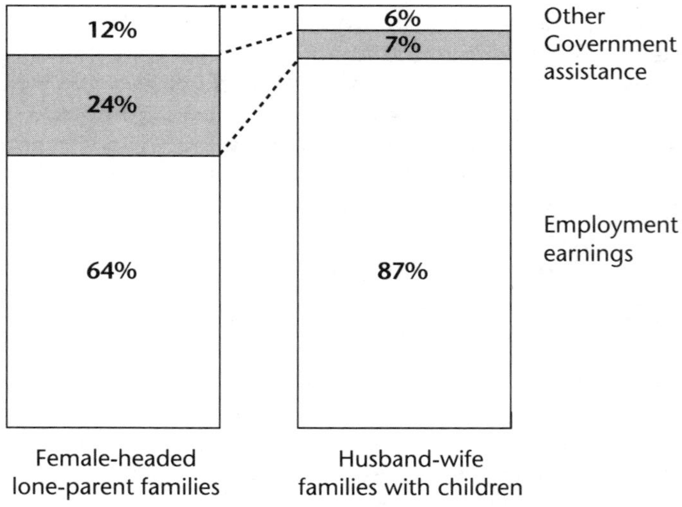

Source: Statistics Canada, Labour and Household Surveys Analysis Division, Survey of Consumer Finances, unpublished data. In Maureen Moore (1987). "Women Parenting Alone," *Canadian Social Trends,* Winter, p. 34.

afford to own their homes and thus most need to live in rented quarters (Moore, 1989). In the United States, never-married mothers experience more severe poverty for longer periods than two-parent families (Besharov & Quin, 1987). Widows probably are the best off financially, since they benefit from pension plans and usually do not have children to care for as young as those of other single parents (Schlesinger, 1990).

In Calgary, 67 percent of single parents were working full-time, 10 percent part-time, and 5 percent were students. Half of these parents felt their marital status resulted in fewer opportunities for promotion. For example, they were unable to travel much for business or work much overtime because of their family responsibilities. However, this is a problem common to many working mothers (Portner, 1983). They also felt that employers regard female single parents as unreliable and unstable. Many of them find dead-end jobs with low pay and little possibility for promotion. Women, rather than men, are hired for these positions because too many employers still assume that women do not need as much money as men because they are not supporting families.

There are a number of barriers to employment for single parents. Lack of choice in day care was seen as a major difficulty by over one-third of single parents interviewed by Edmonton Social Services (City of Calgary, 1985). In Calgary, about one-third reported no child care problems. The remainder stated they had problems with cost of child care, care for a sick child, and problems finding care that matched their hours as shift workers. Many women cannot afford day care (Ross & Shillington, 1989). During classroom discussions, college students (many of whom are single parents) complain also about problems in finding care for children during vacations, before and after school, and on teachers' professional development days.

In spite of its drawbacks, government assistance is often the only reasonable alternative to paid employment for single parents. It does not, however, provide for an adequate standard of living, since benefits fall well below the *poverty line* (Ross & Shillington, 1989). There is also stigma attached to receiving benefits. People who stay home with their children are often regarded as freeloaders. If they are on welfare, they are open to invasion of privacy and judgments on the part of professionals who administer the system. There is also pressure on some mothers to seek employment. For example, in Alberta, single parents are considered employable unless they have a child under four months of age, have two children with at least one under the age of 12, or have a child who is chronically ill or who has a physical impairment (City of Calgary, 1985).

HOUSING

Problems with housing are second only to income difficulties. Housing, as we have seen, is related to income levels. A study in the Maritimes in 1982 found that single mothers often found that they had a poor selection of places they could rent. Affordable housing is often situated in areas that do not have good recreational facilities or good schools. If these families live in low-rent housing, they tend to be in clusters of people like themselves and separated from the rest of society. If they do not have cars, they need to live near transportation routes or within walking distance of jobs and services. This may mean living near the centre of the city, where housing may be run down. Single parents may move frequently. Urban renewal and commercial development can destroy inexpensive inner-city housing. Rent increases may force them to seek more affordable housing, or they may feel that there just has to be a better place somewhere. Almost 60 percent of single mothers moved at least once in an eighteen-month period (City of Calgary, 1985; Doyle, 1989; McLaughlin, 1987; J. Ward, 1989).

A further difficulty reported by some mothers is landlord prejudice. Some fear one-parent families won't meet rent payments or will move without notice (perhaps sneaking out in the middle of the night). They tend to assume that fatherless children will be undisciplined and destructive (City of Calgary, 1985).

A Special Case — The Teen Mother

One of the most-studied groups of single parents is the young adolescent mother. In 1981, for instance, Ontario researchers interviewed single adolescent mothers in Ottawa, Toronto, Windsor, and Sault Ste. Marie (MacKay & Austin, 1983). They described them as being poor, unskilled, and discouraged. Almost all (85 percent) were on social assistance during the first eighteen months after the birth of their baby. Those who did have jobs did not earn much, and most lived well under the poverty line. Three-fifths of the young mothers had Grade 10 education or less, and most had dropped out of school. Many did not even have enough education to qualify for job-training programs. Over one-quarter were aged 14 to 16 years at the birth of the baby, an age usually considered too young for adult responsibility. Quite a number had given up and were not even looking for help to get better education and jobs. Such mothers may have virtually no life outside of being a parent. As a result, they may not develop their own potential, and may stay adolescents psychologically for the rest of their lives. Those who were doing best were white daughters of married mothers in higher-level jobs, who were living with their parents. At the time of the birth, they were older and better-educated than the other mothers in the study.

Very young mothers aged 12 to 15 years make up a very small proportion of all lone mothers. The figures for Ontario, for example, show that in 1988 only about three of every thousand unmarried mothers were that young (Table 7.4). They merit special attention, however, because they are involved more often than others with service agencies. In addition, there are many concerns about how well children can raise children. Young mothers who had children at ages 12 to 15 years were studied in the United States (S. Miller, 1983). Many of the findings were similar to the Ontario study. Since they were so young, they depended either on social assistance or on their parents for support. Many dropped out of

Table 7.4

LIVE BIRTHS IN ONTARIO TO SINGLE MOTHERS, 1988

Mother's Age	Born to Unmarried Mothers	Total Births	% Unmarried
under 15	54	55	98.2
15–19	4 810	6 714	71.6
20–24	6 699	28 431	23.6
25–29	4 036	54 616	7.4
30–34	1 932	35 806	5.4
35–39	622	11 064	5.6
40–44	90	1 337	6.7
45 and over	1	43	2.3
TOTAL	18 244	138 066	13.2

Source: Province of Ontario. *Vital Statistics for 1988*. Toronto: Province of Ontario, p. 14.

school. Some of the difficulties mentioned in the study were lack of understanding on the part of teachers when they could not complete assignments because their babies were sick or crying all night, or when they had to miss school to take their children for doctors' appointments. One out of five had a second pregnancy within eighteen months of the birth of their first child. Only two-thirds were using contraceptives, and these may not have been using them correctly.

Some demonstration programs are available to help young mothers complete their education. These typically last for two or three years (S. Miller, 1983). The very youngest mothers, however, need help for much longer if they are to graduate from high school. Twelve-year-olds, for instance, have not even finished elementary school.

Encouragingly, these very young mothers managed routine care and health care of their babies fairly well. They were, however, not as good at preventing their babies from getting sick. Many infants spent some time in hospital during their first year. One reason that the mothers coped as well as they did was the help and support they received from family members. Many still lived with their parents, and others received a good deal of practical assistance. We should be concerned about the ones who do not have family connections or are estranged from family members. Since they do not have family resources to rely on, both their well-being and that of their children may be endangered (S. Miller, 1983).

The Single Father

In general, there is little information available about the single father beyond a few statistics. In 1986, only 18 percent (less than one in five) of single parents were men. Only 6 percent of single parents under 25 years were men, as compared with 24 percent of those aged 45–64 (Moore, 1987). In 1991, the percentage of male single parents remained the same as that of 1986 (Table 7.1). Fewer single fathers than single mothers live below the poverty line.

There are a number of reasons that there are relatively few fathers with custody of their children. Since women tend to live longer than men and are usually younger than their husbands, they are more likely to become single parents through widowhood. At divorce, custody of children is usually granted to the mother. Now that fathers are increasingly involved in the daily care of their children, they try more often to gain sole custody or shared custody of their children. If this trend continues, we can expect to see more single fathers in the future. Only in unusual circumstances does an unmarried father gain custody of his child. Unless there is a private agreement or he can prove convincingly that the mother is unfit and that he is the father, the mother automatically has custody of her child.

The male partner of an unmarried mother is often a figure in the background, who usually is ignored by both social-service agencies and researchers. A stereotype is of the man who uses a woman for sex and then leaves her holding the baby. Of course, some men do behave in this manner, but research has shown a different side. Nearly half of sexually active male high-school and university students said marriage would be their first choice in coping with their partner's pregnancy; only 28 percent of women felt that way. This reaction is far more likely if the relationship is long-lasting rather than casual. In the latter case, men would prefer adoption or abortion. Few men do, however, get married as a result of a pregnancy. If the partner is young, the mother's family often makes continuing a relationship very difficult. For the most part, many unmarried fathers are themselves very young and have few financial resources, so that it is difficult for them to support a child. Unless the father is living with the mother and child, he usually has little contact (Herold, 1984).

A program serving adolescent fathers in Baltimore, Maryland, works through the schools to ensure contact with children. It features a fathers' support group that meets weekly. The meetings offer not only peer support but also education in parenting, sexuality, and career planning. The fathers' relatives are also included in many of the parent-child activities to help connect the children to the heritage of these families. Although the mothers are included in some activities, the emphasis is on the father and child, not the couple. At the end of the first full year, all of the fathers either had jobs or were continuing their education. They also found satisfaction in their parenting roles (Child Welfare League of America, 1992).

What of the Future?

All statistical forecasts suggest that the number of single-parent families will increase, especially as the result of divorce. Many children will grow up in such families. This fact raises a number of issues for all of us.

First, the level of poverty is high among single parents. As we shall see in more detail in Chapter 15, it has far-reaching effects on children's physical and intellectual development. In addition, children from low-income families tend not to stay in school. Thus they are more likely to end up in lower-paying jobs, with a prospect of raising poor families themselves. Ultimately this cycle will affect all of us through the cost of providing the income-support programs many of these families will need.

Second, fathers are important to children's development. We need to look at ways to encourage the greater involvement of unmarried fathers. This will include looking at the appropriateness of contact with particular fathers. For example, a violent individual may not be a beneficial presence in a child's life. There may be some need to overcome the resistance of mothers who may want no contact with the father, or who fear that he will attempt to gain custody. It may be necessary to establish programs like the one in Baltimore to encourage the youngest fathers to become involved with their children.

Third, many single parents receive much emotional and practical support from their extended families. It is important for agency personnel to encourage this support. Too often they devalue or undermine it (S. Miller, 1983). Relatives will be around long after the agency has bowed out. The future well-being of the family may depend in part on the continuing involvement of relatives and friends.

Finally, it is important, especially for the sake of the children, to eliminate the stigma against single-parent families that remains in society. If society as a whole recognizes that single parents are for the most part as concerned and competent as the majority of other parents, we will have come a long way toward that goal.

SUMMARY

LIFE PATTERNS OF LONE PARENTS. The lone-parent family is the fastest-growing family type in Canada. Members now experience less stigma than in the past. Life patterns vary among the never-married, divorced, and widowed as to the duration of lone parenthood and the likelihood of marriage. Differences in experiences are also related to life-cycle issues. Individuals who become lone parents during adolescence have quite different experiences from those for whom it begins in middle age. The ages and needs of the children also affect parents.

CHILDREN IN LONE-PARENT FAMILIES. Children in single-parent families are often expected to have emotional or behavioural problems. However, difficulties can be explained by financial hardship and family conflict rather than the number of parents. Difficulties may also arise if there are conflicts between the parent and grandparents about child rearing.

QUALITY OF LIFE. Many lone parents have limited emotional support and social activities, partly because of the cost of entertainment, and partly because of lack of time. Most single parents receive emotional support and practical help from relatives and neighbours. A few must depend on social agencies. Many female lone parents, especially young ones, live below the poverty line. They are more likely to receive Family Benefits or Welfare than husband-wife families with children. Those who are employed face barriers such as dead-end jobs and child care difficulties. The quality of housing is related to income levels.

THE TEEN MOTHER. Most adolescent mothers live below the poverty line, since they have limited education and job skills. Very young mothers (aged 12 to 15) experience extreme difficulty completing school. They can usually manage routine care of their children, often under the guidance of older relatives.

THE SINGLE FATHER. There are relatively few single fathers. Following divorce, custody is usually given to the mother, and only rarely do unmarried fathers raise their children. Little is known about fathers without custody. Many, however, are concerned about their children. Their interest needs to be encouraged, since they are important to their children's development.

KEY TERMS

joint custody: custody of children shared by the father and mother

Mother's Allowance: government support originally provided to female lone parents only, now called Family Benefits and available to parents of either sex

poverty line: a level of income below which an individual or family is considered to be living in poverty

social support: practical assistance or emotional back-up provided by others

stigma: any quality that is seen as offensive by the majority

CLASS ASSIGNMENTS

Complete one or more of the following assignments, as directed by your instructor.

1. Some individuals believe that being a single parent is a handicap in our society. Others point out that it has advantages. What arguments can be made for each side?
2. A large percentage of single-parent families headed by women live below the poverty line. What effects might this have on the development of children raised in

such families? Consider both short- and long-term physical, psychological, and social aspects.

3. How does single parenthood differ for men and women? Consider work, child care, school, extended family relationships, and any other aspect that seems relevant.

PERSONAL ASSIGNMENTS

These assignments are designed to help you think about your own family experience.

1. Do you think it is ethical for a woman to choose to become pregnant if she is not married? What factors affected your answer? Does it make any difference if a single person who chooses to adopt a child is male or female?
2. Based on your own experience or that of someone you know, what practical suggestions can you make for developing a satisfying family life for both the single parent and his/her children? Consider relationships within the family and between the family and the rest of society.

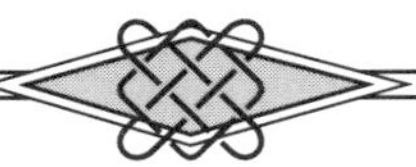

PART 4

Changes in the Family

CHAPTER 8

Coming Apart — The Divorce Experience

OBJECTIVES

- To place the current situation of divorce in historical perspective.
- To look at the developmental stages of divorce and its relationship to the family life cycle.
- To describe the three crises of divorce — emotional, economic, and parental.
- To examine the effects of divorce on children.
- To consider issues around the custody of children.

PUBLIC ANNOUNCEMENT:

John and Jane Smith
announce
an amicable divorce.

Their friends and relatives are asked not to take sides and to please keep in touch with both.

For the time being they are both still at home:

1234 14th Street,
Western City,
Prairie Province, Canada

Source: D.C. McKie, B. Prentice, and P. Reed (1983). *Divorce: Law and the Family in Canada.* Ottawa: Statistics Canada, p. 159.

The most common variation from the traditional family life cycle is *divorce*, or the legal dissolution of a marriage. It is becoming so common, in fact, that it may in time come to be considered a "normal" family event. Divorced families add two or three phases to the life cycle: separation, perhaps remarriage, and finally stabilization in a new family pattern.

A Short History

Divorce has not always been so common. As we have seen, for much of history marriage was considered a way of uniting families, and of providing stability for society. Therefore, divorce was seen as an exception to be undertaken for only very grave reasons. For example, when biological descent for inheritance of property or titles was important, illegitimacy was considered a threat; therefore adultery by a wife once carried much social stigma and was grounds for divorce. Cruelty, on the other hand, was considered part of family life and usually was not considered a reason for breaking up the marriage.

Laws were, at first, influenced strongly by the Church of England in Upper Canada and the Roman Catholic Church in Lower Canada. Since neither church recognized divorce, there was no divorce law. In the Maritimes, although there was pressure to make the Church of England dominant, the movement was resisted. Since the Maritimes had military centres where much of the male population was mobile, many formed temporary relationships with married women. Such relationships were considered "safe" because they had no future. New Brunswick allowed divorce in 1758 on the grounds of adultery and desertion. Three years later the ground of desertion was replaced by that of cruelty. In 1787, Nova Scotia allowed divorce on the grounds of adultery. There is little indication, however, of how many divorces were actually granted (McKie, Prentice, & Reed, 1983).

The situation in the Northwest (what is now British Columbia, Alberta, Saskatchewan, and Manitoba) during 1800 to 1837 was somewhat different. Since the area was owned and administered by the Hudson's Bay and Northwest Companies, there was little concern about marriage and divorce laws. Many traders formed marriages *à la façon du pays* with Indian women. Although such marriages were considered to be as binding as church weddings, many traders abandoned their common-law wives when they left the Company. Sometimes incoming traders replaced departing husbands. Eventually the Company, for financial reasons, introduced a marriage contract in which a husband agreed to support his family and to marry as soon as a clergyman was available. As time went on, European wives became fashionable, and Indian wives were no longer socially acceptable (McKie et al., 1983).

With Confederation in 1867, the federal parliament gained exclusive authority in matters of divorce; yet all it did was allow existing provincial laws to stand. Anyone living in a province without a divorce court could submit a private member's bill to parliament; when it passed, the person was granted a divorce. The rules differed depending on petitioner. Men had to prove adultery on the part of their wives. Women, on the other hand, also had to prove desertion for two years or longer, or extreme physical or mental cruelty. The double standard arose because women were felt to be pure and innocent and unlikely to be motivated by a desire for extramarital sex. Men, however, were presumed to be simply following their "natural" desires. Women also had to sue for divorce in the province in which a man lived. If he had deserted, she had to find him. If he changed his permanent residence, then she would have to start over again in the new province (McKie et al., 1983).

From 1925 on, women could sue for divorce on the same grounds as men. They only had to prove adultery, not adultery and another cause. Finally, in 1930, a woman did not have to sue for divorce in the province in which her husband lived if she could prove he had deserted her for two years. In the same year, Ontario got its first divorce court. There were few other changes to divorce law until the 1960s.

Immediately after World War II, there was a jump in the divorce rate. During the war, many women replaced men in the work force, since the latter were in the military. The freedom and financial independence these women experienced undoubtedly encouraged some divorces, as did hasty wartime marriages and prolonged separations.

Soon, however, the divorce rate dropped off. In the postwar years the idea of family was attractive to many. In the stability following the war, people married in increasing numbers. Advertisers painted glowing pictures of family life in an effort to extend markets. Family size grew to eventually produce the baby boom. Churches opposed change in divorce law. Neither the Roman Catholic nor Anglican churches recognized divorce or remarriage, and the United Church opposed any broadening of the grounds for divorce. The few bills that were introduced in the House of Commons or the Senate in the 1940s did not pass (McKie et al., 1983).

During the 1950s, there was growing realization that family breakdown would not disappear, whether or not divorce was available. Laws were passed in various provinces to allow a deserted or destitute woman to claim maintenance from her husband for herself and their children. An exception was made for the woman who committed adultery without the consent of her husband.

The 1960s saw much change in divorce legislation. Parliament was still handling divorces for Quebec and Newfoundland. Two senators blocked all divorce bills coming before Parliament in order to force a change in law. In 1963, the Dissolution and Annulment of Marriages Act limited the House of Commons to making laws, and provided for a judge of the Exchequer Court to preside over the Senate divorce hearings. In 1966, a Special Joint Committee of the Senate and House of Commons on Divorce held many hearings on the subject. By this time, the churches had changed their position. The Roman Catholic Church stated that its members could vote according to their conscience, and the Catholic Women's League stated that Roman Catholics should not make other Canadians live by their beliefs. Both the Anglican and United Church briefs included marriage breakdown as an advisable cause for divorce. Bill C-187 proposed wider divorce grounds, and transferred parliamentary divorces to the courts. On July 2, 1968, the new divorce law received Royal Assent. The divorce rate subsequently increased dramatically as a result of the wider grounds for divorce (McKie et al., 1983).

In 1986, the law was amended further. Parties to the divorce no longer had to show fault. The waiting period for divorce on the grounds of marriage breakdown was reduced to one year. Once again there was a jump in the divorce rate in response to the shorter waiting period (Statistics Canada, 1989).

The Stages of Divorce

The process of divorcing takes place in several phases. These involve both active and emotional aspects.

THE DECISION TO DIVORCE

The decision to divorce does not usually occur in a single phase. In the first phase, one or both individuals come to realize that there is something wrong with their

Figure 8.1

DIVORCE RATES, 1971–86

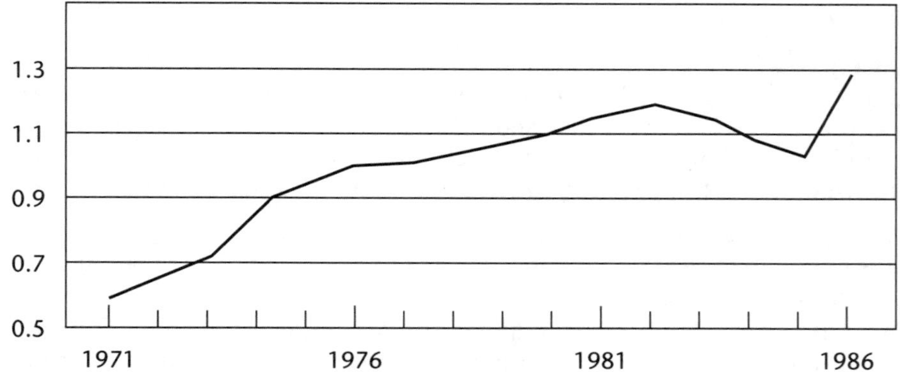

Source: Statistics Canada (1989). *The Family in Canada: Selected Highlights*. January, p. 36.

Table 8.1

SUMMARY STATISTICS FOR THE DIVORCED STATE, BY SEX, CANADA: 1970–1972 AND 1984–1986

	Men		Women	
	1970–72	1984–86	1970–72	1984–86
Percentage of divorced persons remarrying	85	76	79	64
Average time spent divorced (for total population)	1.1	2.6	2.2	4.9
Average length of a divorce	4.9	8.3	10.0	15.8
Average age at divorce	41.5	41.6	38.6	38.8
Average age of divorced population	51.5	53.9	56.8	57.5
Average age at remarriage	42.8	43.8	40.6	41.1

Source: Statistics Canada (1988). *Marrying and Divorcing: A Status Report for Canada*, October, p. 11.

marriage, often following a period of denial. Often the couple will decide to delay the divorce until the children leave home or until some other time they consider suitable. During this period, they may become involved in activities outside the family, in a kind of emotional withdrawal. Later, the entire family begins to realize that the marriage is falling apart and cannot be saved. For some families, this period is one of great uncertainty and stress. The old husband and wife roles are disappearing and new ones, for example those of divorced *coparents*, have not yet been developed. Finally, the couple needs to move past the tendency to blame each other, and to accept the facts that the marriage cannot be saved and that both individuals have played a part in its failure (Ahrons, 1983; Carter & McGoldrick, 1988).

PLANNING THE BREAKUP

In the second stage, the couple must plan the breakup of the system. They need to work cooperatively to settle issues such as *custody* of children, visitation, and finances. They also need to tell extended family members and deal with their reactions. The planning process often does not run smoothly. Many couples separate and reconcile again, sometimes repeatedly. This may be an expression of their mixed feelings or of their guilt over their children's obvious upset. During these temporary separations, there can be a great deal of stress since the family does not know whether the separation will become permanent. As a result, there is a great deal of uncertainty about who is actually part of the family and whether roles should be reorganized. At this stage, the family may also face the reality of what a divorce will mean economically (Ahrons, 1983; Carter & McGoldrick, 1988).

SEPARATION AND FAMILY REORGANIZATION

The third phase is the separation prior to divorce. The couple now need to restructure the family by separating the marital and parental relationships. It is also important to work out new rules for the continuing relationship between the parents, which is so necessary for the welfare of the children. For example, who does a child go to for money for a special event? How will visiting arrangements be worked out in the future? An important aspect of the separation is deciding custody arrangements for children. Many people feel that *joint custody* is best for children, with both parents sharing responsibility and decision-making. Others question their ability to share decision-making if they cannot get along well enough to live together. Couples also need to work out their relationships with the extended family, including the spouse's relatives, so that the children do not lose touch with them (Ahrons, 1983; Carter & McGoldrick, 1988).

Only when the parent without custody fades out of the picture do we have a true one-parent family. When both parents are involved, the children act as links between two connected households. Thus both parents continue to be part of the child's family in an arrangement sometimes referred to as a *binuclear family.* This arrangement can reduce the stress of divorce for children; they do not suffer so extreme a loss. One parent is not cut off from the children, with the other burdened with parenting overload. Occasionally the parents remain good friends; more usually they are able to focus on the children's welfare without open conflict (Ahrons, 1983; Carter & McGoldrick, 1988).

The Crisis of Divorce

The breakdown of a marriage brings with it three crises: emotional, economic, and parenting. A bitter court battle makes all of these crises worse (Payne, 1986). Divorce produces what is called a "transitional crisis," i.e., it produces a temporary crisis as a result of the changes required. Since it interrupts the usual family-developmental tasks, it creates a series of adjustments that throw all family members off balance. This *disequilibrium* lasts for a period of one to three years. The distress surrounding the change is a "normal" short-term stress response. Many factors influence the individual's reaction to divorce: the circumstances of the separation, the quality of life after separation, the person's sex, the length of the marriage, the family's life-cycle stage, the acceptance of their ethnic or religious group, and past experience with stress (Peck & Manocherian, 1988).

THE EMOTIONAL CRISIS

During and after the separation process, individuals suffer the loss of an important relationship. Often it has served as a centre for their lives, whether it was seen as satisfactory or unsatisfactory. The breakup is more painful for a person who does not expect or want it, and easier if both parents have made the decision together. The emotional loss felt in divorce is akin to that felt by the death of a loved one, except that the ex-partner is still around. This continuing presence can lead to a recurring sense of loss, as well as renewed bitterness or anger. Often it takes considerable time for an individual to become emotionally divorced from a partner. Both yearning for the lost relationship and anger over the breakup are signs that this emotional divorce has not occurred. When children are involved, total emotional separation is usually impossible, since the former partners must deal with each other as parents of their children (F.H. Brown, 1988). Often both spouses experience an emotional roller coaster. Just as they weather one emotional crisis, another confronts them.

Separation and divorce usually mean that individuals have to redefine themselves as people. The roles they have filled within the marriage are now lost, and to lose a role is to lose part of oneself. One of the difficulties with divorce is that our society has no readily defined roles for the formerly married. They must work out new ones for themselves as unmarried people, but also often as people with children. There is also little social guidance for how one should behave in a "normal" divorce (F.H. Brown, 1988; Peck & Manocherian, 1988).

Divorced and separated individuals are often socially isolated at first. The relationship with extended family members changes. They are no longer related to their ex-spouse's relatives. They may have limited support from their own relatives. Families that have dealt with divorce before are often more comfortable in dealing with the issues that arise. Some individuals cut themselves off from the extended family to avoid criticism. By doing this, they isolate themselves further.

Divorced women may find social life limited by their lack of a "single" identity. They do not fit into the social pattern of a married person and are not comfortable with being single. Many isolate themselves because they feel overloaded with tasks, others because they feel the sense of failure common after divorce (F. H. Brown, 1988). There is often a sharp decline in support for women from married friends. They may disapprove, may get tired of hearing the same story over and over, or may feel a conflict of loyalty between the two ex-spouses. The social network shifts to new, single, more casual acquaintances (Peck & Manocherian, 1988).

Divorced men often have an easier time socially than divorced women. Although they usually do not have the circle of intimate friends that women have, they often have a social network at their place of employment. Often divorced men are considered a catch and have no shortage of women companions. They will often also seek out women friends for their emotional comfort. Men tend to remarry sooner than women, often to partners much younger than themselves (F.H. Brown, 1988).

Eventually many individuals recognize that the divorce has been an opportunity for personal growth. For many women, this is the first time they have felt in control of their own lives. Some have the new experience of living alone. The result may be a new sense of competence and well-being (Brown, 1988; Peck & Manocherian, 1988). The initial sense of failure and emptiness following divorce may push both men and women into a hurry-up relationship with whoever is available. One divorced woman said, "I wanted a man so badly, anyone looked good." A hasty marriage may not only limit the opportunities for growth, but may also become another marital disaster.

Thus there are three aspects of the emotional crisis of divorce. First, the ex-spouses must accept the loss of the marriage and mourn its passing. They must also become emotionally detached from the other person. Second, they must deal with identity issues. Previously they had defined themselves in terms of their roles in the marriage; now they must take up new roles as single people. Unfortunately, they receive little guidance from social norms. Third, they must build new social networks as single people to replace those that supported the marriage. In successfully accomplishing these tasks, they will find that divorce provided an opportunity for growth.

THE ECONOMIC CRISIS

Divorce usually means a drop in the standard of living, especially for the parent who has custody of any children of the marriage. Even if both spouses have been working outside the home, the income now has to cover the costs of running two homes. Since women are usually granted custody of children, their financial needs following divorce are greater than their husbands'. Yet, as we have seen, they often do not have the ability to earn as much as men. This is partly because they are usually the spouse that takes time out from the work force following the birth of a child, and partly because women are more likely than men to work part-time. Thus they do not have the same seniority as men when they seek full-time work. Women also make up the majority of the lowest-paid groups of workers, such as clerks in small stores (Armstrong & Armstrong, 1988).

Although both parents are held responsible for the financial support of their children, the amount the *noncustodial* parent is required to pay is usually less than the cost of raising the child. In addition, there are often difficulties in collecting the amount due (Cochrane, 1991). Too often the mother is left on her own to support the children. If the husband does not have a steady job or has disappeared, the family may be reduced to living on welfare. This is especially true if the mother has few or no marketable skills. Chapter 15 looks in more detail at the serious implications of poverty on the development of children.

The division of family property was, in the past, often obviously unfair. The case of Irene Murdoch in 1968 is an example.

Jim and Irene Murdoch of Turner Valley, Alberta, separated in 1968 after they had been married for twenty-five years. Mrs. Murdoch had done the usual farm chores such as milking, caring for small animals, and household care. She had also done so much heavy farm work that her husband did not need to hire a labourer, even during his frequent illnesses.

If she were not married, Mrs. Murdoch would have been granted compensation for all the work she had done. The courts, however, including the Supreme Court of Canada, stated that she had done what any farm wife would have done, and refused to grant her any share in the farm. As a result of the outrage prompted by this case, the various provinces passed laws to give a share of property to partners who had contributed work rather than money to the family economy (Kieran, 1986). In spite of changes in legislation, women may still be at a disadvantage when we consider the benefit package attached to men's employment. A woman may lose health insurance, pension, and life insurance benefits upon divorce, especially if the man remarries (Roy, 1989).

THE PARENTING CRISIS

When a family separates, new boundaries must be drawn. Much of the confusion and stress during the separation process arise from an absence of clear boundaries. The old family with its old rules no longer exists, but new ones have not yet taken their place. This is especially true for parenting. Both authority and responsibility concerning the children need to be renegotiated. To do this successfully, parents need to separate spousal roles from parental roles; only the former are ended by divorce. They also need to establish new rules. For example, who does the child ask for money or help with homework? How much participation is expected of a noncustodial parent? Each parent needs to establish a relationship with the children separate from the other parent. How much authority will she, or more usually he, have over the children? If joint custody is decided upon, how will the responsibility for the children be shared? Parents' communication is an important factor as to whether each parent will allow the other to relate to the child without prejudice or interference. If there is no clear understanding of the new rules of the relationship, the child is likely to become the victim of conflicts between the parents (Ahrons, 1983; Messinger & Walker, 1981).

Divorcing parents may be unable to respond to their children's emotional needs. There are several reasons for this. The initial sense of shock may paralyze them. Later on, parents may be too absorbed in their own crisis to be aware of how the divorce is affecting their children. They may also feel that very young children cannot understand what is going on, and may ignore their distress. Often a parent becomes depressed. One aspect of depression is that the individual becomes less sensitive to the feelings of others. For all these reasons children may be emotionally neglected at a time when they need special care.

Figure 8.2

NUMBER OF DIVORCES WITH DEPENDENT CHILDREN AND NUMBER OF CHILDREN INVOLVED IN PETITIONS FOR CUSTODY, 1971–85

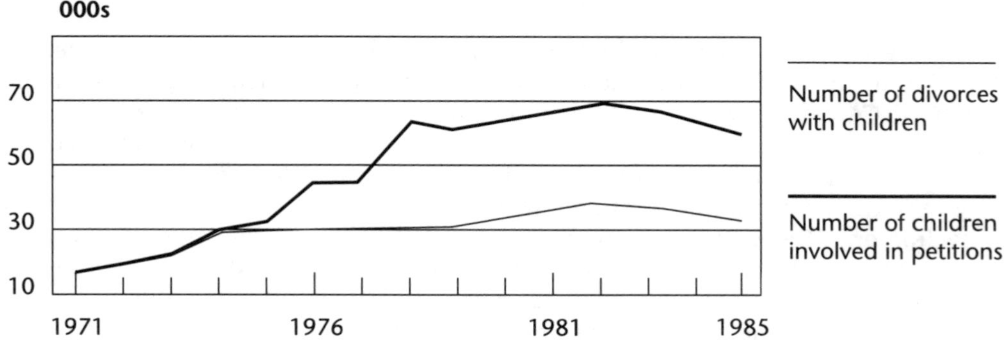

Source: Statistics Canada (1989). *The Family in Canada: Selected Highlights*. January, p. 38.

Children and Divorce

Few children want their parents to divorce, no matter how much tension there has been in the marriage. For them, it means changing the relationship with each parent. Many children cling to a fantasy that their parents will be reunited and the family will be whole again (Peck & Manocherian, 1988).

The impact of divorce on children depends on a number of factors. First, the age of the child is important. The younger children are at the time of divorce (unless they are infants), the greater the short-term impact will be. However, young children who have no memory of pre-divorce life adjust better in the long run than children who consider the divorce the central event of their childhood (Peck & Manocherian, 1988).

Second, divorce affects boys and girls differently. In the immediate post-divorce period, boys have a harder time adjusting to the new situation. There are a number of explanations offered — the loss of the same-sex parent, boys' greater vulnerability to stress, or the less positive nature of mother-son interaction compared with father-son interaction. Mothers tend to be more approving and supportive of daughters. Boys, on the other hand, are more aggressive and tend to act out physically more than girls do; thus they sometimes end up in trouble with their mothers. As a result they act up still more and get their mothers angrier (Peck & Manocherian, 1988). However, researchers describe what they call a *sleeper effect*, a problem that emerges only long after the divorce. Young women whose parents are divorced may display a fear of intimacy or betrayal that will interfere with any attempts to form intimate relationships in young adulthood. In the long term, therefore, daughters may be affected more seriously than sons (Wallerstein & Blakeslee, 1989).

Third, the level of parental conflict both before and after separation is critical. It probably has more impact on children's post-divorce adjustment than the absence of a parent (Peck & Manocherian, 1988). For example, children's self-concept is related to level of conflict in the family, not to family structure (Raschke & Raschke, 1979).

Fourth, life changes after divorce are also important. The number and degree of changes affect the children's ability to adapt. For example, a child who moves from a house to a small apartment in a new neighbourhood and experiences a dramatic lowering of standard of living will probably have more difficulties adapting than a child who stays in the family home and continues to go to the same school with his or her friends. Father absence, as we have already discussed, is related directly to economic instability. The absence will also affect the children's relationship with other relatives, especially grandparents. Without his active participation, the children may have limited access to the extended family members of the *nonresidential parent*. It is suspected that the connection between divorce and greater rates of delinquency, underachievement, and promiscuity in children depends more on stress-inducing changes, including changes in the relationship with parents, than on the divorce itself (Peck & Manocherian, 1988).

Finally, the nature of the new parenting arrangements are important to the children's adjustment. Children want and need an ongoing relationship with both parents, yet many children have little contact with the noncustodial parent one year after the divorce, especially if the parent has remarried (Peck & Manocherian, 1988).

Social supports are important for children, just as they are for adults. Grandparents, friends, teachers, and others may provide the emotional and practical help children need to help them cope with the emotional fallout of divorce. Grandparents hold a special position. If their marriages are intact, they demonstrate that relationships can be lasting, reliable, and dependable. They also show a sense of tradition and commitment to the young. Since the grandparent-grandchild relationship remains stable when the parent-child relationship is undergoing structural changes, it teaches children that not all relationships are temporary and unhappy. In order to be effective supports to children, grandparents must show their concern and involvement without interference or taking sides (Wallerstein & Blakeslee, 1989).

Custody and Parenting

WHO GETS CUSTODY?

As we have already seen in the chapter on single parents, mothers are usually granted custody after divorce. This was not always so. In English common law, which was also followed in English North America, fathers had automatic right to custody of their children. Mothers had few legal rights. During the 19th century changes began to take place. Mothers were gradually given custody, first of young children, then of older children. This shift was partly the result of the Industrial Revolution, during which the workplace and the home became separated. Men had to be free to earn an income and women were expected to stay home and raise their children. Power passed from the father to the family court judge who could decide if the mother deserved to have custody of her children. Custody could be denied her if she was considered at fault in the divorce by committing adultery or by leaving the home (Arnup, 1989; McKie et al., 1983). The current standard used is that of the best interest of the child. This still means that mothers are usually granted custody. There is often, however, reluctance to grant custody to a lesbian mother, especially if she is very open in her lifestyle or is a gay activist, on the grounds that living with her might be harmful for the child (Arnup, 1989).

Although the actual numbers are still relatively small, more fathers are now gaining custody of their children following divorce. Most often this occurs when the mother consents. Frequently, however, her consent is not whole-hearted. Since court cases are often costly, some women cannot afford to hire a lawyer. Others believe that the father can offer the children more stability immediately following the divorce. Still others want to avoid the emotional stress for themselves, and especially for their children, that comes with a contested custody case. Men seek and obtain custody for a number of reasons: some have a strong sense of family or believe that they are better parents than the mother; others seek custody out of revenge; still others are granted custody against their will because they have been deserted by their wives. A few fathers abduct their children because they don't agree with the court granting the mother custody. Fathers with custody who do best tend to be those who have higher incomes; they are also those who wanted custody and were involved with child rearing before the marriage breakup; they do not place the entire blame for the failure of the marriage on either partner; and their ex-wives are also involved with the children on a regular basis, so that the fathers do not carry the full burden of being parents (Greif, 1985; Edwards, 1989).

There is a growing move to joint custody following divorce (Payne & Edwards, 1991). The principle of shared parenting is in theory good for the child, since both parents are involved in decision-making and care. The actual definition of joint custody, however, is still being argued. Does the child have to live an equal amount of time with each parent? Does joint custody mean that both parents have the right to make decisions concerning their child, even if the child lives most of the time with one of them? Arrangements may break down if too great a distance separates parents. A child shifts more easily from one home to another if they are in the same neighbourhood and if the child attends only one school and has one set of playmates. If both parents have decision-making power, the parent who does not live with the child may not have enough day-to-day authority over the child. Joint custody works best if the parents can lay aside their personal disagreements to act together in the best interests of their child. Unfortunately, this does not always happen. Children can and do become pawns in the angry fighting between parents. Although research findings are still scarce, it appears that children do adjust to moving back and forth between homes. Just as boys experience more difficulty than girls following divorce, they also have more problems adjusting to shared custody.

PROBLEM AREAS

There are two major problem areas arising out of custody conflicts — failure to comply with either support orders or with custody provisions. One of the reasons for poverty among divorced mothers and their children is the failure of the father to meet support payments. There are a number of reasons fathers (usually) do not comply with support orders: sometimes they will delay long enough each month that the mother has to go to court to enforce the order; sometimes failure to pay occurs because the father is disgruntled with the custody order; sometimes he does not pay child support in an effort to harass his ex-wife; sometimes he uses it as a method of exerting power over decisions affecting his ex-wife and/or children. Virtually all provinces and territories have established support-enforcement programs. In Ontario, the parent who receives court-ordered support payments for the children can request the Support and Custody Enforcement Office to collect them. One advantage to this is that the Program will try to locate whoever is required to pay support and to garnishee wages or seize property if necessary to enforce the order (Ontario Ministry of the Attorney General). This service, which is the busiest in the country, reports that only 30 percent of support orders are complied with (Cochrane, 1991).

Some parents try to prevent visits if support is not paid. This breach of the terms of custody can actually backfire since the noncustodial parent can request change of custody because access has been denied. Occasionally a noncustodial parent takes the law into his or her own hands and kidnaps the child. Often abductions are discovered when the parent does not return the child after a visit. One of the most urgent steps in abduction cases is locating the child, especially if there is a danger that he or she will be taken out of the country. The Hague Convention on the Civil Aspects of International Child Abduction, which has been accepted by many countries, tries to ensure that an abducted child is returned promptly to the *custodial parent*. It also attempts to ensure that rights of custody and access of one country are respected by other countries. If a child is taken to a country that has signed the Convention, steps are taken to return the child. When the child is taken to a country that does not recognize the Convention, especially one where fathers normally get custody and mothers have few rights, it is much more difficult to get the child back. In such cases, parents can spend large sums on detectives and foreign lawyers in attempts to find and reclaim their children

(Cochrane, 1991; Hoff, 1988; Ontario Ministry of the Attorney General). Occasionally one reads stories of custodial parents re-kidnapping their children.

In both noncompliance of child-support orders and in kidnapping cases, the main victim is usually the child. Regardless of the intentions of the parent, the child suffers in these cases the consequences of poverty, of deprivation of a parent, of being uprooted from a home, and of being forced to live on the run.

PARENTS WITHOUT CUSTODY

Most noncustodial parents are men. Divorce often means for them a loss of a sense of home and family. Women traditionally have been expected to provide for the emotional needs of their families. As a result, they often provide guidance to their husbands in how to parent their children. In many families it is the mother who arranges activities for the entire family; in this way she regulates contact between the father and child. When the marriage is broken, men are sometimes at a loss as to how to manage the father-child relationship on their own. Often visits are seen as play time, with very little discipline involved. Sometimes the father will spend increased time with his parents, since their home provides a convenient place for visits to occur. Visits tend to become fewer and farther apart if the ex-spouses are hostile toward each other or if the father does not make support payments regularly (F.H. Brown, 1988).

There is a great deal of pressure in society for mothers to assume custody of their children following breakup of a marriage. The title of Harriet Edwards' book, *How Could You?* (1989), reflects the stigma experienced by mothers without custody. Mothers who do not have custody often feel, however, that it is in their children's best interests to stay with their father since he can provide a stable home at a time when they cannot. Regardless of their motives, noncustodial mothers are blamed by society for being "unnatural." Edwards found that in a few cases courts awarded custody to the father against the mother's wishes. This often occurred after she had left the children with him temporarily until she could establish her own home. By the time she could take them, the ex-husband could

CUSTODY OF DAD **© 1987 Barry Maguire**

Source: *The Single Parent*, March/April 1992, p. 28.

argue that it would be better if the children were not uprooted. Some mothers felt a custody battle would be too damaging for their children. Many women had no choice in the custody matter; they simply could not afford to raise the children, since they had so little earning power, and their former husbands could afford to raise the children. Often the children lived with the mother for some time before the custody shifted to their father.

Divorce and the Family Life Cycle

Divorce has a different impact at different stages of the family life cycle. The least disruption occurs with the newly married couple with no children. There are fewer people involved and fewer family traditions. Since each partner has been single fairly recently, they are able to slip back into single roles and lifestyle more easily than those married for a long time. As more people are added to the family and the family has a longer history together, divorce becomes more difficult. Traditions build up through years of interaction. Part of the dislocation of divorce after long-time marriage is the loss of these rituals. Elementary-school-age children have a particularly difficult time because they are old enough to understand what is going on but do not have the necessary coping skills. Often they feel they are responsible for the family breakup and have the power to bring parents back together. This is part of the magical thinking of childhood. They feel that the world revolves around them, and that all that happens is a result of their own actions. If divorce occurs when the children are adolescent or adult, they may have difficulty separating from parents who turn to them for support, or they may feel they need to look after the parent (Peck & Manocherian, 1988).

Divorce is especially hard for homemaker women during the time children are leaving home or during the empty-nest stage. Often they feel as if they have no place in society. As we saw in Chapter 7, they may also be faced with the task of finding a job when they have never been in the work force or may have been out of the work force for many years. In addition, older people going through a divorce may suffer a sense of shame and guilt. Since they grew up during a time when divorce was condemned, they often feel the stigma quite sharply (Peck & Manocherian, 1988).

The Future

Divorce shows no signs of going away. In fact, there are predictions that in the future at least half of all marriages will be dissolved. As a society, this phenomenon presents us with a crucial issue: how to best ensure the healthy development of children living in divorced families.

Children tend to do best when they have a continuity in their relationships. This means that they need regular contact with both parents, unless there are overriding reasons to deny it, such as serious abuse. They also need contact with both extended families. In order for this to occur, there must be cooperation of all the adults involved.

Children also need to be assured of adequate financial support. This demands the serious commitment of both parents to the welfare of the children. It also needs to be backed up with effective enforcement laws. This will happen only if the courts, and society at large, take the matter seriously.

Finally, children's interests are best served if their parents receive adequate back-up from their extended families and from society as a whole. If single parents are left to do everything alone — earn a living and raise children — without any assistance, then the phenomenon of single-parent burnout will continue to occur. In the end, it means that society at large must be concerned about the well-being of these families.

SUMMARY

HISTORY OF DIVORCE IN CANADA. New Brunswick and Nova Scotia were the earliest provinces to have a divorce law, with very limited grounds and a double standard favouring men. Following Confederation, in provinces without divorce courts, individuals had to resort to private members' bills in parliament. Following World War II, there was an increase in divorces as a result of prolonged separations, hasty wartime marriages, and women's growing independence as a result of joining the work force. Under pressure for change, a new divorce law, which established wider grounds for divorce, came into effect in 1968. In 1986, a new law allowed for no-fault divorce and a shorter waiting period. Following each legal change there was a dramatic increase in the number of divorces.

STAGES OF DIVORCE. There are several stages in a divorce. The decision to divorce comes with the realization that the marriage cannot be saved. Then couples must plan the breakup: they need to settle custody and financial issues. Finally, following separation, the family must reorganize. They need to separate marital and parental roles in order to allow the children to be part of the families of both parents.

CRISIS OF DIVORCE. There are three crises of divorce — emotional, economic, and parental. In the emotional crisis, the ex-spouses need to mourn the loss of their marriage, establish new identities as single persons, and form new social networks. If these tasks are accomplished, there are opportunities for personal growth. Economically, a divorce usually means a drop in the standard of living, especially for the parent with custody of the children. Both parents are responsible for supporting the children. Property is also divided equally. In addition, the parents need to work out new guidelines for authority over and responsibility for the children. Children fare best if parents can cooperate to ensure their welfare.

CHILDREN AND DIVORCE. The impact on the children depends on several factors. Younger children tend to adjust better in the long run. Boys initially have more difficulty, but some girls may experience serious long-term effects. The parents' level of conflict is probably more important to the adjustment of children than the divorce itself. Lifestyle changes are also significant, including the quality of parenting and the social supports available to the children.

CUSTODY. Mothers are usually granted custody, although joint custody and father custody are increasing. There are two major problem areas regarding custody. One is the failure to comply with support orders; provinces now have support-enforcement programs in place. A second problem area is the failure to comply with custody and visiting provisions. If the custodial parent refuses to allow court-ordered visits with the other parent, this may be grounds for a change in custody. Some parents kidnap their children. The main victim in both support and visitation and custody violations is the child. Many parents without custody lose the sense of home and family. In these cases, visiting and support may taper off. Mothers who give up custody of their children often face stigma, even if they feel they are acting in the best interests of the children.

FAMILY LIFE CYCLE AND DIVORCE. The least disruption occurs when newly-married couples divorce. Individuals who divorce after long-term marriages with school-aged children usually experience the greatest difficulty. In particular, homemaker wives have problems rebuilding their social life.

KEY TERMS

binuclear family: an arrangement where both father and mother act as parents to their child(ren) following divorce while they maintain separate homes

coparent: a divorced person who shares the responsibility for his or her child

custodial parent: an individual who has custody of his or her child

custody: the legal right and responsibility to care for a child in one's own home

disequilibrium: a lack of balance in the family system

divorce: the legal dissolution of a marriage

joint custody: the legal right and responsibility of both parents to make decisions and care for their child

noncustodial parent: the parent who does not have custody of the child

nonresidential parent: the parent who does not live in the home with the child

sleeper effect: a problem that emerges only long after an event such as divorce

CLASS ASSIGNMENTS

Complete one or both of the following assignments, as directed by your instructor.

1. In some communities, mediation is available for couples seeking divorce. How does mediation differ from using the court to solve differences over custody and support? Explain the factors that make mediation most effective. Find out if mediation services are available in your community.

2. Imagine a family with a boy aged 7 years old. The parents are planning a divorce and would like joint custody of their son. Working in pairs, draw up a plan for coparenting. Take into account schooling, residence, holidays, transportation, and any other factor you think is relevant.

PERSONAL ASSIGNMENTS

The following assignments are designed to help you think about your own experience and opinions.

1. Following some divorces, custody of children is split, i.e., one child will stay with the mother and another with the father. What do you feel are the advantages and disadvantages of this arrangement? Do you feel that it is all right for children to be separated in this way? Or do you think they should be kept together? Explain.
2. Do you feel grandparents should be given the legal right to access to their grandchildren and/or custody following the divorce of the parents? Why or why not?

CHAPTER 9

The Second Time Around

OBJECTIVES

- To look at historical changes in remarriage patterns.
- To consider the process of forming a new family system and its relationship to the family life cycle.
- To examine factors leading to success and failure in stepfamily relationships.
- To look at the relationship of the stepfamily and society at large.

Once upon a time there lived a man with a wife and a beautiful daughter. While his child was still young, the man's wife died. The man was at his wit's end trying to make a home for his child.

"I must find a wife," he told himself. "Then we will have a proper home."

So he did as he said, and found a widow with two daughters. They were soon married. His new wife happily moved in, along with her children.

Soon, however, both she and her daughters had turned his child into a servant. The girl had to do all the heavy cleaning, and was at their beck and call all day and all night. Sometimes she crept into the fireplace to rest from the demands of her stepmother and stepsisters, so she was always covered in ashes.

"You're just a cinder girl," they taunted her.

And that is how she came to be called Cinderella.

Remarriage — A New Trend?

The divorce rate is increasing. As a result, there have been many predictions that the rate of remarriage will also increase. The Family History Survey, which was undertaken by Statistics Canada in 1984 to gather information that wasn't available in Census reports, discovered that only a small minority of all adult Canadians have been married more than once, in fact only about 1 in 20. If we consider only those Canadians who have actually been married, fewer than 1 in 10 have been married more than once. Third and fourth marriages are rare (Burch, 1985). More recent figures show that in 1985, more than 20 percent of marriages for both men and women were second or later ones. Divorced people accounted for most of the increase. Between 1975 and 1985, the number of marriages in which at least one partner was divorced doubled. On the other hand, those in which one or both partners was widowed declined (Nagnur & Adams, 1987). In fact, most divorced people do remarry (Adams & Nagnur, 1988).

Table 9.1

PERCENTAGE DISTRIBUTION OF BRIDES AND GROOMS BY FIRST OR LATER ORDER MARRIAGE, 1955–85

	1955	1965	1975	1985
		%		
Brides				
First marriage	91.5	91.1	85.4	79.7
Second or later marriage	8.5	8.9	14.6	20.3
Total	100.0	100.0	100.0	100.0
Grooms				
First marriage	91.7	91.5	84.5	78.2
Second or later marriage	8.3	8.5	15.5	21.8
Total	100.0	100.0	100.0	100.0
Total number of marriages	127 777	145 519	197 585	184 096

Source: Statistics Canada, Catalogue 84–205, *Marriage and Divorces*. In Dhruva Nagnur and Owen Adams (1987). "Tying the Knot: An Overview of Marriage Rates in Canada," *Canadian Social Trends*, Autumn, p. 3.

As these figures show, the faces of both the ending of marriage and of remarriage are changing. Until the end of World War II, taking a second husband or wife tended to follow the death of a spouse. Now remarriage is more likely to follow divorce. More recent statistics reflect this trend. In 1970–72, marriages ended in widowhood for 58 percent of women and in divorce for 19 percent of women. In 1984–86, the proportions were 50 percent widowed and 28 percent divorced. About 22 to 23 percent of men's marriages ended in widowhood at both these times; the figures for divorce parallel women's. Recently there has been a decrease in remarriages among the widowed. Those who did marry again were, on the average, younger when their spouses died than those who did not remarry (Adams & Nagnur, 1988). There are complex factors behind these trends. First, life expectancy has increased; thus there is less likelihood that a person will be widowed at a young age. Second, as we saw in the last chapter, following changes in the law in 1968 and 1986, there has been an enormous increase in the number of divorces. Other factors that may affect remarriage rates are improved pensions, allowing older people to live independently if they choose to do so, and a greater social acceptance of common-law marriages and single living.

Many remarried families are stepfamilies, since about 75 percent of single parents remarry (Morrison & Thompson-Guppy, 1986). Obviously there are generational differences. Younger people are more likely to get divorced. As they age, and as more divorces occur among the coming generations, sociologists expect an increase in the total number of divorced individuals and, as a result, of people marrying for a second or third time.

Remarriage is not a guarantee of happiness. Although most second marriages are stable, they still show a higher rate of divorce than first marriages. One does not have to look far to find explanations. In some cases problems such as family violence, alcoholism, or psychiatric disorders, such as neurosis or schizophrenia, that led to the breakup of the first marriage continue, and create similar difficulties in a later marriage. Another reason lies in the fact that many remarriages include children. Such marriages involve many additional relationships: with the former spouse or spouses (the parents of the children), with extended family

Table 9.2

PERCENTAGE OF ADULTS RAISING STEPCHILDREN

Sex of adult	Age of child			
	0–16	7–20	21+	All ages
Male	3.8%	6.8%	4.7%	4.5%
Female	1.4%	3.1%	2.6%	2.2%

Source: From Thomas K. Burch (1985). *Family History Survey: Preliminary Findings*. Statistics Canada, August, p. 17.

members, and especially with the children themselves. In fact, the divorce rate for stepfamilies lies at about 47 percent, compared with about 30 percent for all marriages (Adams & Nagnur, 1988; Morrison & Thompson-Guppy, 1986).

Forming a New Family System

Unlike nuclear families, *reconstituted* or remarriage families have few norms to guide their formation. If they try to mimic first-marriage families, there can be serious difficulties, since they just do not fit the expected pattern.

STAGES OF REMARRIAGE-FAMILY FORMATION

There are three distinct stages in entering and adapting to a second marriage: entering the new relationship, planning the new marriage and family, and forming the remarriage family (Carter & McGoldrick, 1988).

Before people can successfully enter a new marriage, they need to recover from the loss of the first. Often there is a great deal of anger directed toward the ex-spouse. If it continues, an emotional divorce will not take place, since anger provides a powerful link to the former spouse. The new couple must also commit themselves to forming a new family and be ready to deal with all the complications that will arise.

The second phase involves planning the new marriage. The couple needs to work at open and honest communication. They also must accept the fact that difficulties will not be ironed out overnight. It is important for them to deal with relationships with relatives outside the household. The relationship with the ex-spouse involving coparenting and financial support needs to be maintained. Extended family members must establish relationships with the new spouse and any children he or she brings into the marriage. Plans have to be made for the children to stay connected with the extended families of both ex-spouses. Throughout this phase, the partners must accept their own anxieties and those of the other family members about the new family.

Finally, the new family is formed. This involves renegotiating boundaries and roles, and making room for all the children to keep up their relationships with their biological parents, grandparents, and other relatives. The new family has to share their memories and make new rituals so that they will develop a sense of belonging.

BOUNDARIES

One of the main differences between first marriages and second or later ones involves family boundaries. As we saw in Chapter 1, boundaries mark out who belongs to the family. They must be open enough to allow interaction with the outside world, yet clear enough so that the family feels some sense of unity.

In first-marriage families, boundaries are relatively well-defined. Members live in the same place and are supported by household adults. Authority and responsibility rest with the married couple, who are also the parents of the children. In most families, adults and children are fond of each other (Walker & Messinger, 1979).

Remarriage families do not fit this expected pattern. First, parents and children do not all stay in the same residence. Custody arrangements determine if the children live with one parent and visit with the other, or live at times with one and at times with the other, and if brothers and sisters share the same household. In addition, if both adults in the remarried household have children, the custody and visiting arrangements of the second set further complicate the situation. The number of people living in the home can sometimes vary from week to week. Financial support for children is often provided, in part, by nonhousehold members. The parent paying support may have little control over how this money is used. Authority over and responsibility for the children rest in two households. Who, for example, is in charge of discipline, money, or major decisions? Often the rules vary depending on where the children are currently living (Walker & Messinger, 1979).

Some families respond to this complex and ambiguous situation by attempting to become as much like a first-marriage family as is possible. They may, for example, try to draw a tight boundary of loyalties around the remarriage family, and try to cut off contact with the *nonresidential parent* and his or her relatives. Such an approach is unrealistic. It may throw children into a conflict of loyalties in the face of demands to belong exclusively to one parent's family. In fact, keeping boundaries permeable usually provides the most workable solution; i.e., the new family needs to allow members, such as visiting children, to move in and out, and yet establish its own stable lifestyle. It also needs to allow for necessary contact between households of current and former spouses, at least in respect to the children. *Permeable boundaries* also permit children to move back and forth between households for either custody changes or visits, with the least amount of strain (McGoldrick & Carter, 1988; Walker & Messinger, 1979).

ROLES

The lack of clarity in family boundaries has its counterpart in confusion over roles. Roles in nuclear families are complementary, i.e., they travel in pairs — husband and wife, parent and child. There are also social expectations for the person who fills a role. Role strain occurs if there is a misfit between the individual and the role he or she is expected to fill, or if there is no recognized role for the individual. It was pointed out in Chapter 1, for example, that there are only two *social scripts* for stepmothers to follow — the good mother and the stereotypical wicked stepmother — neither of which fits most families.

One of the main difficulties in remarriage families is that there are too many candidates for the available roles. This fact affects the stepparent in particular.

The children already have two biological parents and are not usually interested in replacing them. If the new spouse tries to take over the role of the parent of the same sex, he or she will meet resistance and resentment from the children. Loyalty issues are involved. Conflict can break out over many issues, from meals that are too different to discipline. A key time for discomfort is the special event involving the child. At graduations and weddings, for example, families have the potentially awkward task of including at least one extra parent figure. Usually such issues underline the fact that the stepparent is not the "real" parent (Morrison & Thompson-Guppy, 1986). Similarly there are "extra" grandparents and other kin.

Traditional gender roles (in which women are expected to take responsibility for the emotional well-being of the family, including rearing the children, and men are expected to manage finances) work against stepfamilies. These roles are unrealistic when some of the children are virtual strangers to the wife and some of the family's income and expenditure is outside the husband's control. Families seem to work best if the responsibility of raising children is established in a way that does not exclude either biological parent. Stepparents need to work out what role is appropriate for them. Often in successful reconstituted families, this involves being an adult friend rather than a parent to the stepchildren (McGoldrick & Carter, 1988; Morrison & Thompson-Guppy, 1986).

A difficulty facing some children is the loss of accustomed roles. This can occur in at least two ways. First, when the new family includes stepsiblings, unless they are widely separated by age, one oldest child loses his or her position, and so does one youngest child. Second, the only boy or girl may gain a same-sex stepsibling and forfeit his or her special status.

Renegotiating family boundaries and roles may take place over a prolonged period of time. Even when the family achieves a comfortable working arrangement, members should expect that it will need continuing adjustment. As children mature and visiting and custody agreements are altered, the relationships will need to be reworked.

Establishing New Family Relationships

THE MARITAL RELATIONSHIP

As in any other marriage, partners in remarriages have the task of commitment to the new family system. They too need to realign relationships with extended family and friends to include the new spouse. In addition, however, they must also adjust the relationship with their children and ex-spouse.

Often couples in second marriages are less romantic and more realistic, honest, and willing to discuss difficulties in the marriage. Remarried couples may be particularly sensitive to conflict following the breakup of an earlier marriage.

This sensitivity can result in more open expression of differences of opinion and greater awareness of the feelings of the spouse. Some couples, however, are so afraid that disagreement will lead to another divorce that they hide differences behind a shield of apparent agreement and thus do not resolve important issues (Hetherington et al., 1988).

The fact that the parent-child bond began before the marriage, not following it, can create difficulties in the relationship between the new spouses. Stepparents may compete with stepchildren for the attention of the spouse/parent. In addition, privacy and time alone for the couple may be lacking. Frequently couple time cuts into children's time at a point when the latter are already feeling left out and confused following the remarriage (Hetherington et al., 1988; McGoldrick & Carter, 1988).

The ex-spouse can also affect the new marriage. The fact that he or she has a continuing relationship with the children means that there is also a continuing relationship with the former partner. Some contacts are necessary to arrange for visits and to discuss issues related to the children's welfare. The influences of ex-spouses can vary widely. Last-minute requests for or cancellation of visits can disrupt the couple's plans or deprive them of needed privacy. Failure of the ex-spouse to meet support obligations on time or requests for additional money can play havoc with financial planning. Occasionally an individual continues to call on an ex-partner to solve daily problems like household repairs and day-to-day discipline; a new spouse can resent such intrusions. Some of these difficulties involve boundaries and appropriate roles and are part of the issues to be resolved during system reorganization. Others are a necessary point of contact for the well-being of the children.

In the early stages of the new marriage, contempt or hostility toward the former spouse is sometimes used to create solidarity because it gives the couple a sense of unity against a common enemy (Hetherington et al., 1988). A more serious problem arises when one partner has not resolved feelings of loss and attachment surrounding the previous marriage, and may be pulled by loyalties to both the old and new spouse. In addition, the new spouse who is unsure of the relationship may be jealous of the earlier spouse.

Sometimes relatives do not accept the new spouse. This may occur if they blame the individual for the breakup of the first marriage, or through the conviction that marriage is for life and that any divorce and remarriage is wrong, if not sinful. If relatives reject the marriage, the couple may lack social support. Thus, when there are normal difficulties in the relationship, relatives may point out the virtues of the first spouse or attack with an "I told you so" approach. Ultimately the couple can become isolated and experience reduced coping resources.

The most common difficulty between spouses, however, is conflict around children. Since the stepparent role is not clearly defined in our society, parents, stepparents, and children alike may have unreasonable and contradictory expectations. Conflict may develop out of parents' differences in attitudes about discipline, or out of children's attempts to play their parents against each other or to appeal to the loyalty of the birth parent. Occasionally conflict takes a different form in families where there are teens or young adults. The biological parent may become jealous of the developing affection between stepparent and stepchild, especially if he or she interprets it in sexual terms.

Partners usually become aware of insurmountable difficulties early in the remarriage; thus most divorces occur quickly. If the marriage is not dissolved quickly, it is likely to be as stable as any first marriage (Hetherington et al., 1988).

RESIDENTIAL PARENT-CHILD RELATIONSHIP

The parent-child relationship often suffers in the early post-divorce period. Given that the *residential parent* is adjusting to the loss of a spouse as well as restructuring his or her life, there is often little emotional or even physical energy available to deal effectively with the child. The child, who is suffering similar difficulties, often takes bad feelings out on the parent through defiance and rebellion or other forms of obnoxious behaviour. As we saw in the last chapter, this pattern is most likely to develop in the mother-son relationship (Hetherington et al., 1988).

Some children face the parent's disorganization by becoming a *parentified child,* i.e., by accepting some of the parent's responsibilities of care and nurturing. With this role comes greater decision-making power. Often the single parent and child will close ranks and become more dependent on each other. The child may become a confidante. This is especially true of a single mother and daughter. When the parent remarries, the child often has to give up some of the responsibility and closeness to the new adult in the family. Naturally the child often feels a sense of both loss and resentment. As a result the child may try to maintain power by becoming more demanding toward the birth parent, with attention-seeking behaviour, or he or she may become depressed and withdrawn (Hetherington et al., 1988).

NONRESIDENTIAL PARENT-CHILD RELATIONSHIP

The relationship between the child and the nonresidential parent varies a great deal from family to family. Some parents have little or no contact with their children. Others are very much involved in decisions about the child and in actual physical care. Variations are related to distance between homes, the length of time since the divorce, the age of the child, and the amount of support paid. If the parent is depressed or feels guilty, he or she may avoid visits because they only aggravate these feelings. More frequent contact is associated with higher income and education, and with reasonably friendly relationships with the ex-spouse. Nonresidential mothers are much less likely to stop visiting children. They are also more likely to keep up regular, frequent visits. If either parent remarries, visits with the nonresidential parent tend to drop off (Hetherington et al., 1988).

Often children's contact with nonresidential parents involves social and fun activities such as going to movies or on trips, while the residential parent is involved in day-to-day activities such as helping with homework and maintaining discipline. Thus, noncustodial parents are seen as the source of pleasure, but they are cut off from the mainstream of daily living. However, custodial parents may become resentful at being forced into the role of disciplinarian and bad guy.

Even though the residential parent may have negative feelings about arranging visits, contact between the children and nonresidential parent is valuable. As we saw in the last chapter, the well-being of children depends on the maintenance of ties with both biological parents.

Dear Ann: I have been divorced from my wife for six years. We have both remarried. Our son chose to live with his mother and her husband, which we agreed was the best thing for all concerned. His stepfather is a rabbi.

We are planning the boy's bar mitzvah, and it is creating a lot of problems. For example, how should our names appear on the invitations?

The really serious difference in opinion centres around the reception. My ex-wife and her rabbi husband insist that the reception be held at his temple after the bar mitzvah service and that all members of the congregation be invited.

Since my family will be travelling a great distance, there will be only about 25 members present. How should we divide the expenses?

I consider it unfair that they expect me to go 50-50 in view of the fact that the great majority of the guests will be members of the congregation who are unknown to me.

It is very important that I maintain an amiable relationship with my former wife and her husband. We all want the day to be a pleasant and happy one for our son. Please advise. — **Somewhere in the East**

Dear Somewhere: The invitation should read: Mrs. (her name) and Mr. (your name) invite you to attend the bar mitzvah of their son (his name). Date, time and place.

My advice is be a mensch and pay half the reception expenses. Five years from now you won't know the difference, and you will be glad you did. Mazel tov!

Source: *The Toronto Star*, 1 June 1987, p. C4.

THE STEPPARENT-STEPCHILD RELATIONSHIP

The relationship between stepparent and stepchild is important for two reasons. First, many marriages founder because problems in this relationship eventually destroy the marriage. Second, adolescents in stepfamilies are at high risk of developing behavioural problems (Hetherington et al., 1988).

To be successful stepparents, adults need to accomplish two tasks: develop an appropriately affectionate relationship with the child, and establish themselves as legitimate parental authorities and disciplinarians. Unfortunately, the tasks are somewhat contradictory. Many families fall short of these goals. A barrier to working out problems is the relative impermanence of the stepparent relationship; it lasts only as long as the marriage does. If the marriage founders, the stepparent generally no longer has any relationship with the child. One factor works in favour of stepfamilies: most children prefer to live in a two-parent family.

Developing a relationship. Stepparents tend to be more successful with younger children, who may transfer their attachment from their biological parent to the stepparent. Both stepfathers and stepmothers report more positive relationships with boys than with girls. The stepmother-stepdaughter relationship suffers from the most severe problems. Often daughters feel responsible for the emotional relationships in the family. Since stepmothers also believe they should nurture emotional relationships, their stepdaughters feel displaced and resist sharing this role (Hetherington et al., 1988; McGoldrick & Carter, 1988).

Some of the problems in stepfamily relationships arise from myths and unrealistic expectations, which place unnecessary burdens on all members. Let's take a look at some of these misconceptions.

1. "One big happy family." In order to prove to themselves and to the world that the new family is a success, some stepparents feel the need to keep all family members happy and contented (Visher & Visher, 1979). Even in first-marriage families it is impossible to satisfy everyone because there are conflicts between needs and desires. It is even more difficult for stepfamilies to achieve this ideal.

2. "Instant love." Often stepfamily members are expected to feel immediate attachment, or even to love one another. This myth is related to the "one big happy family" fantasy. Parents and children who accept this myth have a vision of the ideal child or parent that no human being can fulfil. What makes this situation harder is that the child's ideal is often the nonresident biological parent, who is used as a glowing example of parenting. Both stepparent and child are bound to be disappointed or resentful in this situation. In fact, respect without a deep feeling of love or commitment may be satisfactory for daily living (Schulman, 1972; Visher & Visher, 1979).

3. "The rescuer." This fantasy comes in two versions — making up for what the poor child has been through or straightening the kid out. Neither works.

It is impossible to take away past pain from family upsets or to make up for it. Far healthier is helping the child mourn his or her loss and thus come to terms with it (Visher & Visher, 1979). If the stepparent tries to "correct" what he sees as past failures in discipline with a view to turning the child into a productive member of society, he or she will in all likelihood arouse resentment on the part of the child, and possible conflict with the biological parent (Hetherington et al., 1988).

4. "The wicked stepmother." Stepmothers have bad publicity from way back. The wicked stepmother is a folk figure who stars in the traditional tales, like the Cinderella story, which are told and retold to each generation. Real stepmothers often try to overcome this handicap by trying to be extra nice. Sometimes the "rescuer" or "happy family" fantasy is the result. The problems the stepmother experiences in becoming integrated into the family may partly be the result of her persistence in trying to become a nurturer. When she isn't appreciated, she may become angry or resentful, truly a "wicked" stepmother. If she did not try so hard to counteract the myth, she might actually be more successful (Hetherington et al., 1988; Schulman, 1972; Visher & Visher, 1979).

If people believe the myths, they go into stepfamilies with unrealistic expectations, which may produce disappointment or undeserved suspicion. As a result, they interfere with the development of working relationships.

The degree of acceptance of stepfamily members is often affected by loyalty issues. The child may see the stepparent as an intruder trying to take the "real" parent's place. If attachment does begin to grow, the child may feel that he or she is being disloyal to the same-sex biological parent. In either case, the child

FOR BETTER OR FOR WORSE **by Lynn Johnston**

Source: *The Toronto Star*, 3 November 1988, p. M7.

may be anxious and resentful enough to ward off the new parent by trying to drive a wedge into the marriage (Hetherington et al., 1988). Stepparent adoption may also involve loyalty issues. It seems to work best when the children are young at the time of the marriage and have little contact with the nonresident biological parent. Stepparents may also feel disloyal if they become attached to their new spouse's children. Men who leave their children from a former marriage in the custody of their ex-wife do not relate as well to stepchildren as do men who were bachelors. Part of the reason, some researchers believe, is that the fathers' sense of guilt over leaving their own children interferes with the new relationship (Duberman, 1975).

Finally, there may be complications between opposite-sex stepparent and stepchild because there is no explicit incest taboo surrounding this relationship. Stepfathers may find it easier to express affection verbally or through granting special privileges than physically. Sometimes conflict is used to keep a safe distance, since showing fondness may arouse sexual feelings (Hetherington et al., 1988).

Discipline. Discipline is another potential area of conflict. One of the difficulties is that stepparents are not seen as "real" parents, since they are not the children's birth parents, and only "real" parents are entitled to be disciplinarians. The issue can be complicated by differences in child-rearing styles and strategies, or by the failure of the residential birth parent to act as a disciplinarian. Discipline is also a key area in which a jealous birth parent may undermine the position of the stepparent. The most successful stepparents are those who first develop a friendly relationship with the child and then assert their authority (Duberman, 1975; Hetherington et al., 1988).

RELATIONSHIPS BETWEEN STEPBROTHERS AND STEPSISTERS

A marriage between divorced parents creates stepsiblings. Many stepsiblings do not live together since the most common pattern is for children to live with their mothers. Unless visits are arranged so that only one set of children is in the house at one time, there is periodic interaction between resident and visiting children. With more fathers being granted custody of their children, the likelihood of two sibling groups being combined in one household has increased. For these children, adjustments have to be made on a more permanent basis (M. Ward, 1984b).

Children expect their birth parents to consider them special; thus when there are conflicts, children expect their own parent to side with them. If there are any differences in treatment among stepsiblings, it is usually interpreted by children as favouritism. A key ingredient in this mix is a sense of loss and jealousy because the birth parents are spending time with the other children, often at the expense of time with their own.

If one set of children visits or moves into the family home permanently, there may be problems over turf. When children are expected to share space and toys, there are numerous opportunities for friction. This may centre on both the use of space and on possessions. The conflict is made worse if the two sets of children have different attitudes towards such aspects of daily life as tidiness or the use of others' property.

Children's roles in families may conflict. Two only children, for example, may have difficulty getting used to having another child around, especially if they are the same age and sex. There can only be one oldest and one youngest in a family. Often parents discount the sense of loss a child experiences if he or she has to give up an important role.

When there are adolescents of opposite sexes in the family, there may be conflict in order to maintain a safe distance between them. The incest taboo between stepsiblings ranges from weak to nonexistent, and such conflict provides a safe buffer against sexual attraction.

On the positive side, stepsiblings can provide one another with emotional support, for example, if visits with the nonresidential parent fall through. Since they have all had similar experiences of losing their original family and having to adjust to living in a new blended family, they can form a mutual self-help group.

Remarriage and the Family Life Cycle

The experience of remarriage differs according to the life-cycle stage of each partner. If they are in the same phase, they share common problems. Their greatest strain involves responsibilities to their children. This is especially difficult when they have adolescents. Some issues are common in families with adolescents: there is conflict between the family's need to form attachments and the adolescent's normal need to separate from the family; there are also difficulties arising out of the teen's ability to manipulate parents and out of adolescent sexuality. In later life-cycle stages, grown children may complain about having to shift from a "normal" image of parents/grandparents to that which includes a stepparent. They may also have concerns about inheritance. There are particular problems if one spouse is considerably older than another, and life-cycle stages differ. For instance, some men marry women roughly the same age as their children. In general, the greater the difference in life-cycle stage, the harder it is to adapt to the new family because husband and wife are dealing with different life-cycle issues (McGoldrick & Carter, 1988).

The Stepfamily and Wider Society

The relationship of the stepfamily to society is somewhat confused. In some ways these families are indistinguishable from first-marriage families. They have two parents in the household, for instance, living with their children. This invisibility helps the family blend in, at least superficially. Yet the fact that they seem the same leads to the expectation that they will actually be like other families. Some of the differences seem almost petty, yet they can create problems, e.g., school officials are often unhappy about sending duplicate report cards and school notices to each parent (Ahrons, 1983).

Stepfamilies also experience role ambiguity. They do not receive clear messages from society. On the one hand, they are expected to have something wrong with them. In part, this is realistic since many children in these families do display problems in relationships with peers and authority figures because of unresolved anger; yet expecting problems often becomes a self-fulfilling prophecy. On the other hand, society often expects the stepfamily to act like one big happy family.

Given the number of children involved, it is important for all of us to develop a model of stepfamily health rather than stepfamily disturbance. With such a model, we will be able to support parents in creating a stable and nurturing environment.

SUMMARY

HISTORICAL CHANGES. The nature of remarriage has changed in recent years. In the past, most stepfamilies were formed after one spouse died. Now they more commonly follow divorce. As a result, the remarriage is complicated by the existence of a living ex-spouse.

FORMING A NEW FAMILY SYSTEM. Forming a reconstituted family occurs in several stages. First, the couple needs to recover from the loss of their first marriages and commit themselves to their new one. Second, anxiety about remarrying and arrangements for children's continued contact with the other parent and his or her relatives need to be worked out. Third, boundaries and roles need to be renegotiated. Since the children belong in two households, boundaries need to be flexible enough to allow for their coming and going. In addition, financial support and parental authority are also divided. There is often lack of clarity over roles in stepfamilies, in particular over the stepparent role.

ESTABLISHING NEW FAMILY RELATIONSHIPS. Members of reconstituted families must work out relationships with old and new family members.

The parental relationship. Often the resident parent cannot respond to the child's needs immediately after the divorce. As a result, some children take on the parent's responsibilities for care and nurturing other family members. When the parent remarries, the parentified child experiences both a loss of power and feelings of resentment.

The relationship with the nonresidential parent may vary from no contact to frequent visiting. Continuing contact, in most cases, improves the well-being of the children. Stepparents need to accomplish two tasks: to develop an appropriately affectionate relationship with the child, and to establish themselves as legitimate disciplinarians. They are hampered by myths that suggest either that everything will work out smoothly or that stepparents are cruel. Children often resist becoming attached to their stepparent because of loyalty to the same-sex birth parent. Discipline is another area of conflict, since children may not accept the stepparent's authority.

Stepsibling relationships. Often stepsiblings do not live in the same household, but have contact on periodic visits. Whether they visit or share a home, there may be conflict over space, possessions, rules, and attention from parents.

REMARRIAGE IN THE LIFE CYCLE. As in divorce, the impact of remarriage depends partly on the life-cycle stage of the new partners. For example, the age of the children has an effect on family life. There may be additional pressures if the new couple is in different life-cycle stages.

STEPFAMILIES AND SOCIETY AT LARGE. Since stepfamilies superficially resemble first-marriage families, they are often expected to be like them. On the other hand, they also are expected to have something wrong with them. Society still needs to develop positive models of stepfamily roles.

KEY TERMS

nonresidential parent: the parent with whom the child does not live

parentified child: a child who takes on an unusual degree of parental roles

permeable boundaries: family boundaries that allow members to move through them

reconstituted family: a remarriage family

residential parent: the parent with whom the child lives

social script: cultural rule that tells us what, where, when, how, and why we should do something

CLASS ASSIGNMENTS

Complete one or both of the following assignments, as directed by your instructor.

1. Many of the problems of remarriage families centre on power issues. Identify areas where power or control might be a problem. What difficulties can these issues cause and how might they be avoided?
2. One issue that sometimes arises is the possibility of a stepparent adopting a step-child. What is the law in this regard? Explain the advantages and disadvantages of stepparent adoptions.

PERSONAL ASSIGNMENTS

These questions are designed to help you reflect on your own experience.

1. In stepfamilies you are acquainted with, what factors made for relatively harmonious relationships? Explain why. How do you think such relationships can be encouraged in other families?
2. Often little things, or hassles, are a major source of friction in families. Identify some of these apparently small difficulties that you feel can cause serious problems in stepfamilies. Explain your answer.

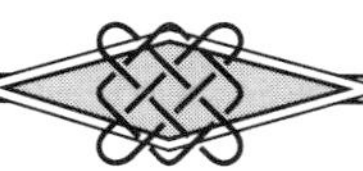

PART 5

Midlife and Beyond

C H A P T E R 1 0

Middle Age and the Empty Nest

O B J E C T I V E S

- To show the place of the middle years as a transition in the family life cycle.
- To explore the transitions that occur for both children and parents during the middle years.
- To describe the stresses on the parents from both the child and grandparent generations.

When I was in my 20s, 40 seemed ridiculously far off — a venerable middle age at which I envisioned myself taking a crash course in bridge and migrating south to avoid the cold. Now, having rocketed to that age zone with astonishing speed, it seems the archetypal middle age about which I was so patronizing isn't quite so venerable after all.

For one thing, the much hyped decline of the body, while not exactly welcome, is neither devastating nor inevitable. Sure, I've had to make the acquaintance of the color technician at the hairdresser and I sport some lines on my face that surprise me every time I pass a mirror. But the overall physical plant is holding up just fine. Good genes may play a part here, but they don't tell the whole story. A better explanation is that I'm representative of the "new middle age," a generation that has radically changed what the 40s look and feel like. I exercise — something I never did in my 20s or even 30s — I eat sensibly and slather on the sunscreen. Happily, I can report that all these efforts really pay off. Without question, I'm in better shape now than I've ever been before.

Lesley Barsky (1990). "40 Something: The New Exciting Middle Age?" *Chatelaine*, January, p. 34.

The middle years of life — for men a time of fulfilment, of reaching the pinnacle of their careers; for women only physical deterioration and uselessness once they have accomplished their mission of bearing and raising children. Any meaning left for their lives is in caring for their husbands and living out their hopes in their grandchildren. This double vision is the result of the traditional view of marriage and family.

In fact, middle age in this sense is a fairly recent idea. For example, Robert and Ann Miller, who lived in the Niagara peninsula in the 1800s, had fourteen children. The oldest was born when Ann was 20, the youngest when she was 45. By the time her youngest daughter was married, Ann Miller was in her sixties. Child rearing consumed about forty-five years of her life. Robert died at the age of 62 when the youngest child was 15. A busy middle age came for the Miller parents somewhere between the last birth and the time most of their children were independent.

With their smaller nuclear families, parents nowadays are usually finished active child rearing earlier in their lives (Table 10.1). Since longevity has increased, people can expect to live longer than their ancestors did. Thus, many years of life (about 13 years) remain after the children have moved out and before retirement (McCullough & Rutenberg, 1988). Population projections show that the number of middle aged will increase by 25 percent from 1987 to 2011 (Figure 10.1). Just as other attitudes about family relations have changed over the last few decades, so have attitudes about the post-child years. Lesley Barsky's comments on turning 40 reflect these new values.

Table 10.1

AVERAGE AGE OF PARENTS WHEN CHILDREN LEAVE HOME

	Male Parent	Female Parent
First child	46.7 years	44.9 years
Last child (2–5 children)	52.9	52.2
Last child (8 or more)	58.0	56.7

Source: From Thomas K. Burch (1985). *Family History Survey: Preliminary Findings*. Ottawa: Statistics Canada, p. 25.

The Family Stress Bomb — The Middle Years

The middle years have now joined child rearing as the longest stage in life. The midlife group is very diverse. Since their ages span twenty to twenty-five years,

Figure 10.1

ONTARIO'S POPULATION AGED 25–54, 1987 TO 2011

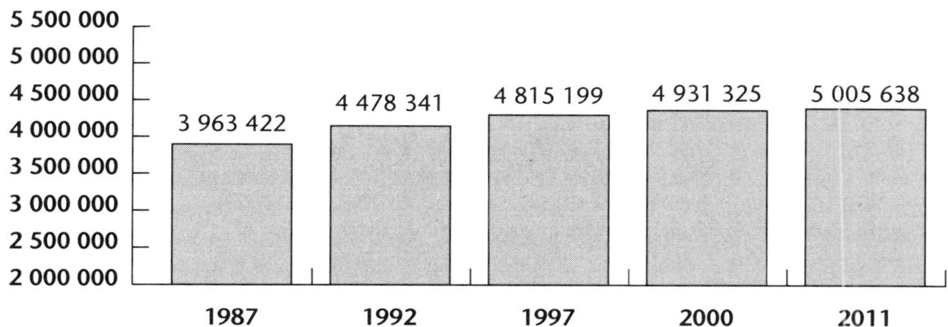

The population aged 25–54 will grow 25% by 2000, and these maturing baby boomers will want retraining so they can respond better to the increased pace of technological change and global competitiveness.

Source: *Looking Forward* (Vision 2000), Vol. 1, No. 2, March 15, 1989.

they may include parents of young children as well as great-grandparents. At the beginning of the midlife period, many will be approaching the peak of their careers, while those at the end will be nearing retirement. Women in this group may have been employed outside the home throughout their adult lives, they may be entering the work force for the first time, or they may be re-entering the work force after a long interval devoted to child rearing. Therefore, any generalizations about this group will fit only parts of the population.

These years of the family life cycle are transitional. There is a shift from active child rearing at the beginning of this stage to the post-child family at the end. This period often marks the splitting of one family into two or more, as children form their own nuclear families. The process involves a major readjustment of the family system. New boundaries must be drawn as to who is a family member. Relationships need to be worked out between the family of origin and the new families of procreation. New roles need to be established to reflect these changes.

Like all major life changes, family adaptation in the middle years contains a series of stressors. A *stressor* is a life event, e.g., parenthood or death, that can produce change in the family system (McCubbin & Patterson, 1983). Losing family members, gaining family members, and any new responsibilities that fall on family members can all act as stressors. How families cope with the stress will probably set the pattern for the quality of the remainder of their lives (F.H. Brown, 1988).

TASKS OF THE PARENT GENERATION

The tasks that confront the parent generation at this stage fall into three groups, all of which involve redrawing the family boundaries and redefining individual roles. First, the relationship with their children changes as they move from adolescence into young adulthood. Parents need to allow their children the freedom to grow up and move out. Once the children have become independent, parents need to learn how to relate to the children as adults rather than as parents and children. As the members of the younger generation begin to form their own families, the parents need to accept new individuals into their extended families. These may include sons- and daughters-in-law, grandchildren, and perhaps step-grandchildren. With these new members come new roles — those of parents-in-law and grandparents.

Second, there is a new focus on the marital relationship. Now that the couple is alone, they must renegotiate their marital system as a dyad, or pair, rather than as part of a larger family system. This process may give rise to new sources of conflict. The role patterns they assumed as a young couple or as parents of young or adolescent children may not reflect their needs in maturity. For instance, they may have avoided talking about problems in the marriage by becoming involved with their children. This buffer is now lost. There may be friction over the reallocation of the functions that were filled by children, e.g., the wife may object to assuming those household tasks that were previously looked after by children, and the husband may feel that the household is her domain.

Third, if any members of the grandparent generation are in ill health, the parents may need to deal with their disability and possible death. At this time, there may be a shift in focus for caregiving activities from children to parents. Again, there may be boundary and role difficulties if the middle-aged adults take over decision-making for their parents.

TASKS OF THE CHILD GENERATION

At the same time as these adjustments are taking place in the parent generation, corresponding changes are occurring in the child generation. They need to differentiate themselves from their family of origin and develop their own values and goals for life. This is the period for developing close peer relationships with both sexes; these may be either friends or potential mates. Young adults also need to establish themselves in the work world so that they can attain financial independence.

Several things can interfere with this process. For example, when young people cannot find employment, it is obviously difficult for them to support themselves. If parents divorce or one is chronically ill or dies while there is an adolescent or young adult in the home, the child may feel obliged to stay and care for one or both parents and siblings in the home. This sense of obligation may hold the young person tightly to the family, instead of allowing the mutual separation of parents and children that is the major life-cycle task (F.H. Brown, 1988).

The Parent Generation at Midlife

As we saw in Chapter 1, when families try to solve problems, they first use methods that have worked in the past. For example, when children are no longer present to do certain household chores, the wife may extend her caregiving activities to include these chores. If the workload becomes too imbalanced, especially if she is newly employed out of the home, she may make demands on her husband to help. If this solution is not effective, the couple may fall into a vicious cycle, or develop some new method of handling household tasks, i.e., develop new rules through the process of *morphogenesis* (Broderick & Smith, 1979). The same process holds true for both practical difficulties and problems in relationships.

One characteristic of the middle years is the re-examination of the individual's life course and family relationships. Just as there are differences in the experiences of men and women, so there are differences in their process of self-evaluation.

MEN AT MIDLIFE

For most men, there are two main areas on which their lives focus: family and work. The middle years are often transitional in both areas. For some men, the strain is so extreme that the period has been dubbed the *midlife crisis*. Daniel Levinson and his colleagues, who studied middle-aged men, describe this period as one of the major transitions of life, along with the early-adult and late-adult transitions (Figure 10.2). As we have seen, all occur at about the same time in the three generations (Levinson, 1978).

Men and work. According to Levinson (1978), a young man forms a dream of what he wishes to accomplish in life. By midlife, it should be apparent whether that dream is attainable. If he has not achieved it, he must alter his plans to fit reality. If he has achieved it, he needs to find another goal to give his life direction. For many in the baby-boom cohort the dream may be an illusion. The members of that generation were socialized to expect that they would achieve more than their parents. Their likelihood of making it into management positions, however, is 10–25 percent less than those of people a little older or a little younger than themselves because of the many people competing for the few available positions. On top of that, recessionary times may bring layoffs instead of promotion. As a result, we can anticipate that this group will experience considerable frustration and anger because their dreams have not been fulfilled (Kettle, 1980).

Often parents have looked forward to having their children become independent so that they will have some financial freedom. This may allow the option of a new job or career. When young people have problems finding work, however, they remain dependent longer, and the parents' hopes do not come to pass.

Figure 10.2

DEVELOPMENTAL PERIODS IN EARLY AND MIDDLE ADULTHOOD

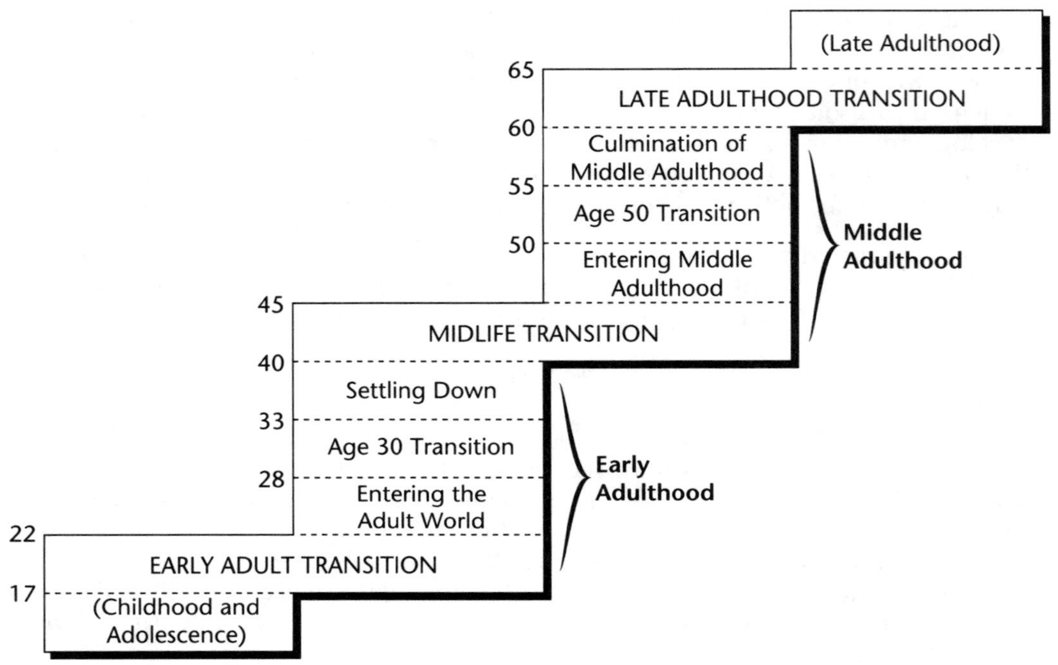

Source: Daniel J. Levinson (1978). *The Seasons of a Man's Life*. New York: Alfred A Knopf, p. 57.

Men and their families. Due to frustrations and disappointments in the realm of work, many men look for satisfaction from their families. Yet these relationships are also undergoing shifts during the middle years. As children become independent, move out, and establish their own families, men are confronted with three dimensions of change in family relationships.

First, they are now moving up one generation. This fact is emphasized if they become grandparents. If their parents die, they become the senior generation. They are obviously becoming older physically. This is underlined by the fact that a number of men die at these ages. So men are faced with the fact that their lives too must end some day, and that day may not be far off. In contrast, in spite of some minor complaints, most still feel vigorous. Some men express this tension in lifestyle changes. Fitness and other aspects of healthy living may concern them. They also may change their style of dress, or acquire the proverbial sports car (Levinson, 1978).

Second, they are faced with the prospect of spending the rest of their lives alone with their wife, without having children as a buffer between them. In addition, she too is growing older and reminds him of his own age. Some men conclude that this relationship is not rewarding, and choose to divorce. Many remarry, often a woman younger than their first wife. Others choose to remain in the marriage. Often, as they adjust to the childless household, there is a shifting of roles of both husband and wife toward greater *androgyny*, or a balance between the masculine and feminine roles. Men at this age often become more concerned with relationships and may give up some of the masculine gender trait of competitiveness. Women, on the other hand, become more interested in achievement. Those couples who stay together and modify their relationship usually experience an increase in marital satisfaction (Campbell, 1989; Levinson, 1978). This is not surprising because, as we saw in Chapter 4, androgynous couples tend to be the happiest.

Third, men's relationships with their children are in transition as they separate from each other. This process may be made more difficult both by the characteristics of the young person, and by pressures from a man's relationship with his parents. Often during the midlife transition, a man's children are adolescents. Their vitality is more likely to arouse envy and resentment than delight and forbearance by their contrast with his own aging process. A man may also be preoccupied with unresolved grievances against his own parents that have resurfaced with their increasing dependency. He may therefore be even more intolerant of the grievances of his children. Some men do maintain contact with youth by becoming a mentor, i.e., they act as a close advisor for someone younger whom they help achieve their life dream. In this way, they make a contribution to society and are involved second-hand in a young man's achievements (Levinson, 1978). Erikson (1982) sees both the involvement with children and the mentor relationship as an expression of the generativeness of adulthood.

WOMEN AND TRANSITIONS AT MIDLIFE

The study of women's transitions at midlife came later than that of men's. Most of the research deals with homemaker wives, since many women currently at or just past middle age were never employed outside the home or spent large segments of time in child rearing. One important issue for these women is the shift in social expectations for women that has occurred during their lifetime. When they were young, it was usual for women to remain in the home. If they worked at all, they did so before children were born, and a small number worked after children were grown. Thus they did not have careers in the same way as their husbands. With the increase today in the number of working wives, there is both pressure on these women to find a job, and a sense of opportunity to become more independent. The women's movement has made women more aware of new possibilities for fulfilment, both within marriage and in the wider world, through work and volunteer activities (McCullough & Rutenberg, 1988).

Maturity often involves integrating the earlier emphasis on social relationships and intimacy with independence and self-determination (Campbell, 1989).

Complicating the issue is the woman's age. Menopause is a marker event with no parallel in men's lives. For those who see a woman's primary fulfilment as motherhood, menopause signals an end to her most rewarding years. In general, women are considered to be old at a younger age than are men. This can affect both their employment and remarriage prospects. Since middle age is usually considered to last from about 40 to 55 years and old age from 65 and beyond, women in their late fifties and early sixties are in a never-never land between the two. This fact itself is stressful (Campbell, 1989).

Like men, women's transitions also involve job and family, but the emphasis is different. In most families, it is the woman who has had the major responsibility for household duties, even if she has been in the work force. As children move out and she is not involved in active child rearing, she may feel liberated. Yet there may also be a sense of loss. Women have been socialized to concentrate on family needs, often at the expense of their own needs (Heller, 1986). If this has been the centre of their lives, children's growing independence leaves them feeling lost and dislocated. The resulting depression and sense of uselessness that women experience is often referred to as the *empty nest syndrome*.

Women, especially mothers, need to find a new centre for their lives. Campbell (1989) refers to this process as a time of personal and sexual identity formation that had been put on hold during the child-rearing years. There are three possible areas for the new focus: the extended family, marriage, and work.

Some women seek to maintain their traditional caregiving roles by either having a last-chance child or by looking after others within the extended family.

FOR BETTER OR FOR WORSE **by Lynn Johnston**

Source: *The Sudbury Star*, 29 September 1990, p. A7.

They may do this through involvement with their children and grandchildren, for example by providing child care while the young parents are at work. Although this arrangement often works well, it can also lead to conflict over child-rearing standards and other control issues. Some women care for their parents or other relatives. In either case there may be problems over where boundaries should be drawn between families.

This may be a time for renewal in marriage. As we have already seen, if the union survives the transition, it is often happier than in the child-rearing years. Women, however, are more likely than men to suffer family breakup. Given the increase in the divorce rate over the last few years, more middle-aged women will suffer personal loss or rejection. Some, of course, will themselves leave marriages that have been unsatisfactory since they no longer have children to hold them there. In addition, about half of all widows are under the age of 60; the majority of these are in their fifties. Thus a woman in midlife is in danger of finding herself without children, husband, sex, and accustomed social and financial support (Campbell, 1989).

A third option is to begin or resume a career. Researchers have found attitudes toward careers differ between mothers and nonmothers. The latter appear to have a life pattern more similar to that of men. Mothers, however, find the forties a liberating time rather than a period of reassessment since they no longer need to be absorbed in child-rearing activities. For them it is a time for career changes or returning to school (Mercer, Nichols, & Doyle, 1989). Unlike the younger women, those in their fifties have difficulty finding jobs, unless they have already been involved in the work force. They may lack marketable skills or recent experience and are at an age when extensive training or education may no longer be practical (Campbell, 1989).

MARRIAGE AND SEXUALITY

Once there are no longer children in the home, the marriage relationship becomes more important. Couples need to review their marriages and often work out new arrangements. This is especially true if children have been the centre of the marriage. If there have been strains between the partners, they are more obvious when there are no longer children to distract attention from them. There can be an imbalance in the marriage as a result of the developmental stages the husband and wife are going through. For example, the husband may want to change the relationship to fit his new values after midlife and the wife may want to cling to the way the marriage has been. If the wife has been a family caregiver, the husband may have difficulties adjusting to the fact that she now wants to concentrate on a career rather than on just the family (McCullough & Rutenberg, 1988).

The sexual relationship of the couple may change. For some couples, there is increased interest. Now that children are grown, there is more private time available and fewer interruptions. Many couples become experimental at this time. After menopause, there is no need to fear pregnancy. Men's slowed response time allows a more relaxed approach, and often more pleasure for the woman. On the other hand, interest may drop off through boredom. One couple who swore off sex spoke of how "the habit of sex" interfered with the companionship they both enjoyed in their marriage (Amiel, 1987). Some couples accept the social stereotype that older people are asexual beings (Hammond, 1987). This goes hand-in-hand with the idea that sexual relations are intended only for procreation. According to this notion, once a woman has passed menopause and there is no possibility for more children, there is no reason for continuing sexual relations.

The Younger Generation — Moving Out, and the Revolving Door

While parents of families are experiencing the transitions of midlife, their children are also going through the early-adult transition. The period from early adolescence to the early twenties is marked by growing independence until finally the young person lives independently and perhaps establishes his or her own nuclear family.

During adolescence and early adulthood, major changes occur in four areas: sexuality, identity, autonomy, and attachment/separation (Preto, 1988).

SEXUALITY

The young person changes physically. The upsurge in sexual thoughts can produce confusion and even fear in all family members. To younger siblings, the adolescent suddenly is no longer the familiar brother or sister they grew up with. Parents may be upset by their children's interest in sexual activity. Many mothers have become upset when they discover their daughters have bought contraceptives. Sometimes the opposite-sex parent has incestuous feelings toward the child. In order to protect against these impulses, there is an increase of conflict with this parent. Conflict with the same-sex parent may arise out of competition. If parents are not open about sexuality or if they themselves are experiencing conflicts and anxieties about their own sexuality, then they are likely to be either too permissive with their children or to set unreasonably strict limits (Preto, 1988).

IDENTITY

During adolescence, young people must shape their own identity (Erikson, 1982). They no longer accept others' views of who they are. The process of identity formation can be very exciting, but it may also be a source of conflict with parents. During the process, young people often question and challenge their parents' rules and standards for behaviour. At times, they may criticize parents for being hypocritical, since the standards they set out for their children are different from the way they have actually lived. This challenge from their children may come at the same time as the adults are evaluating their own lives and questioning their own values, and can be an added source of conflict and stress (Preto, 1988).

AUTONOMY

Adolescents need to learn to be responsible for their own decisions. Many parents have difficulty achieving a balance between trying to control the young person and allowing sufficient opportunity to make decisions, even if they are wrong. This is especially hard if they feel that they are being judged by their own children.

ATTACHMENT, SEPARATION, AND LOSS

The move of the young person away from the family toward the peer group, and eventually toward an intimate relationship with another individual, is often felt as a loss by the family. The other members are no longer needed in the same way as they were when the child was younger. Some families respond to this sense of loss by being overprotective and overcontrolling. In others, the young person may be forced to leave before he or she is really ready so that this stage can be over and done with.

Parents must learn to relate to their grown children as adults. The parent generation also needs to develop flexible family boundaries to allow young people to leave, and to welcome their sons' and daughters' partners and children into the extended family (McCullough & Rutenberg, 1988).

THE NOT-SO-EMPTY NEST

Young adulthood used to be almost synonymous with moving out and living on your own. This was part of growing up. In fact, from 1971 to 1981, a growing number of unmarried men and women in their twenties chose to live alone or with nonrelatives (Boyd & Pryor, 1989). Recently, however, a new trend has emerged. From 1981 to 1986, there was a noticeable increase in the number of unattached young adults aged 20–29 who continued to live with their parents. (See Table 10.2.)

There seem to be a number of reasons for this change. One is related to the fact that young people are now getting married later. Single young adults have two options: to live with their parents or to live somewhere else. More are choosing to continue to live with their parents or to return home after a period of being on their own. Thus there is a longer transitional period from child rearing to the empty nest. Why do young adults choose to live at home? More young adults now are in full-time post-secondary education than in the mid-1970s. During a recession, finding and keeping a job that pays enough to allow independent living is difficult. In 1986, fully 43 percent of the unemployed youth in Calgary lived with their parents (Table 10.3) (City of Calgary, 1986). Since many of these young adults are the younger members of the baby boom, larger numbers are competing for fewer jobs. In addition, the cost of establishing a separate household can be extremely high, especially in urban areas like Toronto or Vancouver

Table 10.2

PERCENTAGE OF UNMARRIED PERSONS AGED 15–34 LIVING WITH PARENTS

	Men		Women	
Age	**1981**	**1986**	**1981**	**1986**
15–19	91.9	92.0	90.5	91.4
20–24	68.1	71.2	59.3	63.3
25–29	40.0	44.6	27.2	31.6
30–34	27.8	28.8	17.1	17.7

Source: Monica Boyd and Edward T. Pryor (1989). "Young Adults Living in Their Parents' Homes," *Canadian Social Trends*, Summer, p. 18.

(Boyd & Pryor, 1989). Similar trends were reported in Nova Scotia in the late 1800s. The young adults then were the product of another baby boom, and began hunting for jobs during another recession. Men did not marry until the age of 27 or later. There were also differences from the situation today. Most of the families lived on farms and could provide work and maintenance for their unmarried young adults. Those choosing employment and independence (more often men than women) had to leave the area to find work (Brookes, 1982).

Different life courses may produce similar effects in the late teens and early twenties. One group of young adults continue their education; during this period, they may continue living at home. Others become pregnant at a young age, and continue to live at home with their children (Fulmer, 1988). Often the middle-aged (or younger) grandmother takes over full care of the grandchild (Heller, 1986). Eventually the young woman marries or moves in with a partner, sometimes after she has had another child. In either case, the young adult does not move out of the parents' home until the middle or late twenties.

Some young people move away from home and come back again, a phenomenon that has been called *the revolving door*. This return may be the result of job loss, poor employment prospects, or marriage breakdown. In the latter case, both the child and grandchildren may move in, and the grandparents are often faced with renewed child-care responsibilities to allow their adult child to enter the work force (Schlesinger, 1989).

Having children continue living at home or returning home as young adults can be stressful for parents and means a new adjustment of roles, since the old parent-child ones may now be inappropriate. This situation may interfere with their own plans. If their marriage is difficult, the return may create extra strains, which might be the final straw before a complete breakdown. There are many

Table 10.3

RESPONDENTS' EMPLOYMENT STATUS BY LIVING ARRANGEMENTS (PERCENT OF EMPLOYED AND UNEMPLOYED)

	Employment Status	
Living Arrangements	**% of Employed***	**% of Unemployed***
Alone	10	13
Parent(s)	35	43
Sibling(s)	33	28
Other relative(s)	2	17[1]
Spouse (including common-law)	15	18
Children	10	17
Friend(s) (including boy/girlfriend)	23	7[1]
Roommate(s)	5	5
Other	0	2

*Percentages total more than 100 because respondents could be living with more than one class of individual.

[1]Denotes a statistically significant difference (≤.05) between employed and unemployed youth.

Source: City of Calgary Social Services Department (1986). *The Effect of Youth Unemployment in Calgary.* Calgary: Author, p. 26.

practical issues which arise in this situation: privacy for both parents and adult children, the use of the family car, family rules and regulations, sharing of expenses, the use of the house for parties and other forms of socializing. The whole situation is ambiguous. On the one hand, parents feel the need to maintain control of their own home. On the other, the adult "children" have a need to control their own lives (Schlesinger, 1989). In fact, the revolving door has become so common that there are now how-to books on coping with adult children who return home (for example, Okimoto & Stegall, 1987).

The Sandwich Generation

At the same time as middle-aged individuals are experiencing pressure from their in-and-out children, they may also be trying to cope with the fact that their parents are aging and need assistance. As we shall see in the next chapter, the conflict between the need for help on the part of infirm elderly parents and their desire for independence is similar in some ways to adolescent-parent conflicts. Thus the middle generation is subject to stress from both the younger and older generations. Benjamin Schlesinger (1989) refers to this as the *sandwich generation*.

Although most elderly people live by themselves or with a spouse, they tend to live near relatives. As their age increases and their health declines, they become more dependent on their children for assistance and are, in fact, more likely to live with a child (City of Calgary, 1983; National Advisory Council on Aging, 1983). The burden of caring for elderly parents tends to fall on women. Middle-aged and older women provide most of the home health care. In some ways the daughters of sick parents are needed at home almost as much as mothers of preschool children. Women also provide part-time health care to aged relatives living elsewhere, even to those living in nursing homes (Heller, 1986). In addition, many families provide assistance such as shopping, home maintenance, and home care. Even when adult children do not provide many actual services for a parent, they may be involved in the time-consuming and frustrating task of locating required help. There may be a problem with increasing demands placed on the middle-aged child so that she feels she cannot do enough for a parent, and becomes plagued with a sense of guilt. If she does do enough, she may come to resent the demands. If she cannot admit to resentment, she may eventually experience burnout (Rhodes, 1989).

The Social Time Clock

In our society, many aspects of life are governed by age. For example, there are minimum ages at which one can begin school, drive, drink alcohol, or vote. Marriage and family life are also affected by legal restrictions, e.g., individuals wishing to marry have to reach a certain age to do so without their parents' consent. There is also a minimum age for marriage with parents' consent. People who wish to adopt usually have to be over a given age, and children being adopted must consent to their adoptions at ages varying from 7 to 12 years depending on the jurisdiction.

There are also social norms for life events. People say things like "I was young when I had my first baby," and "I was pretty old when I graduated from school," or "She was widowed very early." These statements indicate that we expect certain events to occur at a particular time in life.

Distinctions between life periods have become blurred (Neugarten & Neugarten, 1986). It is very difficult, for example, to define when middle age begins or when old age takes over. Yet people are more likely to experience a crisis if life events occur "off time" (McGoldrick & Gerson, 1985). There are social scripts, i.e., expected patterns of behaviour, for these events. People can anticipate them and think about what they will do when the time comes. For instance,

A GRANDMOTHER AT 27

Most women don't expect to become grandmothers until they are in their 40s or 50s. But some women become grandmothers in their late 20s or early 30s when their daughters, products of teenage pregnancies themselves, become teenage mothers.

To see how young grandmothers handle their out-of-sync roles, sociologist Linda Burton interviewed mothers, grandmothers and great-grandmothers from black working-class families in Southern California. Eighteen of the grandmothers were in their late 20s through their late 30s; 23 were "on-time" grandmothers in their 40s and 50s.

Burton compared the responses of the early grandmothers with the "on-time" grandmothers and found that women who became grandmothers later in life were happier with their roles. They were more likely to have established careers, as well as the time and money to spend on their grandchildren. Most of those who became grandmothers at a youthful age felt that they were too young to be grandmothers, did not like the "old" connotation it bestowed on them and resented being saddled with a grandchild when they wanted to get on with their lives.

One 28-year-old grandmother told Burton, "I could break my daughter's neck for having this baby. I just got a new boyfriend. Now he will think I'm too old. It was bad enough being a mother so young — now a grandmother too!"

Since many of the teenage mothers were too immature to care for their babies, they turned them over to their mothers, as their mothers had done with them. But quite a few of the young grandmothers refused to care for their grandchildren and instead handed them over to their mothers. So these great-grandmothers — the youngest was 46 years old — found themselves caring for the babies of the granddaughters they had also raised.

Not surprisingly, some great-grandmothers were unhappy with this situation. One 56-year-old told Burton, "My daughter and granddaughter keep making these babies and expect me to take care of them. I ain't no nursemaid; I ain't old; and I ain't dead yet." The burden was especially hard on great-grandmothers in five-generation families who were also caring for their ailing parents.

Burton did find a few young grandmothers who were content with their roles. One 38-year-old mother who was caring for seven children at home felt that the addition of a grandchild was no burden at all. "This baby has only added joy to my life... I take pride in being a grandmother."

And a 91-year-old great-great-great-grandmother, who gave birth to her first child at age 14, likes the idea of being able to meet and know the many generations of her family that followed her. "Then you have more people to look out behind you when you [are] old like me."

Source: Elizabeth Stark (1986). *Psychology Today,* October, p. 18.

parents can look forward to and plan for the "empty nest." If, however, the children do not leave home at the socially appropriate time, both parents and adult children experience stress. Widowhood at age 35 is more of a crisis than at 65. Becoming a grandmother at 27 may be a crisis, but becoming one at 60 may be impatiently anticipated.

Strains of the Middle Years

The major theme of the middle years is the triple transition within the extended family. The main focus in young adulthood is separation from the family of origin; in late adulthood, there is increasing dependence on their children; the middle-aged generation is pulled between separating from the young and accepting more responsibility for the old. In the process family boundaries must be redrawn and family roles redefined. For many, it is a time of extreme stress.

With the need for both greater education and reduced opportunity for employment, young people are remaining for longer periods in their parents' homes. There is no prescribed role for these young people and no specific marker event to label them as adults; therefore there is increased stress on all family members. Society as a whole needs to rethink the place of young adults within the family.

Another issue is how to make the middle years fulfilling, especially for women. This issue is particularly relevant for those who have never, or have only temporarily, been in the workplace. There is now an increasing number of single women, especially the separated and divorced. They do not have families who require their attention. Psychological and financial independence can be an important issue during the middle years. Since many younger women are now employed outside the home, problems in this area may not be as pressing in coming years.

To conclude, the transitions of the middle years are a source of stress. However, they open the possibility of building more satisfactory relationships on which to base the rest of life.

SUMMARY

THE MIDDLE YEARS. The middle years are a time of transition, marked by a shift from active child rearing to the post-child family. This life stage has emerged fairly recently as the result of smaller families and the shorter time span devoted to raising children. The major task facing adults is the formation of new family boundaries and redefinition of roles for both the parent and child generation.

THE PARENT GENERATION AT MIDLIFE. During this time, middle-aged adults often re-examine their life course and family relationships. Men tend to focus on two areas.

In the realm of work they may question whether they can achieve their goals, or if they should change them. In relation to the family, they realize that they are moving up one generation and have a sense that they are aging, especially as they look at their maturing children. They also face the prospect of spending the rest of their life alone with the same wife. As a result there is a greater concern with relationships. Middle-aged women experience the shift of changing social expectations for women away from homemaker toward career person. It is a source of both pressure and opportunity. Some of those who mourn the end of their child-rearing days, in the so-called "empty nest syndrome," continue caregiving in other ways. This is also a time of either renewal of the marriage or its dissolution through divorce or death. If the marriage survives, the couple's sexual relationship may change, either becoming more satisfying or diminishing.

THE YOUNGER GENERATION. During the adolescent and early adult years, the younger generation is moving away from their parents. This occurs in a variety of ways: by seeking to establish an identity, by being responsible for their decisions, by shifting toward the peer group and away from the family of origin, and by forming an intimate relationship. There are obstacles, however, to living independently, such as later marriage, employment difficulties, single parenthood, and marriage breakdown with a return to the parents' home. When young people move back home, there may be friction over rules, privacy, and appropriate roles.

SANDWICH GENERATION. Middle-aged adults may become caught between the continuing dependency of their children and the increasing disability of their parents. The pressure may be increased by off-time events such as the pregnancy of an adolescent daughter. The burden of providing care for both young and old tends to fall on women. The middle years are marked by triple transitions within the extended family which may produce high levels of stress as the members attempt to adjust

KEY TERMS

androgyny: balance of masculine and feminine characteristics in one's personality

empty nest syndrome: the depression and sense of uselessness some women experience when the last child leaves home

midlife crisis: extreme strain as a person re-evaluates his or her life in middle age

morphogenesis: developing new forms of behaviour

revolving door: young people's repeated moving in and out of their parents' home

sandwich generation: middle-aged adults who experience the stress of continuing dependency of their children and increasing disability of their parents

social time clock: the period in which it is believed life events ought to occur in a particular society

stressor: a life event which can produce change in the family system

CLASS ASSIGNMENTS

Complete one or both of the following assignments, as directed by your instructor.

1. Explore the opportunities for education and retraining available in your community for women in their forties and fifties. How likely are they to find employment? In what fields? Explain.
2. How is midlife different for people who have children when in their late thirties or forties? Think about couples with afterthought children, remarried couples wanting a child of the second marriage, and single parents who become pregnant or adopt.

PERSONAL ASSIGNMENTS

These assignments are designed to help you look at your own family experiences.

1. Thinking about your experience or that of someone you know, explain both the advantages and disadvantages of the revolving door, i.e., of children moving in and out of their parents' home.
2. Who looks after older relatives in your family? Describe both the frustrations and rewards.

CHAPTER 11

Grey Power and the Sunset Years

OBJECTIVES

- To look at aging and death in relation to the family life cycle.
- To examine the lifestyle and family relationships of younger and older elderly people, including variations among minority groups.
- To discuss the implications of terminal illness and death for family members.
- To explore policy issues around services for the elderly.

When is Old??
When is old?
When you're 20 it's 40
But 40 can be naughty.
At 30 it's 50
But at 70
50 is nifty.

At 40, 60 is a sage
But 80 says
60 is a wonderful age.

Wherever you are
it's on the way
But definitely
it's not today.

Janet Neuman (1983). In *Guidebook for Intergenerational Planning*. Toronto: Ministry of Tourism and Recreation, p. 3.

What Is Old?

The elderly — almost immediately the popular image springs before our eyes: we see Granny in a rocking chair, she is plump and soft, her hair is pulled back into a bun, and she spends her time knitting for family members. Popular mythology paints a picture of the three-generation family of the past, where parents, children, and grandparents lived together in a large cooperative family. Both these stereotypes are deceptive.

In fact, these images do not and never did fit the realities of most Canadian families and their older members. We need only look at statistics to understand why. In the past, many people did not live to old age. i.e., to what we usually consider normal retirement age — 65 years (Table 11.1). Those who did usually chose to live near, not with, other family members. Three-generation families have always been a minority in Canadian society. When such households existed, they resulted either from the control the oldest generation kept over land or from the financial and physical dependence of the aged on their children (Baker, 1988; Connidis, 1989). Both are situations where there can be extreme conflict. In fact, past generations were aware of this potential for conflict, as we can tell from the will of Robert Miller of South Grimsby Township, Ontario. He carefully outlines just what rights his widow will have in the house she will share with their youngest son.

The image of Granny in the rocking chair is also deceptive. Most societies have what is referred to as a "social time clock" (Neugarten & Neugarten, 1986). This reflects the age range in which certain life events are "supposed" to happen. As a very simple example, think of children starting school. If they start at a very early age or at a late age, parents are often called upon to explain why. The time

Table 11.1

PROJECTED LIFE EXPECTANCY

Year	Women	Men
1931	62	60
1961	74	68
1986	80	73
2011	84*	77*

*Assumptions in latest projections

Source: Statistics Canada data. In *Royal Bank Reporter,* Winter 1989, p. 3.

THE ELDERLY IN THE PAST

The following is an excerpt from the will of Robert Miller, a farmer from South Grimsby Township, Ontario, dated February 1, 1871. He died March 26, 1871, aged 63 years, 11 months.

"I give and bequeath unto my Wife Ann Miller, in addition to Her legal claims of Dower all my household furniture of every kind including beds and bedding, Stoves and pipes, wearing apparel, including the Geese, the fowl, the bees and Two Cows, Two Sheep, and Two Hogs to choose any She likes, and feed for them through the Winter. I also give unto her One half of the growing Wheat to be given to Her in clean grain, One third of the Apples and also all the wood She wants for house use, To have free access to the well at all times and to any or all the buildings about the premises. My said wife to have the free and exclusive use of the front door, Yard, and Three rooms in the front part of the House."

Sixty acres and the building were left to Robert Miller's youngest son, with the understanding he would support his two youngest sisters, aged fifteen and seventeen until they were married or of age.

clock for becoming old is less clear-cut, but it still exists. As a result, life events that occur "on time" usually seem less traumatic than those that come too early or too late. For example, widowhood is probably less of a crisis for the woman who is 65 than for the one who is 30. When events such as retirement and grandparenthood come at expected ages, they can be prepared for mentally.

Dimensions of Aging

Our society recognizes several aspects of becoming old: chronological, biological, psychological, and social (Baker, 1988). All are involved with our notions of the social time clock.

1. CHRONOLOGICAL AGE. *Chronological age* is the number of years a person has lived. Certain privileges and responsibilities go along with age, e.g., receiving a pension or having to take an annual driving test.

Does old age begin at retirement? If so, does that mean we now become old sooner than in the past? Retirement age has been decreasing over the last few decades. In the 1950s, nearly 20 percent of the population over 65 years of age were employed. By 1986, only 7 percent of the elderly were working. The change can be credited mainly to improved pension plans, which make it financially possible for people to retire younger (Methot, 1987). With options for early retirement now available, many people leave their employment at ages from 55 to 64 years. Obviously, most are not ready for the rocking chair or the nursing home.

Many people who write about old age use 65 years as the cut-off mark. In fact, 65 is a relatively new standard. For example, in 1952 the government old-age pension was given to all residents over the age of 70. It was not until 1966 that the age was lowered to 65 (Baker, 1988). Prior to the establishment of pension plans, many aging people worked as long as they could. For many, to admit that they were so old and weak that they could not work meant becoming dependent on their children or on charity.

2. PHYSICAL AGE. Physical changes occur during the aging process. White hair, wrinkles, and slowing movements are often equated with old age. These changes affect how we perceive ourselves and how others treat us; as a result they also affect our self-esteem. There are sex and class differences in how physical changes are regarded. Men in professional and managerial positions are considered to have greater knowledge based on experience; grey hair is thus a mark of distinction. On the other hand, men who do manual labour or play sports professionally see physical aging as a sign of failing ability. Aging can be an even greater crisis for women, especially if they have depended on physical attractiveness to fill esteem needs (Baker, 1988). If we are to believe television commercials, instead of becoming distinguished, women become only wrinkled and old.

Some social scientists suggest that old age begins when physical disability sets in. If we use this standard, we would have to exclude many people in their seventies or even eighties because they still remain vigorous (Neugarten & Neugarten, 1986).

3. PSYCHOLOGICAL AGE. Other people argue that old age is a frame of mind, i.e., that old age is defined psychologically. They point to "old" behaviour such as grandmother sitting in the rocking chair knitting. Attitude differences between the elderly and the not-so-old can be explained in part, of course, by the experience the former have gained by moving through the life cycle. Some characteristics are cohort effects (Baker, 1988), i.e., they are most likely the result of being raised during particular historical events such as the Great Depression and World War II, and of the values that were prevalent during their early lives. Yet, it is difficult to find qualities that are characteristic of most elderly. They show more differences than similarities, as do much younger people.

4. SOCIAL AGE. Aging also has a social aspect. This is related to cultural norms, which specify how we should act when we are a certain age and how we should interact with people older and younger than ourselves (Baker, 1988). The boundaries between periods of life are, however, becoming blurred. The timing of marker events such as retirement, grandparenthood, and widowhood are changing. On the one hand, many people see earlier retirement as a desirable goal; on the other, there are attacks on mandatory retirement at a specific age. Since

women have first children as early as 12 or as late as 45, there is also a wide range in the age at which they become grandparents. Women born during the 1800s could expect to be widows in their late fifties; the corresponding figure today is almost 70 (Gee, 1987; Neugarten & Neugarten, 1986). As a result, our expectations of appropriate behaviour are also changing. Retirement, for example, has lost its link with physical frailty. Grandmother also is probably not in her rocking chair; she is more likely to remain actively involved with her family and in the community.

Since people are now living longer than they used to, they are more likely to survive to ages where they can experience later life-cycle stages. When the average person died at the age of 60, many did not experience retirement or grandparenthood. In our society, women are more likely to experience life changes because they tend to live longer than men (Gee, 1987). More generations have the opportunity to know each other now than in the past. This fact can also create problems over who is eligible to fill certain age-related roles. One study of five-generation families found that there was some confusion as to who had the rights and privileges of old age (Hagestad, 1986). Was it the very oldest, who were in their eighties and nineties? If so, where did it leave their children, who were in their sixties and seventies (an age often considered "old")? Traditionally children keep an eye out for their parents and provide assistance to them, even if they do not live together. In these five-generation families, elderly people were looking out for still more elderly parents and were missing out on the benefits of old age themselves.

Figure 11.1

PERCENTAGE CHANGE OF POPULATION FOR SELECTED AGE GROUPS, CANADA, 1961 TO 1986

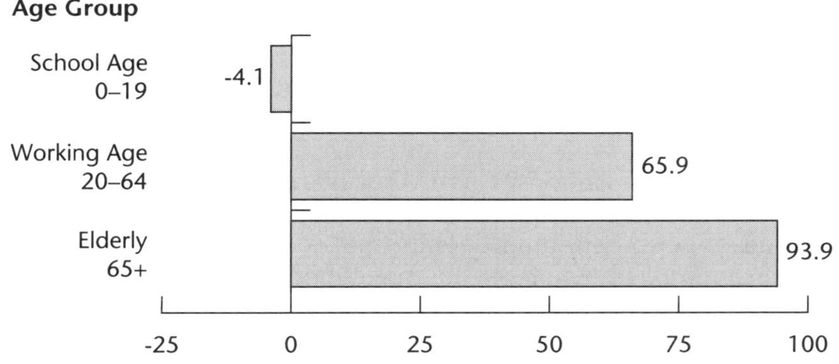

Source: Census of Canada, 1961 and 1986. In *Human Settlements in Canada: Trends and Policies 1981–1986*. Ottawa: Canada Mortgage and Housing Corporation, 1987, p. 10.

Increased longevity has resulted in new terminology for the older members of our society. Sociologists are beginning to describe individuals over 65 as young-old (65–74 years), middle-old (75–84 years), and old-old (85 years and over).

In spite of some vagueness as to when old age really begins, one fact is clear: the population of Canada is becoming older. This is the combined effect of a number of factors. As we have seen, people are living longer. In a few years, the oldest members of the baby-boom bulge will be starting to retire and will swell the number of seniors. Since the birth rate is down, there are fewer young members of Canadian society to offset the increase among the elderly. In fact, the North American population is aging faster than the European population because the birth rate is lower on this continent (Dumas, 1987). It is obvious that the increasing proportion of older people in Canada will have far-reaching effects on our social and political institutions.

Developmental Tasks of Old Age

As members age, the family faces important changes and adjustments in both family systems and roles. The key task for older people is accepting the shift of roles to allow the next generation to take over leadership in various areas of private and public life. This task involves a number of smaller changes. As people retire, they make room for younger ones to take over management jobs. Grandparents usually do not have the primary responsibility for raising the new generation of children. Nevertheless, older people have a vital role in providing both moral support and practical help to the middle generation as its members take over the central position. Their children, however, must in turn value the wisdom and experience of the elderly without taking over the day-to-day tasks of living that their parents and grandparents can still manage. The older generation must also adapt to their own physical decline. They must deal with the loss of spouse, brothers and sisters, and friends and acquaintances. Ultimately they must prepare for their own death (Carter & McGoldrick, 1988).

Erik Erikson (1963) describes the psychosocial task of old age as integrity vs. despair. As individuals look back on their lives, they look for order and meaning. Each society has its own definition of what makes a good life; thus the kind of meaning a person finds in his or her life may differ from one society to another, but the attempt to find meaning is common to all. Without a sense that life has had meaning and purpose, i.e., integrity, an individual sinks into a final despair. Time is now too short to start another life in order to make some mark on the world. With a sense that life has had meaning, on the other hand, a person need not fear death.

The "Young" Old

Any division of people into categories of old age such as "young-old" or "old-old" is artificial. Many of the variations among individuals have more to do with functioning than with age itself. Decisions and events that occur earlier in life can also make major differences in the lifestyles of the elderly and in their options for the future. For example, a man who has a first child at the age of 25 may well be a grandfather, possibly even a great-grandfather, at 65. On the other hand, a man who has a child when he is in his fifties will have parenting responsibilities that will continue into his old age.

ECONOMIC FACTORS

In the past, pensions were often not available. Even when employers offered contributory plans, they were often optional. Under such circumstances, men continued to work as long as they were able. If they had a large enough income, they were able to put aside money for retirement. Otherwise, they were dependent on the support of their children or, at the extreme, of the community. In 1951, the Old Age Security Act provided for pensions for all Canadians aged at least 70. From 1966, most workers have been covered by either the Canada Pension Plan or the Quebec Pension Plan. In addition, many employers now offer private plans and individuals can set up their own Registered Retirement Savings Plans. It has become economically feasible for larger parts of the population to enjoy travel and other leisure activities following retirement. In fact, they are sometimes referred to as "Woopies" — well-off older people (Royal Bank, 1989).

Retirement age has fallen over the years. Many pension plans are set up so that the employee may take early retirement and still have an adequate income. Some individuals making this choice go on to second careers or to fulfilling forms of humanitarian service, including volunteer work.

In spite of these changes, there are still many inequities in pensions, and it is women who are disadvantaged (Cohen, 1984). Most pensions are related to the individual's earnings. Women usually do not work as many years as men; they may take time off to care for children. Many retire at the same time as their older husbands (City of Calgary, 1983). Women often earn less when they do work. Pensions continue the inequities in pay. More women than men work part-time or work in service occupations where there are no pensions. The Old Age Security pension and its accompanying income supplement were never designed to be the sole source of income in old age. Yet many women live below the poverty line since the government pension is the only one they have.

A divorced woman may be at a further disadvantage, especially if her husband has remarried. Canada Pension Plan, for example, will pay widow's benefits to only one spouse or former spouse. This policy may mean that a wife of many years will be passed over in favour of her short-term successor.

Figure 11.2

WHY PEOPLE RETIRED

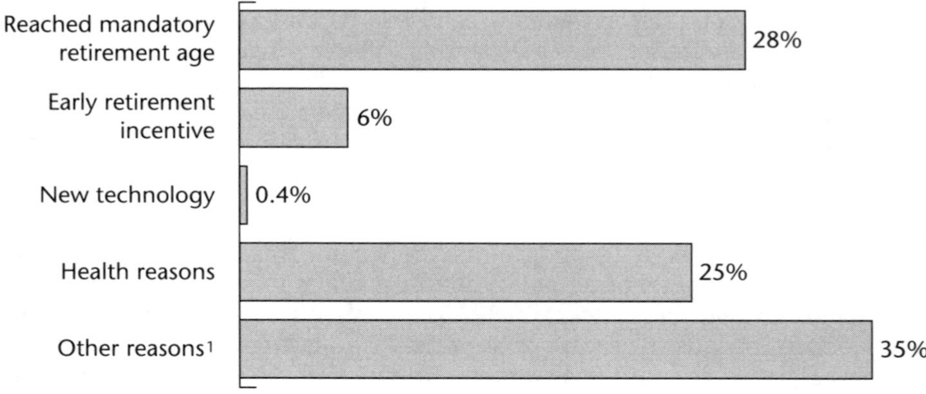

[1]Includes personal choice; marriage or family responsibilities.
Source: Statistics Canada. General Social Survey, 1989. In Graham S. Lowe (1992). "Canadians and Retirement," *Canadian Social Trends,* Autumn, p. 21.

ACTIVITIES AND INTEREST

State of health is an important factor in the amount of activity people undertake. Most of the "young-old" are still in good health. In fact, the older man who feels he is reasonably healthy is more likely to be satisfied with his life. Although good health is also important for women's outlook on life, they tend to value the relationship with their children; if it is satisfying, then life is satisfying (Baker, 1988).

Retirement usually marks a major change in activities. This can be a problem for those who define their value as individuals by their occupations. The disappearance of meaningful job roles, the sense of not being productive, and the loss of workplace relationships can lead to a loss of self-esteem (National Advisory Council on Aging, 1983; Walsh, 1988). Working women may not feel as much displacement as men, since many of them continue the homemaking role for which they have been responsible during their working years. On the other hand, many individuals feel that working is a burden, but that it is necessary for survival. For these, retirement is a welcome opportunity to spend their time in more enjoyable activities.

A husband's retirement can mean important changes for a woman. Some homemaker wives complain of having a man underfoot all day when they have been used to being alone and directing their own time. The couple needs to renegotiate their areas of responsibility. If they do not work out a comfortable arrangement, then there may be an increase in marital conflict. In his search for something to do, for instance, a man may start to take over household responsibilities that have been an important source of his wife's self-esteem. Some working wives also choose to retire early when their husbands do, so that retirement demands a double adjustment.

FAMILY RELATIONSHIPS

For older people, as for younger, family relationships depend on a number of factors. First, a person must have relatives in order to have any interaction. Obviously, a man cannot have a spousal relationship if he has no wife. Second, the frequency and variety of contact matter. Does a woman see her children once a week or once every six months? How often do they phone each other? Third are the possibilities for providing, receiving, and exchanging services and aid. If an individual has no money or is in poor health, then it is difficult to provide financial help or physical assistance in cleaning or babysitting. Finally, the quality of family relationships is important. This aspect can include mutual affection and shared opinions and values. It is possible for relatives who see each other on a daily basis to spend the time fighting or belittling each other. There may actually be a closer relationship with someone who has less frequent contact (Connidis, 1989; Rosenthal, 1987).

1. Spouse. The majority of older people live with a family member, especially a spouse. Many of those who are married report a high level of marital satisfaction (Baker, 1988; Connidis, 1989; Lupri & Frideres, 1981). Marriages that have survived to this point may have fewer pressures on them — no teenagers in the house, more time for each other, a more relaxed attitude toward life, and men's desire for greater emotional connectedness.

More men than women over the age of 65 are married. This fact results mainly from women's longer lifespan — 49 percent of women aged 65 and over are widowed compared with 14 percent of men. An increasing number of women are divorced. For a number of reasons, more widowed and divorced men than women remarry. Men more than women depend on their spouse for social and emotional support. Women have more close relationships with others since they are the ones who usually keep up contact with relatives. Thus they are not dependent on a spouse for emotional support. There are also more eligible women available than men because men tend to die earlier; so it is easier for men to find a new partner (Baker, 1988; Connidis, 1989). Adult children may also play a role in remarriage. Some may actively discourage remarriage because they see it as disloyalty to the deceased parent or because they are worried about their inheritance. Certain economic and legal constraints, such as pensions that are discontinued on remarriage, may make marriage financially disastrous. The easing of attitudes toward cohabitation may also contribute to the increase of older as well as younger people living together without marriage (Walsh, 1988).

2. Children. Most older people (80 percent) have at least one living child. Like people now in their child-rearing years, a sizable proportion have just one or two children (Connidis, 1989). At least one of these children lives quite close to the parents so that most older people see one of their children at least once a week. Usually contact is made by telephone, followed in frequency by personal visits and letter writing. Those who live nearby have shorter but more frequent visits than those who live at a distance (City of Calgary, 1983). The closest relationship is usually between mothers and daughters (Connidis, 1989), partly because women are seen as "kin-keepers," i.e., they have the responsibility of keeping up contacts with relatives (Hagestad, 1986).

The parent-child relationship is not one-sided; rather, they help each other. For example, adult children may provide practical assistance in house and yard maintenance. When adult children have crises such as divorce, widowhood, or the birth of a child with health problems, parents are key providers of support (Connidis, 1989; Vadasy et al., 1986). Financial aid can flow in either direction.

3. Grandchildren. The relationship between grandparents and grandchildren is often considered special because it is not complicated by the responsibilities and conflicts of being a parent. Over three-quarters of those aged over 65 years have at least one grandchild (over 90 percent of those with children). Unlike the relationship with grown children, the emotional closeness is affected by how near grandchildren live to grandparents and how often they see one another (Connidis, 1989). Being grandparents or great-grandparents can give the elderly a new lease on life since they see a part of themselves that will survive. Having grandchildren is also an opportunity to come to terms with both the satisfactions and disappointments of raising one's own children, and adds the pleasure of seeing them experience the fulfilment of being parents (Vadasy et al., 1986).

The impact of divorce on grandparents has only recently received much recognition. The relationship between grandparents and their adult children is important, because the latter control access to the grandchildren. This connection is doubly important if the child's ex-spouse has custody of the grandchildren. Grandparents can have both positive and negative effects in these circumstances. They can provide support and a haven for grandchildren when problems at home are too difficult to live with. Yet they can be drawn into the conflict between the estranged spouses or try to play grandchildren against parent(s). The expectation that they be a resource for the family but do not interfere can be a burden for some seniors. Often family counselling ignores grandparents, although they may play a vital role in family interactions. Information concerning right of access to grandchildren, even when there has been an ongoing relationship, may not be readily available. If this is cut off, both grandparents and grandchildren may lose an important emotional resource (Ontario Advisory Council on Senior Citizens, 1989; Walsh, 1988).

4. Siblings. Most older people have at least one living brother or sister. Usually, there is less interaction with siblings than with children and grandchildren. As might be expected, those who have never married and the childless widowed are especially dependent on siblings, who appear to hold third or fourth rank in relationships. When they do associate, they seem drawn together by interest rather than by the sense of obligation that is true for parents and children (Connidis, 1989). In general, however, little is known about sibling relationships among adults.

GAY MEN

There are apparently few differences in adjustment to old age between homosexual and heterosexual men. As with elderly males in general, the life satisfaction of elderly gay men is connected to how they perceive their state of health. One study (Lee, 1987) found that 38 percent of elderly gay males had been married at some time and 13 percent of those over 50 were still living with their wives. Most had married before 1960, when there was a great deal of stigma against homosexuality. The few who remained married reported being afraid of a lonely old age. Their marital status was not, however, related to life satisfaction because there were major differences in the level of conflict in their marriages. As might be expected, those with a lover, especially a live-in lover, were the most satisfied. Friends tended to substitute for family members as the main source of social support.

There are few guidelines as to how gay males should behave in old age. Those who had role models of successful gay aging tended to be happier than those who did not. There is little data available regarding aging lesbians so that we have not included them in our discussion.

The "Old" Old

HEALTH AND SELF-CARE

As people grow older, physical well-being and concern about possible or actual illness become more important. This is realistic. Those over the age of 75 are more likely than younger people to have a chronic health problem (City of Calgary, 1983). Physical and mental deterioration can be made worse if an individual becomes depressed, feels helpless, and fears losing control over his or her life. Loss of hope can lead an individual to give up (Walsh, 1988).

Catherine Hill (1984) studied fifty elderly people in Guelph, Ontario, who were unable to live on their own. In most cases, their children began to look after them because they were sick and needed nursing care (38 percent) or because they were alone and needed comfort and emotional support (36 percent). Often this care continued much longer than the caregiver, usually a daughter, had

FOR BETTER OR FOR WORSE **by Lynn Johnston**

Source: Lynn Johnston (1987). *It's All Downhill From Here*. Kansas City: Andrews and McMeel, p. 110.

expected. Often the caregiving ended when the mental or physical health of the elder made it impossible for the family to cope any longer. Some aspects of chronic illness can be extremely difficult to live with, e.g., a person who has sleep disturbance and roams the house during the night, is incontinent, makes delusional statements, or behaves aggressively (Walsh, 1988). When an elder entered an institution, it did not mean that family contacts were cut off. Some women actually went to the nursing home every day to feed or provide other care for a parent.

Whether seniors live in their own homes, with a child, or in an institution, family members, especially daughters, feel a duty to provide care, even if they have other responsibilities such as children or a job (Connidis, 1989). This can result in very mixed feelings. Some women are afraid they are neglecting their husbands or children; some feel they can never quite do enough to satisfy their elderly relative (C.J. Hill, 1984). They may feel guilty for not doing enough, and become overprotective and interfere unnecessarily with their parent's independence (Rhodes, 1989).

THREE KEY ISSUES

The National Advisory Council on Aging (1983) has identified three key areas of conflict involving older people and their family members: independence vs. dependence, connectedness vs. separateness, and openness vs. privateness.

Independence vs. dependence. Life satisfaction of older people is related to the degree to which they can control their own lives (City of Calgary, 1983). Stress may come from two sources: frustration at not being able to do accustomed tasks, and a shift in their social roles. Giving up control means that older people must also change their social roles.

The ability to remain independent is related to both the financial status and the physical and mental condition of the older individual. These factors work alone or in combination. For example, older people who cannot manage to do repairs to a house or clean an apartment can still live on their own if they have enough money to pay someone to do these things for them. This factor is especially important for never-married women. They, more than other groups, depend on paid help. Unmarried men, by contrast, more often receive help from neighbours and friends (Minister for Senior Citizens' Affairs, 1985). Government services can help keep older people in their own homes, for example, through the provision of grants to help finance renovations to make homes accessible to disabled persons, and through the provision of homemaker and home-nursing services to reduce the need for institutionalization. Of course, living in a seniors' residence or a nursing home greatly reduces independence (Robichaud, 1989). Due to rules and routines, there can also be problems practising the traditions and rituals of one's cultural background, which tend to become more important as one ages (McGoldrick, 1988a).

Dependence can also be related to the attitude of relatives or nursing-home staff. If they see a person's condition to be worse than it is, and think that he or she is incompetent, they will try to make decisions for the older person and discourage any independence he or she might show. As a result, the older person is taught to be helpless (Rhodes, 1989).

Connectedness vs. separateness. The struggle for independence often reflects tension between the desire for connectedness and separateness. In many ways this is reminiscent of adolescent-parent conflicts, except that this conflict occurs between adult child and older parent. Older people value their relationships with their children and grandchildren, yet they also wish to maintain their uniquely personal lifestyle. As parents become older and frailer, there is often a tendency on the part of their children to worry about them and to try to limit their independence unnecessarily. For example, some children will be afraid that a parent will fall or become ill and lie helpless for hours, or even days, without being able to call for help. As a result, they will urge their parent to move in with them or to move to an institution where they can be supervised more closely, rather than working to arrange a check-up system or a method of summoning help. Since many older people resist being managed to this degree, the result is family conflict.

Openness vs. privateness. Privacy may become precious in the face of retirement, widowhood, sickness, and institutionalization. In some cases, the older person may fear family members' disapproval of new ways of behaving and become secretive. Living in a nursing home makes a private life virtually impossible so that residents are deprived of their sexual rights. For example, husbands and wives sometimes do not share the same room. Even if they do, it is difficult for them to engage in any sexual activity without fear of interruption, or even in

Aunt Martha began acting strangely a year ago, after her husband's death following a long illness. Not only would she refuse invitations to go out but was very reluctant to allow us to visit any more. While she was downstairs, I saw she had replaced her twin bedroom set with a gigantic king-size bed!

I teased her about it: "What is a 74-year-old widow doing with a new king-size bed?" She got very angry and said she didn't think it was any of my business. She was sick and tired of the family's moral judgments which she had endured all her life! Then she calmed down and told me. The man next door, a retired physician whose wife had died several years before, had begun "calling" on her. She felt so good about it. "I was a loyal wife for 53 years and it wasn't no picnic, believe me, especially when Andy got sick. Now I'm having some fun for a change."

Source: National Advisory Council on Aging (1983). *Family Role and the Negotiation of Change for the Aged*. Ottawa: Author, pp. 24-25.

safety, if they are not provided a double bed. The situation is even more difficult for couples who meet at the home (Hammond, 1987).

Minority Groups and Aging

IMMIGRANTS

There are major differences among cultures in their views regarding how responsible the middle generation should be for looking after the elderly. Certain groups, such as Italians and Chinese, have strong beliefs about not "abandoning" relatives to nursing homes. Others are more likely to accept the nursing-home solution. Given the need for women to add to the family income, however, it is increasingly difficult for families to care for their older members even if they so desire (McGoldrick, 1988a).

It is possible that with time ethnic groups may change their attitudes toward care of the elderly. We can look at the Japanese as an example. The traditional Japanese culture emphasizes the duty of children to care for their parents. This is a form of social exchange — parents are repaid in their old age for the care they gave their young children. Nowadays, even first-generation immigrants do not rely solely on their children for support, but rather make use of government and other pensions. Second-generation Japanese prefer not to depend on their children. There are a number of reasons for this change in values. Social services are now available that were not an option in traditional culture; increased lifespan may place an intolerable burden on children; caring for a parent for five or even ten years might be acceptable, but twenty or thirty years is too stressful. Even with this shift in attitudes, language problems and the cultural value of not expressing feelings make it difficult for the Japanese to tap into social and economic support systems (Ujimoto, 1987).

ABORIGINAL PEOPLES

Traditionally, the grandparent generation among native peoples in North America was responsible for socializing the children. They had both practical knowledge and a wealth of cultural information they could pass on. Much of their teaching of core values and survival techniques was transmitted through storytelling. In return, their grandchildren had the honoured responsibility of helping them to remain independent. If they had no grandchildren themselves, then they became informal grandparents to other children, who filled the grandchild role (Vanderburgh, 1987).

The elder role was eroded through the coming of Christian missions, with their accompanying boarding schools, which removed children from their homes and cultures. In addition, during the 1960s and 1970s, many children were apprehended by child-welfare authorities and placed with white foster and adoptive families. As a result, elders were no longer vital members of society because socialization of children had passed to other people. Since children were no longer available to provide practical assistance, it also became more difficult for the old to retain their independence. Many ended up in nursing homes, out of touch with their culture (Vanderburgh, 1987; M. Ward, 1984a).

In recent years there has been a renewal of interest in traditional native ways. Elders are once again valued as transmitters of culture. They are, however, filling a place somewhat different from the traditional role. They no longer act only within the confines of their family, but rather in the context of voluntary groups such as an Elders' Circle. Valuable life experience has been redefined to include how to deal with schools, social-service agencies, health-care facilities, and the legal system. Indeed, such knowledge may be just as important for survival as traditional methods of hunting, fishing, or agriculture. In addition, elders are seen as custodians of the traditional culture, from which the younger generations are alienated (Vanderburgh, 1987).

Death of Family Members

There has been a shift in the social time clock of dying. In the past, death lurked around every corner and could occur at any age. With medical advances and increased life expectancy, death is now regarded as belonging mainly to old age. Serious illness and death that occur earlier are seen in terms of an incomplete life. The death of the last member of the oldest generation now more clearly marks a shifting of generations, so that the next generation is now the oldest and next in line for death (Walsh, 1988). As life expectancy has increased, so has the incidence of long and debilitating illnesses such as cancer and Alzheimer's disease. As a result, when we talk about death, we need to distinguish between the actual death and the events leading up to it (F.H. Brown, 1989; Riley & Riley, 1986). Both have a profound but different impact on families.

TERMINAL ILLNESS

The final illness can be very stressful for families. First, both the dying person and his or her relatives must face the deterioration of physical or mental powers. Elderly people tend to fear prolonged illness and dependency more than death itself. This fear is related to the desire for independence, and in extreme cases may be expressed by refusing treatment. Part of the stress involved in terminal illness comes from the changes in lifestyle needed to deal with the illness. These affect the older person and his caregivers alike. For example, if a person cannot control bladder or bowels, someone has to clean and change the person. A key stress factor for relatives is the time needed for the physical care of the dying person or for repeated hospital visits (F.H. Brown, 1988; Riley & Riley, 1986).

Second, the family, especially the husband or wife, has to prepare for the actual death and for the changes that must occur in lifestyle and relationships. Individuals who know they are dying have the opportunity to look over their lives, to make plans for their families, and to say final goodbyes and make peace with people they have been alienated from. Family members also have a chance to say farewell. Such preparation for a spouse's death can aid the long-term adjustment of a husband or wife. This is more likely if friends have also been widowed and provide role models (Baker, 1988). The ability to prepare for death is affected by the information the family is given and by their degree of openness in talking about it. Sometimes, of course, death comes suddenly. While there may be little physical suffering, there is no opportunity for goodbyes. Part of the surprise element may come from a lack of honesty on the part of doctors. Sometimes they do not want to admit to themselves that they can do nothing more; and sometimes they feel it is easier for people not to know the worst. By the 1980s, most doctors treating patients with a terminal illness said it was generally their policy to tell the patient that he or she was dying. Often if the patient or family is not told, they will still suspect that the illness is terminal. They are prevented from talking openly, however, by the hope that they are wrong. Even if they do know, they may still not communicate freely, pretending that the family member is not dying (Riley & Riley, 1986). Denial, silence, and secret-keeping prevent family members from grieving in advance (Walsh, 1988). As a result, survivors may feel cheated.

Openness may also affect the ability to talk about such matters as prolonging life once the quality of life is destroyed. Most people now feel that a person has a right to die with dignity rather than be subjected to painful or humiliating treatments, which may prolong life by a matter of days or weeks (Riley & Riley, 1986). The growing hospice movement has also encouraged humane care for the dying. In these institutions, the concern is to make the patients' last days as comfortable as possible. Staff are trained to be supportive to both the dying and the members of their families.

THE FACT OF DEATH AND ITS AFTERMATH

There are ethnic and class differences in the way people deal with death. Many in the majority culture prefer death to occur in hospitals. This is part of the North American tendency to deny death, as is seen in the transfer of responsibility for looking after the body to a funeral home. For other ethnic groups, however, to die away from one's home and family compounds the tragedy of death (McGoldrick, 1988a).

Funerals are family times. Often these events, even more than weddings, are occasions when all the relatives gather together. Until the funeral is over, family members usually forget their differences and offer assistance to one another (Baker, 1988). A funeral is also the occasion for formal leave-taking of the person who has died. As such it is an important aspect of mourning. North American culture, however, is moving toward minimizing everything that has to do with death. This is reflected in the hospital as the preferred place for dying, in the control of the ceremonies by the funeral industry, and in the short time allowed for bereavement leave from work. Such practices make it difficult for some cultural groups to retain their traditional customs (McGoldrick, 1988a). They may also interfere with the grieving process by encouraging family members to distance themselves from the death.

Adjustment to widowhood. Widowhood initially involves a sense of loss, disorientation, and loneliness. Women who have centred their lives on their husbands and families often feel a loss of identity. They may also feel a loss of status. Over the years, the couple has built up a family identity with shared customs and habits. As married people, they have a recognized status within society. With the death of the spouse, all that is gone. Women tend to manage better than men after the death of a spouse, probably because they depend on children and friends for social and emotional support. Working-class women tend to turn more to children and grandchildren, and middle-class women more often to friends or organizations, for help and companionship. Men fare worse, since they usually have depended on their wives for emotional support. In the crisis of death they are often left isolated. Especially in the first year following the death of a spouse, men more than women suffer an increase in death and suicide rates (Baker, 1988; Walsh, 1988).

The psychological task confronting widowed people is grief over the loss, and then commitment to their own continuing life. Typically they go through three stages. First, they need to loosen their bonds to their spouse and accept the fact he or she is dead. Second, they must pay attention to day-to-day living such as job and household management. Finally, they shift to new activities and interests in others. During this period family relationships must be reworked to create a new balance. For example, a widow may now tell her worries to a daughter, when in the past she confided in her husband. The process of mourning and adaptation to the new life typically takes one to two years (Walsh, 1988).

The economics of death. Often the death of a spouse means a drop in family income. This is especially true when an employed partner dies. As has already been discussed, long-term hardships tend to be greater for women, since they often have limited financial resources such as pensions and are less likely to find a new marriage partner. There are also the costs surrounding death itself. There may be a drop in income during the final illness because the sick person cannot work and the partner may need to take a leave of absence from his or her job. Funeral expenses may run very high because the family may try to show their love and respect to the deceased by making elaborate arrangements. Add to these the cost of cemetery plot and grave marker. Too often people involved in the "death" business play on the emotions of survivors when they are at their most vulnerable.

Often there is a period of uncertainty following death as financial affairs are sorted out. A widow may not know for some time to what income she is entitled. Some survivors' pensions, for example, are based on the widow's age. If a person dies intestate, i.e., without making a will, there is much greater delay and confusion. As a result, survivors may experience continuing distress until financial affairs are settled.

What Does the Future Hold?

In coming years, we will probably see a great but temporary increase in the proportion of the elderly in the Canadian population. In part, this increase will be the result of a gradually increasing life expectancy. Since much of the change will, however, be due to the aging of the baby boom, the numbers of old people will decrease again once the wave has passed by (Baker, 1988).

The greater number of elderly in the population will call for changes and create conflicts in society. Many of our myths will be challenged. We can expect an increase in "grey power." It is already reflected economically in the increasing number of television advertisements aimed at older people. We can also expect pressure to be brought on governments to improve pensions and health care.

Some economists believe that the younger generations will be weighed down with the taxes needed for these services, but will probably not protest vehemently since they too will benefit eventually from improved services (Baker, 1988). Availability of services will also reduce the individual financial burden of aging parents and grandparents. With the move to eliminate compulsory retirement, older people may keep working longer. There will be two effects of such a trend: seniors will contribute to the tax base that will pay for better services, and opportunities for promotion for the young may be limited.

MYTHS

Ageisms and resulting age biases are the result of myths and stereotypes which have their root more in fiction than in fact.

For example:

For many younger people, most older people are:

- — inflexible, rigid and set in their ways
- — over-conservative in dress, conduct, politics and popular viewpoint
- — a homogeneous group of persons 65 years of age and older
- — weak, feeble, in poor health, institutionalized, dependent and lonely
- — if not senile, definitely declining in intelligence and the ability to learn
- — non-productive
- — sexless

On the other hand, many older persons see the majority of younger persons as:

- — immature, lazy and playful
- — disrespectful of authority and property
- — careless, impulsive and irresponsible
- — extreme in dress, manners, behaviour and popular viewpoint
- — loud, boisterous and irritating
- — lacking in experience and general knowledge

Mythical and stereotypical portraits of persons such as the ones mentioned here continue to be an integral part of the general images the young and old have of one another.

These images have given rise to the popular concept of Generation Gap.

Source: *A Guidebook for Intergenerational Planning*. Toronto: Ministry of Tourism and Recreation, 1983, p. 11.

Economists also talk of the *dependency ratio*, i.e., the proportion of the population that needs to be supported by the rest. Most dependent people are children and senior citizens. This ratio has remained relatively constant in the past and will continue to do so in the future because the decrease in the number of children will offset the increase in the number of elderly. The reduced need for services for the young, such as education, will counterbalance the growing need for health services and pensions for the elderly. The picture is not that simple, however. Costs for the elderly run about two-and-a-half times per person those for children and adolescents. Resources cannot readily be switched from the young to the elderly population. For example, school buildings would need major modifications before they could serve as nursing homes. In addition, the jurisdiction for services is spread among different levels of government and there would have to be a difficult renegotiation of cost sharing (Seward, 1987). Then, when services for the elderly are well established, the baby-boom bulge will pass and the need for services for the elderly will shrink.

One fact remains: our society will be faced with major adjustments as we adapt to the increasing numbers of older people. Legislators and service providers will need to come up with innovative plans if needs of all citizens are to be met.

SUMMARY

THE AGING POPULATION. The population of Canada is growing older as a result of the aging baby-boom generation and a low birth rate. Old age is, however, difficult to define because it consists of several dimensions. Chronological age refers to the years an individual has lived; physical age to changes in the body; psychological age to emotional and cognitive aspects of aging; and social age is related to social norms. The developmental tasks of old age include allowing the next generation to take over leadership, and finding order and meaning in life as its end approaches.

THE "YOUNG" OLD. People in their early retirement years now enjoy better pensions than in the past. There are, however, many inequities. Women, in particular, are disadvantaged because of their lower employment rate and lower pay with fewer benefits. The interest of older people shifts from employment to other activities. When men are at home, there are changes in family roles. Family relationships are an important source of social support. Men are more likely than women to be married. Women live longer, and widowed or divorced men are more likely to remarry. The relationship with children is often based on mutual help. The relationship with grandchildren can be close, but it is affected by distance or by custody following divorce. The unmarried and childless tend to have the closest ties with brothers and sisters. Gay men's adjustment is similar to that of heterosexual men, with the exception that their main source of social support comes from friends rather than family.

THE "OLD" OLD. Health and self-care becomes an issue as people grow older. Chronic illness becomes more of a concern to both the elderly and their children, who may have to care for their parents. Life satisfaction is related to the degree older individuals can control their own lives. Their ability to do so is affected by financial, physical, and mental factors, as well as the attitudes of family members and professional helpers. Most older people wish to maintain their own lifestyle while keeping up relationships with their relatives. Privacy may become precious as individuals become more dependent on the care of others.

MINORITY GROUPS. There are major differences among cultural groups in their attitudes toward the elderly. There may also be differences between first- and second-generation immigrants. Among aboriginal peoples in the past, elders held an important role in transmitting cultural values to the young. This has been eroded through the influence of the majority culture. Recently, however, elders are becoming more valued once again.

DEATH OF FAMILY MEMBERS. Often a prolonged illness and dependency is feared more than death itself. If possible, both the dying person and family members need to prepare themselves and say their farewells. Although funerals draw family members together, the trend toward minimizing death may make ethnic observances difficult. The adjustment to widowhood involves dealing with the loss of identity and status, grieving the loss of one's partner, and then commitment to continuing one's own life. There may be economic hardships related to death, both in funeral costs and drop in income.

THE FUTURE. It is predicted that there will be a large but temporary increase among the elderly in the future. This will place more political power in their hands. One issue that still needs to be addressed is how to meet the cost of providing care for the growing population of elders.

KEY TERMS

chronological age: the number of years a person has lived

dependency ratio: the proportion of the population that needs to be supported by the rest

physical age: changes that occur in the body as a result of the length of time a person has lived

psychological age: the attitudes and beliefs about one's age

social age: cultural norms which specify appropriate behaviour for people of a given age

CLASS ASSIGNMENTS

Complete one or both of the following assignments, as directed by your instructor.

1. Discover what facilities and services are available in your community for senior citizens. Did you find any gaps? What are the difficulties in acquiring needed services?
2. Three options for the care of frail elderly people are going to an institution, living with relatives, and receiving services in their own homes. Describe the advantages and disadvantages of each of these options for older people and their relatives.

PERSONAL ASSIGNMENTS

These assignments are designed to help you explore your own family experiences and your expectations for the future.

1. Among the people you know, whom do you think of as old? What characteristics, in your opinion, distinguish between old and not old? Why?
2. Even though it seems far in the future, describe what you feel would make life worthwhile once you are retired. Be realistic! What steps can you take beforehand to make these plans attainable?

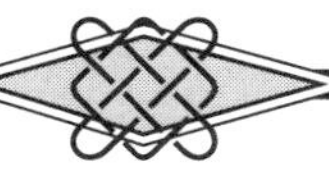

PART 6

Social Problems in the Family

C H A P T E R 1 2

The Family Beleaguered—When Problems Come

O B J E C T I V E S

- To consider the definition of a problem within the family context.
- To describe the response of the family system to problems using the ABCX model.
- To examine two problems (chronic illness and alcoholism) in relation to the family's problem-solving ability.
- To look briefly at the part communication plays in problem-solving.

A mother writes ...

When the police charged my son and his friend with break, enter, and theft, we were angry but didn't realize how difficult the whole experience would be for us. Since he was a young offender, at least one parent was expected in court. And it wasn't just the one time. There was a preliminary interview with the lawyer. There were repeated returns to court over the next several months because there was a second charge pending and it would be to his benefit to have both tried together. Then someone in the Crown Attorney's office mixed things up, and scheduled hearings on the charges at the same time in different courts. That meant further delays while the mess got sorted out. And all this so that he could plead guilty.

I kept having to ask for time off work. It got pretty awkward after a while to explain where I needed to be. My husband could just as easily have taken time off, but he argued that he would lose more pay than I would, so I was the one who had to go to court.

It was a real worry when our son broke the conditions of his probation, such as the curfew that was imposed. When it appeared that he was dealing drugs out of the house, we asked him to move out. After all, we were worried about the effect on our other children if we overlooked his behaviour. He quit school. That was a further violation of his probation. I can't understand how he got away with it, but his probation officer never called him to task.

In all those months, we didn't talk about it with our friends or relatives. It was embarrassing to say the least. We also felt some guilt. After all, parents are supposed to control their children, aren't they?

Families have problems. Since many problems are related to deviance or being different in some way, they have a social dimension to them. We have already considered many aspects of minority and majority relationships (Chapter 2). In this chapter, we will look at when being different becomes a problem.

What exactly is a social problem? A useful definition is "that a social problem exists when a significant number of people believe that a certain condition is in fact a problem" (Coleman & Cressey, 1984, p. 3). Yet this definition raises a number of issues. When there are competing views, who decides what is a problem? For whom is it a problem? How do social problems affect families? We will look at each of these issues in turn.

Who Decides When a Problem is a Problem?

The simplest answer is that the public decides what is a problem. Public opinion does not always remain the same however. For example, harsh physical discipline of children has at times been encouraged so that they may grow into law-abiding adults. Sayings like "Spare the rod and spoil the child" (which many people wrongly assume is a quote from the Bible) are used to justify such practices (Greven, 1990). In contrast, a major concern nowadays is the damage that can be done to children as a result of physical violence.

Similarly, over the years, homosexuality has been seen as sin, crime, mental illness, or simply a variation on family living. As a sin, it was linked with other forms of sex, such as masturbation and *bestiality*, in which reproduction was not a goal. Originally, homosexuality was dealt with by the Church rather than criminal courts. In 1535, Parliament in England passed a law making male homosexuality a crime. There were later laws established against gross indecency.

Convicted homosexuals were often referred to psychiatrists, who undertook research to learn more about what they considered a psychological and sexual disorder. Early researchers also suspected that "self-abuse," i.e. masturbation, could produce homosexuality. This is probably the source of the myth in the early 1900s that masturbation leads to insanity (Kinsman, 1987). Even though many gay and lesbian individuals argue that homosexual couples are a form of family, there are still many people who feel that such relationships are abnormal (Weston, 1991).

Obviously, a problem is something that is undesirable in some way. Behaviour that might physically harm oneself and, more important, others is almost always seen as a problem. Yet some individuals are not felt to deserve as much protection as others.

For example, in the past aboriginal peoples have been treated as an exploitable resource to aid the economic development of a dominant society. Their traditional livelihood has been destroyed and their ancestral lands taken over so that newcomers to the land might prosper. The British, for example, believed that whites were destined to rule large parts of the world. During early contacts with native peoples, charters gave aboriginal lands to traders and settlers and spoke of waging war on the barbarians. One of the results was the destruction of the Beothuk Indians (Frideres, 1983). Through the residential schools, the newcomers taught native children the values of white society, in the process telling them that *indigenous* peoples were savage and incompetent. By destroying native culture and values in this manner, the newcomers attempted to gain control of both people and resources (Ryser, 1984).

Over the centuries family members have not received as much protection against assault as other individuals. The idea that a family is entitled to privacy behind its closed doors has protected abusers. Most family violence takes place in private without witnesses. Even when others know about the abuse, they are reluctant to report incidents to child-welfare authorities or police because they do not consider it their business. In the past, police often unintentionally protected men who battered their wives or children because they failed to intervene in domestic disputes (Guberman & Wolfe, 1985).

The public is made up of many groups that often have competing interests. One or more groups in society usually have been quite successful compared with others. They are often referred to as *vested interests,* since they have a stake in keeping society as it is. These powerful groups tend to have the greatest influence in defining problems. Since they tend to be among the wealthiest and thus pay more taxes, they may be concerned with the cost of problems to society (Coleman & Cressey, 1984). For example, child abuse can be very expensive. If the abuse is left undetected and untreated, victims can become a continuing financial burden on society. They may have to receive repeated medical treatment. If they are severely damaged, they may even need life-long care.

Adults who were abused as children may require psychiatric services or welfare assistance because of emotional damage that prevents them from becoming productive members of society. They may also emotionally or physically damage their own children, thus extending the cost to another generation (Tower, 1989).

Often *gatekeepers*, i.e., individuals who are recognized as having special expertise in identifying problems, are given the authority to label individuals or groups as being the source of a problem (Coleman & Cressey, 1984). Some of these gatekeepers in Canadian society are doctors, police officers, judges and juries, and social workers. For example, doctors decide if an individual's mental condition is dangerous enough to require confinement. They are the ones who decide if a person is sick or injured enough to be admitted to hospital. The actions and decisions of police officers, judges, and juries determine if an individual is labelled as a criminal. Child-welfare workers are entrusted with deciding if children are in sufficient danger to remove them from their homes. All of these people work within laws, regulations, and guidelines that they are held responsible for following, even if they personally disagree with them. In this way they support the power of the dominant group in society.

Not everyone in society defines problems in the same way. Two groups may see a particular situation as containing a problem, but they may differ drastically as to just what the problem is (Coleman & Cressey, 1984). In the case of homosexuality, for instance, many in society (such as conservative religious groups) see homosexual behaviour as bad or sick. On the other hand, gay-rights activists see the problem not in their own behaviour, but in the intolerance of society. Groups like those advocating gay rights, rights for the physically or mentally challenged, or rights of fathers to have custody of their children are referred to as special-interest groups. Often they want regulations or laws supported by vested interests to be changed. When the special interests of two groups are similar, they may work together to force change. For example, although they disagree on some issues like trapping fur-bearing animals, conservationists and native peoples have cooperated in trying to prevent lumber companies from cutting old growth forests in northern Ontario.

The Impact on Families

When society or the family itself decides a situation is a problem, individuals and families as a whole are affected. The social definition of a problem can create internal problems for the family, e.g., when the father in a family is charged by the police, this may affect the relationship of spouses and of parents and children.

DEALING WITH A NEW PROBLEM

Families differ in the way they respond to a stressful situation. We have all met those who seem to handle far more than their share of misfortune and still keep a positive outlook on life. Other families seem to fall apart at the slightest difficulty. Reuben Hill (1958) proposed what he called the ABCX model of response. In this model, *A* refers to the stressor event, the arrest of the family breadwinner, for example.

The impact of the stressor is affected by the family's resources (the *B* factor). Do they have money for day-to-day living? Can they afford a lawyer? Do they know how to go about finding one with some expertise in the particular sort of crime? They probably want someone who has specialized knowledge of criminal law, as opposed to business or family law. Do they know anyone they can ask for advice? Usually a family will try to solve problems in ways that have worked before. Some families may have a good deal of experience in dealing with the justice system; thus they have a level of practical know-how other families do not.

The response of the family is also affected by the way the family members view the event (the *C* factor). For instance, does the wife see herself as a social outcast if her husband is charged with a crime? Or does she see him as the victim who needs to be defended from a racist society? Or does she feel that he no longer deserves to be a family member? The viewpoint of the children in the family may differ from the parents' viewpoint. They may consider a father's exploits

Figure 12.1

A SCHEMA FOR DEPICTING THE INTERPLAY OF STRESSOR EVENT, CONTRIBUTING HARDSHIPS, AND FAMILY RESOURCES IN PRODUCING A FAMILY CRISIS

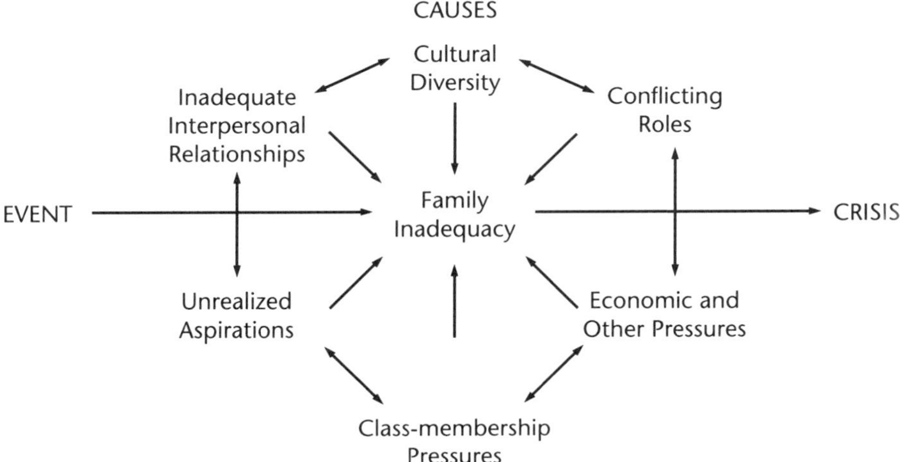

Source: Reuben Hill (1958). "Social Stresses on the Family," *Social Casework*, 39: 139–150. In Marvin B. Sussman, (ed.), (1968). *Sourcebook in Marriage and the Family*. 3rd ed. Boston: Houghton Mifflin, p. 446.

an interesting adventure, and plan to avoid the same pitfalls with the law. On the other hand, they may be ashamed and try to hide or even deny a connection with him.

These three factors interact to produce the *X* factor — the crisis. When a family is in *crisis*, it means that there is an imbalance in the demands placed on the family and their ability to meet the demands (McCubbin & Patterson, 1983). Once the familiar methods of problem-solving fail, the family boundaries are loosened enough to allow for new information, rules and roles become confused, and tension between family members increases (Pittman, 1987). At times like this, the family is open to try new ways of finding solutions. These solutions may be *functional* or *dysfunctional*, i.e., they may increase the family's ability to solve new problems (functional) or they may temporarily reduce family tensions but create new problems in the future (dysfunctional). Functional solutions might involve a stay-at-home spouse finding a job, learning of sources of practical help such as counselling services, or developing skills in dealing with the justice system. Dysfunctional solutions may involve blaming the husband and father for all the family's difficulties, or centering all interactions around his needs. Thus the couple might not talk about their own conflicts, but only about his court appearances and defence.

LONG-TERM PROBLEMS

Usually a family does not experience a problem as a single bolt-from-the-blue stressor. Family crises evolve over time and pressures from various sources accumulate. This fact led to an expansion of the ABCX model, as shown in Figure 12.2, (McCubbin & Patterson, 1983).

According to this expanded model, there are five general types of stressors that can pile up (McCubbin & Patterson, 1983). First there is the initial stressor and its hardships, e.g., a breadwinner in the family is charged and convicted. Second, there are normative stresses in the family, i.e., changes that most families go through and can be expected. The growing independence of an adolescent or young adult is one of these "ordinary" stressors. If the mother has relied on one of her children for emotional support after her husband was charged, she may become very anxious if that child wants to move away from home. Third, families may also experience strains that began before the particular stressor. Perhaps the husband had been involved with earlier criminal activities for which he had not been charged. Perhaps the wife is alcoholic, or there has been a pattern of continuing family violence. Fourth, there are the efforts of the family to cope. If they deny the problem, for example, they may cut themselves off from outside help or they may be unable to discuss the situation to come up with a concrete plan for dealing with the issue. Fifth, there may be *ambiguity*, i.e., the situation within the family or within society may not be clear. Some convicts' wives, for example, have been propositioned by "friends" of their husband who think they must be lonely and anxious for a new sexual relationship. The stigma toward

Figure 12.2

THE DOUBLE ABCX MODEL

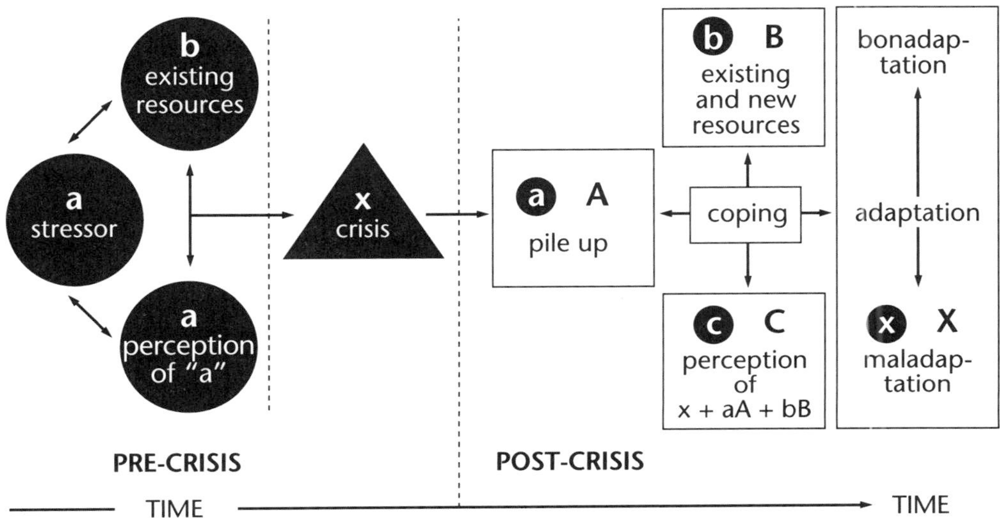

Source: Hamilton I. McCubbin & Joan M. Patterson,"Family Transitions: Adaptation to Stress" In Hamilton I. McCubbin & Charles R. Figley (1983). *Stress and the Family. Volume 1: Coping with Normative Transitions*. New York: Brunner/Mazel, p. 12.

criminals within society may also affect the family by virtue of their association with a convict. All these stressors work together to cause pile-up (the *aA* factor).

The family resources that help them adapt to the situation make up the *bB* factor. This can include personal resources of individual family members, such as education, health, money, and, most important, self-esteem and a sense of mastery. It also includes the resources of the family system, such as flexible role relationships and the ability to share power. If the family breadwinner, for example, is sent to the penitentiary, is the partner able to find a job to support the family? Finally, it includes social support, which can provide practical help, emotional support, and foster a sense of self-esteem in family members.

Families may also have *snag-points*, or areas of difficulty, that interfere with constructive efforts to cope with problems (Pittman, 1987). There may be rules about open communication, e.g., in some families, talking about the convict father may be taboo, or lies may be told about why he is no longer present. Another snag-point may be related to the level of intimacy in the family. In some families, members are so distant that no one feels involved in anyone else's life. Thus family members might not stand behind one another. In other families, members are so enmeshed in one another's lives that it is unclear who really owns the problem. In such families, everyone feels as disgraced as if they themselves had been convicted. When families are very rigid about roles, e.g., men's and women's duties, there may be a crisis when someone is imprisoned or absent and cannot fulfil the role. Sometimes a family's unrealistic goals and values fail to make allowance for changed circumstances, and therefore interfere with problem-solving ability.

Some of these snag-points are also related to the *cC* factor, the family's definition of the situation and the meaning they find in it. For example, goals and values are reflected in the assessment of the situation. Some families feel it is a disaster if they cannot meet a cherished goal because of the *chronic illness* or disability of a family member. Others see it as a challenge, or give the crisis a special meaning. Parents of children with severe mental challenges, for instance, sometimes say that they have learned the value of human life and love through knowing their child. One father commented, "No matter what else goes wrong with my life, I know he will always be the same. He creates a calm centre." However, a healthy attitude does not deny the reality of the situation or minimize what needs to be done to meet the situation.

All these factors combine to create the *xX* factor, the family adaptation to the problem. Family efforts need to be coordinated so that members can create a new

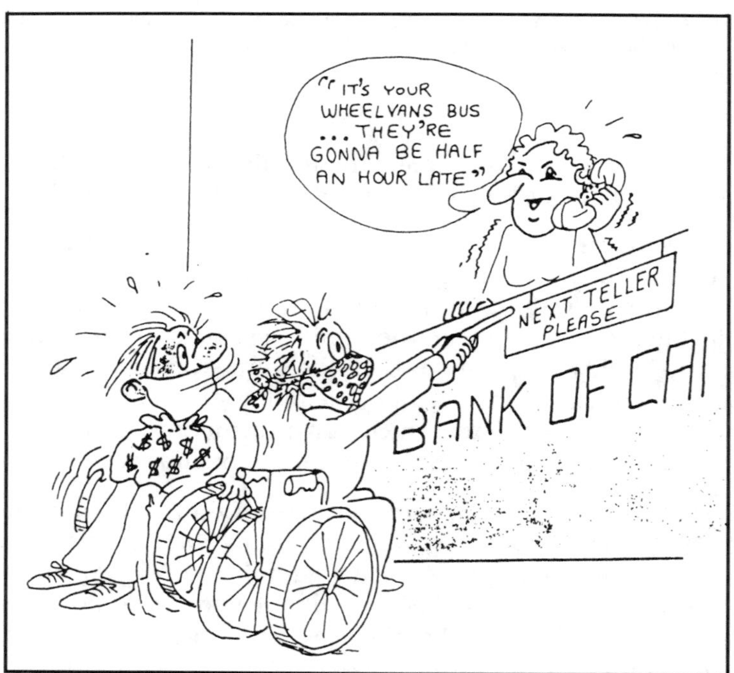

Source: Audrey J. King (1987). *There's Lint in Your Bellybutton!"* Toronto: Canadian Rehabilitation Council for the Disabled, p. 54.

lifestyle to suit the changed circumstances. They need to work out a new "fit" between themselves and the community. Sometimes the solution isn't ideal, but family members support it because they recognize that it is the best they can do. Members also need to feel that the family relationship is worth the effort of making all these changes. If the needs of the family are ignored for too long, the result may be family breakdown.

Two Specific Family Problems

The double ABCX model fits the way families respond to many crises and ongoing problems. As we saw in Chapter 11, for instance, the death of a husband or wife is a situation that requires fundamental changes in lifestyle and in relationships. The eventual adaptation of survivors depends not only on their own resources but also on the social support they receive and the interpretation they place on their loss. As we shall see in the next chapter, the same factors hold true for family violence. In this section, we shall look at two situations that both society and families define as being problems.

THE IMPACT OF CHRONIC ILLNESS OR DISABILITY ON THE FAMILY

Chronic illness or disability usually starts in one of two ways — suddenly, or over a period of time. Although in many ways the effect on the family is similar in both situations, there are also differences.

The initial shock. Sudden awareness of the problem may come about as the result of an accident or the birth of a child with obvious problems. After the initial shock, the first concern may be with the individual's survival. Soon there is an increase in energy, visiting in hospital perhaps, or taking the family member for tests, providing the new care that is necessary, taking over the responsibilities for which the ill member used to be responsible. The *a* factor includes the acute illness, the diagnosis, the first attempts at medical treatment, and the energy rush used to meet the new demands on the family (Jacobs, 1991).

Later, there will be a period of assessment to determine just what level of functioning is likely. Sometimes this cannot occur until there has been time allowed for healing, followed by extensive testing. During this process, the problem becomes a chronic one, extending over a period of time.

During the initial phase of illness, the needs of other family members are often ignored. Meals may become catch-as-catch-can. Laundry may pile up. Children may receive very little attention and supervision. If the illness lasts more than a few days, however, one or more family members may become burned out. They no longer have the energy to respond to the physical and emotional demands placed on them. As a result, they become irritable and tend to withdraw from others. They may in turn become ill themselves. The family system itself starts to break down as family resources can no longer meet the demands of illness. The family goes into crisis.

In other cases, the onset of illness is gradual and takes place over a period of time. Little by little the family, or others, come to believe that something is wrong. This may take place when an older member is showing memory loss and changes in personality, a baby is not meeting developmental stages, or an individual has a series of illnesses. At the point when the disorder is diagnosed as chronic, e.g., Alzheimer's Disease, a chromosomal disorder leading to physical and mental delays in development, or AIDS, the family faces a crisis similar to the acute onset of an illness. In addition, they have a history of living with the long months or years of worry and fear that have created other stressors as they have tried to cope.

In both cases, the meaning the family places on the illness is important; this is affected by a variety of factors. Do they have experience with a similar disorder? If so, do they feel their experience has given them the power to cope or do they dread living through the problem once again? How do they see the prognosis? Do they feel that an individual can live a rewarding life if he or she is confined to a wheelchair or is facing death? Or do they dread the process? The reason they give for the illness or disability is also important. Do they blame themselves because they were not more careful, or do they see an accident or a genetic disorder as occurring in spite of all their precautions? Do they blame the sufferer? This may be important with an illness like AIDS that is often stigmatized by society.

The long haul. As an illness becomes chronic, there is a pile-up of stressors on the family (Patterson & McCubbin, 1983). These can come from many sources. First, within the family itself, members may approach burnout and are no longer able to handle the everyday hassles of family living. Relationships with other family members can become strained. There may also be resentment over the demands of the ill member, and often a feeling of guilt about not being more patient. Sometimes the needs of well family members are felt to be a burden. Overall, there may be an increase in tension and conflict.

Family activities and goals may need to be changed. These changes may, in part, be due to financial limitations, either as a direct result of needs of the patient or the impact the illness has on other members' employment options. If an illness is unpredictable, such as asthma, it may be difficult to count on family rituals and customs since they may be interrupted by the medical needs of the individual. When a parent is emotionally disturbed, the family environment may also be unpredictable. Sometimes the person will fill his or her roles well. At other times, the family will be thrown into chaos when there is a flare-up of the parent's disorder (Guttman, 1989). In a progressive illness, such as multiple sclerosis, the family has the strain of repeatedly adjusting to new care and role demands (Rolland, 1988). Planning for the future may also be difficult if the prognosis is uncertain. Will the patient recover? If not, when is death likely to occur — tomorrow or five years from now? (Jacobs, 1991). Social activities may

I used to be the kind of person who would say (and sincerely believe) you could do everything and anything that you can for a child, especially a child with problems. Now I'm not sure, I mean, it's much more complicated than that. Lots of time I wonder if we wouldn't all be better off if she died. You know, at times I think that we have all reduced ourselves to her level of living — just barely surviving from moment to moment, constantly struggling, using all of our energy just to get through a meal.

Please don't misunderstand, no one could love a child more than I love her! It's just that my whole life could be devoted to taking care of her and nothing more. The best advice that I got from anybody this year came from a check-out girl. It was really quite simple and self-evident, but I had lost the thread and needed to hear it. She said, "You've got to continue living your own life — giving up on who you are is not helping your daughter, and it's destroying you. You have a right to a full life, too, you know!"

I still haven't been able to do what she said — it's real hard. When I think of myself, I get real worried about my daughter being short-changed; when I ignore my own needs, I worry that my life is just slipping away. Sometimes the pressure gets so bad that I forget my marriage, friends, and everything, and when I see that that's happening, I get even more upset. Somehow all this pressure has got to stop!

Source: Siegfried M. Pueschel, "Parental Reactions and Professional Counseling at the Birth of a Handicapped Child." In James A. Mulick & Siegfried M. Pueschel, eds. (1983). *Parent-Professional Partnerships in Developmental Disability Services*. Cambridge, MA: Academic Guild Publishers, p. 18.

also change. If the illness demands a great deal of time from the caregiver or if it carries stigma, such as disfigurement or AIDS, the family may become socially isolated.

Added to all these stressors are *normative changes*, i.e., family changes that come about through the normal changes in the family life cycle. These include puberty, the growing independence of young people, finding a mate, having children, or retiring. Chronic illness can have a different effect depending on the stage of the family life cycle of either the parents or children (Jacobs, 1991). For instance, a young person's chronic illness or disability may influence his or her decision (or even opportunity) to marry and, if the person does marry, whether to have children. Illness can also interfere with the growing independence of a young person. If the adolescent or young adult is ill, he or she may remain dependent on the family of origin long past the time most young people are living on their own. If a parent is ill, the young person may feel duty-bound to stay home and help with care. In later life, illness of a partner can disrupt plans made for activities such as travel after retirement. Middle-aged children, often referred to as the sandwich generation, can also feel trapped through parents' need for care.

As already mentioned, the resources an individual can call on affect the ability to cope. Some resources, however, create their own demands and difficulties. Dealing with the medical system, especially if it is not very sensitive to the needs of family members, can be an added source of stress. Supplementary health insurance can help relieve the financial burden of chronic illness. At times, however, its rules make it unclear whether all or even some of the costs are covered, and thus increase anxiety among family members (Jacobs, 1991). Similarly, friends and relatives can play a key role in protecting children from the periodic neglect of a mentally ill parent. If, however, they take responsibility for areas which the parent can still manage, they may undermine the individual's position in the family and push the individual to the sidelines (Guttman, 1988).

Over time, families may change their perception of the illness. For example, one family with a child with severe physical challenges started out by blaming one another for his problems. Eventually, they came to see him as a force which pulled them together because he was so dependent on them for survival. Some couples who have had a mentally or physically challenged child born to them, or who nurse a chronically ill child, have adopted other children with similar problems because they feel that the skills they have gained in dealing with their birth child should not be wasted but should be used for the welfare of others. This is also true of parents with physical challenges who have adopted or fostered children like themselves because they have learned how to lead rewarding lives (Sandness, 1983).

As a result of the interplay of these factors, family coping patterns emerge. Dysfunctional coping can include overprotection of the ill or disabled member, denial of the reality of the illness, anger and resentment toward the ill person or toward other family members. In general, the family feels out of control and victimized. Functional coping, on the other hand, helps the family feel in control of the situation. They try to understand the medical situation through communicating with others in a similar situation and with medical personnel. They work at keeping the family together and emphasize cooperation. They do not cut themselves off from social support. As a result of their sense of control, their self-esteem is high and they remain psychologically stable (Patterson & McCubbin, 1983).

THE ALCOHOLIC FAMILY

Why do we refer to an alcoholic family rather than a family with an alcoholic member? One of the difficulties with alcohol abuse, as we shall see, is the fact that so much of family life focuses on the alcohol abuse that it becomes the main organizer, i.e., the entire family system is involved with alcoholism.

Alcoholism has a number of factors similar to chronic illness. Given his or her physical condition, and in the case of alcoholism his or her behaviour, one family member cannot fill the usual family roles and responsibilities. Others have to adjust their behaviour to account for this. Alcohol abuse itself adds stresses in terms of changed behaviour, depending on physical state, income difficulties if drinking interferes with work, and social isolation. Further stresses are also created by developmental demands on the family and attitudes of society.

There are also important differences between alcoholism and chronic illness. Unlike many chronic illnesses, alcoholism does not start suddenly; rather it develops over a period of time. Since it is considered *discreditable* by society, the family, along with the alcoholic member, often go to great lengths to avoid acknowledging the problem. As a result family members often assume stereotyped roles in alcoholic families. One or more may be *enablers*, i.e., their behaviour allows the individual to continue drinking without suffering the most extreme consequences (Copans, 1989). This can include a wife phoning in to say that her husband is sick or young children looking after their drunk or hung-over mother. These members tend to become overly responsible as the drinker becomes increasingly irresponsible. Others can become superachievers and still others scapegoats, who can be blamed for family problems. These and other roles are shown in Figure 12.3. All cover up the anger, guilt, and pain that family members feel. Since the problem of alcohol abuse is not addressed, family life seems to be in a continuing state of crisis (Krestan & Bepko, 1988).

Members of alcoholic families learn a number of lessons about family life (Copans, 1989). In such families, individuals spend their time worrying if the alcoholic member will come home drunk, covering up drinking behaviour, or not inviting friends home because a parent may be drunk. The first lesson, then, is that alcohol is the centre of family life. A second lesson is that alcohol can make things better. Often the alcoholic member is more loving and warm while drinking than while sober. Also the drinker will demonstrate that alcohol will make unpleasant withdrawal symptoms go away. A third lesson is that alcohol abuse is a family secret to be denied and covered up.

This pattern of coping has its costs. It may lead to a variety of symptoms in the nonalcoholic member, e.g., anxiety, depression, shame, and anger. In addition, *codependence* or enabling on the part of children often continues into adulthood. Daughters, in particular, tend to marry men who are substance abusers or who underfunction in some other way. They may also raise substance abusers (Copans, 1989). On the positive side, some adult children of alcoholics are drawn to the helping professions where they can care for others in a socially approved manner. Yet they may have difficulty with particular kinds of clients or patients as a result of their early experiences. For example, one psychiatrist, who as a teenager was sent to find his alcoholic father and bring him home, found that he was impatient and ineffective when he tried to treat an alcoholic patient.

Figure 12.3

THE CHEMICALLY DEPENDENT FAMILY

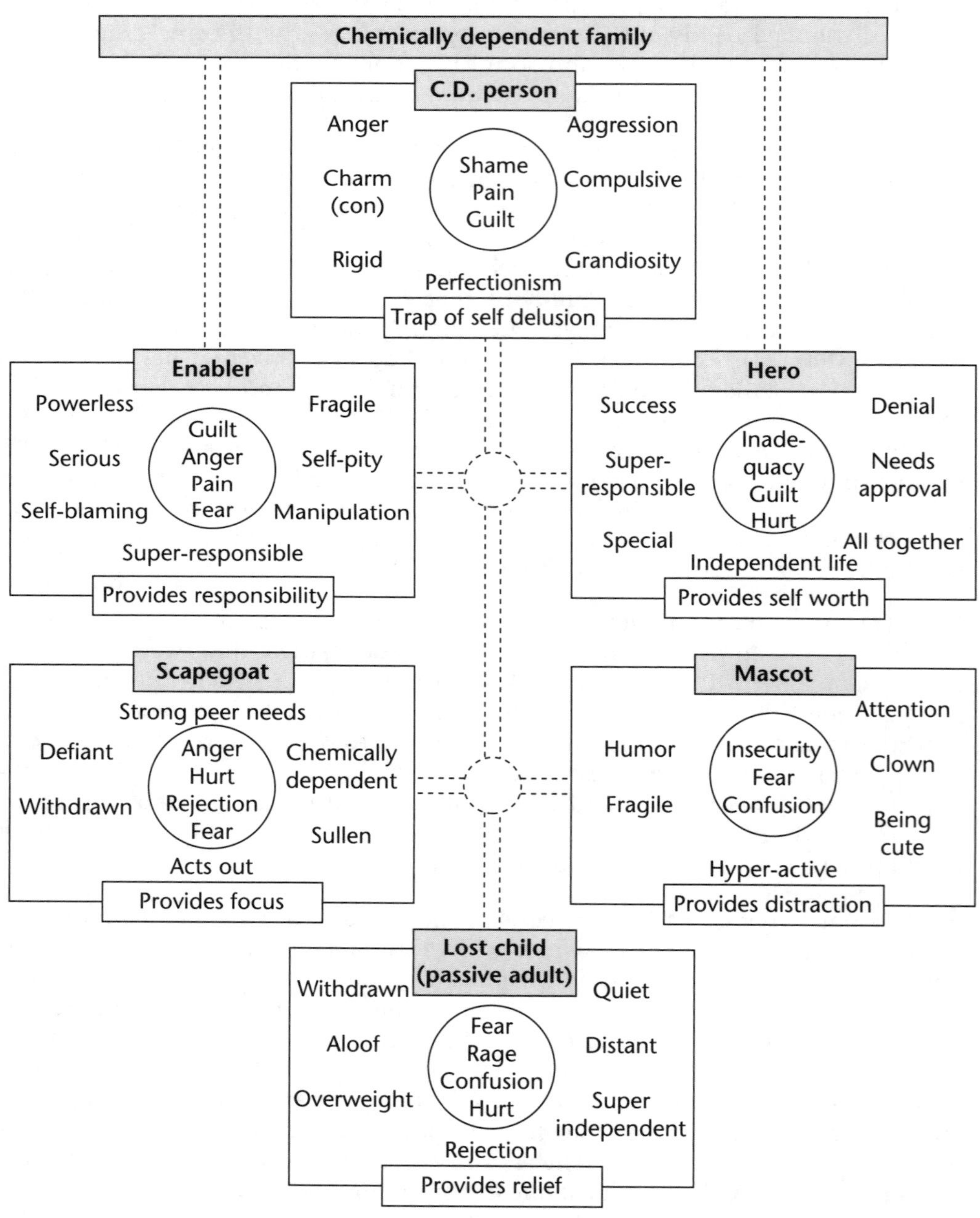

Source: St. Joseph's Treatment Center, North Bay, Ontario.

Often the alcoholism is not admitted until there is a decisive event that makes denial impossible. This event may differ for the alcoholic and family members. For example, the alcoholic may not experience drinking as a problem until his wife leaves him. Obviously there has been an earlier event or series of events that created a crisis for her.

When the alcoholic member stops drinking, there may be a "crisis" of sobriety. The family still has its old patterns, and has to learn new ones. The period of adjustment typically lasts from six months to two years. All family members may need to have counselling or be involved in mutual support groups such as Alcoholics Anonymous, Alanon, and Alateen. The irresponsible family member needs to learn to take responsibility for his or her behaviour, and overly responsible members need to learn how to stop taking on responsibility that is not theirs. Both lessons may be extremely difficult because they involve creating a completely different family pattern.

Communication and Problem-Solving

As families encounter problems, they must find solutions if they are to cope. As we have seen, communication helps couples and families change their system in order to find solutions. In families where there is less positive communication, there is less change and lower levels of adaptability than in families with more balanced communication (Olson, 1990).

Families with more effective problem-solving skills usually communicate clearly. This occurs both in words and through a wide range of interpersonal messages. When they encounter a problem, they try out a variety of patterns of interaction that have already worked in an attempt to solve the problem. If they are unable to do so right away, they do not feel helpless, but look for new solutions. On the other hand, families that are less effective in solving problems often have more limited patterns of interpersonal communication and often seem to be talking at cross-purposes. Since they also attempt to keep things the same and resist change, they are unable to adapt to new circumstances (Benjamin, 1982).

The Long View

All families are changed by the problems they experience. The way they change is shaped by what they themselves, and society as a whole, believe about the situation. Old patterns of problem-solving, the resources available, and other pressures all contribute to striking a new balance. Some families break under the stress; others develop strengths they never dreamed possible.

SUMMARY

WHAT IS A PROBLEM? A social problem exists when a significant number of people believe it is a problem. What is considered a problem has changed over the years. For example, homosexuality has been described at different times as a sin, a crime, a mental disorder, and an alternate lifestyle. Often the dominant group in society has the greatest influence in deciding what a problem is.

THE ABCX MODEL. The way families respond to a problem depends on the stressor itself (*A* factor), the family's resources (*B* factor), and their interpretation of the situation (*C* factor). These factors work together to produce a crisis (*X* factor), which calls for new ways of problem-solving. If the problem is long-term, stressors can pile up. Again family resources and interpretation affect the outcome — the eventual adaptation of the family to the problem. This second pattern has been called the double ABCX model.

TWO FAMILY PROBLEMS. Two long-term problems that affect families are chronic illness and alcoholism.

Chronic illness. Chronic illness can have either a sudden or gradual onset. In either case, the illness and diagnosis create stress, which is affected by both the coping resources of the family and the meaning they attach to the illness. Often members respond to the crisis with high levels of activity. When the illness is prolonged, other stressors are also involved, such as changes in family lifestyle and ordinary life-cycle changes. Different resources may be required to cope in the long term, and the family's interpretation of the situation may change over time. These combine to produce new coping patterns.

Alcoholic family. Like chronic illness, alcohol abuse is a family stressor. As in chronic illness, the family's coping resources and the meaning members place on alcohol abuse will affect the severity of the crisis. Various attempts at coping may combine with other stressors to produce pile-up. Eventually the family may adapt by making alcohol abuse part of the family pattern through enabling behaviours. If the alcoholic member stops drinking, the family may go through a further crisis because the old coping patterns are no longer appropriate.

COMMUNICATION AND PROBLEM-SOLVING. Positive communication is important for helping families change in a positive way. Often those who are less effective in solving problems have limited or negative patterns of communication.

KEY TERMS

ambiguity: lack of clarity

bestiality: sexual relations between a person and an animal

chronic illness: an illness that lasts for a prolonged period of time

codependence: the tendency for nonalcoholic members of an alcoholic family to display a variety of psychological symptoms

crisis: an imbalance in demands placed on an individual or family and their ability to meet the demand

discreditable: damaging to one's reputation

dysfunctional: decreased ability of family to solve problems

enabler: a person whose behaviour allows another to act in a certain way; the term is often used in reference to nonalcoholic members of alcoholic families

functional: increased ability of the family to solve problems

gatekeepers: individuals who are recognized as having special expertise in identifying problems

indigenous: aboriginal or native

normative changes: changes that are expected as part of life

snag-points: areas of difficulty that interfere with constructive efforts to cope with problems

vested interest: group of people involved in working for personal advantage

CLASS ASSIGNMENTS

Complete one or both of the following assignments, as directed by your instructor.

1. By reading newspapers and/or watching TV, discover two current issues that present the family with problems. Explain what stresses they place on the family and solutions that have been proposed. What are the advantages and disadvantages of these solutions?
2. Explain why an individual in a helping profession would find the double ABCX model useful. Illustrate your answer by applying the model to a specific problem.

PERSONAL ASSIGNMENTS

These assignments are designed to help you think about your own experience.

1. What problems has your family experienced? How have they affected family relationships and roles? Did they change the day-to-day organization of family life? Explain.
2. When you have personally experienced problems, what methods have you used to try to resolve them? Did these methods work? Why or why not? What other means might you have used?

CHAPTER 13

Home Dangerous Home: Abuse and Violence in the Family

OBJECTIVES

- To place the problem of family violence in historical perspective.
- To look at the incidence of child abuse, characteristics of victims and abusers, and the response of society to child abuse.
- To look at the incidence of partner abuse, characteristics of victims and abusers, reasons people stay in abusive relationships, and the response of society to such abuse.
- To look at the incidence of abuse of the elderly, characteristics of victims and abusers, and the response of society to elder abuse.
- To consider causes of abuse, including the cycle of abuse.
- To think about ways of preventing family violence.

The story of a former shelter resident

by Colette

Nearly 15 months have passed since that autumn — that time in my life when everything went wrong. When my husband threatened to kill me, I panicked

— I wanted to hide — I wanted to run away. But where could I go and how could I get there with hardly any money? Besides, I was obsessed with images of my own head exploding from a rifle shot — I was afraid of going crazy and afraid of dying.

After many telephone calls, I found the Maison du Reconfort. They would take us in, my two children (aged 9 and 16) and I. The fear of going there grabbed at me: what is a shelter? Maybe it would be a big, solid building like a convent, with bars, and maybe a big heavy door that would shut behind us....

My big son wasn't any braver than I. He imagined that there might be two or three hundred aggressive women who would attack him because he looked like a man.

And I was afraid — for myself, and for my children.

As we made our way to the shelter, the idea of it tormented me. I had never heard anything about it. What would happen to my freedom? Would I be swallowed up by the system? Were they going to take all responsibility for me? Would I have to submit to excessive authority? And would I be seen as a good mother? Would they take away my children? As a battered woman, how would they look at me? Would they pity me or disapprove? It was the unknown ... and we were afraid.

We got out of the taxi, the children and I, at a house that looked like all the others in the neighbourhood. The welcome was simple but very warm. After a little tour of the house, we were introduced to some of the residents, and a room was assigned to us, the room that became our tiny home for a month.

The part of the shelter I came to know best was the kitchen, where I spent most of my time. Around the table, with the other resident women and the workers, I began to break my silence. I told my story and I never felt I was being judged. I was okay. They listened to me and I listened to them. I could identify; I was no longer alone. One of the workers was assigned to me; I wanted to take a few days to think this over and she respected my need to breathe quietly at my own pace.

With her, I worked through my fears, my insecurities, my guilt and my shame. I got rid of some of it: I say "some" because these emotions had been rooted deep within me for over 20 years. They didn't fly away, but dissipated enough that I could reach the level of clarity I needed, to take stock of myself and make a decision about divorce.

Once the worker knew what my decision was, she was able to tell me how to go about it and help me through the process, as well as help me face the emotions that arose within me.

Finally, for me, my time in the shelter was a time of peace, reflection and identification with other women and that was what I really needed.

I found comprehension, good listeners and moral support. I — who was so afraid to go in — was almost afraid to leave. I felt very secure there, well-protected and supported by the workers. Then, when I returned home and when I went to court, I was not going desperately alone. I could count on the friendly presence of my worker, who watched over me even after I went home.

My time in the shelter was truly a moment when time stopped, an important stage in my life. It was there I discovered that I wanted to live freely and without fear. Now the time of silence and solitude is over — and the time of violence.

Source: Written for the Regroupement provincial des maisons d'hébergement pour femmes victimes de violence (provincial association of shelters for abused women) *Vis-à-vis,* Summer 1989, pp. 8–9.

"A haven in a heartless world" (Lasch, 1979) is how the family is described. Home is the one place of all places where we are protected and safe. Yet for too many people, the family home is the most dangerous of places. They are the victims of family cruelty and violence.

What Is Family Violence?

Family violence wears many faces. It is the baby who is battered, the child who is sexually assaulted, the woman who is punched and kicked by her husband, the elderly gentleman who is attacked and exploited by his children.

We all recognize these individuals as abused. Yet the whole area of family violence and abuse suffers from confusing definitions. Violence can refer to many actions, ranging from throwing things, to shoving and punching, to using a knife or gun. Although it is not usually recognized as violent, verbal abuse through yelling and screaming is common and intimidating. Some people make a distinction between "normal" violence (such as pushing and slapping) and "abusive" violence (such as beating up a person). The same act, however, may have an entirely different effect depending on who does it and against whom it is directed. For example, a small woman may shove a large man without any particular damage. On the other hand, a strong man's shove may send someone smaller (e.g., a child or a woman) slamming into a wall. Abuse is similarly subject to differences in definition. Some people may feel that any physical punishment is child abuse. Others go by the saying "Spare the rod and spoil the child" (Frankel-Howard, 1989).

Definitions are important. Levels of reporting depend on what one considers abuse. Does one count explicit sexual language or walking about naked in front of a child as forms of sexual abuse? Does slapping a child rate as child abuse? Is belittling a person a form of abuse? A broad definition would mean earlier involvement of authorities. As a result, more families could face social or legal intervention and agencies would need to provide more services.

For our purposes, *violence* is defined as an act intended to physically hurt another person. *Abuse* is a more general term, which refers to a situation in which a person takes advantage of a less powerful person. Thus abuse can include neglect, sexual and emotional abuse, and financial exploitation, as well as physical violence (Frankel-Howard, 1989).

Although family violence has been around for a long time, concern about it is relatively recent. Historically, the first type of abuse to catch public attention was child abuse, followed by wife beating and elder battering.

Child Abuse

HISTORY AND CHILD ABUSE

For centuries, children were considered the property of their parents, especially their fathers. Not only were fathers able to decide, as we saw in the chapter on mate selection, who their children could marry, they also often had the power of life and death. *Infanticide*, the killing of babies and young children, has occurred from early times. Some cultures have viewed the practice as a form of birth control or of ensuring the survival only of strong and healthy individuals who could contribute to society. Sometimes babies were used as religious offerings. There are records of young children sealed in the foundations of buildings or bridges to ensure a strong structure (Frankel-Howard, 1989; Tower, 1989).

Both parents and teachers were encouraged to physically punish children. The saying, "Spare the rod and spoil the child" was often quoted as a guideline. This belief is reflected, among other places, in nursery rhymes. The old woman who lived in a shoe with her many children, for example, "whipped them all soundly and sent them to bed." Children were seen as basically bad. Through punishment they could be transformed into God-fearing individuals (Frankel-Howard, 1989; Tower, 1989). The result was that many children were not only whipped but were physically injured, all in the name of turning out good citizens.

Sexual exploitation of children was also common. In ancient times, fathers often arranged the marriages of their young daughters to gain some financial advantage. These marriages were sometimes consummated before the girls reached puberty. In ancient Greece, it was common for men to use boys for sexual pleasure. In fact, most boys of noble families had to take adult lovers who would train them to be soldiers. Finally, in 1548, England passed a law protecting boys from forced *sodomy* and, in 1576, prohibiting forcible rape of girls under the age of ten (Tower, 1989).

In spite of laws and social criticism of the sort found in Charles Dickens' novels like *Oliver Twist,* most abuse of children was overlooked. A man's home was his castle. Outsiders had no business poking their noses into what went on in the privacy of his four walls.

In 1874, the case of Mary Ellen caught popular attention in North America. The New York child was battered by her foster parents. Initial attempts to remove her from the home failed because there was no law against child abuse. Eventually advocates argued that laws against cruelty to animals also referred to children, since they are a part of the animal kingdom. Following the Mary Ellen case, Societies for Prevention of Cruelty to Children were formed in New York State and child-abuse legislation was passed (Wachtel, 1989). The focus of early child protection was on cruel employers and foster or adoptive parents. Very rarely did Societies intervene to remove children from abusive natural parents (Pagelow, 1984).

In Canada, the first Children's Aid Society was formed in Toronto in 1891. "An Act for the Prevention of Cruelty to and Better Protection of Children" was passed in Ontario in 1893, followed by a similar act in Manitoba in 1898. There was little change in legislation for many years. For example, British Columbia kept most of the wording of the 1893 act into the 1970s (Wachtel, 1989).

Following the popularization of the term "battered child syndrome" by C. Henry Kempe in the early 1960s, mandatory reporting laws were passed. By the late 1970s, nine of twelve provincial and territorial jurisdictions had passed such laws and the remainder had set up monitoring programs (Wachtel, 1989).

WHAT IS CHILD ABUSE?

The area of child abuse, like all aspects of family violence, suffers from some confusion over its definition. The most obvious forms — battering which produces serious physical injuries, severe neglect, and flagrant sexual abuse — are generally recognized as abusive. All definitions assume that there are appropriate standards of behaviour for parents. Abusive acts violate these standards. The problem is that these standards vary over time, e.g., concerning appropriate discipline. They also vary across cultures and between social and cultural groups. Thus what is seen as abusive or neglectful by one group is considered responsible parenting by another (Wachtel, 1989).

Since some forms of abuse are difficult to detect or prove, they may not be included in official definitions. Emotional abuse, for example, can be just as damaging to a child as physical abuse. Yet it is difficult for an outsider to prove that a parent is rejecting, cold, or inconsistent enough to be abusive; thus few cases of emotional abuse are reported (Wachtel, 1989). There are other grey areas. Most laws, for example, allow parents to use "reasonable force" against their children. When does force stop being reasonable and become abusive? Is exhibitionism included in sexual abuse? In one police report, for example, 46 percent of sexual abuse cases involving children involved indecent exposure (Kempe & Kempe, 1984).

HOW MANY PARENTS ABUSE THEIR CHILDREN?

The true level of child abuse is unknown. However there has been a dramatic rise in the number of reported cases recently. In the ten years from 1974 to 1983, there was a more than 1100-percent increase in British Columbia of reports of serious abuse (Table 13.1). The increase was particularly high for physical and sexual abuse. There were similar increases in other parts of Canada. This change is usually attributed to publicity about abuse and to compulsory reporting laws (Wachtel, 1989). In the area of sexual abuse, for instance, the level has remained the same over the past fifty years, although reporting has increased (Finkelhor, 1987).

Usually, only the most extreme cases of abuse are reported to police or child-protection agencies. A variety of explanations are given for low reporting and recognition rates. First, since child abuse is frowned on by society, it is often a secret behaviour. For this reason, it may not come to anyone's attention. Second, professionals who see signs of abuse may not report the incident. Teachers or day-care staff may fear antagonizing parents. Doctors may feel bound by the duty to maintain confidentiality regarding their patients. Third, a parent's or caregiver's

Table 13.1

FOUNDED CASES OF CHILD ABUSE IN B.C. 1974–83

	No.	Year to Year Change (%)	Cumulative Change (%)
1974	145	—	—
1975	262	80.7%	80.7%
1976	417	59.2	187.6
1977	450	7.9	210.3
1978	605	34.4	317.2
1979	791	30.7	445.5
1980	987	24.8	580.7
1981	1286	30.3	786.9
1982	1536	19.4	959.3
1983	1751	14.0	1107.6

Source: Andy Wachtel (1989). *Discussion Paper: Child Abuse*. Ottawa: Health and Welfare Canada, p. 30.

explanation for injuries may seem plausible, so that no one becomes suspicious. Fourth, people may feel it isn't their business, and therefore fail to report the abuse they know about (Frankel-Howard, 1989; Wachtel, 1989).

There are many variations in estimates of abuse. The differences are the result of definitions used, of reporting laws, and of the attitudes of service providers. In the area of sexual abuse, for example, estimates vary widely. A figure that is commonly cited comes from the Badgley Report on the Sexual Abuse of Children: one in two girls and one in three boys will be the victims of unwanted sexual acts by the time they are 18. These numbers are the result of a wide definition of sexual abuse, ranging from indecent exposure to forced intercourse. Another estimate, using a narrower definition, is that 25 percent of women and 10 percent of men in the present adult population were sexually abused before the age of 16 (Frankel-Howard, 1989).

The huge growth in the reported cases of abuse has strained the resources of social-service agencies. Even when abuse is not confirmed, many families have problems that require counselling. For the most part, the increase in staff, if any has occurred at all, in no way matches the increase in reported cases.

WHICH CHILDREN ARE AT RISK OF NEGLECT AND ABUSE?

Many abused and neglected children are doubly disadvantaged. The abuse itself, of course, endangers them. Children at risk of being abused include unwanted children, children living in non-nuclear families (such as foster and stepfamilies), those born prematurely or suffering *perinatal* complications, those with physical or mental challenges, or those in poor health. Often abused children are very young. The most dangerous age for physical abuse is 3 months to 3 years. Sexual abuse often occurs first between the ages of 3 and 8 years. Thus, abused and neglected children are often particularly helpless (Frankel-Howard, 1989; Senn, 1988).

In addition, neglected children were often born during a stressful period in their parents' lives. Sometimes they remind parents of themselves or of a significant person in their lives with whom they have had unpleasant experiences (Frankel-Howard, 1989). Children who are particularly vulnerable to sexual abuse are often emotionally deprived and socially isolated. They usually know and trust the adult who abuses them and have a special fondness for that person, (usually a male). Sometimes the *perpetrator* is the only person who shows the child affection, and is often a person expected to be protective. Girls, in particular, are sexually abused by family members (Senn, 1988).

Early writers in the field of abuse have mentioned other characteristics of abused children. The physically abused, they said, often behaved in a provocative manner in order to get parents' attention, no matter how brutal. Sexually abused girls behaved in a seductive manner. More recently people have come to realize that such behaviour is described from the perspective of the abuser rather than the victim, and point out that many children with similar behaviour are never abused. Indeed, such ideas blame the victim rather than the culprit for the abuse.

WHAT KIND OF PEOPLE ARE CHILD ABUSERS?

We have problems drawing a composite portrait of the child abuser. There can be no single picture. Perpetrators are of different ages, sexes, and relationship to the child. They include mothers, fathers, siblings, stepparents, babysitters, and others who have contact with the child. They come from all parts of society. Originally it was thought that sexual abusers were mainly from the lower socioeconomic level of society. This view, however, was probably based on the fact that people who are on welfare, who come in contact with social agencies, and who live in apartments rather than houses, are more open to observation and are thus more likely to be reported. If this is so, many middle-class abusers probably fail to be identified (Maidman, 1984).

Physical abuse. Early studies produced a stereotype of the abusive mother based on these biased findings. Those at particular risk of abusing children were felt to be disadvantaged and to have poor self-esteem. Particular groups that were identified were the young (under 20 years) and the unmarried. Often the child was unwanted. A woman whose parents separated before she was 15 years old, or who lived in a foster home because she or her siblings were neglected or abused, was considered to be at particular risk. Often she was at the time the abuse occurred, or at some time in the past, grossly overweight or underweight. She lacked social support. Many times she could not bring the child's father to the interview with the child protection worker (Frankel-Howard, 1989).

Nevertheless, abusive parents seem to have some characteristics in common, which can be explained in terms of the ABCX model (Chapter 12). Often they are under high levels of stress. Stressors may be of many kinds, e.g., problems in the marriage, unemployment, or illness or disability of a family member. Often the coping resources of abusive parents are poor, e.g., many abusive families are isolated from relatives and have few close friends. Some live in areas with little community feeling (Maidman, 1984). Others lack financial resources. Abusive parents often perceive parenting as very stressful, e.g., they believe that they have little control over the situation. They also have difficulty seeing the relationship from the children's point of view, i.e., they lack awareness of children's age-appropriate emotional states and needs. When there is a crisis, they give first claim to their own needs, with the children's needs sometimes not considered at all. In addition, many believe that their children deliberately set out to defy or sabotage them. Often they also have standards for children's behaviour well beyond their developmental level. These negative attitudes toward their children help feed the parents' feelings of stress and loss of control, and thus act as a trigger for aggression (Acton, 1990).

FOR BETTER OR FOR WORSE **by Lynn Johnston**

Source: *Sudbury Star*, 20 February 1992, p. B4.

Sexual abuse. It is difficult to get a clear picture of the parent who sexually abuses his or her child because known cases are probably only the tip of the iceberg. Most of the studies on sexual abuse have looked at father-daughter incest; even less is known about other forms, such as father-son abuse. What has appeared in the research so far is not a single picture, but rather a series of pictures.

Sexually abusive families do tend to have a few features in common. First, many are isolated. Therefore, they have little relief from a poor marital relationship and relatively few opportunities for sexual activity, such as having an affair or going to a prostitute. The isolation can be physical, e.g., living on a farm or in a remote area; it can also be social and psychological (Waterman, 1986). Some fathers are authoritarian, e.g. they live an outwardly correct life, but have no close friendships. Other families are multi-problem or chaotic and cannot relate well with the outside world (Kempe & Kempe, 1984). Second, the marital relationship is often emotionally and sexually unsatisfying. Frequently the wife is not interested in sex or is ill, disabled, or absent. Often the power distribution in the family is unequal, with one domineering parent and the other passive (Waterman, 1986). Since the spouses cannot recognize and meet each other's needs, one will turn to the child for warmth and affection (Kempe & Kempe, 1984). Third, the oldest daughter is often at risk, especially if she has become a parentified child. Her father may regard her as a partner in a sexual as well as a parental sense. Often abusive fathers interpret young daughters' normal attachment to them and their curiosity about physical differences in an inappropriate sexual way (Waterman, 1986).

Some writers also cite the way males are socialized in our society as a cause of sexual abuse. There is heavy emphasis on sexual success, rather than a loving relationship, as the mark of a "real man." As part of this picture, little distinction is made between sexual and nonsexual forms of affection. Males are also socialized to regard younger and smaller individuals as being appropriate sex partners. Carried to an extreme, younger and smaller means children (Finkelhor, 1987; Frankel-Howard, 1989).

Contrary to popular notions, women do sexually abuse both boys and girls. Sometimes they go along with the idea of their male partner, at times in fear of being abused themselves. Such abusers tend to abuse very young children and to combine physical abuse with the sexual (Frankel-Howard, 1989). Sexual abuse of young boys by their mothers or grandmothers is, according to some authorities, more damaging than father-daughter incest, although they cannot explain why it should be so. They speculate that it may occur only when the mother-child relationship is particularly disturbed (Kempe & Kempe, 1984).

Abuse by siblings. Although brother-sister sexual abuse may be five times as common as father-daughter incest, society often fails to recognize it as a problem. It frequently occurs along with physical and emotional abuse (Wiehe, 1991). Violence between siblings is often considered part of the normal experience of growing up. As Pagelow says, "Violence by children is seen, but it is not seen as violence" (p. 341). She suggests that this is the reason that there is little research into either *incidence* or after-effects. What evidence is available suggests that boys tend to be more violent than girls. In one study, 89 percent of the 150 females questioned reported that they had been abused by siblings, most often by their brothers (Wiehe and Herring, 1991). Part of the reason behind the lack of research can be found in the general attitude about violence and sexual activity, that "boys will be boys" (Pagelow, 1984).

OFFICIAL RESPONSE TO CHILD ABUSE

As we have seen, there are child-protection laws in place at both the national and provincial levels. These require cases of child abuse to be reported. There are, however, problems with the lack of a standard definition of child abuse. If the abuse is severe, the abuser is prosecuted. In less severe cases, social-service agencies, such as Children's Aid Societies or provincial child-welfare departments, deal with the matter. They may remove the child permanently or on a temporary basis until the home can be made safe. They may provide counselling and treatment to the various family members to teach proper parenting or to deal with the after-effects of abuse.

There are contradictory pressures on protection agencies. On the one hand, they are expected to prevent abuse from occurring again. If a child is returned home, and is severely abused or killed, there is a public outcry. On the other hand, these agencies may be accused of child snatching and intruding unjustifiably on family life. It is impossible to predict in every case whether the child will be safe at home. Children who are removed from their homes may be damaged further by the system designed to protect them. Many children are moved repeatedly while they are in foster or residential care. Many are further physically or sexually abused, either by caregivers or by other children in the same placement (Wachtel, 1989).

Abuse Between Partners

Violence between partners is usually referred to as "wife abuse." The victim is most commonly a woman living in a marriage or marriage-like relationship with the abuser. Violence does occur in other situations: women in dating relationships and men in general are also abused. Abuse can take many forms, and often occurs in combination. It can comprise physical assault (hitting, punching, kicking), psychological abuse (belittling, threatening, destroying possessions), restriction of movement (locking in or out of the dwelling), economic deprivation, and sexual abuse (Frankel-Howard, 1989).

Like child abuse, woman abuse is rooted in history. Women have long been seen as possessions of men. In England, women and children were considered the property of the husband and father, who had the obligation to control and discipline them. A man was allowed to beat his wife as long as the stick he used was no thicker than his thumb. This law was not repealed until 1820. From 1909 to 1960, the Canadian Criminal Code included the separate offence of wife battering. The victim had to demonstrate a greater degree of bodily harm than was required in cases of assault by a stranger (Guberman & Wolfe, 1985; MacLeod, 1989).

Abused children received protection under the law earlier than did abused wives. The latter had to wait for the women's movement to publicize their plight. In 1983, a man could finally be charged with raping his wife. In the same year, changes to the Canada Evidence Act meant that a spouse could be compelled to give evidence in cases of wife battering. Since then, procedures and programs have become more sensitive to the needs of the victims of crime (MacLeod, 1989).

HOW MANY WIVES ARE ASSAULTED?

Since violence against a female partner was considered a private family matter and was tolerated for centuries, it has largely been a hidden crime. Figures are usually based on estimates and, as in child abuse, vary according to the definition used. In the following discussion, there is no distinction made between married and cohabiting couples since violence in these relationships is similar.

The most frequently quoted number is that one in ten women are abused, both physically and psychologically. An Alberta study in 1987 estimated that in 11.2 of 100 couples, the man abused his partner and that severe violence (kicking, hitting, using a weapon) occurred in 2.3 of 100 couples (MacLeod, 1989). A national study conducted by Lupri in 1986 found that one man in ten had committed at least one serious offence against a female partner in the last year. Spousal assault rates were highest in the Western provinces and the Atlantic region and lowest in Quebec. More cases were reported in urban than rural areas. Over one million wives or female partners were physically abused by their partners in 1986 (Lupri, 1989).

Table 13.2

CHARACTERISTICS OF THE VICTIMS AT THE TIME OF ABUSE

Total Number	254
By sex	
Female	243
Male	11
By region	
Atlantic	28
Quebec	27
Ontario	90
Prairies	74
British Columbia	22
Yukon	1
NWT	2
Didn't specify	10
By age	
Under 16	53
16–25	117
26–35	50
36–45	21
46–55	4
56–64	0
64+	1
Didn't Specify	8
By Income	
Low	114
Average	137
Wealthy	3
By education level	
Pre-school	20
Primary	24
Secondary	128
College/University	75
Didn't specify	7

Source: Chantal Goyette and Nahid Faghoury (1989) "A Window on Family Violence in Canada," *Vis-à-vis,* Autumn, p. 8.

HUSBAND ABUSE

There is some controversy about how serious a problem abuse of a male partner really is. Those who see it as a serious problem point out that in one study more women than men in Edmonton admitted to hitting their partner or throwing things. In the United States, the rates of spousal homicide are equal for women and men. Others reply that although husband abuse exists, it is not as serious as wife battering. First, most serious assaults by women are in response to attacks by their partners. In 60 percent of cases in which women killed their partners, they were reacting to violence against themselves or another family member. Unlike figures reported for the United States, in 1987, 6 percent of homicides in Canada involved women killing partners and 15 percent involved men killing partners. Figures from both Minnesota and Ontario show that in about 95 percent of the domestic-assault cases where police are called, women are the victims (MacLeod, 1989; Pagelow, 1984). Men are usually in less danger than women. Men are, on the average, stronger than women. They are not as likely to be injured by a blow from their partners as vice versa. Men also escape from violence more easily; because of their strength, they can usually force their way out of the house (Pagelow, 1984).

DATING VIOLENCE

Relatively little is known about dating violence. Yet, as we saw in Chapter 3, this can be a serious problem between unmarried couples. There are no national statistics available. One survey by DeKeseredy asked male students at four Ontario universities if they had physically or psychologically abused a girlfriend, lover, or casual date. Sixty-nine percent reported psychological abuse and 12 percent physical abuse. Most of the physical abuse was minor (11 percent of students), although 6 percent reported one or more acts of severe violence and 2.6 percent reported sexual abuse. These figures, especially for sexual abuse, are probably low because they depend on self-reporting. The men were more likely to have abused women they lived with than women they dated either casually or seriously (DeKeseredy & Hinch, 1991).

THE VICTIMS OF WIFE BATTERING

Many researchers have concentrated their attention on the battered woman rather than on the violent partner. They have tried to find characteristics that put her at risk of becoming a victim. They have looked for ways in which she brings violence on herself. They have tried to figure out why she stays with a man who assaults her. They have even tried to show her how to change her own behaviour in order to avoid being beaten. This approach to the problem reflects the notion that women are somehow responsible for their own abuse. Victims also blame themselves and feel guilty about the violence, as if it were their fault.

All the studies have failed to find typical characteristics of abused women, with one exception. They have all married or are living with an assaultive man (Frankel-Howard, 1989).

Three groups of women are at particular risk if they are victims of spousal abuse (MacLeod, 1989). Those who live in rural or isolated areas may have difficulty getting to a shelter, if there is one available in the area. Often poor communities cannot take advantage of federal or provincial funding because they cannot provide local funds. Since everyone knows everyone in a small community, it may be hard for the woman to ask for help, especially if the doctor or police officer are friends of the husband. Immigrant women may face language difficulties in getting help. They may also fear that they will be rejected by their communities or even be deported. Women with physical challenges make up the third group of those at particular risk. They are twice as likely to be physically and sexually assaulted as the able-bodied. Since they are largely dependent on their caregivers, they may have to be institutionalized if they complain of abuse. Those who do go for help may find that they cannot even enter the building because it has no wheelchair access, or that they are not believed (especially if they report sexual abuse) (MacLeod, 1989; McPherson, 1990).

WHO ABUSES THEIR PARTNERS?

At first, researchers concentrated on finding individual psychological disorders that occur commonly among men who abuse their partners. Their search was unsuccessful. Recently they have found that certain social and psychological characteristics are fairly common among these men (Frankel-Howard, 1989).

1. They tend to accept fully the traditional male and female roles and to draw strict lines between what is masculine and feminine. Part of their image of the "ideal" man is someone who is in control of all aspects of his life. This includes wife and children. Such men feel that they have the responsibility for the behaviour and attitudes of all family members and therefore have the right to keep their women in line.

2. They use violence as a way of solving problems and of controlling others.

3. They have difficulty dealing with emotions. This is shown in their inability to see the difference between their partner's needs and their own. They appear to believe that "real men" do not express softer emotions such as tenderness or fear. All that is left is anger, and this they cannot control.

4. These men have trouble trusting others, including their partners. As a result, they do not have anyone to whom they feel close enough to share personal concerns.

5. Often women abusers have poor self-images. A sense of being in control of the people around them makes them feel more adequate. Thus they depend on their partners to make them happy, but because they do not trust them, they are often excessively jealous.

6. They do not take responsibility for their actions. Instead they blame stress, an alcohol problem, or their partners for the violence. This is easier for

them to do since at first the violence happens only occasionally and usually only at home. Often they appear to be "nice guys" to the outside world.

Many spouse abusers suffered abuse when they were children. Rather than following a cycle of violence, however, they appear to be caught in a "cycle of sexism." They and their fathers are believers in sex-role stereotypes and try to enforce these roles in intimate relationships (Frankel-Howard, 1989).

WHY DO WOMEN STAY?

There are three basic reasons women stay in abusive relationships (Frankel-Howard, 1989). First, they are committed to the wife/mother role. Second, they are afraid of the results of leaving. Third, they have learned a sense of powerlessness and guilt.

Commitment to the wife/mother role. Many women in abusive relationships have fully accepted traditional male/female roles. Some believe they have married "for better or for worse" and must keep their vows. For some, it is so important to have a partner that they view a violent one as better than none at all. Girls are still socialized to see their most important contribution to society as being a wife and mother. They are also taught that it is a woman's responsibility to make an intimate relationship work and to keep family peace. Therefore, to ask for help means to admit that they have failed in their main responsibility in life. Since she is ashamed, the victim may also cut herself off from family and friends to keep the violence secret. Some women also feel that a mother should sacrifice herself for her children and that a single-parent home would harm them. Often the last straw before leaving is a physical attack on her children.

Since attacks usually occur only once in a while and are followed by apologies and promises that it will never happen again, many women hope the violence will stop. In addition, many women love the "nice" side of their partners. Often they will try to change their own behaviour so that they will please their husbands.

Fear of the consequences of leaving. There are many things for these women to fear. Some men threaten to severely injure or even kill their partners if they leave. A woman may fear poverty and isolation. Often abused women have been homemakers and have been out of the work force for some time. It is impossible to support themselves or their children on the low wages they can earn, if they can even find a job. Many fear going on welfare. If she has been working, her partner has often kept control over the finances, so that the woman has no resources and yet is not eligible for social assistance. Immigrant women may fear deportation if they apply for financial aid.

Some men try to control their partners through their children. They may make threats in regard to the children — either of injury or of custody suits. Some try to undermine their children's respect for their mother by calling her names or telling them that she is stupid. If the woman threatens to leave, or actually does so, her partner may inform the children she does not love them. This indoctrination campaign to alienate the children from their mother has been described as a form of emotional abuse of both woman and children (Taylor, 1993).

A sense of powerlessness. Many abused women feel helpless. In some ways their situation is similar to that experienced by prisoners of war in Vietnam. When the captives returned, they were plagued with persistent guilt feelings. This was the result of a number of aspects of their imprisonment. They were subjected to verbal and physical abuse by their captors; they also felt powerless. Because they had grown up believing that punishment was the penalty for wrong-doing, they felt that they must have done something wrong to deserve the abuse they received; they also felt guilty because they were unable to live up to their own standards, because they hadn't fought hard enough, or because they had signed a confession (Hunter, 1983). Many abused women go through a similar process. When they find that all their attempts to escape violence are unsuccessful, they not only stop trying but give up all hope of change. They also feel guilty. Girls may be especially vulnerable to an irrational sense of guilt because traditionally they have been socialized to be quiet, submissive, and pleasing to men.

Helplessness may, in fact, be a reality. Many women find no source of help. One study found that police were called in only 44 percent of cases of spousal abuse. Six out of ten women who did not report assault believed that the police could do nothing about it (Johnson, 1988). Some men physically prevent their partners from seeking help by locking them in the house or removing telephones. The victims of abuse cannot get social assistance until they have their own address and they cannot get an address without money. If there is no shelter nearby or it is full, they may literally have nowhere to go.

There is sometimes further victimization by the people the abused woman turns to for help. Clergy, family members, or friends may assume it is her fault if the relationship isn't working and may urge her to go home and try harder. The result is that the woman feels even more guilty for somehow failing at her proper role. She may feel guilty for her natural anger and frustration. The insensitivity of those around her also fuels her sense of helplessness.

HOW DOES SOCIETY RESPOND TO SPOUSAL ABUSE?

In the past, our society has not been very responsive to wife abuse since we have tended to regard it as a private family matter. In the past ten years, however, there has been increased demand for spousal assault to be taken as seriously as any other violence.

Abused women's first need is for protection. This can be provided in two ways: through the police and courts, and through places of safety such as shelters. In a recent survey (Harris & Dewdney, 1991), women were asked where a battered woman could go for help. Less than half suggested police. Nine percent actually stated that the police should be avoided. In an earlier study, 60 percent of the battered women who had called police found them unhelpful because they did not provide suitable information, they did not take the danger seriously, or they put down or blamed the women (Harris & Dewdney, 1991).

In the past, police have not always laid charges in cases of spousal abuse. Three factors for this failure have been suggested: (a) the belief that what happens in the home is private, (b) the belief that couples should try to reconcile rather than expose their problems in court, and (c) the fear that the victim will refuse to testify. Police viewed their task as one of quieting down the situation so that there would be no more violence that day (Frankel-Howard, 1989).

Since 1982, all provincial and territorial governments have issued directives to police and, in most cases, to Crown Attorneys that encourage a more careful investigation and prosecution of spousal-assault cases. The growing concern about spousal abuse has resulted in improved training throughout the justice system. Larger police forces have also established special units to respond to family violence (MacLeod, 1989). According to one study conducted after these changes took place, among those women who called the police, 63 percent rated their performance favourably and 68 percent said they had responded quickly (Johnson, 1988).

Often a pressing need for abused women is safe housing. Part of the need is met by transition houses and other temporary shelters, but their numbers fall far short of the need. Although there has been increased funding during the 1980s for shelters, there has been little money provided for counselling and similar supportive services that are needed by the residents. There has also been very little money provided to upgrade the low salaries paid shelter workers (MacLeod, 1989). Funding cutbacks would make it impossible to maintain even the present inadequate level of service (Bruger, 1988).

Housing for the longer term is also important. Yet in 1988, for example, there were only twenty-two special *second-stage housing* projects across Canada, which provided a protective environment and necessary emotional support and counselling (MacLeod, 1989). Many abused women have poor coping skills, since their partners have severely limited their power to make decisions. They need legal advice as well as skills upgrading so that they can support themselves (Alberta Social Services, 1988).

Women may have difficulty finding the help they need. Often they do not know who to ask, or they may contact agencies that do not provide the kind of help they need. In general, they know only a few agencies and these might not provide the services needed. Listing in telephone books may not be helpful. An individual needs to know the correct section to refer to in the directory, and even then the names of agencies may not be informative enough. For example, a woman who calls a counselling centre may find that financial counselling is all that is provided. Agency staff are not always well-informed about the services of other organizations. The result is a series of frustrating referrals, which feel like a run-around. The situation is made worse if women expect services that individuals or organizations are not set up to provide, e.g., physicians are often expected to give referrals, counselling, emotional support, and advice, yet many fail to even recognize abusive situations (Harris & Dewdney, 1991).

In many large centres, treatment is available for all family members. Women, of course, suffer emotional as well as physical damage when they are abused. Children from violent families may have problems managing their own anger and may need therapy. Recently, treatment for abusive men has received much attention. Often they attend groups because they are afraid of losing their wives or because they are ordered to do so by the courts. Although there is some question about how well such treatment works, many people feel that it is the only way to reduce marital violence (MacLeod, 1989).

Abuse of the Elderly

Elder abuse is the most recent kind of family violence to be recognized. The great increase in the number of older people is partly responsible for the incidence of elder abuse. What was a rare event is now much more common simply because there are now so many more seniors than in the past. Also, more people now are professionally concerned with older people. Since they make up a larger portion of the population, older people have more political power. Society as a whole has become concerned about protecting its vulnerable members, such as the weak and disabled (Gnaedinger, 1989).

There is still no standard definition of elder abuse. Most studies include physical and psychological abuse. There is disagreement, however, whether spouse abuse should be included in the definition since most such abuse started long before old age. Some researchers also include neglect and financial abuse. The latter involves the theft or conversion of money or objects of value, most commonly by cashing pension or social-insurance cheques and not giving the senior the money (Gnaedinger, 1989). Neglect can be classified as active or passive, depending on whether the failure to provide care is intentional or unintentional (Douglass, 1987).

In spite of the popular term, "granny bashing," most abuse is nonphysical in nature. There is, however, disagreement as to the most common variety — financial abuse or passive neglect. Estimates, in general, vary widely, partly because of lack of agreement as to the definition. Much of the reported abuse occurs in institutions rather than in families, yet only 10 percent of seniors live in such facilities. Figures from Quebec suggest that 43 percent of mistreatment occurs in institutions and 25 percent in families (Frankel-Howard, 1989). Based on her studies in Manitoba, Shell (n.d.) estimates that 2.2 percent of the elderly living at home are abused. Figures from the United States indicate that from 2.5 percent to 10 percent of the elderly population is abused (Frankel-Howard, 1989; Gnaedinger, 1989).

IS ELDER ABUSE LIKE OTHER FAMILY VIOLENCE?

Elder abuse is, in many ways, similar to other forms of family violence (Gnaedinger, 1989). It tends to occur most often when both victims and families are socially isolated. Like other victims of abuse, the elderly abused are weak, powerless, and dependent. In addition they are looked down on for being old. Much abuse occurs when family members do not have practical or psychological resources to deal with the older person and yet are expected to be responsible for that person. Often the abuser has a history of alcohol abuse, unemployment, and low self-esteem. In many families there has been a history of violence.

There are also aspects unique to elder abuse. Many older people feel that there is a stigma in raising a child who mistreats them; thus they do not want to admit the abuse. The older person may be dependent on the child for daily needs, because of either a physical disability or a cognitive impairment, such as Alzheimer's disease. The social contacts of older people may disappear either because friends and relatives die or because they themselves cannot get around. Sometimes the caregiver is an old person caring for a still older one. Finally, the caregiver may become discouraged because of the elder's physical and mental deterioration (Gnaedinger, 1989).

VICTIMS AND ABUSERS

The victim is most likely to be female, frail or disabled, over the age of 70 (often over 80), and living with the abuser. This picture is just what one would expect. As we saw earlier, most of the oldest part of our population is made up of women (Frankel-Howard, 1989; Gnaedinger, 1989). Few people in our society have less power than older women. They are looked down on both for being women and for being old. They are likely to have spent their lives in the traditional wife and mother role and, as a result, are likely to be financially dependent on others (Mastrocola-Morris, 1989).

There is considerable disagreement as to who is a typical abuser of the elderly. This is partly the result of the definition used, especially whether spouse abuse is included. Overall, about 60 percent of abusers are males (husbands and sons), followed by daughters. Often the abuser is dependent on the victim, e.g., an adult child who is supported by a parent. Many abusers feel trapped by a sense of family obligation (Frankel-Howard, 1989). In institutional abuse, most perpetrators are women, since they make up most of the staff. Sometimes in long-term care facilities, the abuser may be another resident (Gnaedinger, 1989).

Few victims report the abuse. They may believe that they have caused the abuse and deserve it. They may be ashamed. Often they are afraid — that they will be further abused because of the report, that they will be institutionalized, or

Allen, a retired railroad worker, age 66, lived two miles from his parents who were both 85 years old and reasonably healthy. They had hoped to stay in their own home until they died, but it was more than two miles from the nearest shopping center and neither parent could drive because of poor vision. So the couple decided to move into a small apartment two blocks from Allen's home.

Allen was concerned about his own family's financial future and his difficulty in meeting the payments for an expensive home and tuition for three children still in college. To all appearances, Allen was a model husband and father but in reality he was a long-term spouse abuser who had also been arrested twice on charges of assault. In both cases the charges were dropped by the victims — neighbors who had tried to come to the aid of Allen's wife while he was abusing her. Allen's wife also refused to file charges against him or to consider divorce or separation. Allen had been abused as a child by both of his parents, as were all four of his siblings. The parents, however, paid for his college education and provided the down payment for his home.

With his parents living closer, Allen's wife encouraged him to visit daily. This resulted in Allen visiting his parents during the monthly financial crisis which plagued his household. Three months after his parents moved into their apartment Allen asked them for a large sum of money to help him reduce his indebtedness. When his father said the money wasn't available, Allen beat him and threw his mother through a glass door. There were no witnesses and no charges were filed. After three similar violent assaults, Allen's mother was hospitalized with a cerebral hemorrhage. An emergency room nurse suspected domestic violence and after a police investigation Allen's father filed assault charges. Allen was jailed for 90 days. During that time, his parents moved to a senior citizens' apartment complex and obtained a restraining order that prohibited Allen from visiting them alone.

Source: Richard A. Douglass (1987). *Domestic Mistreatment of the Elderly — Toward Prevention*. Washington, DC: American Association of Retired Persons, p. 16.

that they will not be believed. Some are incapable of reporting the abuse because of mental deterioration, serious illness or disability, or because they do not know how to get help (Gnaedinger, 1989).

ELDER ABUSE AND SOCIETY

Just as some professionals in the community are unaware of the high levels of spousal abuse, they are also unaware of the high levels of elder abuse. One study in Ontario, for example, found that in 1984 only 41 percent of Ontario Provincial

Police officers knew about elder abuse. The most knowledgeable professionals were health-unit staff (Moore & Thompson, 1987). The number of service providers who know about elder abuse has, however, probably increased because of the publicity given the problem in recent years. Some professionals may not believe complaints of abuse. Disbelief may be the result of ageism, e.g., some individuals cannot imagine any old person being attractive enough to be sexually assaulted. They may also see an older person's symptoms as part of the aging process rather than abuse.

Some individuals feel that there should be mandatory reporting of elder abuse, just as there is for child abuse. Such legislation has already been introduced in Newfoundland, New Brunswick, Nova Scotia, and Prince Edward Island (Gordon & Tomita, 1990). One concern about making reporting mandatory is that such laws may violate the rights of the elderly under the Charter of Rights and Freedoms, i.e., they would have little more ability to direct their own lives than do children. For example, mandatory reporting may deprive them of the choice of where to live. It might mean that elderly people will end up in nursing homes or other institutions against their will (Gordon & Tomita, 1990; Moore & Thompson, 1987).

Is There a Cycle of Violence?

According to systems theory, patterns of violence continue from one generation to the next (Pagelow, 1984). If children are abused or see their mother abused, they are likely to become child abusers, according to this theory. Boys who see their mothers abused grow up to be spouse abusers; girls in such a family grow up to be abused. Quite apart from any cycle of violence, it is clear that children of violent partnerships are negatively affected in many ways (Elbow, 1982).

Do abused children become child abusers? There is little evidence to either prove or disprove the theory. In one study, 24 percent of a group of persons who had been abused as children were considered highly likely to become abusive parents, compared with 6 percent of a nonabused group. Yet, over three-quarters of the abused group were not considered a high risk. Many abusers come from multiproblem families where they have experienced poor socialization and are emotionally unstable as a result of damaging experiences in childhood. There is no single cause of abuse (Pagelow, 1984).

Do abused girls become battered women? Some do. There is no support, however, for the theory that they have been socialized to expect or invite violence (Pagelow, 1984). Rather, they have had the misfortune to mate with violent men.

Do abused children become spouse abusers? Abuse by men, according to a study by Pagelow (1984), seems to be related more to the way they handle stress than to the fact that they themselves were abused. Most of their brothers and sisters, even though they grew up in the same abusive home, do not become abusers. On the other hand, children who are abused are taught that violence is an appropriate way of settling conflicts within the family. We still need to learn why some boys model their adult behaviour after their fathers and others do not (Jaffe et al., 1986).

Why Do People Abuse Family Members?

There have been many attempts over the years to explain why abuse occurs. Most theories fit into one of two basic varieties (Frankel-Howard, 1989).

THE INDIVIDUAL IS RESPONSIBLE

There have been a number of explanations that look at the characteristics of the individual abuser and victim. The first type of individual-responsibility theory has tried to find a typical psychological disorder in abusers. For example, child abuse has been blamed on "role reversal." That is, some abusive parents expect their children to provide them with the kind of love, approval, and sense of importance that they should really provide their children. When children fail to live up to these standards, they are assaulted. Others have blamed failure in bonding of the mother to the child. Alcohol and drug abuse are involved in many cases of family violence. They cannot, however, be considered causes, rather they are used to excuse violence. Alcohol and drug abuse may affect the nature, timing, and extent of the abuse.

Sometimes victims are blamed for provoking the violence. This can be direct in statements such as, "If she had made supper on time, he wouldn't have hit her." There can also be indirect blaming and sharing of blame in such concepts as the "cycle of violence," where abuse is believed to run in families. These views overlook the fact that, regardless of the circumstances or family background, the abuser chooses to use violence.

There has also been some attempt to look for genetic causes of abuse, e.g., men with two or more y-chromosomes (so called "super-males") were at one time considered more violent than men with only the one. The findings are suspect since there were few comparisons made with nonviolent men. There was also little attempt made to explain why some "super-males" are violent and others are not.

SOCIETY AND THE FAMILY ARE RESPONSIBLE

Some sociological explanations of family violence focus on family dynamics. If families are under extreme stress, according to these theories, members take out their frustration in abuse. The stress may come from a variety of sources: from outside the family as through unemployment, from value and role conflicts within the family, and from life-cycle changes. Abuse has also been related to power and status within the family based on age and sex. The abuser may need to assert or maintain superiority, especially if he or she feels it is challenged too far. For example, if a man strongly believes that the male partner should be the breadwinner in a family and he is unemployed, he may fear he is not quite a man because he cannot fill the conventional male role. If his partner does anything he considers a challenge to his superiority, he may assault her. People will use violence in families if the costs do not outweigh the rewards. Thus if the victim tries to appease the abuser and does not call the police, the abuse is likely to continue.

Society itself has been blamed for abuse. As we have seen, many identified abusers are from lower socioeconomic classes. Their violence may be a response to the stress of social factors such as poverty, unemployment, poor and crowded housing, and often a sense of powerlessness. In addition, our society is a violent one, as we can see any day of the week on our television screens. Use of considerable force in families is permitted, or even approved, e.g., parents are expected to physically restrain or punish their children in order to control their behaviour. Society also has built-in norms of male dominance over women and children. In family violence, most victims are female and most abusers are male. This pattern reflects the way men and women are socialized.

Many of the individual and social theories about violence in our society are attractive. Although there is evidence to support most of them to some degree, not one fully accounts for violence. There is no simple explanation. Rather, violence is probably the result of a complex interaction of many factors: the individual characteristics of the abuser, the stresses resulting from both family relationships and from society itself, and the manner in which people are socialized to accept the values and norms of society.

Preventing Family Violence

Although there are differences in the forms family violence takes, there are two basic approaches to prevention.

The most common approach is referred to as secondary prevention. This is treatment or some other intervention to keep abuse from occurring again. These include, for example, services to battered women which empower them to leave an abusive situation, such as shelters, second-stage housing, and skills training. It can also include treatment of perpetrators. Some of these programs include teaching parenting skills to abusive parents (Acton, 1990), providing group therapy for violent husbands (Ontario Medical Association, 1988), and treating behaviour problems, such as aggression, in children from abusive homes (Watson, 1986).

Another approach is through primary prevention which aims to keep abuse from occurring at all. One of its principal methods is education. Some is directed at particular populations, e.g., the elderly can be taught how to keep the risk of financial exploitation, neglect, and abuse to a minimum as they plan for their future care. Family members can also be instructed in ways to protect their older relatives (Douglass, 1987). Another target group is children. There have been programs with the goal of streetproofing them and teaching them the difference between good and bad touch. Yet these have been criticized as making children feel unsafe about the world in which they live (Kraizer, 1986). School courses in parenting help equip young people with knowledge about child development and appropriate methods of child rearing. Primary prevention also tries to make the community more supportive to families. For example, elder abuse can be reduced if there are relief programs so that caregivers do not become overwhelmed (Douglass, 1987). Supportive programs for parents of young children or children with severe health problems can serve the same function. Another approach focuses on high-risk groups, e.g., therapy for children from violent homes can help teach them better ways of managing anger than attacking family members (Jaffe et al., 1986).

One difficulty with primary prevention is its cost. Since it is broad-based, and since we cannot predict accurately who is likely to abuse a family member, many education or community-based programs are unfocused. Yet, because they reach so many people, they provide the best hope for making the family home the one place of all places where members are protected and safe.

SUMMARY

WHAT IS FAMILY VIOLENCE? The whole area of family violence and abuse suffers from confusing definitions. In this book, "violence" refers to an act intended to physically hurt another person and "abuse" refers to a situation where a person takes advantage of a less powerful one. Due to problems with definitions and reporting, actual levels of abuse are unknown.

CHILD ABUSE. Historically, child abuse has been part of society. In North America, the first laws against it were passed in the late 1800s. Child abuse is commonly considered to include physical and sexual abuse. Some people also include emotional abuse. Abused children are often young, unwanted, and physically or mentally disadvantaged. Abusers come from every class in society. Often they are under high levels of stress, are isolated socially or physically, and perceive parenting as stressful. Sexual abusers, in addition, tend to have unsatisfactory marital relations. While sibling abuse is common, little is known about it. When abuse is reported, the perpetrator may be charged, the child may be removed from the home, and/or the family may receive therapy.

PARTNER ABUSE. Violence between partners became a social concern more recently than did child abuse. Although there is disagreement about how serious a problem abuse of male partners is, in general men are less likely to be injured than women. Couple violence can begin before marriage, where it occurs more commonly among cohabiting couples than in more casual relationships. Victims of spousal abuse do not fit a single description. Perpetrators tend to have some or all of the following characteristics: acceptance of traditional gender roles, use of violence as a method of control, difficulty dealing with emotions, problems with trust, a poor self-image, and reluctance to take responsibility for their actions. Some women spend many years in an abusive relationship. They may be committed to the wife/mother role; they may fear the consequences of leaving, which may include fear of further injury, fear of economic hardship, or fear of having their children turned against them. They also have a sense of powerlessness, which can be reinforced by society. In the past, spousal assault was often considered a private matter. Now police are directed to charge abusers when there are reasonable grounds to do so. Although they do not meet the demand, shelters are available for abused women and their children.

ABUSE OF THE ELDERLY. Elder abuse has only recently received much attention. In addition to neglect and physical and sexual abuse, it also includes financial exploitation. Both partners and children may be perpetrators. In some families, elder abuse is part of a longstanding pattern of violence. In others, it may result from frustration with the needs of the older person, and the lack of resources and support to help the caregiver meet those needs. There is controversy over whether reporting elder abuse should be mandatory or whether it infringes on the rights of the older person.

WHY DO PEOPLE ABUSE FAMILY MEMBERS? There have been many attempts to explain why abuse occurs. Some researchers have suggested that there is a cycle of violence in which each generation of the family in turn abuses members. While abusers are more likely than others to have been abused themselves, there is no explanation as to why some who have been abused are violent and others are not. Other researchers have looked for individual causes for abuse in either the perpetrator or the victim. Still others look at social influences, such as unemployment or low socioeconomic status. Our society also condones violence. There are, however, no clear patterns; violence is probably the result of many complex factors.

PREVENTING VIOLENCE. There are two basic approaches to prevention. One is to treat abusers or separate them from their victims to keep the violence from happening again. The second is to prevent violence altogether through education, or by encouraging society to be supportive to families.

KEY TERMS

abuse: a situation in which a person takes advantage of a less powerful person

incidence: percentage of cases in the population

infanticide: the murder of a baby

perinatal: around the time of birth

perpetrator: person who is guilty, in this case of abuse

second-stage housing: longer-term housing for abused women

sodomy: anal intercourse between two males

violence: act intended to physically hurt another person

CLASS ASSIGNMENTS

Complete one or both of the following assignments, as directed by your instructor.

1. What facilities exist in your community to assist abused women? Are they adequate? Why or why not? Are there gaps in the services available? Explain.
2. There are two basic approaches to dealing with families that abuse children. One is to leave the child in the home while the family receives treatment. The second is to remove the child from the home. Give the advantages and disadvantages of each approach.

PERSONAL ASSIGNMENTS

These assignments are designed to help you think about your own experience.

1. Do you know anyone who is (was) abused? What effect has the abuse had on the individual, either in the short term or the long term? How could the abuse have been prevented or stopped earlier?
2. Do you believe that it should be compulsory to report abuse of the elderly? (Yes, no, maybe)? Why do you think so?

CHAPTER 14

The Family and the World of Work

OBJECTIVES

- To consider the history of day care and its relation to women's work.
- To examine sources of stress in the interface between work and family life.
- To explore the effect of unemployment on the family.
- To look at the impact of worker burnout on the entire family.

What a shock when I went back to work! My reason was the usual one: our growing family needed more money. Teenagers are more expensive than toddlers and my husband's pay hadn't kept pace with inflation, so I got a job filling in for a teacher on maternity leave.

I knew it would mean major changes for my family. A stay-at-home mother does chores and deals with family problems during the day. No more! We assigned chores and planned schedule changes. These took hold after early resistance. What none of us had counted on was that my work almost paralyzed me as a family member. I came home exhausted and didn't have the physical energy to deal with the many hassles and concerns that crop up in any family. Even more trying was the fact that I worked with teenagers and when I came home I couldn't escape them. I wasn't much good as either a wife or a parent.

More and more families are affected by the conflict between work and family responsibilities. As we saw in Chapter 4, a major trend in our society is the increase in the number of women employed outside the home. This has grown sharply since the mid-1970s. The greatest increase has been among those aged 25 to 44, i.e., among women with children at home. In November 1992, 59 percent of married women with children under age 3 whose husbands were employed worked outside of the home, as did about 70 percent of those with children aged 6 to 15 (Statistics Canada, 1992). This trend has produced two major problem areas: care for young children and juggling two family jobs along with household responsibilities.

Day Care in Canada

Day care in Canada is closely tied with social attitudes toward women's work. There has long been the assumption that children are best off at home looked after by their mothers. In pre-industrial times, as we have seen, children worked along with their parents in the family business. Day-care centres were established only when it was seen to benefit society, either from the desire for better supervision of children or from the need for the mothers to join the work force.

Figure 14.1

PERCENTAGE OF WOMEN AND MEN EMPLOYED, 1975–88

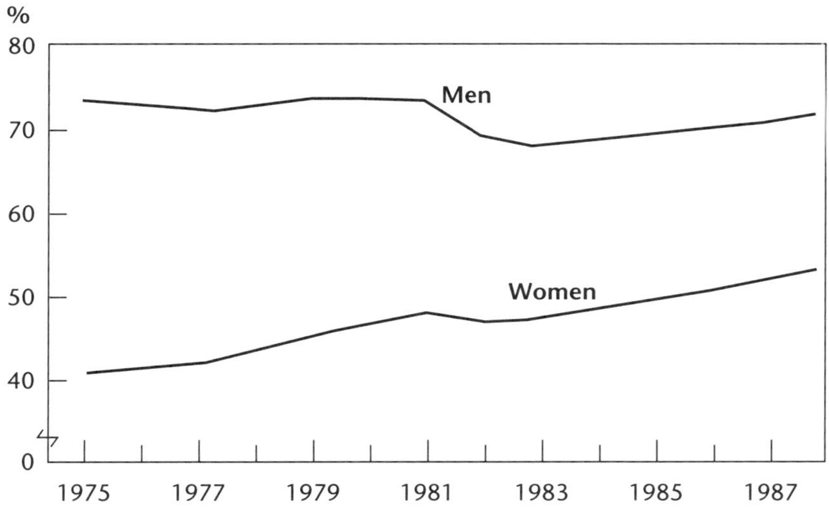

Source: Statistics Canada. Catalogue 71-529. In Jo-Anne B. Parliament (1989). "Women Employed Outside the Home," *Canadian Social Trends*. Summer, p. 3.

Once families moved to towns and cities as a result of industrialization, children no longer worked alongside their parents in the home or on the land. Their behaviour was no longer shaped under the watchful eyes of the neighbours in a small community. Child rearing became more difficult for parents since they had to work away from the home in places that children were not welcome. The situation was especially difficult for single mothers. Some children were left with older brothers or sisters; this came to be seen as a problem after school attendance was made compulsory. Other young children were left alone, sometimes tied to the bedpost so that they could not wander. Officials were concerned that the lack of supervision and training might produce a large group of criminals (Schulz, 1978).

The first day-care centres were established under various auspices, such as schools and children's hospitals, in response to these problems. Most, however, were developed by religious organizations, such as the earliest day nurseries in Montreal, or by volunteer women's organizations. Partly because of the level of knowledge about child development and partly because of limited funding, the care was mainly custodial with few educational activities provided (Schulz, 1978).

These services were never planned from the user's point of view. They were always seen as an emergency service to meet the needs of society. As a form of welfare, they allowed mothers to work to support themselves and their children. In connection with the centres, some organizations set up employment agencies. The mothers were regarded as a source of domestic labour for the women who set up the child-care services and their friends. Rules tended to represent the employers' rather than the day-care users' interests. Day-care services were also seen as a method of preventing future social problems for which society would have to pay. They also allowed older brothers and sisters to attend school. Children in these centres received training to turn them into productive members of society. The emphasis was on manners, cleanliness, obedience, and religion. There was a continuing sense, however, that such care was second-rate, lagging far behind care at home (Schulz, 1978).

During World War II, there was an urgent need for women with children to join the work force. In 1942, the federal government agreed to enter cost-sharing agreements with the provinces to provide day care on the condition that at least 75 percent of the spaces were reserved for the children of mothers working in essential industries. Only Ontario and Quebec took advantage of this arrangement. In these provinces, there was an enormous expansion of day-care services. Once the war was over, federal funding was discontinued. Women were expected to stay at home now that men were once again available to fill jobs. In Quebec, many centres were closed on October 1, 1945. Ontario planned to do the same, but the public outcry was so great that the province passed the Day Nurseries Act in 1946, which provided funding and established minimum standards. However, a number of centres did close, because of inadequate resources (Schulz, 1978).

Presently there are differences in the levels and types of day care provided. There are several reasons for such differences. First, the current attitude in society toward day care is mixed. Some people point out that high quality day care should be a right granted to working parents and their children. It is also seen as remedial, or as an aid to the development of children with special needs, e.g., of the developmentally challenged. Subsidized day care is part of the welfare system. On the other hand, day care is seen as a cost to the parent (especially the mother) that allows the indulgence of a job, since the tax credit provided by the government does not equal the actual cost of care.

Second, there is no national policy regarding day care because day care is a provincial responsibility. A national policy assumes that the majority of Canadians share the same goals and values. There are, however, too many family types and traditions for such agreement. In addition, there is the underlying belief that families should take on full responsibility for raising their children; therefore, subsidized day care is seen as an exception rather than something all families should have. To add to the confusion, because care of children is considered a private rather than public affair, there has been little information collected on either the need for or quality of day care in Canada (Lero & Kyle, 1991).

Work and Family Stress

There are many other ways that families and work are interrelated. One of these is the stress that results from the conflicting demands of job and home. This is a two-way street. The tensions from paid work carry over into the home, and the family issues affect the job (Armstrong & Armstrong, 1987).

EXPECTATIONS

One of the major stressors in dual-income families is the expectations of family members and the people around them. Social values affect individuals, e.g., women complain that if they stay home, they are seen as failing to live up to their potential, and if they work outside the home, they are criticized for neglecting their children. This problem results in part from the fact that there are many mothers in each camp who are defending their own decisions. In addition to pressure from social expectations, individuals are affected by their own expectations, e.g., some are perfectionists who place themselves under unnecessary stress because they want to do everything well. Others are workaholics and deprive the family of their participation (Portner, 1983).

The expectations of employers and fellow employees may be anti-family. Employers frequently expect employees to work more than an eight-hour day and five-day week, especially if they want to advance in their careers. Job transfers, part of the cost of promotion, disrupt relationships with relatives and friends. If a spouse refuses to move, he or she can be blamed for holding the partner back (Portner, 1983).

ON THE FASTRACK

Source: *Sudbury Star*, 20 February 1992, p. B4.

In a study of male officers in an American police department (Maynard & Maynard, 1982), researchers found that although the department had no specific policies about families, there were actually a number of policies that did directly affect families. The value of stable family life was understood but not encouraged. Many of the officers seemed to have the attitude that it was better to be single or divorced than married. In fact, the divorce rate among the officers was 70 percent within the first five years on the police force. Nearly half the wives felt that the department expected wives and families to adjust their lives to the demands of police work, but did little in return to help the family. About half the wives had to give up job opportunities or other plans of their own because of the work schedules of their husbands. This was most likely to happen when there were children whose needs had to be considered. It was often difficult to plan activities too far ahead because work hours could change at the last minute. Many wives felt their husbands should put the family first. Most of the men, however, felt that their career was more important than family life and would not get another job even if the going got rough for their wives and children. This conflict arises in part from the emphasis placed on esprit de corps. Police are encouraged to place their loyalty to the force and to fellow officers ahead of other priorities since their lives may depend on such loyalty. As a result, families come second.

While this study focused only on men working in law enforcement, women police officers probably experience even more job-related stress than male officers. Researchers found that, in addition to the same stressors affecting men, women were often subject to lack of acceptance and to sexual harassment. The female officers interviewed reported that if one made a mistake, all women were stereotyped as incompetent. Male officers often had negative attitudes to the extent that sometimes they would not speak to women or refused to have them as partners. The movement to provide equal opportunity was also a source of resentment. In some cases, men believed that a woman was hired just because she was a woman, rather than because she would make a good officer. In addition, women were subjected to many allegations concerning their sexual orientation and habits (Wexler & Logan, 1983). All these stressors could contribute to possible burnout and the resulting family stress.

JUGGLING TIME AND ENERGY

Many individuals have problems balancing the demands of work and family. First, there never seems to be enough time and energy for individuals to accomplish all they wish to in either their work or family roles. This may result in short-term difficulties in getting day-to-day work completed or it can result in failure to achieve overall goals. Second, there can be difficulties over scheduling of time. Shift work, frequent travel, and long hours may mean that family members get to spend little time with one another (Portner, 1983).

There has been some research, mainly in the United States rather than Canada, about the way family responsibilities spill over into the workplace and vice versa. Workers with young children seem to experience the most interference. For example, 68 percent of mothers and 51 percent of fathers with children under the age of 6 report this difficulty. The juggling of responsibilities affects both work and family life. In a Toronto study, 43 percent of parents felt they did not have enough time to spend with their children. When there was a conflict, family or personal well-being was usually sacrificed to the job. Over one-third of women studied reported that when there was conflict between motherhood and their job, they resolved it by cutting back on leisure time and sleep. Those workers who seem most at risk of conflict are mothers of children younger than 12, single parents, and parents of babies. Women are more likely than men to stay home, to care for sick children or parents, or to deal with other crises. They may take this time as sick leave, and may not have any left if they themselves become ill. If they take too much time off for family reasons, they may also fear losing their job (Lero & Kyle, 1991).

On the other side, about three-quarters of both men and women in the study had dealt with family issues during working hours. Nearly half the women and one-quarter of the men had lost work time because of child-care difficulties. Even though over two-thirds of Toronto workers felt that the fit between family and work was good, many felt drained at the end of the day and worried about their children while they were at work (Lero & Kyle, 1991).

CHILD-CARE RESPONSIBILITIES

Working parents are concerned about the possible negative effects of their employment on their children. There is more attention paid to the impact of working mothers because it is generally assumed that all men work and that women are responsible for the care of family members. Although quality time is generally seen to be more important than the actual hours spent with a child, it is difficult to both define quality time and to make it happen on schedule (Portner, 1983).

Two facts are clear — child care consumes a great deal of time, and it is usually women's work. It is estimated that women working full-time in the home spend 1.3 hours per day solely caring for children. This does not count the time that they supervise activities such as watching television or playing. It also does not include taking children to and from activities such as music lessons or recreational sports, waiting for them to finish the activity, or watching the activity (Armstrong & Armstrong, 1987). In fact, children now require more time and attention from their parents than ever before. There are not as many adults to share child-care responsibilities, such as grandparents or unmarried female relatives. Families are also shrinking so that there may not be older siblings to care for younger ones. Even though parents working outside the home do use various child-care resources, when they are home they still must spend time with the children. When there are children in the home, women extend the time spent in household chores by nearly three-quarters of an hour and men by only twenty minutes (Marshall, 1990). Even when a husband helps with child care, he may take over the enjoyable tasks, like playing with the children, and the mother may not feel any relief (Lowe, 1989).

HOUSEHOLD RESPONSIBILITY

As with child care, women assume primary responsibility for household work (Figure 14.2). Admittedly, housework is not the hard labour it once was. One needs only to consider the appliances now available. The microwave is a real advance over the wood stove that was once used for cooking. There are dishwashers, automatic washers and dryers, and central vacuum cleaners. For those who do not want to cook, there are restaurants, and take-out and delivery services. House cleaning, laundry, and yard work can be done by others for a fee.

The relationship between housework and marital roles, however, is not that simple. Housework, despite modern appliances, still requires many hours per week. The actual time spent is related to such factors as income levels, and age and quality of the housing, as well as personal standards for meal preparation and cleanliness. Older buildings usually require more effort in cleaning as do crowded quarters and those with inadequate storage. Not everyone can afford modern appliances. Those with low income levels must spend more time in planning and in finding bargains to make ends meet. Buying meals out or hiring help are beyond the reach of those living near the poverty line (Armstrong & Armstrong, 1987).

As we saw in Chapter 4, the shift from wage-earner husband to wage-earner spouses has not meant an equal shift in household responsibilities. Rather, there have been conflicts over just how household work and child care should be divided. Since women traditionally have been the caregivers in our society, they often expect (and are expected) to be responsible for most of the family's physical care and emotional well-being. Many women spend more hours each day in combined paid employment and family care than do men or homemaker wives

Figure 14.2

PERCENTAGE OF WOMEN AND MEN PERFORMING SELECTED HOUSEHOLD CHORES, NOVEMBER 1986

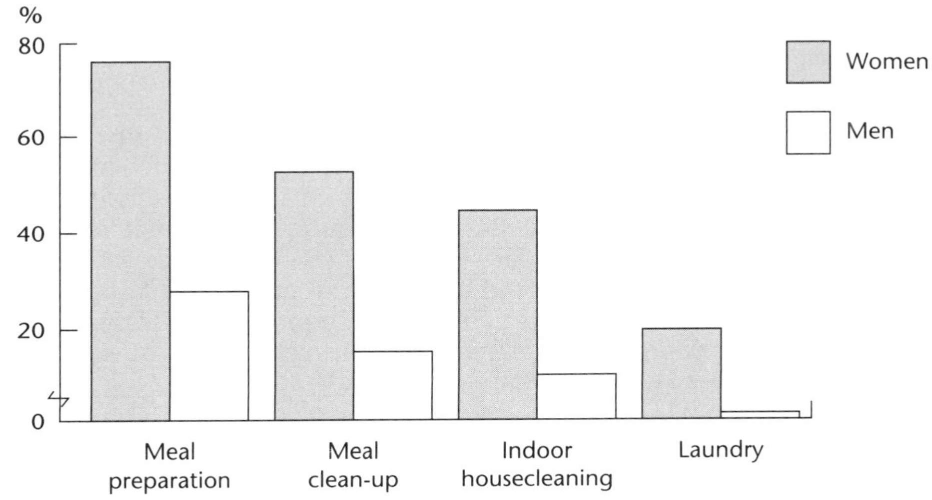

Source: Statistics Canada, General Social Survey, 1986. In Katherine Marshall (1990). "Household Chores," *Canadian Social Trends,* Spring, p. 18.

(Parliament, 1989). Since men traditionally have not had to concern themselves with family care responsibilities, some have difficulty in seeing housekeeping chores as being masculine; thus they feel demeaned if they do traditional "women's" work. On the other hand, a husband may well be aware of the overload the wife is suffering, and be concerned for her well-being. The norm appears to be undergoing change. There is evidence that men, especially younger ones, are now assuming a greater share of household responsibilities than they used to (Luxton, 1986).

PAID WORK AND HOUSEHOLD WORK

For women, since they have such a heavy responsibility for child rearing and household work, paid and unpaid work are often similar. Both may involve boring, repetitive tasks, little opportunity for self-fulfilment or promotion, and little opportunity to unionize to defend their interests. Often the jobs available to women take for granted that they will be caregivers — waitress, shop clerk, nurse, teacher, and day-care worker all fall into this category. Women's work in the marketplace is thus mainly geared to ensuring the well-being of others. This responsibility is related to burnout (de Koninck, 1984).

Losing a Job — The Effects of Unemployment

A different kind of job-related stress comes with unemployment. Of course, whether expected or sudden and unpredictable, unemployment has a financial impact on the family, even if it does not result in outright poverty. If a family lives in an area with one major industry that drastically reduces its work force or even closes, there may be widespread layoffs or business closures; other jobs may be difficult to find, forcing the worker to relocate.

Work serves many functions beyond the financial. It structures time — sleeping and eating times, weekdays and weekends, work and vacation. With unemployment, this framework suddenly disappears, not only for the unemployed individual but also for the rest of the family. Work also provides for regular contact outside the family. Often one of the first ways families cut back financially is in the area of recreation, thus reducing social contact still further. Work provides an outlet for a person's inborn need for activity. Finally, it provides a person with status and identity. For young people, in particular, having a job means being counted an adult (City of Calgary, 1986; Voydanoff, 1983).

Often unemployment undermines an individual's sense of identity. If a man or his family holds the traditional value that a man provides financially for the family, then losing a job means that he has failed as a person. The individual whose personal identity depends on his or her profession (a police officer or a surgeon, for example) may also feel a deep sense of loss. A common response to the need for income is for the spouse of the unemployed individual to find a job or to increase work hours. This strategy further alters the power of family members. The ease with which the family makes the shift depends largely on their attitudes. Does a wife resent having to support the family? Is the husband willing to take on homemaking responsibilities? Is the man's authority tied to economic factors or to the affection family members have for him? Adaptation is also dependent on the financial resources and social support available (Voydanoff, 1983).

Burnout and the Family

Although many families manage to juggle work and family responsibilities, others find the task extremely stressful. One danger is the possibility of burnout. *Burnout* is a state that occurs when a person, often in a helping profession, experiences prolonged stress without learning how to cope with it (Maslach, 1982). One psychologist believes that women are at particular risk of burnout because of the daily stresses and pressures under which they operate (Freudenberger & North, 1985).

Burnout produces physical and emotional exhaustion because of the excessive demands placed on the individual. People may impose extremely high standards on themselves, their families, employers, and friends, or society itself may impose high expectations. For example, if an employed woman with young

Ralph Brown was numb, barely able to comprehend that after 10 years he was suddenly indefinitely laid off from his job. Sure, he had heard rumors of impending layoffs, but he had reasoned that certainly 10 years of seniority would prevent him from being affected. Soon he would have to face his family with the word. What would happen to all of their plans — the addition he was going to build on the house, skis for his daughter, camp for his son, the new freezer for his wife? How could he explain that he had no job, no plans for getting one, and no knowledge as to whether or when he would be called back to his old job? What would they think? What would they say? Of course, they knew times were tough. Several friends and neighbors had already been laid off. But that was different. What would happen to **him, his** family? What if his wife were laid off too?

Source: Patricia Voydanoff, "Unemployment: Family Strategies for Adaptation." In Charles R. Figley and Hamilton I. McCubbin, eds. (1983). *Stress and the Family.* Vol 2. New York: Brunner/Mazel, p. 90.

children is a perfectionist at work, and her husband expects her to keep the house spotless and take the children to numerous recreational activities in which they are involved, she may be a candidate for burnout. Her first response probably will be to try harder, but she will find that she still cannot keep up with the many demands on her time and energy. As a result, she is likely to become exhausted and depressed, a condition that makes it difficult for her to respond to the emotional needs of her husband and children or to be productive at work (Freudenberger & North, 1985).

INDIRECT EFFECTS

Some of the effects of burnout on the individual have an indirect impact on the family. Often emotional exhaustion goes hand in hand with physical exhaustion. As a result the individual becomes susceptible to illness. Stress is a direct factor in some illnesses such as heart disease and ulcers. The individual may also suffer psychologically. The reduced sense of accomplishment and self-esteem that goes with burnout, and the loss of zest for life, are the central characteristics of depression. In attempts to deal with the emotional effects of burnout, the individual may take to alcohol or drugs. These physical and emotional disorders affect the family if the burned-out member cannot take part normally in family life. For example, we have already seen the effects of chronic illness and alcoholism on family members (Chapter 12). In the extreme, of course, death completely deprives the family of one of its members (Maslach, 1982).

Often individuals in caregiving positions find it difficult to admit they themselves need care. Nurses are prone to burnout, which has been correlated with both drug abuse and mental illness. Programs are now in place to deal with drug problems. Yet many nurses feel there is a stigma attached to admitting to psychiatric problems. As a result, some delay seeking help for so long that they become sicker and sicker, and the chances of full recovery are reduced (Powell, 1989).

DIRECT EFFECTS

There are also direct effects of burnout on the family. The overstressed individual's growing dislike of interacting with others may lead to irritation and anger at family members. When they are emotionally drained, individuals cannot handle calmly everyday hassles at home. They are less able and willing to spend time or become emotionally involved with family members. Instead they want to be left in peace and quiet. Because they feel bad, they may demand extra attention and understanding by the family and then feel guilty for needing such. If other family members expect them to interact as they did in the past, the burned-out person may withdraw out of a sense of hurt and neglect. This reaction may lead in turn to injured feelings on the part of spouse or children. Sometimes the desire for a hassle-free home leads to pressure on other family members to be perfect. The burden may be particularly difficult for children of police and correctional officers, judges, and clergy. Often society adds to the pressure by expecting such children to display model behaviour (Freudenberger & North, 1985; Maslach, 1982).

Burnout may reduce individuals' ability to cope with stress or to use proven methods of stress reduction. Some take chances and expose themselves to risks.

Figure 14.3

WEB OF RELATIONSHIPS

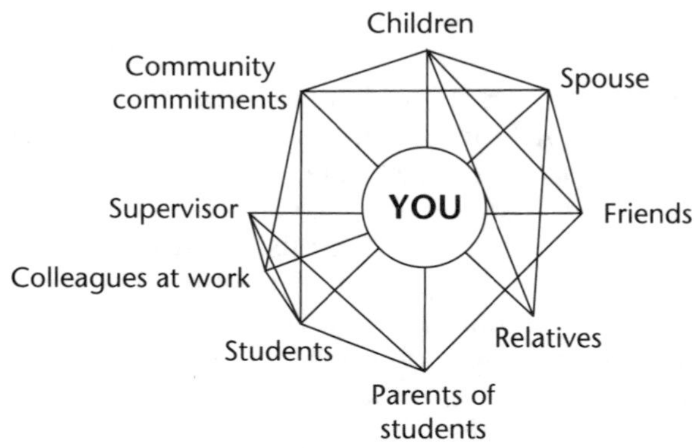

This diagram illustrates the different people and loyalties that can pull a day-care worker in many directions. A similar diagram can be drawn for other professions.

Source: Paula Jorde (1982). *Avoiding Burnout: Strategies for Managing Time, Space, and People in Early Childhood Education.* Washington, DC: Acropolis Books.

Some are resistant to therapy. The latter reaction seems to occur especially among doctors and mental-health workers who do not want to admit to the same kinds of problems their patients and clients display. Often they are too tired to make active efforts such as exercising to reduce stress, especially if they have worked ten- or twelve-hour shifts (such as some correctional officers and nurses are required to do). Many are unable to open up emotionally to their spouses. Some may feel that to do so may be a breach of professional confidentiality. Others may wish to protect their family from the grim realities of the job. Some may also be trying to protect themselves (Maslach, 1982).

What is the effect of burnout on the family? As we saw in our discussion of family systems, a change in the behaviour of one member affects the rest of the members of a family. The increased irritability and lower levels of patience and tolerance of the burnout victim may lead to squabbling and bickering which escalate into serious marital and family conflict. The resulting separation or divorce may be blamed on problems in the marital relationship rather than on the job stress where it originated. Burnout may also be catching. Some partners may be nurturers; they will respond to the obvious distress on the part of their spouse by increased nurturing. In spite of this, the burned-out person does not feel better, so the partner tries harder. The burnout victim's apathy and unwillingness to communicate tend to make the spouse feel rejected. If the situation continues for some time, the partner may burn out too (Freudenberger & North, 1985). If the workplace is unsympathetic to family needs (like the police department described earlier), the stress on family members is even greater.

Flexible Work Arrangements

One way that employers and families have tried to address the problem of competing work and family demands is by setting up alternative work arrangements. These take three forms: flexible time, flexible workplace, and reduced hours of work. Most such arrangements are designed on the assumption that women are principal caregivers for children and other family members. They allow hours to be adjusted to family demands. Some men have been finding such arrangements helpful also (Rothman & Marks, 1987). Although theoretically these arrangements can be of particular advantage to women, they do have some drawbacks.

FLEXIBLE TIME ARRANGEMENTS

A number of employers have established alternatives to the traditional eight-hour day. One arrangement is *flexitime*, in which all employees are expected to be at work during a core period in the middle of the day but may decide for themselves when they will arrive or leave, provided they work the usual number of hours. Theoretically this allows parents to better meet family needs as well as workplace responsibilities. In practice, however, when a woman has the full responsibility for child care, even flexitime does not alleviate stress sufficiently. In addition, some professions still demand that anyone expecting promotion should not pay attention to the clock; therefore those using flexitime may lose out on promotions (Ontario Women's Directorate, 1991; Rothman & Marks, 1987). Some individuals prefer longer periods off work. Their needs may be met by a *compressed work week,* in which they work ten- or twelve-hour shifts for three or four days, and then have several days free. The long hours may, however, contribute to exhaustion and burnout. Others are able to accumulate credits through working longer hours and then take extra time off at the beginning and end of summer weekends (Ontario Women's Directorate, 1991).

FLEXIBLE WORKPLACE

With the growing use of computers and communication technology, it is possible for people to work outside the office, an option sometimes referred to as "telecommuting." Some families view this type of arrangement as one way of solving the conflict between work and child care. Too often, according to researchers, women who choose to work at home are not considered regular employees and are not only paid less than regular employees but receive no fringe benefits. Since they are at home, they are commonly seen first as homemakers and second as paid workers. Often many such women work early in the morning, late at night, and when their children are asleep during the day. Thus this arrangement does little to reduce stress (Christensen, 1987). The Ontario Women's Directorate (1991) recommends that individuals working at home should be considered part of the regular work force, and encouraged to attend meetings and social events with other employees so that they maintain contacts that might lead to promotion.

REDUCED HOURS OF WORK

Part-time work allows the individual to fulfil care responsibilities for children or older relatives. However, it can mean that the individual loses opportunities for advancement. Labour unions are also concerned with the trend to converting full-time jobs into part-time jobs without benefits. Protected part-time work occurs when salaries and benefits are prorated according to the hours worked. The arrangement can be either permanent or temporary. Another plan is *job-sharing,* in which two employees share one full-time job, again with prorated salary and benefits. Reduced work hours do not appeal to everyone since few can afford to live on less than a full-time salary (Ontario Women's Directorate, 1991).

The Family, Work, and Society

Some of the tensions between family and the workplace can be better understood in terms of Garbarino's ecological model of interacting systems (Chapter 1). In the macrosystem we find conflicting values. For example, women are felt by some to find their greatest fulfilment as wives and mothers. Others consider that women can best achieve their potential in the work world through careers. Thus no matter what choice women make, someone will tell them that they are wrong.

Another source of tension in families is the unequal value placed on men's and women's work. This can be seen, for instance, in levels of pay, and the concern over the effect of working mothers, but not working fathers, on their children's development.

In the exosystem, institutions such as the workplace and day-care centres also seem to present conflicting values. On the one hand, women are encouraged to find employment. On the other, there is the unfriendly attitude of many employers toward families. Day-care centres are planned as a service for working parents, yet it is difficult to find one with hours that will accommodate shift work.

Some of these conflicts are played out in the mesosystem. Teachers, for example, may feel that children's failure to do homework arises from inadequate supervision when two parents are employed out of the home. Parents, for their part, may feel that the expectations of the school are unrealistic. All of these pressures work together to produce stress in the family microsystem around such matters as child care and household chores. In turn, the marital and parental subsystems are also affected.

Many individuals feel that the only real answer to some of these problems is a shift in values in our society. There are signs, small and slow though they are in coming, that norms are changing to accommodate the needs of two-earner families.

SUMMARY

DAY CARE. Day care is closely tied to social attitudes toward women's work. When mothers' paid employment has been seen as important for society, day care has been provided. Current levels of day care reflect conflicting attitudes. Some believe that affordable high-quality care is a right of working parents and their children, and others are convinced that families should assume full responsibility for their children.

WORK AND FAMILY STRESS. An important way in which work and families are interrelated is through conflicting demands. One of the major stressors for families comes from expectations of society and of employers. Women receive conflicting messages about motherhood and work. Not all workplaces are responsive to family needs. Often the demands of both family and employment need to be juggled. Often family responsibilities are handled on work time. Yet family or personal well-being, especially leisure time, are frequently sacrificed to the job. Parents must care for children outside day-care hours and also look after the household. Despite modern appliances, these duties still consume a great deal of time, with women usually assuming the major responsibility for them. Many women experience stress because their jobs also require caregiving activities. Unemployment affects families, not only through loss of income, but also through changes in time management and family roles, which may affect the unemployed individual's self-esteem.

BURNOUT. Burnout is the result of extreme stress, often job-related. It results in physical and emotional exhaustion, poorer job performance, and reduced ability to deal with the demands of others. As a result, it has serious effects on the family. Indirectly, an individual's stress-related illness or substance abuse creates additional stress for the family. Directly, individuals may withdraw from family life or be much less tolerant of family-related stressors.

FLEXIBLE WORK ARRANGEMENTS. One solution for the conflict between family and employment is adapting work hours to family needs. These include flexible work hours, flexible workplace, and reduced hours of work. While all permit individuals more leeway in handling family needs, all have drawbacks. Full-time work, regardless of hours or workplace, still produces high levels of stress among parents of young children. Income levels and promotion opportunities may be reduced with flexible work arrangements.

FAMILY, WORK, AND SOCIETY. Many of the tensions can best be understood in terms of the ecological model, where there are interactions among social values, institutional attitudes, and family needs.

KEY TERMS

burnout: a state of physical and emotional exhaustion resulting from prolonged stress

compressed work week: a job with long work hours concentrated in three or four days per week, allowing for several days in succession off work

flexitime: a full-time job in which employees can determine when they arrive and leave

job-sharing: a situation in which two employees share one full-time job

CLASS ASSIGNMENTS

Complete one or both of the following assignments, as directed by your instructor.

1. Explore in more detail different options such as flexitime and job-sharing that might help individuals manage both family and work responsibilities. What are the advantages and disadvantages of each?
2. What are the various day-care options available in your community? Who offers them? How are they supervised? What advantages do each of the various choices offer children? What are the potential problems?

PERSONAL ASSIGNMENTS

These assignments are designed to help you reflect on your own experience.

1. Students often experience high levels of stress, especially if they have family responsibilities. What do you consider the main sources of stress? Describe the effect they have on families. What suggestions can you offer for reducing such stress?

2. Select an occupation in which you are interested. What do you feel may be the main sources of stress in this occupation? How might these particular stressors affect a family?

CHAPTER 15

Poverty and the Family

OBJECTIVES

- To place poverty in Canada in historical perspective.
- To look at poverty among the four poorest groups in the population—young people, older women, female-headed single-parent families, and the working poor.
- To consider the characteristics of the poor.
- To examine the effect of poverty on children.
- To look at homelessness in Canada.

They begin gathering in front of the church doors before 8:00 a.m. on Wednesday morning. Around 8:30 a.m., someone unlocks the door to the gym, and the men and women jostle to get to the head of the line. At a table, a tall man checks their IDs, takes their names, and assigns each a number. Some lift chairs from the stacks along the wall and sit down to wait. Others go outside to smoke or stand around visiting with friends and acquaintances. Soon someone puts out coffee and stale buns and people drift to the table to help themselves. Two small children run around, and the adults smile indulgently at them.

Around 9:00 a.m., helpers are ready to start the distribution, and people are called up in turn to receive a few cans of food, perhaps some limp and bruised fruit and vegetables, and an assortment of stale loaves and rolls. New clients are interviewed by a social worker. If latecomers are lucky, the food will hold out until they get to the tables. They have already run short several times this year. By 11:00 a.m., it's all over.

Next Wednesday, before 8:00 in the morning, the crowd will be waiting at the door.

Most poor people do not use food banks. Yet they may have serious difficulties making ends meet. In general, poverty is defined almost entirely in terms of income. Financial levels alone do not accurately reflect the ability of some people to manage better than others the money they have available. For example, some are able to grow or gather food to supplement what they can buy. Others have developed shrewd management skills. Yet most families require a certain minimum level of income to create satisfying lives in our society.

There are two basic ways of defining poverty (Ross & Shillington, 1989). One is to consider what it would take to provide what is absolutely necessary for physical survival. The most extreme definition would apply to the family that used food banks, hostels, and second-hand clothing to survive, and received only the most basic health care. Historically this has been the kind of criterion used in deciding if someone needed social assistance. The other approach to defining poverty is based on social well-being in addition to physical survival. Most measures of poverty in Canada use the latter type of definition.

Helping the "Worthy" Poor

In the early years, the poor depended almost entirely on their families or on other private individuals for help. Up until World War I, public assistance was provided by local governments or charities on an emergency basis only. Most of the help involved the provision of grocery hampers, second-hand clothing, and vouchers for fuel. Very little cash was provided, partly because poverty was believed to result from bad budgeting (along with a variety of vices such as drinking). It was generally felt that help should be at a level lower than the earnings of the most poorly-paid labourer, so that handouts were barely enough to survive on. There was also the notion that asking for help should be so unpleasant that a person who did not need it would not ask. For example, homeless elderly people were kept in local jails on charges of vagrancy because there was no other place they could go. Some places demanded that people live in a workhouse if they were to receive assistance (Guest, 1985).

Gradually what is called the social *safety net* began to develop. Mothers' pensions (later called Mothers' Allowances) were set up in order to help needy children. However, eligibility depended on the mother. The criteria varied from province to province. In British Columbia, for example, mothers were eligible if their husbands were in a tuberculosis sanatorium, mental hospital, or prison, or if they themselves were chronically ill or disabled or widowed. Applicants had to be of good character, even providing letters of reference, and had to pass a strict *means test* to prove that they needed help. Once they received the allowance, such mothers were subject to intrusion into their personal lives — no man in the house (except a close relative), permission needed to move from city to country or vice versa. In 1927, old-age pensions were established for the needy, again with a strict means test (Guest, 1985).

Beginning around the time of World War I, the idea of a social security net for all began to take hold, although it developed slowly. Worker's compensation came into being; minimum-wage legislation was passed by the 1920s. Following World War II, the pace of change picked up — family allowances, universal old-age pensions, medical insurance, Canada and Quebec Pension Plans. There continue to be services provided to those with low incomes, e.g., the Guaranteed Income Supplement for the elderly and pensions for the disabled. To receive these, individuals or families must pass a means test, administered either by service providers or through income tax returns. The responsibility for providing social programs has shifted from the municipality to the provincial and federal governments by means of cost-sharing arrangements (Guest, 1985). In order to reduce the cost of providing universal programs, the government has established what is called the *clawback*, i.e., defining benefits as income and then taxing such benefits.

Poverty, Officially Defined

Currently, poverty is considered in relation to the income of the "average" Canadian. One of the most commonly used definitions is the Statistics Canada low-income cut-off point, which is updated annually. This takes into account family size, up to five members, and community size. The result is thirty-five separate low-income cut-off points. The poverty lines are set at a level where a family spends significantly more of its income on food, clothing, and shelter than the average family (Table 15.1). These cut-off points are artificial. A family with an income 10 percent above the poverty line could afford only a couple of extra bus tickets or cups of coffee per day than those at the poverty line (Ross & Shillington, 1989). In an attempt to simplify the poverty lines, Statistics Canada has proposed leaving community size out of the calculations. If this takes place, it would appear as though the number of poor people in cities has decreased, and those in rural areas has increased, without circumstances actually changing (Ross, 1992).

Two factors that influence the impact of poverty on families are its depth and duration. Depth of poverty refers to the amount a family or individual income is below the poverty line. The further below, the more difficult it is to provide the basic needs. Duration refers to how long the poverty lasts. Short-term low income is easier to weather than prolonged periods because individuals usually have some resources to help tide them over a bad period. When poverty is prolonged, however, everyday resources are eventually depleted and need to be renewed. For

Table 15.1

STATISTICS CANADA LOW-INCOME CUT-OFFS (1986 BASE), ESTIMATED 1992

		Size of Community	
Family Size	**Over 500 000**	**100 000/ 499 999**	**Rural**
One	$15 428	$13 552	$10 504
Two	20 914	18 370	14 240
Three	26 584	23 349	18 099
Four	30 608	26 881	20 837
Five	33 441	29 371	22 767

The cut-offs do not differentiate between adults and children. Table 15.1 is an abbreviated version of the cut-offs: there are actually 35 separate lines calculated for five different-sized communities and seven family sizes.

Source: David Ross (1992), "Current and Proposed Measures of Poverty, 1992,"*Perception* 15 (4):60.

example, income could initially be used almost entirely for food and living expenses. Eventually it must stretch to cover replacement costs for clothing and for household supplies such as furniture, bedding, and towels. Thus, the longer poverty lasts, the harder it is for the family to make ends meet (Ross & Shillington, 1989).

Who Are the Poor?

For a number of reasons, it is difficult to determine how many poor people exist in Canada. First, the number will vary depending on the definition used. Second, the very poorest of the poor are almost impossible to count because they include the homeless.

Between 1973 and 1989, the figures were somewhat encouraging. Although the total number of Canadians living in poverty increased, the percentage decreased from 16.8 percent to 13.6 percent. In 1990, however, the rate increased to 14.6 percent, a reflection of worsening economic times (Ross, 1992). Four groups stand out—young people, older women, female-headed single-parent families, and the working poor. We will look at each in turn.

UNATTACHED ADULTS

The rate of poverty among unattached adults is high. Since 1973, there has been a dramatic shift in the makeup of this group. Earlier, the largest numbers were the elderly, especially older women. Now the largest segment is those under 35.

The official number probably underestimates the level of poverty among the youngest adults, since it does not include the many who cannot afford to move out of their parents' homes.

1. The elderly. The decrease in poverty among the elderly is the result of improved pensions and government benefits. The majority receive most of their income from public programs. If the individual had been employed, Canada or Quebec Pension Plans provide an income. Old Age Security is paid to all seniors. For those with low incomes, there are also benefits provided through the Guaranteed Income Supplement. The combination of these income sources has served to move many older people above the poverty line. A large number, however, are among the near poor. Many of the elderly poor are women. They are less likely to have contributed to the Canada/Quebec Pension Plans and are more dependent on the Supplement. Among the elderly, 43 percent live in poverty (about 47 percent of women) and 21 percent in near poverty (Ross, 1992; Ross & Shillington, 1989).

2. Young adults. The shifting of poverty from old to young is in part the result of the baby boom reaching employable age. It is, however, also due to the fact that the growth of jobs in the economy has not kept pace with the population increase. The types of jobs available to young people have shifted from the well-paying areas of resource development (e.g., mining), manufacturing, and government to consumer services, which pay less (Wannell, 1991). In addition, many young people can find only part-time work. There has been growing concern over the increase in "employable" people receiving welfare, especially if they have no dependents, since they are considered a drain on the taxpayer's pocket. Recent welfare reforms have reduced benefits available to this group. This trend appears to be a revival of the concept of the "deserving" poor (e.g., the mentally and physically challenged) and the "undeserving." Unfortunately, such moves only drive young people deeper into poverty when there are no jobs available (Torjman & Battle, 1989).

FAMILY POVERTY

Poor families increased in numbers, but their percentage of all families declined from 1979 to 1986. For families headed by someone of working age, however, both the total numbers and rate increased. Since 1986, the trend toward more poor families has continued in all provinces except Nova Scotia, Alberta, and British Columbia. Ontario, in particular, suffered a 21-percent increase in family poverty, a reflection of the permanent loss of manufacturing jobs (Ross, 1992; Ross & Shillington, 1989). Two groups have been most affected.

1. Young couples with children. Although families with parents under 25 are especially at risk, much of the increase in poor families that occurred after 1981 has been in two-parent families with the head aged 25 to 44. Larger families

Table 15.2

CHANGES IN THE COMPOSITION OF FAMILY POVERTY, 1973 AND 1986—STATISTICS CANADA DEFINITION

	Percentage of the Poor Population	
Characteristic	**1973**	**1986**
Province		
Quebec	30.8	33.5
Ontario	29.8	25.4
British Columbia	7.3	12.4
Age of Head		
under 35	27.9	40.2
65 and over	22.6	10.8
Family type		
lone-parent female	19.5	27.4
elderly couple	16.9	6.7
couple/children	38.7	35.1
Education		
less than 9 years	54.0	27.7
university degree	1.9	4.8
Number of earners		
one	45.4	39.6
two or more	16.9	22.9

Note: The percentages are for selected characteristics and do not add to 100 percent.

Source: David P. Ross and E. Richard Shillington (1989). *The Canadian Fact Book on Poverty—1989*. Ottawa: Canadian Council on Social Development, p. 47.

with three or more children are also in danger of poverty (Clarke, 1988). Families with two earners are obviously better off financially than one-earner families.

2. Lone-parent families. Hardest hit are lone-parent families headed by mothers, with 56 percent living below the poverty line. The poverty rate for families headed by women is four times that for families headed by men. The situation is worst for young mothers. These statistics reflect the lower pay women traditionally receive and the fact that many single mothers receive Family Benefits, either because they cannot afford day-care costs or cannot find a job (Ross, 1992; Ross & Shillington, 1989). Due to the growing number of single-parent families, many children are growing up in poverty. In 1984, for example, 68 percent of all children living with only their mothers were poor.

SPECIAL GROUPS

Two groups are not singled out in Statistics Canada figures — aboriginal peoples and the mentally and physically challenged. In 1985, among native peoples with incomes, 54.2 percent were poor, compared with 39.1 percent of all Canadians. These figures do not include natives who live on reserves. One estimate which included all native peoples was that over 62 percent live in poverty. Those with mixed ancestry were somewhat better off, although their poverty levels were also above the Canadian average (Ross & Shillington, 1989). Another minority group affected are blacks in Nova Scotia (Keyes, 1989).

In 1986, 68 percent of disabled Canadians had an annual income under $10 000 and accounted for about one-third of all Canadians on welfare. Only 5 percent earned over $30 000. Often their costs of living are higher than average because of their special physical needs. Government assistance for the disabled comes from a confusing variety of sources, which are governed by many conflicting rules (Muszynski, 1989; Torjman, 1989).

What is Beyond the Numbers?

One of the most striking facts about poverty in Canada is that many people who live in poverty have jobs. In 1990, the working poor accounted for 27.7 percent of all poor families (Ross, 1992). Who is the typical working-poor family? They most likely live in Western Canada, probably in Saskatchewan, they haven't had as much schooling as their more affluent neighbours, and they have more children (even the family with one or two children is twice as likely to be poor as a childless couple); they are probably young, with parents aged 25 to 34; only one family member is employed. The nonpoor are far more likely to have two or more adult earners. In families with one child, however, even if both parents work full-time at the minimum wage, the family will still fall below the poverty line. Obviously single parents are at an even greater disadvantage (Ross & Shillington, 1989).

HAGAR THE HORRIBLE **by Dik Browne**

Source: *Sudbury Star*, 20 June 1992, p. B4.

Young people aged 16 to 24 have a much higher rate of joblessness than older adults. They are usually the last hired and the first fired. Often they are shunted into part-time jobs. Even if they find what they believe to be full-time work, they may find their hours cut due to poor economic times or other circumstances. Many end up with just enough work to qualify for unemployment insurance. Girls often take courses that limit them to jobs with homemaker-like skills, work that has traditionally been underpaid. The average real wage (what money will buy) has dropped for younger workers, especially those aged under 25. Young people face a number of barriers to employment. They have little or no job experience. As a result, they have fewer interpersonal and job-related skills and fewer contacts to help them find work (Senate Committee on Youth, 1986; Wannell, 1991).

Education is a factor in poverty. In 1986, a person with less than nine years education was four times as likely to be poor as a university graduate. Four out of ten without a high-school education are unemployed. Recently, having post-secondary education has been no guarantee of finding employment. Although researchers are not sure what factors make the difference, they speculate that some better-educated individuals do not have steady employment because of factors such as disability, ill health, or psychiatric problems (Ross & Shillington, 1989).

Individuals who cannot read well enough for practical use are likely to have much lower incomes than those who can read well. Since they cannot read instructions, they may require more training time, suffer avoidable accidents, or turn out substandard work. Therefore they may have problems holding jobs when they can find them. More than half of those people on welfare in Ontario are illiterate. Parents may lack the language skills to read to children and to help them with their homework. As a result their children may also have difficulties in school (Swan, 1990; Weiler, 1989).

A lack of affordable housing has made living more difficult for those with low incomes. Cheaper housing near city cores is being "gentrified," i.e., renovated into stylish and expensive homes far beyond what the original residents can afford. Less subsidized housing is being produced. Most of what exists is available to families and seniors, with a small number reserved for those with disabilities. Usually young unattached individuals are not eligible for such housing. As a result many of the poor must depend on the "for profit" rental market. Many spend at least half of their income for accommodation (Doyle, 1989; McLaughlin, 1987; J. Ward, 1989).

Since housing is so expensive, people are using food banks in ever greater numbers. During 1989 in Metropolitan Toronto, nearly 80 000 people relied on food banks each month (Doyle, 1989). Current estimates are about 162 000 in Toronto and 320 000 in Ontario (Aarsteinsen, 1993). A survey of food-bank users in Edmonton and Calgary late in 1985 found that many were waiting for money, usually unemployment or welfare. Some ran out of funds before the end of the month, especially if they had some emergency expense. Most had already used the food bank at least once that year (Edmonton & Calgary Social Services, 1986). There is also increasing pressure on other services such as soup kitchens. Some funds intended originally to help individuals with unexpected expenses have been diverted to helping stock food banks. The result is that there is less variety in the emergency help available. Critics of food banks point out that they allow the government to avoid responsibility for providing adequate financial resources to those in need. Others suggest that food-bank operators know better than most the effects of welfare policies and are highly regarded in society; they should therefore lobby government for the right of all Canadians to have their basic needs met (Riches, 1989).

What is Poverty Doing to Children?

Children make up the largest single group of the poor people in Canada — over 1.5 million. Both the rate and the total number increased between 1973 and 1990. Although most poor children are members of two-parent families, a growing proportion have single mothers. Lone-parent families often cannot compete well in an economy that requires two incomes for each household. By splitting family resources, separation and divorce tend to make the ex-partners poorer. The lack of accessible and affordable housing and high-quality day care also contribute to the problem (Glossop, 1989; Ross, 1992; Ross & Shillington, 1989).

Poverty affects two major areas of life: health and education. To some degree the two are related.

HEALTH

Health of poor children is affected even before birth. When money is tight, the food budget often suffers and with it the health of children, even before they are born. Babies with low birth weight are more commonly born to low-income mothers than to more affluent mothers. This is associated with a greater number of birth defects and higher infant mortality. In Alberta, for example, babies from poor families die at twice the rate of those from wealthy families. Among native families, the rate is 4.5 times the average (James, 1989; Clarke, 1988).

The effects of poverty continue into school age. Children living in poverty suffer a wide range of health problems. Often they have inadequate nutrition which lacks essential vitamins. If a family lives in substandard or crowded housing, children may be exposed to more illnesses to which they are less resistant because of their diet. If a family is not covered by insurance, dental care may suffer. More poor children also suffer from psychiatric disorders than others (Clarke, 1988).

In 1988, the Nova Scotia Nutrition Council released a report which showed that welfare rates in the province provided only between 50 and 80 percent of the cost of a nutritious diet. The council recommended raising food rates to reflect the cost, providing milk and juice to pregnant women, and offering nutrition education to welfare recipients. As a result, food rates were increased and pregnant women can now receive a nutrition supplement (Dyer, 1989).

EDUCATION

Many children from low-income families do not do well in school. More repeat grades and drop out without completing high school. Fewer go on to post-secondary education. There are several reasons for this. Since they are ill more frequently, poor children miss more time from school and may have trouble catching up. If they go to school hungry, they may also have difficulty concentrating on class activities. Crowded homes may mean that there is no suitable place for homework or studying. When housing is substandard, poor families tend to move more often. As a result, children must adapt to new schools and different curriculums. They are also at a disadvantage since there is less income for cultural opportunities such as museum visits or music lessons. They may also be stigmatized if they cannot pay for school outings and activities or if they wear unfashionable clothing. For many children, schooling is so unpleasant that dropping out is a relief (City of Calgary, 1985; Clarke, 1988). There may also be pressure on adolescents to get jobs to reduce economic strain on the family. School dropout rates for 16- and 17-year-olds from poor families are more than twice those for the nonpoor (Ross & Shillington, 1989). As we have seen, 16- to 24-year-olds make up a large proportion of the poor. Since they have only limited education, they have difficulty getting jobs. Those they do find do not pay well and may be only temporary. Thus it is difficult for them to break out of poverty. In this way the cycle of poverty is carried from one generation to the next.

Homelessness

There are no exact figures for the number of homeless people in Canada. This is in part a result of the difficulty in counting them. It is also due to the fact that the homeless population changes from day to day. Estimates vary from 10 000 in Toronto alone to 10 000 for the entire country (J. Ward, 1989). A head count of people staying in shelters was conducted on January 22, 1987 (during the Year of the Homeless). Three hundred and five shelters participated. Using the average of these agencies, it was estimated that 10 672 people spent that night in a shelter. The number in Vancouver was lower than usual because welfare cheques had just been issued. Of course, the homeless who did not use a shelter remained uncounted (McLaughlin, 1987). Who are the homeless? The picture of the 1930s transient, unemployed man is no longer appropriate (Table 15.3). Instead the homeless include families, single parents and their children, single women, and young people. Many are receiving social assistance. They have lost their homes because of misfortune, such as fire or lack of rent money. Among the homeless are psychiatric patients and individuals with disabilities (Halsey, 1987).

There are a number of causes of homelessness. The shortage of affordable housing is a key, but it does not explain the whole phenomenon. Changes in employment patterns have had an effect. Many men now using shelters found casual and seasonal labour in the past. Homeless women, especially those who

Table 15.3

PERSONAL SITUATIONS OF PEOPLE WHO SOUGHT SHELTER ON JANUARY 22, 1987

Situation	People	Percent of Sample
Unemployed	4 239	54.7
Current or ex-psychiatric patient	1 556	20.1
Receiving social assistance	3 995	51.5
Evicted	726	9.4
Alcohol abuser	2 580	33.3
Drug abuser	1 163	15.0
Physically handicapped	237	3.1

Source: Mary Ann McLaughlin (1987). "Homelessness in Canada: The Report of the National Inquiry." Special insert in *Social Development Overview*, Vol. 5, No. 1, p. 5. (published by Canadian Council on Social Development).

have been married, tend to have fewer skills in demand by the labour market. Since shelter residents cannot find suitable housing, they are staying on in what are supposed to be temporary and emergency shelters; as a result, others are turned away (McLaughlin, 1987; J. Ward, 1989).

Conditions in shelters do not favour family living. Men's shelters are generally worse than women's, which receive six times the funding per person. Many men's shelters are in old buildings, including former warehouses and factories. There is little privacy because beds are in dormitories. Lice, dirt, and odour are common. Part of the reason for the difference in men's and women's shelters is the idea that men are to blame for their homelessness, while women are regarded as victims of society. The latter are thus seen as worthy recipients of assistance (McLaughlin, 1987; J. Ward, 1989).

Psychiatric patients make up a sizable portion of shelter users and cut down on spaces available for others. When large mental institutions were closed during the 1960s and 1970s following the advent in the 1950s of new drugs to treat mental illness, it was planned that patients would live in the community in regular housing or in group homes. They would be treated in community-based mental-health centres. Unfortunately, governments did not allocate adequate funding to make the system work, and increasing numbers of psychiatric patients are among the homeless. As a result of their disorders, those living in community-based group or boarding homes find it difficult to live according to community expectations. Some are therefore evicted and have no place to go. The shelters do not have the trained staff to deal with their violent and disruptive behaviour (McLaughlin, 1987; J. Ward, 1989).

Like other poor children, those living in shelters suffer in both their health and education, but the effects are more extreme. Usually by the time families reach shelters, they have already moved several times, staying with friends and relatives, perhaps even sleeping in a car. As a result children often have a high number of respiratory infections and other illnesses. They also suffer psychologically. Two-thirds of homeless parents report an increase in their children's acting-out behaviour. In-depth interviews of homeless children in Boston found that many as young as 5 years old had problems. Nearly half were delayed in language skills and motor and social development. The majority of school-aged children were suffering from serious emotional difficulties — 51 percent were depressed, 54 percent had repeated a grade in school, and 11.5 percent needed immediate psychological attention (Gewirtzman & Fodor, 1987; Maza & Hall, 1988).

The feeling of having no roots has its effect. Homeless children frequently see life as temporary. People, places, and schools come and go. So do families. Many children are separated from parents and/or brothers and sisters. Some stay with relatives, a few in foster care. With impermanence as a fact of life, there is no urge to complete projects. Homeless children have not developed a sense of their space or possessions. If they ever had any toys, they have been lost or stolen along the way. Thus many lack the experiences with toys and places that help develop a knowledge of size, colour, and spatial relationships (Gewirtzman & Fodor, 1987; Maza & Hall, 1988). As in other forms of poverty, children are the chief victims of homelessness.

What Can be Done?

Providing people with adequate income is, of course, the goal of the many suggestions made for reducing poverty. There have been a variety of proposals that tackle one or more problem areas. Some would provide an adequate income through direct grants and by increasing the supply of affordable housing. Such proposals also include individualized funding for those with physical or mental challenges to cover both their basic survival as well as special needs. Universal disability insurance would reduce the number needing social assistance. Others would provide better job training and retraining so that individuals could support themselves and their families. Still others focus on the needs of children. They would ensure that they receive adequate nutrition starting during their mother's pregnancy and are involved in early educational enrichment programs to prepare them for school and to reduce dropout levels. Yet others suggest overcoming the difficulty of finding good affordable day care by extending parental leave.

The will to make these and similar changes may be lacking in our society. There are a number of difficulties with expanding the benefits available to the poor. Even if increased benefits would reduce welfare dependency in the future, it would further burden taxpayers now. In fact, rather than increasing assistance, governments have been cutting back on unemployment benefits and monitoring the welfare system more rigidly to catch people who abuse it. Many individuals point to welfare fraud as a justification for reducing the level of assistance. If the circumstances of the poor are to improve, there must be a dedicated effort toward public education and lobbying on the part of their advocates.

SUMMARY

WHAT IS POVERTY? There have been two ways commonly used to define poverty. The first is using as a standard the minimum required to ensure physical survival. The second is based on the standard of social well-being. In North America, the focus was initially on providing the barest essentials to the deserving poor. Often this was given by charitable groups. Gradually the government provided more income-support services until the definition of poverty today is closer to the well-being standard. One of the most-used definitions is the Statistics Canada low-income cut-offs.

WHO ARE THE POOR? There are four principal groups of poor people. Older women often have not been employed and are solely dependent on the government pension.

Young adults aged 16 to 24 are affected by the shift of employment from well-paying areas to poorer-paying consumer services. Often these jobs are part-time. Young working couples make up a third group. These tend to be single-earner families with several children. The hardest hit are female-headed single-parent families, especially young mothers. Those with low educational levels tend to be the worst off. Two other groups with extremely high poverty levels are native peoples and those with disabilities. The situation of the poor is made worse by the lack of affordable housing. With much of their income going for shelter, individuals have little left for food and other essentials. There has been an increase in the use of food banks during the last several years.

POVERTY AND CHILDREN. Children are the largest single group of poor people. Poverty affects both health and education. Since so much of family income goes for shelter, nutrition may be inadequate and resistance to illness low. Substandard and crowded housing may expose children to more illnesses. Many children from low-income families do poorly in school. This tendency may be linked to both health and living conditions. Many who drop out of school have poor job prospects and continue poverty into a new generation.

HOMELESSNESS. There are widely varying estimates of the number of homeless. Shelter residents are a varied population. Shelter conditions do not favour family living, both because of the lack of privacy and because some residents have problems that disturb others. Often shelters are a last resort after several moves. Children in shelters suffer health, educational, and emotional difficulties more severe than other poor children.

WHAT CAN BE DONE? A number of remedies that address parts of the problem have been suggested. Unfortunately, there does not appear to be a consensus in our society that tax money should be spent to implement these solutions.

KEY TERMS

clawback: the practice of defining social-security benefits as income and then taxing such benefits

means test: a method of screening applicants to ensure that only those who need financial assistance receive it

safety net: basic social-security programs needed to support family life

CLASS ASSIGNMENTS

Complete one or both of the following assignments, as directed by your instructor.

1. Many students live in poverty. What strategies do they use to make money go further? Would these strategies work for a family over a long period of time? Explain.
2. What is the minimum wage in your province? If a person works forty hours per week, what will the take-home be after Unemployment Insurance, Canada Pension Plan, and taxes (if any) are deducted? How much will have to go for rent (a) for a

single person, (b) for a single parent with one child? Draw up a budget to cover other costs such as food, clothing, transportation, and child care. What occasional expenses may occur? How will they be met?

PERSONAL ASSIGNMENTS

The following assignments are designed to help you think about your own experience.

1. Based on your own experience or on that of parents you know, explain the differences between those who manage reasonably well financially and those who have extreme financial difficulties.
2. Describe what you feel are the effects of poverty on the parent-child relationship. Explain your answer.

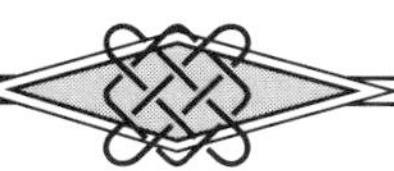

PART 7

The Future of Canadian Families

C H A P T E R 1 6

The Crystal Ball: Predicting the Future of the Family

O B J E C T I V E S

- To consider the implications of an aging population for the future.
- To look at what forms families will likely take in the future and what changes in roles will follow.
- To suggest possible shifts in the relationship between family and society.

2025

[They] now live in the Eaton Centre, which was converted from a shopping centre a few years back. What is left of its open space retains something of the building's original character; it is now the city's central bartamart.

It is spring, and New Class Action is making a last effort to influence the retirement referendum ... The generation of the post-Second-World-War baby boom is the core of this last-ditch move to restore retirement pensions, but now for the first time they are fighting a younger portion of the electorate that is almost as numerous as they are and much brighter and better organized — a population that most definitely does not want to support the millions who could lay claim to a pension.

Source: John Kettle (1980). *The Big Generation*. Toronto: McClelland and Stewart, p. 16.

What will the Canadian family look like in ten years? In thirty years? Will we be able to recognize it as a family? Will families even exist at the beginning of the 22nd century? Or will the forms we already know survive?

We can make educated guesses about the future of the family by looking at statistical trends. Such predictions are more likely to be accurate ten years down the road rather than thirty or forty. We can even attempt to explain what these trends may mean in terms of family experiences, but this is shakier ground. There are so many unknowns in the situation that in twenty years predictions made today may seem absolute foolishness. In spite of that risk, let's look into the crystal ball to try to ascertain the future of the family.

An Aging Population

Unless there is a catastrophe that kills off senior citizens or a massive increase in births, Canadians can expect the population as a whole to become older. There are two major factors working together to produce this trend: first, the changing birth rate and, second, advances in medical technology. In the last fifty years, there have been large swings in the birth rate. From the end of World War II until the early 1960s, the rate was high — the so-called baby boom. The older members of this generation are moving out of childbearing age and will start reaching retirement age in about twenty years. The boom was followed by a "baby bust." The birth rate has now dropped below the level necessary to replace the population (Statistics Canada, 1986). These trends are working together to push up the average age of Canadians.

Advances in medical technology have also had their impact at both ends of life. The development of relatively easy and safe contraceptives has made it easier to avoid having children. More women now have children later in life, and have fewer than in the past, or have none at all. A decrease in infant mortality means that it is no longer necessary to have several children to ensure the survival of one or two. At the other end of life, people are living longer. Combined with the numbers of the big generation, the increased life span will magnify the effects of the dropping birth rate.

What Does an "Old" Canada Mean?

The aging of the population will have a number of consequences in the future. One result of increased longevity is already obvious: children nowadays are more likely to know their grandparents and great-grandparents than in any previous generation. More generations are alive now than at any other time in history.

The elderly will have more political power in the future since they will have a larger share of the vote. There will be an increased demand for housing, community services, and residential care for the elderly. This shift in social service needs is already reflected in gerontology — the study of aging. The whole area of providing services to the elderly is an expanding field of employment, yet tax dollars are limited. It is difficult to guess, however, what programs will lose out as funds are shifted to provide for the elderly. However, the need for added facilities will be only temporary just as the need for more and larger schools was temporary as the baby boom passed through the educational system. Eventually the demand for all of these services will diminish.

Even though there are improvements in private pensions, the cost of providing government pensions, medical care, and other services is expected to mushroom in the future. A smaller work force will have to shoulder the costs of supporting the elderly. This fact can have two results. First, the tax burden may become even heavier than it is now. Second, families may be expected to provide more of the care their elderly parents and grandparents require. There may, however, be a conflict over time demands since a growing number of women are employed outside the home. It is also possible, as Kettle suggests in his prediction, that younger generations may choose not to support the elderly.

As the population ages, the total number of births will fall and the death rate will rise. Unless there is a rapid increase in the birth rate or a dramatic growth in immigration, the population of this country will start to shrink (Dumas & Peron, 1992). This trend would have many economic consequences for the country, including changes in employment patterns as a result of shrinking and altered markets (Burke, 1986). It is obvious that economic changes of this kind would have an impact on the family, but it is difficult to predict what form it would take.

Different Types of Families

The "traditional" family — husband, wife, and their biological children — has been considered the norm in Canadian society, although there have always been variations on the theme, for instance, never-married individuals living alone or with their relatives, widowed parents and their children, and childless couples. Since the late 1960s, however, the numbers of these "different" family forms have shown a marked increase, a trend that is expected to continue into the future.

There are now more people living alone than in the past. The increase has been greatest among older women and young people. With increased life expectancy, women are outliving their husbands in greater numbers. They are enabled to live alone rather than with family members because of the improvement in pensions. This trend will probably continue. As more women enter the work force, they will be eligible for private pensions as well as Old Age Security. Among young people aged 15 to 34, many are delaying marriage or not getting married. Others are divorcing in greater numbers. The result is that fewer members of this age group are now living with either parents or spouse.

Marriage patterns are changing. There has been an increase in unmarried cohabitation. Although in many cases this is a prelude to marriage, many of these relationships are temporary. This group also includes relationships among homosexual individuals, who are pressing to have their unions recognized. Marriages are now occurring later in life. Since most children are born to married couples, childbearing is also postponed, a possible factor in the falling birth rate. There has been an increase in divorce in recent years. Following divorce, some individuals permanently join the population that lives alone; others remarry and form new family groupings. However, the ideal in our society is still one exclusive relationship at a time (serial monogamy).

Children's living situations have changed. A growing number of children are affected by the new birth technologies. They may have to cope with the differences surrounding their conception and birth. Many children live with just one parent, either because their parents never married or because they have separated or divorced. This is a change from as recently as the 1950s, when most single parents were widows. Lone-parent families now make up the fastest growing family grouping. More children now live in stepfamilies than in the past. While it is true that many widowed parents remarried, the children in such families were not faced with the conflicting loyalties of having a parent outside of the home.

Since 1967, there has been a change in patterns of immigration. The number of individuals coming from Europe and countries with populations of European origin has dropped, while the number coming from countries in Asia, the Caribbean, and Central and South America has increased (Badets, 1989). The new immigrants have brought different traditions with them, including those involving the family. Some, for instance, rely more strongly on the extended family for social life and for practical and moral support. A number of traditions encourage arranged marriages. Thus these immigrants and their children are contributing to the variety of family forms.

Changes in Family Roles

A young person can no longer count on going through the traditional family life cycle, which includes marriage, having and raising children, the empty nest, and shared retirement and old age, with appropriate roles established for each phase. New stages are added as individuals cohabit, marry, separate, divorce, and re-couple. With second and third marriages, the social time clock is becoming more and more blurred. Parents may have two sets of children widely separated in age, complicated perhaps by the assistance of reproductive technology. There are already signs that new social scripts are emerging that specify behaviour appropriate for the new life stages. We can also expect new laws to clarify grey legal areas surrounding birth technologies, lone parenthood, and remarriage. There will continue to be societal pressure to respect the differences in families of racial, ethnic, and sexual minorities. There will also be demands for social institutions such as schools and the legal system to be more sensitive to these differences.

There is now increasing role flexibility between the sexes. The breadwinner husband and homemaker wife have become a minority of families as more and more women are working outside the home. The increase in the cost of living and high levels of employment call for at least two wage-earners per family if they are to avoid poverty. With high levels of separation and divorce, women can no longer depend on a spouse for lifelong financial support. Having a job provides a certain level of insurance. The responsibilities of both earning a living and looking after the home and children are shared by spouses, although often not equally. Advocates call for greater equality both in women's pay and in men's participation in homemaking. There is also pressure for more day care and a greater variety in the forms it takes to better meet the needs of working parents and their children.

Children will have more parent figures in coming years. These will of course include the biological parents, but may add parents' lovers, adults with whom mother or father share accommodation, surrogate mothers, stepparents, babysitters, and day-care personnel. As a result, socialization of children may be less strongly under parents' control, even though they may choose many of the socializers. Experts disagree over the effect this trend will have on children.

Although at the moment the two forms exist side-by-side, there appears to be a basic shift in society from a *patrilineal* to a *matrilineal* family organization (Dumas & Peron, 1992; Segalen, 1986), i.e., kinship is being counted through the mother rather than the father. In "traditional" families, patrilineal descent is reflected in the wife taking the husband's name at marriage and in the desire to give birth to a son "to carry on the family name." When parents divorce, custody of the children is now usually awarded to mothers. The number of mothers with

HI AND LOIS **By Walker & Brown**

Source: *Sudbury Star*, 22 June 1992, p. B8.

custody is swelled by never-married parents. Although many fathers do keep in touch with their children, for many others the contact becomes only occasional or dies out completely within a few years. When mothers remarry, children acquire a new father figure with a new set of relatives; they may even take his name. Through all the family changes the children experience, the connection with the mother's extended family is the most enduring.

The Family in Society

There will probably be further changes in the relationship of the family and society in the future. In the past, what occurred within the family was considered a private matter. There is now greater openness about intimate matters, for instance about sexual practices and problems and difficulties in having children. We can expect legislation and other forms of official control in several areas. First, there are many grey areas in the new reproductive technologies concerning ethics and custody rights. There have already been several government commissions established to consider changes to the law. We can also expect clarification concerning who is responsible for the support of children conceived through these technologies.

Second, we can expect society to be more involved in the regulation of family relationships. More and more, homes are developing see-through walls. Children are cared for by those other than family either in or out of their homes. Social services are available to seniors in their own homes. There is a growing concern that many children and adults alike are receiving substandard care by family members or other caregivers. For example, there is some pressure to make reporting of elder abuse mandatory. There is also a move toward more licenced day-care centres and private homes. The cost of providing such services is, however, a major stumbling block.

The Unknowns

The predictions made so far have been based on statistical trends in Canadian society. These do not take into account the many unknown influences that can produce profound changes. These include global factors such as widespread economic recessions, wars, or natural disasters (including the AIDS epidemic). Political action within Canada will also affect families in the future. Immigration policies influence the age, family composition, origin, and occupation of varying segments of the population. Social and economic policies at the federal, provincial, and municipal levels determine what services are available to families and who can benefit from them. Through taxation and income-distribution programs like pensions, they will also affect the disposable income of families. Finally, it is impossible to predict the decisions of individuals and their families. These can have an enormous influence on society, as we have already experienced in the case of the baby-boom generation.

Will the Family Survive?

The traditional patriarchal extended family system (in which the nuclear family of parents and children are a part of the larger family) is under siege. It has suffered gradual erosion since at least the beginning of the Industrial Revolution. Once the nuclear family left the small community of friends, neighbours, and relatives and moved to the city, it had to rely more on its own resources. The change began in the cities, but spread at different rates to different parts of the country. For example, rural areas and traditional religious groups have been slower to change.

There are many signs of this movement in current society (Segalen, 1986). There is a strong emphasis on the couple, rather than on the wider family. If the emotional needs of the partners can no longer be met, then the family is dissolved. The family uses rather than produces goods and services. In keeping with this shift, fewer families provide the services that were seen as their responsibility in the past: the care of the sick, the elderly, the disabled, and the mentally ill. Even the functions the family has kept, such as the socialization of children or the financial support of family members, it shares with people and institutions outside the family. Day-care centres, babysitters, and schools all share the responsibilities of raising children; governments provide pensions and family benefits. Analysts suggest we are now questioning the rules governing the social life of society, including marriage, childbearing, and even the entire concept of the family (Dumas & Peron, 1992).

On the other hand, the family has become the focus of emotional life (Lasch, 1979; Segalen, 1986). In the past when people lived in small communities, warm social relationships were spread among a wide range of relatives, neighbours, or friends. As a result, close relationships within marriage were not of vital importance. Now, however, it is mainly within the family circle that feelings can be expressed, which must be concealed in a society that seems to ignore human values. As a result, the nuclear family has become extremely powerful. The central focus is the couple, with secondary concentration on the children. If unions do not fill members' emotional needs, they are dissolved. There has been a movement away from marriage (a public event that includes the community) toward a pact between individuals (a private event), which does not require legal sanction (Dumas & Peron, 1992).

Will the family survive? The answer depends on how we define the family. If we consider the traditional patriarchal family, the answer may well be no. However, its disappearance is by no means certain. At the end of the 19th century, the American press looked with alarm at the state of the family. The concerns sound familiar: the divorce rate was rising; middle-class women were having fewer children; women's position was changing as they attended university and demanded the vote; morals were declining (Lasch, 1979). Yet following World War II, there was a blossoming of traditional family values (Dumas & Peron, 1992). We cannot be certain if the changes now occurring in society are the result of a long-term trend or are another swing of the pendulum.

Throughout history the family has proven itself highly adaptable. It has taken many forms, but it has never disappeared. The family thus far has been the most efficient way of meeting individual needs. These include economic needs, the need for intimate relationships, and the need for a connection to society through socialization of all members. At different points in time, the family has given up all of these functions, but it has always retained at least one. Currently its primary task is to meet intimacy needs, although to some degree it still retains both economic and social functions. The balance between them helps shape the form the family takes in different times and places.

Although the family of the future may be quite different from that we have known to date, yes, the family will survive.

SUMMARY

Although it is impossible to predict the future, we can make some educated guesses in relation to the state of the family in Canada.

First, we can expect an older population as the result of the aging baby boom, increased longevity, and reduced birth rate. As a result, the elderly will have increased political power. There may, however, be a financial crisis in providing care and support for them.

Second, family types will probably become, if anything, more varied in the future. More people will live alone. Unmarried cohabitation will likely continue to delay marriage and childbearing. Children will live in varied family settings. Given the number of immigrants from third-world countries, new traditions will be brought to Canada.

Third, there will be changes in family roles to accommodate family variety. There will also be greater role flexibility between the sexes as both husband and wife work outside the home. Children will have more parent figures. Due to the high divorce rate and the number of single parents, there may be a basic shift from a patrilineal to a matrilineal society.

Fourth, society will probably be more involved in the family by regulating reproductive technologies and supervising family relationships.

There are, however, unpredictable factors that may affect the family, such as economic trends, wars, or natural disasters. In addition, government actions that affect immigration and income-distribution policies cannot be forecast.

Although the traditional patriarchal extended family may not survive, the family will adapt to meet new challenges.

KEY TERMS

matrilineal: counting descent through one's mother

patrilineal: counting descent through one's father

CLASS ASSIGNMENTS

Complete one or both of the following assignments, as your instructor directs.

1. What solutions are available to increase the proportion of young people in the Canadian population? Explain benefits and drawbacks of each of the choices.
2. What is meant by "a shift from a patrilineal to a matrilineal society"? Describe the possible impact of this shift on institutions such as schools, day-care centres, or the workplace.

PERSONAL ASSIGNMENTS

These assignments are designed to help you explore your own feelings and opinions.

1. In the year 2025, what do you expect your family situation will be? Give reasons for your answer.
2. Do you think that the family will disappear? Give reasons for your answer.

REFERENCES

Aarsteinsen, Barbara

1993 "Foodbanks Want a New Place at the Table," *The Toronto Star,* 13 February, p. D.1.

Acton, Robert G.

1990 "The Treatment of Aggressive Parents: An Outline of a Group Treatment Program," *Canada's Mental Health,* 38(1/3): 2–5.

Adams, O.B., and D.N. Nagnur

1988 *Marriage, Divorce and Mortality: A Life Table Analysis for Canada and Regions.* Ottawa: Statistics Canada.

Adler, Ronald B., and Neil Towne

1990 *Looking Out, Looking In,* 6th ed. Fort Worth: Holt, Rinehart & Winston.

Ahrons, Constance

1983 "Divorce: Before, During, and After." In Hamilton I. McCubbin and Charles R. Figley, eds., *Stress and the Family.* Vol 1. New York: Brunner/Mazel.

Alberta Social Services

1988 *Second Stage Housing and Short Term Crisis Accommodation Projects in Canada.* Edmonton: Alberta Social Services.

Amato, Paul R.

1987 "Family Process in One-parent, Stepparent, and Intact Families: The Child's Point of View," *Journal of Marriage and the Family,* 49: 327–37.

Ames, Michael M., and Joy Inglis

1976 "Tradition and Change in British Columbia Sikh Family Life." In K. Ishwaran, ed., *The Canadian Family,* 2nd ed. Toronto: Holt, Rinehart and Winston.

Amiel, Barbara

1987 "No Sex Please, We're British," *Chatelaine,* June, pp. 52, 147–48.

Archer, Sally L.

1985 "Career and/or Family: The Identity Process for Adolescent Girls," *Youth and Society,* 16: 289–314.

Armstrong, Pat, and Hugh Armstrong

1987 "The Conflicting Demands of 'Work' and 'Home'." In *Family Matters.* Toronto: Methuen.

1988 "Women, Family and Economy." In Nancy Mandell and Ann Duffy, eds., *Reconstructing the Canadian Family: Feminist Perspectives.* Toronto: Butterworths.

Arnup, Katherine

1989 "'Mothers Just Like Others': Lesbians, Divorce, and Child Custody in Canada," *Canadian Journal of Women and the Law,* 3: 18–32.

Badets, Jane
1989 "Canada's Immigrant Population," *Canadian Social Trends,* Autumn: 2–6.

Bagnell, Kenneth
1980 *The Little Immigrants: The Orphans Who Came to Canada.* Toronto: Macmillan.

Baker, Maureen
1988 *Aging in Canadian Society: A Survey.* Toronto: McGraw-Hill Ryerson.

Baltes, Paul B., Hayne W. Reese, and John R. Nesselroade
1977 *Lifespan Developmental Psychology: Introduction to Research Methods.* Monterey, CA: Brooks/Cole.

Bank, Stephen P., and Michael D. Kahn
1982 *The Sibling Bond.* New York: Basic Books.

Barrett, F. Michael
1980 "Sexual Experience, Birth Control Usage, and Sex Education of Unmarried Canadian University Students: Changes Between 1968 and 1978," *Archives of Sexual Behavior,* 9: 367–90.

Barsky, Lesley
1990 "40 Something: the New Exhilarating Middle Age?" *Chatelaine,* January, 33–37.

Baucom, Donald H., Clifford I. Notarius, Charles K. Burnett, and Paul Haefner
1990 "Gender Differences and Sex-role Identity in Marriage." In Frank D. Fincham and Thomas N. Bradbury, eds., *The Psychology of Marriage: Basic Issues and Applications.* New York: Guilford.

Baumrind, Diana
1980 "New Directions in Socialization Research," *American Psychologist* 35: 639–52.

Beigel, Hugo G.
1951 "Romantic Love," *American Sociological Review* 16: 326–34.

Belsky, Jay
1990 "Children and Marriage." In Frank D. Fincham and Thomas N. Bradbury, eds., *The Psychology of Marriage: Basic Issues and Applications.* New York: Guilford.

Benjamin, Michael
1982 "General Systems Theory, Family Systems Theories, and Family Therapy: Towards an Integrated Model of Family Process." In Allon Bross, ed., *Family Therapy.* Toronto: Methuen.

Berger, David M.
1980 "Infertility: A Psychiatrist's Perspective," *Canadian Journal of Psychiatry,* 25: 553–59.

Berndt, Thomas J.
1983 "Correlates and Causes of Sociometric Status in Childhood: A Commentary on Six Current Studies of Popular, Rejected, and Neglected Children," *Merrill-Palmer Quarterly,* 29: 439–48.

Besharov, Douglas J., and Alison J. Quin
1987 "Not All Female-headed Families Are Created Equal," *The Public Interest,* No. 89, Fall: 48–56.

Bhargava, Gura
1988 "Seeking Immigration Through Matrimonial Alliance: A Study of Advertisements in an Ethnic Weekly," *Journal of Comparative Family Studies,* 19: 245–59.

Birch, Richard, and Betsy Matthews
1990 *13 Financial Reasons Not to Marry.* Toronto: McClelland-Bantam, 1990.

Blood, Robert O.
1955 "A Retest of Waller's Rating Complex," *Marriage and Family Living,* 17: 41–42.

Blum, Heather Munroe, Michael H. Boyle, and David R. Offord
1988 "Single-Parent Families: Child Psychiatric Disorder and School Performance," *Journal of the American Academy of Child and Adolescent Psychiatry,* 27: 214–19.

Bohman, Michael, and Soren Sigvardsson
1980 "Negative Social Heritage," *Adoption & Fostering,* 101(3): 25–31.

Bossard, James H.S. (with Eleanor Stoker Boll)
1956 *The Large Family System.* Philadelphia: University of Pennsylvania Press. Reprinted in 1975 by Greenwood Press, Westport, CT.

Boyd, Monica, and Edward T. Pryor
1989 "Young Adults Living in Their Parents' Homes," *Canadian Social Trends,* Summer: 17–20.

Braverman, Lois
1989 "Beyond the Myth of Motherhood." In Monica McGoldrick, Carol M. Anderson, and Froma Walsh, eds., *Women in Families: A Framework for Family Therapy.* New York: W.W. Norton.

Brinkerhoff, M.B., and Eugen Lupri
1989 "Power and Authority in the Family." In K. Ishwaran, ed., *Family and Marriage: Cross-Cultural Perspectives*. Toronto: Wall & Thompson.

British Agencies for Adoption & Fostering
1984 *AID and After.* London: Author.

Broderick, Carlfred, and James Smith
1979 "The General Systems Approach to the Family." In Wesley R. Burr, Reuben Hill, F. Ivan Nye, and Ira L. Reiss, eds., *Contemporary Theories About the Family.* Vol. 2. New York: Free Press.

Brodribb, Somer
1984 "The Traditional Roles of Native Women in Canada and the Impact of Colonization," *Canadian Journal of Native Studies,* 4(1), 85–103.

Brookes, Alan A.
1982 "Family, Youth, and Leaving Home in Late Nineteenth-Century Rural Nova Scotia: Canning and the Exodus, 1868–1893." In Joy Parr, ed., *Childhood and Family in Canadian History.* Toronto: McClelland and Stewart.

Brown, Fredda Herz
1988 "The Impact of Death and Serious Illness on the Family Life Cycle." In Betty Carter and Monica McGoldrick, eds., *The Changing Family Life Cycle: A Framework for Family Therapy,* 2nd ed. New York: Gardner Press.

Brown, Jennifer S.H.
1982 "Children of the Early Fur Trades." In Joy Parr, ed., *Childhood and Family in Canadian History.* Toronto: McClelland and Stewart.

Bruger, Nancy Randall
1988 *A Profile of Battered Women Who Use Shelters in Alberta.* Edmonton: Alberta Social Services.

Burch, Thomas K.
1985 *Family History Survey: Preliminary Findings.* Ottawa: Statistics Canada.

Burgess, Ernest W., and Harvey J. Locke
1960 *The Family: From Institution to Companionship,* 2nd ed. New York: American Book Company.

Burke, Mary Anne
1986 "Families: Diversity the New Norm," *Canadian Social Trends,* Summer: 6–10.

Burke, Peter J., Jan E. Stets, and Maureen M. Pirog-Good
1988 "Gender Identity, Self-Esteem, and Physical and Sexual Abuse in Dating Relationships," *Social Psychology Quarterly,* 5: 272–85.

Buss, David M.
1988 "The Evolution of Human Intrasexual Competition: Tactics of Mate Attraction," *Journal of Personality and Social Psychology,* 54: 616–28.

Cahill, Bette
1992 *Butterbox Babies.* Toronto: McClelland-Bantam.

Campbell, Shirley
1989 "The 50-Year-Old Woman and Midlife Stress." In Thomas W. Miller, ed., *Stressful Life Events.* Madison, CT: International Universities Press.

Canadian Council of Catholic Bishops
1980 *Marriage and the Family: Working Paper.* Ottawa: Canadian Council of Catholic Bishops.

Carter, Betty, and Monica McGoldrick
1988 "Overview: The Changing Family Life Cycle: A Framework for Family Therapy." In Betty Carter and Monica McGoldrick, eds., *The Changing Family Life Cycle: A Framework for Family Therapy,* 2nd ed. New York: Gardner Press.

Castellano, Marlene Brant
1989 "Women in Huron and Ojibwa Societies," *Canadian Human Studies,* 10 (2 & 3): 45–48.

Cheal, David
1989a "The Meanings of Family Life: Theoretical Approaches and Theory Models." In K. Ishwaran, ed., *Family and Marriage: Cross-Cultural Perspectives.* Toronto: Wall & Thompson.

1989b "Theoretical Frameworks." In G.N. Ramu, ed., *Marriage and the Family in Canada Today.* Scarborough, Ontario: Prentice-Hall Canada.

1991 *Family and the State of Theory.* Toronto: University of Toronto Press.

Chess, Stella, and Alexander Thomas
1987 *Origins and Evolution of Behavior Disorders from Infancy to Early Adult Life.* Cambridge, MA: Harvard University Press.

Child Welfare League of America
1992 "Florence Crittenton Division Launches National Adolescent Fathers Program," *Children's Voice,* August: 23.

Christensen, Kathleen E.
1987 "Women, Families, and Home-Based Employment." In Naomi Gerstel and Harriet Engel Gross, eds., *Families and Work.* Philadelphia: Temple University Press.

City of Calgary
1986 *The Effects of Youth Unemployment in Calgary.* Calgary: Author.

1985 *A Profile and Needs Assessment of Calgary's Single Parents.* Calgary: Author.

1984 *Native Needs Assessment.* Calgary: Author.

1983 *A Profile of the Elderly in Calgary: A Demographic Profile and Needs Assessment.* Calgary: Social Services Department.

Clarke, Michelle
1988 "Wasting Our Future: The Effects of Poverty on Child Development" (a position paper). Ottawa: Canadian Council on Children and Youth.

Clausen, John A., and Suzanne R. Clausen
1973 "The Effects of Family Size on Parents and Children." In James T. Fawcett, ed., *Psychological Perspectives on Population.* New York: Basic Books.

Cochrane, Michael G.
1991 *The Everyday Guide to Canadian Family Law.* Scarborough, Ont.: Prentice-Hall Canada.

Cohen, Leah
1984 *Small Expectations: Society's Betrayal of Older Women.* Toronto: McClelland and Stewart.

Coie, John D., and Kenneth A. Dodge
1983 "Continuities and Changes in Children's Social Status: A Five-Year Longitudinal Study," *Merrill-Palmer Quarterly,* 29: 261–82.

Cole, Elizabeth S.
1984 "Societal Influences on Adoption Practice." In Paul Sachdev, ed., *Adoption: Current Issues and Trends.* Toronto: Butterworths.

Coleman, James William, and Donald R. Cressey
1984 *Social Problems.* New York: Harper and Row.

Connidis, Ingrid Arnet
1989 *Family Ties and Aging.* Toronto: Butterworths.

Conway, John F.
1990 *The Canadian Family in Crisis.* Toronto: Lorimer.

Copans, Stuart
1989 "The Invisible Family Member: Children in Families with Alcohol Abuse." In Lee Combrinck-Graham, ed., *Children in Family Contexts: Perspectives on Treatment.* New York: Guilford.

Correctional Service of Canada
1982 "Private Family Visiting Program." Ottawa: Author.

Cowan, Carolyn Pape, and Philip A. Cowan
1992 *When Partners Become Parents: The Big Life Change for Couples.* New York: Basic Books.

Crocker, Allen C.
1983 "Sisters and Brothers." In James A. Mulick and Siegfried M. Pueschel, eds., *Parent-Professional Partnerships in Developmental Disability Services.* Cambridge, MA: Academic Guild.

CRTC (Canadian Radio-television and Telecommunications Commission)
1990 *The Portrayal of Gender in Canadian Broadcasting: Summary Report 1984–1988.* Ottawa: CRTC.

Cruickshank, David A.
1991 "The Child in Care." In Nicholas Bala, Joseph P. Hornick, and Robin Vogl, eds., *Canadian Child Welfare Law.* Toronto: Thompson Educational Publishing.

Day, Catherine F., Samuel A. Kirk, James J. Gallagher
1985 *Educating Exceptional Children.* Canadian Edition. Scarborough, Ont.: Nelson Canada.

D'Costa, Ronald
1987 "Recent Immigrants Slow Down Population Aging," *Perception,* 10(5): 30–31.

DeKeseredy, Walter S., and Ronald Hinch
1991 *Woman Abuse: Sociological Perspectives.* Toronto: Thompson Educational Publishing.

de Koninck, Maria
1984 "Double Work and Women's Health," *Canada's Mental Health,* 32(3): 28–31.

Department of Public Health, Toronto
1922 *The Care of the Infant and Young Child.* Toronto: Author.

Dodge, Kenneth A., David C. Schlundt, Iris Schocken, and Judy D. Delugach
1983 "Social Competence and Children's Sociometric Status: The Role of Peer Group Entry Strategies," *Merrill-Palmer Quarterly,* 29: 309–36.

Douglass, Richard L.
1987 *Domestic Mistreatment of the Elderly — Towards Prevention.* Washington, DC: American Association of Retired Persons.

Douthitt, Robin A., and Joanne Fedyk
1990 *The Cost of Raising Children in Canada.* Toronto: Butterworths.

Doyle, Robert
1989 "Provincial Report: Ontario," *Perception,* 13(2): 39–40.

Doyle, Robert, and Livy Visano
1987 "Toronto Social Agencies Don't Meet Needs of Minorities," *Perception,* 10(5): 12–13.

Dreyer, Cecily A., and Albert S. Dreyer
1973 "Family Dinner Time as a Unique Behavior Habitat," *Family Process,* 12: 291–301.

Duberman, Lucile

1975 *The Reconstituted Family: A Study of Remarried Couples and Their Children.* Chicago: Nelson-Hall.

Duffy, Ann Doris

1988 "Struggling with Power: Feminist Critiques of Family Inequality." In Nancy Mandell and Ann Duffy, eds., *Reconstructing the Canadian Family: Feminist Perspectives.* Toronto: Butterworths.

Dumas, Jean

1987 *Current Demographic Analysis: Report on the Demographic Situation in Canada 1986.* Ottawa: Statistics Canada.

Dumas, Jean, and Yves Peron

1992 *Marriage and Conjugal Life in Canada: Current Demographic Analysis.* Ottawa: Statistics Canada.

Duvall, Evelyn Millis, and Brent C. Miller

1985 *Marriage and Family Development,* 6th ed. New York: Harper and Row.

Dyer, Sandy

1989 "Les pauvres ont-ils les moyens de manger?" *Perception,* 13(4): 14–16.

Edmonton and Calgary Social Services

1986 *Calgary/Edmonton Survey of Food Bank Users.* Edmonton & Calgary: Authors.

Edwards, Harriet

1989 *How Could You? Mothers Without Custody of Their Children.* Freedom, CA: Crossing Press.

Eichler, Margrit

1987 "Family Change and Social Policies." In *Family Matters.* Toronto: Methuen.

1981 "The Inadequacy of the Monolithic Model of the Family," *Canadian Journal of Sociology,* 6: 367–88.

Elbow, Margaret

1982 "Children of Violent Marriages: The Forgotten Victims," *Social Casework,* 63: 465–71.

Elkin, Frederick

1964 *The Family in Canada.* Ottawa: Canadian Conference on the Family.

Elliott, S.A., and J.P. Watson

1985 "Sex During Pregnancy and the First Postnatal Year," *Journal of Psychosomatic Research,* 29: 541–48.

Epstein, Elizabeth, and Ruth Guttman
1984 "Mate Selection in Man: Evidence, Theory, and Outcome," *Social Biology,* 31: 243–78.

Erikson, Erik H.
1963 *Childhood and Society.* 2nd ed. New York: W.W. Norton.

1982 *The Life Cycle Completed: A Review.* New York: W.W. Norton.

Finkelhor, David
1987 "New Myths About Child Sexual Abuse." Ottawa: National Clearinghouse on Family Violence.

Ford, Mary, and Joe Kroll
1990 *Challenges to Child Welfare: Countering the Call for a Return to Orphanages.* St. Paul, MN: North American Council on Adoptable Children (NACAC).

Fowlkes, Martha R.
1987 "The Myth of Merit and Male Professional Careers: The Roles of Wives." In Naomi Gerstel and Harriet Engle Gross, eds., *Families and Work.* Philadelphia: Temple University Press.

Frankel-Howard, Deborah
1989 *Family Violence: A Review of Theoretical and Clinical Literature.* Ottawa: Health and Welfare Canada.

Freudenberger, Herbert J., and Gail North
1985 *Women's Burnout.* New York: Penguin.

Frideres, James S.
1983 *Native People in Canada: Contemporary Conflicts.* 2nd ed. Scarborough, Ont.: Prentice-Hall Canada.

Fulmer, Richard M.
1988 "Low-Income and Professional Families: A Comparison of Structure and Life Cycle Process." In Betty Carter and Monica McGoldrick, eds., *The Changing Family Life Cycle: A Framework for Family Therapy,* 2nd ed. New York: Gardner Press.

Gaffield, Chad
1982 "Schooling, the Economy, and Rural Society in Nineteenth-Century Ontario." In Joy Parr, ed., *Childhood and Family in Canadian History.* Toronto: McClelland and Stewart.

Garbarino, James
1982 *Children and Families in the Social Environment.* New York: Aldine.

Gay Fathers of Toronto
1981 *Gay Fathers: Some of Their Stories, Experience, and Advice.* Toronto: Author.

Gee, Ellen M.

1987 "Historical Change in the Family Life Course of Canadian Men and Women." In Victor W. Marshall, ed., *Aging in Canada: Social Perspectives,* 2nd ed. Markham, Ont.: Fitzhenry & Whiteside.

Gerson, Kathleen

1987 "How Women Choose Between Employment and Family: A Developmental Perspective." In Naomi Gerstel and Harriet Engle Gross, eds., *Families and Work.* Philadelphia: Temple University Press.

Gewirtzman, Rena, and Iris Fodor

1987 "The Homeless Child at School: From Welfare Hotel to Classroom," *Child Welfare,* 66: 237–45.

Gilligan, Carol

1982 *In a Different Voice: Psychological Theory and Women's Development.* Cambridge, MA: Cambridge University Press.

Glick, Ira D., John F. Clarkin, and David R. Kessler

1987 *Marital and Family Therapy,* 3rd ed. Orlando: Grune & Stratton.

Glossop, Robert

1989 "Putting Families First," *Perception, 13*(2): 48–49.

Gnaedinger, Nancy

1989 *Elder Abuse: A Discussion Paper.* Ottawa: Health and Welfare Canada.

Goldberg, Gary David

1990 "TV's Extended Family," *New Perspectives Quarterly,* 7(1): 58–59.

Golombok, Susan, Ann Spencer, and Michael Rutter

1983 "Children in Lesbian and Single-Parent Households: Psychosexual and Psychiatric Appraisal," *Journal of Child Psychology and Psychiatry,* 24: 551–72.

Goode, William J.

1959 "The Theoretical Importance of Love," *American Sociological Review,* 24: 38–47.

Gordon, Robert M., and Susan Tomita

1990 "The Reporting of Elder Abuse and Neglect: Mandatory or Voluntary?" *Canada's Mental Health,* December: 1–5.

Graff, Joan, ed.

1987 "Strength Within the Circle," *Journal of Child Care* (Special Issue, Fall): i–v, 1–53.

Greif, Geoffrey L.

1985 *Single Fathers.* Lexington, MA: Lexington Books.

Greven, Philip

1990 *Spare the Child: The Religious Roots of Punishment and the Psychological Impact of Physical Abuse.* New York: Vintage Books.

Gross, Wendy L.

1986 "Judging the Best Interest of the Child: Child Custody and the Homosexual Parent," *Canadian Journal of Women and the Law,* 1: 505–31.

Guberman, Connie, and Margie Wolfe, eds.

1985 *No Safe Place: Violence Against Women and Children.* Toronto: The Women's Press.

Guest, Dennis

1985 *The Emergence of Social Security in Canada.* Vancouver, University of British Columbia Press.

Guimond, A.

1983 *Responsible Procreation: Reflections from a Personalist Perspective.* Ottawa: Canadian Conference of Catholic Bishops.

Guttman, Herta A.

1989 "Children in Families with Emotionally Disturbed Parents." In Lee Combrinck-Graham, ed., *Children in Family Contexts: Perspectives on Treatment.* New York: Guilford.

Hagestad, Gunhild O.

1986 "The Family: Women and Grandparents as Kin-keepers." In Alan Pifer and Lydia Bronte, eds., *Our Aging Society: Paradox and Promise.* New York: W.W. Norton.

Hall, Edward T.

1973 *The Silent Language.* Garden City, NY: Anchor Press/Doubleday.

Hall, Elizabeth

1987 "All in the Family, Profile: Eleanor Maccoby," *Psychology Today,* November: 54–60.

Hall, Judith A.

1984 *Nonverbal Sex Differences: Accuracy of Communication and Expressive Style.* Baltimore: Johns Hopkins University Press.

Halle, David

1987 "Marriage and Family Life of Blue-Collar Men." In Naomi Gerstel and Harriet Engel Gross, eds., *Families and Work.* Philadelphia: Temple University Press.

Halsey, Bruce

1987 "Housing the Homeless: Everyone's Concern," *Perception,* 10(4): 13–15.

Hammond, Doris B.
1987 *My Parents Never Had Sex: Myths and Facts of Sexual Aging.* Buffalo: Prometheus Books.

Harris, Roma M., and Patricia Dewdney
1991 "Exchanging Information About Wife Assault: A Mismatch of Citizen Needs and Social Service System Response," *Canadian Library Journal,* 48: 407–11.

Havighurst, Robert J.
1952 *Developmental Tasks and Education,* 2nd ed. New York: Longman's Green.

Heller, Anita Fochs
1986 *Health and Home: Women as Health Guardians.* Ottawa: Canadian Advisory Council on the Status of Women.

Hepburn, Bob
1989 "Couple Feuds Over Test-tube Embryos' Right To Be Borne," *The Toronto Star,* August 6: H1, H5.

Herberg, Edward N.
1989 *Ethnic Groups in Canada: Adaptations and Transitions.* Scarborough, Ont.: Nelson Canada.

Herman, Robert D.
1955 "The 'Going Steady' Complex: A Re-examination," *Marriage and Family Living,* 17: 36–40.

Herold, Edward S.
1984 *Sexual Behaviour of Canadian Young People.* Markham, Ont.: Fitzhenry & Whiteside.

Hertz, Rosanna
1987 "Three Careers: His, Hers, and Theirs." In Naomi Gerstel and Harriet Engel Gross, eds., *Families and Work.* Philadelphia: Temple University Press.

Hetherington, E. Mavis, Jeffrey D. Arnett, and E. Ann Hollier
1988 "Adjustment of Parents and Children to Remarriage." In Sharlene A. Wolchik and Paul Karoly, eds., *Children of Divorce: Empirical Perspectives on Adjustment.* New York: Gardner Press.

Hicks, Sharon, and Carol M. Anderson
1989 "Women on Their Own." In Monica McGoldrick, Carol M. Anderson, and Froma Walsh (eds.), *Women in Families: A Framework for Family Therapy.* New York: W.W. Norton.

Higgins, Paul C., and Richard R. Butler
1982 *Understanding Deviance.* New York: McGraw-Hill.

Hill, Catherine J.
1984 "Caring for an Elderly Relative," *Canada's Mental Health,* 32(1): 13–15.

Hill, Reuben
1958 "Generic Features of Families Under Stress," *Social Casework,* 49: 139–50.

1971 "Modern Systems Theory and the Family: A Confrontation," *Social Science Information,* 10(5): 7–26.

Hobart, Charles W.
1984 "Changing Profession and Practice of Sexual Standards: A Study of Young Anglophone and Francophone Canadians," *Journal of Comparative Family Studies,* 15: 231–55.

Hoff, Patricia M.
1988 *Parental Kidnapping: How To Prevent An Abduction and What To Do If Your Child Is Abducted,* 3rd ed. Revised by Janet Kosid Uthe and Patricia M. Hoff. Washington, DC: National Center for Missing & Exploited Children.

Hogan, M. Janice, Cheryl Buehler, and Beatrice Robinson
1983 "Single Parenting: Transitions Alone." In Hamilton I. McCubbin and Charles R. Figley, eds., *Stress and the Family.* Vol. 1. New York: Brunner/Mazel.

Humphrey, Michael
1975 "The Effect of Children Upon the Marriage Relationship," *British Journal of Medical Psychology,* 48, 273–79.

1986 "Infertility as a Marital Crisis," *Stress Medicine,* 2: 221–24.

Humphrey, Michael, and Rhona Kirkwood
1982 "Marital Relationships Among Adopters," *Adoption & Fostering,* 6(2), 44–48.

Hunter, Edna J.
1983 "Captivity: The Family in Waiting." In Charles R. Figley and Hamilton I. McCubbin, eds., *Stress and the Family. Volume II: Coping with Catastrophe.* New York: Brunner/Mazel.

Imber-Black, Evan
1989 "Women's Relationships with Larger Systems." In Monica McGoldrick, Carol M. Anderson, and Froma Walsh, *Women in Families: A Framework for Family Therapy.* New York: W.W. Norton.

Insel, Paul, and Henry Lindgren
1978 *Too Close for Comfort: The Psychology of Crowding.* Englewood Cliffs, NJ: Prentice Hall.

Jacobs, Jane S.
1991 "Families with a Medically Ill Member." In Fredda Herz Brown, ed., *Reweaving the Family Tapestry: A Multigenerational Approach to Families.* New York: W.W. Norton.

Jaffe, Peter, Susan Wilson, and David A. Wolfe
1986 "Promoting Changes in Attitudes and Understanding of Conflict Resolution Among Child Witnesses of Family Violence." Ottawa: National Clearinghouse on Family Violence. (Reprinted from *Canadian Journal of Behavioural Science,* October 1986).

James, Gayle Gilchrist
1989 "Provincial Report: Alberta." In *Perception* 13(3):9.

Johnson, Holly
1988 "Wife Abuse," *Canadian Social Trends,* Spring: 17–20.

Johnston, Basil
1976 *Ojibway Heritage.* Toronto: McClelland and Stewart.

Johnston, Patrick
1983 *Native Children and the Child Welfare System.* Ottawa: Canadian Council on Social Development.

Jones, Marshall B., David R. Offord, and Nola Abrams
1980 "Brothers, Sisters and Antisocial Behaviour," *British Journal of Psychiatry,* 136: 139–45.

Kallen, Evelyn
1989 *Label Me Human: Minority Rights of Stigmatized Canadians.* Toronto: University of Toronto Press.

Katarynych, Heather L.
1991 "Adoption." In Nicholas Bala, Joseph P. Hornick, and Robin Vogl (eds.), *Canadian Child Welfare Laws.* Toronto: Thompson Educational Publishing.

Kaulback, Brent
1984 "Styles of Learning Among Native Children: A Review of the Research," *Canadian Journal of Native Education,* 11(3): 27–37.

Kempe, Ruth S., and C. Henry Kempe
1984 *The Common Secret: Sexual Abuse of Children and Adolescents.* New York: W.H. Freeman.

Kendrick, Martyn
1990 *Nobody's Children: The Foster Care Crisis in Canada.* Toronto: Macmillan of Canada.

Kettle, John
1980 *The Big Generation.* Toronto: McClelland and Stewart.

Keyes, Michael
1989 "Provincial Report: Nova Scotia," *Perception,* 13(2): 38.

Kiecolt, K. Jill, and Alan C. Alcock
1988 "The Long-term Effects of Family Structure on Gender-Role Attitudes," *Journal of Marriage and the Family,* 50: 709–17.

Kieran, Sheila

1986 *The Family Matters: Two Centuries of Family Law and Life in Ontario.* Toronto: Key Porter Books.

King, Alan J.C., Richard Beazley, Wendy K. Warren, Catherine A. Hankins, Alan S. Robertson, and J.L. Radford

1988 *Canada Youth & AIDS Study.* Kingston, Ont.: Queen's University.

Kinsman, Gary

1987 *The Regulation of Desire: Sexuality in Canada.* Montreal: Black Rose Books.

Kirk, H. David

1984 *Shared Fate: A Theory and Method of Adoptive Relationships,* 2nd ed. Port Angeles, WA: Ben-Simon Publications.

Kirsh, Sharon

1984 "Working with Unmarried Parents." In Frank Maidman, ed., *Child Welfare: A Source Book of Knowledge and Practice.* New York: Child Welfare League of America.

Klein, Luella

1986 "Our Willy-Nilly Childbearing: Unintended and Teenage Pregnancy in the United States," *The Pharos,* Fall, 27–29.

Kopelman, Richard E., and Dorothy Lang

1985 "Alliteration in Mate Selection: Does Barbara Marry Barry?" *Psychological Reports,* 56: 791–96.

Kraizer, Sheryll Kerns

1986 "Rethinking Prevention," *Child Abuse and Neglect,* 10: 259–61.

Krestan, Jo-Ann, and Claudia Bepko

1988 "Alcohol Problems and the Family Life Cycle." In Betty Carter and Monica McGoldrick, eds., *The Changing Family Life Cycle: A Framework for Family Therapy,* 2nd ed. New York: Gardner Press.

Lachapelle, Rejean

1988 "Changes in Fertility Among Canada's Linguistic Groups," *Canadian Social Trends,* Autumn, 2–8.

Ladd, Gary W.

1983 "Social Networks of Popular, Average, and Rejected Children in School Settings," *Merrill-Palmer Quarterly,* 29: 283–307.

La Gaipa, John J.

1981 "A Systems Approach to Personal Relationships." In Steve Duck and Robin Gilmour, eds., *Personal Relationships. I: Studying Personal Relationships.* London: Academic Press.

Lamb, Michael E.
1978 "The Development of Sibling Relationships in Infancy: A Short-Term Longitudinal Study," *Child Development,* 49: 1189–96.

Lang, Denise V.
1988 *The Phantom Spouse: Helping You and Your Family Survive Business Travel or Relocation.* White Hall, VA: Betterway Publications.

Larson, Lyle E.
1976 *The Canadian Family in Canadian Perspective.* Scarborough, Ont.: Prentice-Hall of Canada.

Lasch, Christopher
1979 *Haven in a Heartless World: The Family Besieged.* New York: Basic Books.

Lee, John Alan
1987 "The Invisible Lives of Canada's Gray Gays." In Victor W. Marshall, ed., *Aging in Canada: Social Perspectives,* 2nd ed. Markham, Ont.: Fitzhenry & Whiteside.

1975 "The Romantic Heresy," *Canadian Review of Sociology and Anthropology,* 12: 514–28.

Leman, Kevin
1985 *The Birth Order Book: Why You Are the Way You Are.* New York: Dell.

Lero, Donna S., and Irene Kyle
1991 "Work, Families and Child Care in Ontario." In Laura C. Johnson and Dick Barnhorst, eds., *Children, Families and Public Policy in the 90s.* Toronto: Thompson Educational Publishing.

Levin, Eric
1987 "Motherly Love Works a Miracle," *People Weekly,* October 19: 39–43.

Levinson, Daniel J.
1978 *The Seasons of a Man's Life.* New York: Alfred A. Knopf.

Lipman, Margaret
1984 "Adoption in Canada: Two Decades in Review." In Paul Sachdev, ed., *Adoption: Current Issues and Trends.* Toronto: Butterworths.

Lowe, Graham S.
1989 *Women, Paid/Unpaid Work, and Stress: New Directions for Research.* Ottawa: Canadian Advisory Council on the Status of Women.

Lundy, Katherina L.P., and Barbara D. Warme
1990 *Sociology: A Window on the World,* 2nd ed. Scarborough, Ont.: Nelson Canada.

Lupri, Eugen
1989 "Male Violence in the Home," *Canadian Social Trends,* Autumn: 19–21.

Lupri, Eugen, and James Frideres

1981 "The Quality of Marriage and the Passage of Time: Marital Satisfaction Over the Family Life Cycle," *Canadian Journal of Sociology,* 6 (3), 283–305.

Luxton, Meg

1986 "Two Hands for the Clock: Changing Patterns in the Gendered Division of Labour in the Home." In Meg Luxton and Harriet Rosenberg, eds., *Through the Kitchen Window: The Politics of Home and Family.* Toronto: Garamond Press.

McCubbin, Hamilton, I., and Joan M. Patterson

1983 "Family Transitions: Adaptation to Stress." In Hamilton I. McCubbin and Charles R. Figley, eds., *Stress in the Family: Vol. I. Coping with Normative Transitions.* New York: Brunner/Mazel.

McCullough, Paulina G., and Sandra Rutenberg

1988 "Launching Children and Moving On." In Betty Carter and Monica McGoldrick, eds., *The Changing Family Life Cycle: A Framework for Family Therapy,* 2nd ed. New York: Gardner Press.

MacDonald, John A.

1984 "Canadian Adoption Legislation: An Overview." In Paul Sachdev, ed., *Adoption: Current Issues and Trends.* Toronto: Butterworths.

Macdonald, Robert

1985 "The Hutterites in Alberta." In Howard Palmer and Tamara Palmer, eds., *Peoples of Alberta: Portraits of Cultural Diversity.* Saskatoon, Sask.: Western Producer Prairie Books.

Macfarlane, Aidan

1977 *The Psychology of Childbirth.* Cambridge, MA: Harvard University Press.

McGoldrick, Monica

1988a "Ethnicity and the Family Life Cycle." In Betty Carter and Monica McGoldrick, eds., *The Changing Family Life Cycle: A Framework for Family Therapy,* 2nd ed. New York: Gardner Press.

1988b "The Joining of Families Through Marriage: The New Couple." In Betty Carter and Monica McGoldrick, eds., *The Changing Family Life Cycle: A Framework for Family Therapy,* 2nd ed. New York: Gardner Press.

1988c "Women and the Family Life Cycle." In Betty Carter and Monica McGoldrick, eds., *The Changing Family Life Cycle: A Framework for Family Therapy,* 2nd ed. New York: Gardner Press.

McGoldrick, Monica

1989 "Women Through the Family Life Cycle." In Monica McGoldrick, Carol M. Anderson, and Froma Walsh (eds.), *Women in Families: A Framework for Family Therapy.* New York: W.W. Norton.

McGoldrick, Monica, and Betty Carter
1988 "Forming a Remarried Family." In Betty Carter and Monica McGoldrick, eds., *The Changing Family Life Cycle: A Framework for Family Therapy*, 2nd ed. New York: Gardner Press.

McGoldrick, Monica, and Randy Gerson
1985 *Genograms in Family Assessment*. New York: W.W. Norton.

McIntosh, Robert
1987/88 "Canada's Boy Miners," *The Beaver*, December 1987/January 1988, 34–38.

MacKay, Harry, and Catherine Austin
1983 *Single Adolescent Mothers in Ontario*. Ottawa: Canadian Council on Social Development.

Mackay, Ronald, and Lawrence Myles
1989 *Native Student Dropouts in Ontario Schools*. Toronto: Ontario Ministry of Education.

McKie, D.C., B. Prentice, and P. Reed
1983 *Divorce: Law and the Family in Canada*. Ottawa: Statistics Canada.

McLaughlin, Mary Ann
1987 "Homelessness in Canada: The Report of the National Inquiry," Special Insert, *Social Development Overview*, 5 (1). (Published by Canadian Council on Social Development).

MacLeod, Linda
1987 *Battered But Not Beaten...Preventing Wife Battering in Canada*. Ottawa: Canadian Advisory Council on the Status of Women.

1989 *Discussion Paper: Wife Battering and the Web of Hope: Progress, Dilemmas and Visions of Prevention*. Ottawa: Health and Welfare Canada.

McPherson, Cathy
1990 "Justice for the Disabled," *Vis-à-vis*, 8 (2): 7.

McRoy, Ruth G., Harold D. Grotevant, and Kerry L. White
1988 *Openness in Adoption: New Practices, New Issues*. New York: Praeger.

McWhinnie, Alexina M.
1984 "The Case for Greater Openness Concerning AID." In *AID and After*. London: British Agencies for Adoption & Fostering.

Maidman, Frank
1984 "Physical Child Abuse: Dynamics and Practice." In Frank Maidman, ed., *Child Welfare: A Source Book of Knowledge and Practice*. New York: Child Welfare League of America.

Makepeace, James M.
1986 "Gender Differences in Courtship Violence Victimization," *Family Relations,* 35: 383–88.

Marshall, Katherine
1990 "Household Chores," *Canadian Social Trends,* Spring: 18–19.

Maslach, Christina
1982 *Burnout: The Cost of Caring.* Englewood Cliffs, NJ: Prentice Hall.

Maslove, Allan, and David Hawkes
1989 "The Northern Population," *Canadian Social Trends,* Winter: 2–7.

Mastrocola-Morris, Elaine
1989 "Woman Abuse: The Relationship Between Wife Assault and Elder Abuse." Ottawa: National Clearinghouse on Family Violence.

Maynard, Peter E., and Nancy E. Maynard
1982 "Stress in Police Families: Some Policy Implications," *Journal of Police Science and Administration,* 10: 302–14.

Mayard, Rona
1987 "Here Come the Brides," *Report on Business Magazine,* June, 24–30.

Maza, Penelope L., and Judy A. Hall
1988 *Homeless Children and Their Families: A Preliminary Study.* Washington, DC: Child Welfare League of America.

Mazor, Miriam
1979 "Barren Couples," *Psychology Today,* May, 101–108, 112.

Mercer, Ramona, Elizabeth G. Nichols, and Glen Caspers Doyle
1989 *Transitions in a Woman's Life: Major Life Events in Developmental Context.* New York: Springer.

Messinger, Lillian, and Kenneth N. Walker
1981 "From Marriage Breakdown to Remarriage: Parental Tasks and Therapeutic Guidelines," *American Journal of Orthopsychiatry,* 51: 429–38.

Methot, Suzanne
1987 "Employment Patterns of Elderly Canadians," *Canadian Social Trends,* Autumn, 7–11.

Miall, Charlene E.
1987 "The Stigma of Adoptive Parent Status: Perceptions of Community Attitudes Toward Adoption and the Experience of Informal Social Sanctioning," *Family Relations,* 36: 34–39.

Miller, Darla Ferris
1989 *First Steps Toward Cultural Difference: Socialization in Infant/Toddler Day Care.* Washington, DC: Child Welfare League of America.

Miller, Shelby H.

1983 *Children as Parents: Final Report on a Study of Childbearing and Child Rearing Among 12- to 15-Year-Olds.* New York: Child Welfare League of America.

Miner, Horace

1939 *St. Denis: A French-Canadian Parish.* Chicago: University of Chicago Press (1979 reprint).

Minister for Senior Citizens Affairs

1985 *Elderly Residents in Ontario With Particular Focus on Those Who Are Single.* Toronto: Seniors Secretariat, 1985.

Minuchin, Salvador

1974 *Families and Family Therapy.* London: Tavistock.

Mishra-Bouchez, Therese, and Lise Emond

1987 "The Marital Status of Gatineau Mothers Between 1976 and 1984 or the Rapid and Deep Change of a Society," *Canadian Journal of Public Health,* 78: 381–84.

Money, John

1986 *Lovemaps.* New York: Irvington.

Montgomery, Lucy Maud

1908, 1935 (copyright) *Anne of Green Gables.* Toronto: McClelland-Bantam.

Moogk, Peter N.

1982 *"Les Petits Sauvages:* The Children of Eighteenth-Century New France." In Joy Parr, ed., *Childhood and Family in Canadian History.* Toronto: McClelland and Stewart.

Moore, Maureen

1987 "Women Parenting Alone," *Canadian Social Trends,* Winter: 31–36.

1988 "Female Lone Parenthood: The Duration of Episodes," *Canadian Social Trends,* Autumn: 40–42.

1989 "Dual-earner Families: The New Norm," *Canadian Social Trends,* Spring, 24–26.

Moore, Terence, and Victor Thompson

1987 "Elder Abuse: A Review of Research, Programmes and Policy," *The Social Worker/Le Travailleur social,* 55: 115–22.

Moore, Timothy, Debra Pepler, Brenda Weinberg, Liz Hammond, Janice Waddell, and Liza Weiser

1990 "Research on Children from Violent Homes," *Canada's Mental Health,* 38(2/3): 19–23.

Morgan, S. Philip, Diane M. Lyle, and Gretchen A. Condran
1988 "Sons, Daughters, and the Risk of Marital Disruption," *American Journal of Sociology,* 94: 110–29.

Morris, Monica B.
1987 "Children's Perceptions of Last-Chance Parents: Implications of Current Trends Toward Late Childbearing," *Child Welfare,* 66: 195–205.

Morrison, Kati, and Airdrie Thompson-Guppy, with Patricia Bell
1986 *Stepmothers: Exploring the Myth.* Ottawa: Canadian Council on Social Development.

Murphy, M.J.
1984 "Fertility, Birth Timing and Marital Breakdown: A Reinterpretation of the Evidence," *Journal of Biosocial Science,* 16: 487–500.

Murstein, Bernard I.
1980 "Mate Selection in the 1970s," *Journal of Marriage and the Family,* 42: 777–92.

Muszynski, Leon
1989 "An Idea Whose Time Has Come," *Perception,* 13(2): 55–56.

Nagnur, Dhruva, and Owen Adams
1987 "Tying the Knot: An Overview of Marriage Rates in Canada," *Canadian Social Trends,* Autumn: 2–6.

National Advisory Council on Aging
1983 *Family Role and the Negotiation of Change for the Aged.* Ottawa: Author.

Nett, Emily M.
1988 *Canadian Families: Past and Present.* Toronto: Butterworths.

Neugarten, Bernice L., and Dail A. Neugarten
1986 "Changing Meanings of Age in the Aging Society." In Alan Pifer and Lydia Bronte, eds., *Our Aging Society: Paradox and Promise.* New York: W.W. Norton.

Nicholas, M.K., and J.P.P. Tyler
1983 "Characteristics, Attitudes and Personalities of AI Donors," *Clinical Reproduction and Fertility,* 2: 47–54.

Nihmey, John, and Stuart Foxman
1987 *Time of Their Lives: The Dionne Tragedy.* Toronto: McClelland-Bantam.

Okimoto, Jean Davies, and Phyllis Jackson Stegall
1987 *Boomerang Kids: How to Live with Adult Children Who Return Home.* Boston: Little, Brown.

Olson, David H.
1990 "Commentary: Marriage in Perspective." In Frank D. Fincham and Thomas N. Bradbury, *The Psychology of Marriage: Basic Issues and Applications*. New York: Guilford.

Ontario Advisory Council on Senior Citizens
1989 *Annual Report 1988/1989*. Toronto: Queen's Printer for Ontario.

Ontario Law Reform Commission
1985 *Report on Human Artificial Reproduction and Related Matters*. Toronto: Ministry of the Attorney General.

Ontario Medical Association
1988 "Approaches to Treatment of the Male Batterer and His Family." In *Reports on Wife Assault*. Toronto: Ontario Medical Association.

Ontario Ministry of the Attorney General
n.d. *Support and Custody Enforcement Program*. Toronto: Author.

Ontario Ministry of Community and Social Services
1987 *Single Parents: A Resource Guide*. Toronto: Queen's Printer for Ontario.

Ontario Women's Directorate
1991 *Work and Family: The Crucial Balance*. Toronto: Ministry of Community and Social Services.

Page, W.E.
1989 "Study Recommends Increasing AIDS Awareness Among Canadian Youth," *Ontario Medical Review*, November: 22–23.

Pagelow, Mildred Daley
1984 *Family Violence*. New York: Praeger.

Papp, Peggy
1988 "Single Women: Early and Middle Years." In Marianne Walters, Betty Carter, Peggy Papp, and Olga Silverstein, *The Invisible Web: Gender Patterns in Family Relationships*. New York: Guilford.

Parekh, Navin
1989 "Cultural and Racial Diversity in Canada: An Urgent Challenge," *Perception*, 13(2): 43–44.

Park, Norman
1991 "Child Care in Ontario." In Richard Barnhorst and Laura C. Johnson (eds.), *The State of the Child in Ontario*. Toronto: Oxford University Press.

Parliament, Jo-Anne B.
1989 "How Canadians Spend Their Day," *Canadian Social Trends*, Winter, 23–27.

Parsons, Talcott, and Robert F. Bales
1955 *Family, Socialization and Interaction Process.* Glencoe, Illinois: The Free Press.

Patterson, Joan M., and Hamilton I. McCubbin
1983 "Chronic Illness: Family Stress and Coping." In Hamilton I. McCubbin and Charles R. Figley, eds., *Stress in the Family: Vol II. Coping with Catastrophe.* New York: Brunner/Mazel.

Payne, Julien D.
1986 "Whither the Broken Family?" *Transition,* March: 4, 10.

Payne, Julien D., and Brenda Edwards
1991 "Cooperative Parenting After Divorce: A Canadian Legal Perspective." In Jay Folberg, ed., *Joint Custody and Shared Parenting.* 2nd ed. New York: Guilford Press.

Peck, Judith Stern, and Jennifer R. Manocherian
1988 "Divorce in the Changing Family Life Cycle". In Betty Carter and Monica McGoldrick, eds., *The Changing Family Life Cycle: A Framework for Family Therapy.* 2nd ed. New York: Gardner Press.

Peter, Karl
1976 "The Hutterite Family." In K. Ishwaran, ed., *The Canadian Family.* 2nd ed. Toronto: Holt Rinehart & Winston of Canada.

Petersen, David
1969 "Husband-wife Communication and Family Problems," *Sociology and Social Research,* 53: 375–84.

Piddington, Ralph
1976 "A Study of French-Canadian Kinship." In K. Ishwaran, *The Canadian Family,* 2nd ed. Toronto: Holt, Rinehart & Winston of Canada.

Pincus, Lily, and Christopher Dare
1978 *Secrets in the Family.* London: Faber & Faber.

Pineo, Peter C.
1976 "The Extended Family in a Working-Class Area of Hamilton." In K. Ishwaran, *The Canadian Family,* 2nd ed. Toronto: Holt, Rinehart & Winston of Canada.

Pittman, Frank S., III
1987 *Turning Points: Treating Families in Transition and Crisis.* New York: W.W. Norton.

Poling, Daniel A., II
1976 "Socio-Sexual Distance: The Emotional, Social, and Sexual Obstacles the Disabled Encounter when Interacting with the Able-Bodied." In Michael

Barrett and Neville Chase, eds., *Sexuality and the Disabled.* Ottawa: Sex Information and Education Council of Canada.

Porter, Elaine
1987 "Conceptual Frameworks for Studying Families." In *Family Matters: Sociology and Contemporary Canadian Families.* Toronto: Methuen.

Portner, Joyce
1983 "Work and Family: Achieving a Balance." In Hamilton I. McCubbin and Charles R. Figley, eds., *Stress and the Family.* Vol 1. New York: Brunner/Mazel.

Powell, Van C.
1989 "Caring for Colleagues," *The Canadian Nurse,* February: 14–17.

Pressman, Barbara M.
1984 *Family Violence: Origins and Treatment.* Guelph, Ont.: Children's Aid Society of the City of Guelph and the County of Wellington.

Preto, Nydia Garcia
1988 "Transformation of the Family System in Adolescence." In Betty Carter and Monica McGoldrick, eds., *The Changing Family Life Cycle: A Framework for Family Therapy,* 2nd ed. New York: Gardner Press.

Price, Anne, and Nancy Dana
1987 *How to Find Romance in the Personals.* New York: Meadowbrook.

Raschke, Helen J., and Vernon J. Raschke
1979 "Family Conflict and Children's Self-Concepts: A Comparison of Intact and Single-Parent Families," *Journal of Marriage and the Family,* 41: 367–74.

Reid, Joseph H.
1963 "Principles, Values, and Assumptions Underlying Adoption Practice." In I. Evelyn Smith, ed., *Readings in Adoption.* New York: Philosophical Library.

Reiss, Ira L.
1960 *Premarital Sexual Standards in America.* New York: Free Press.

1965 "Social Class and Premarital Sexual Permissiveness: A Re-examination," *American Sociological Review,* 30: 747–56; reprinted in Marvin B. Sussman, ed., *Sourcebook in Marriage and the Family,* 3rd ed. Boston: Houghton Mifflin, 1968.

1980 *Family Systems in America,* 3rd ed. New York: Holt, Rinehart & Winston.

Rhodes, Ann
1989 *Guidance and Support in Caring for the Elderly.* Montreal: Grosvenor House Press.

Riches, Graham
1989 "Banking on Political Action," *Perception,* 13(4): 11–13.

Riley, Matilda White, and John W. Riley, Jr.
1986 "Longevity and Social Structure: The Potential for the Added Years." In Alan Pifer and Lydia Bronte, eds., *Our Aging Society: Paradox and Promise.* New York: W.W. Norton.

Robichaud, Jean-Bernard
1989 "Les responsibilités étatiques face au vieillissement de la population," *Perception,* 13(2): 51–54.

Rodgers, Roy H., and Gail Witney
1981 "The Family Life Cycle in Twentieth Century Canada," *Journal of Marriage and the Family,* 43: 727–40.

Rolland, John S.
1988 "Chronic Illness and the Family Life Cycle." In Betty Carter and Monica McGoldrick, eds., *The Changing Family Life Cycle: A Framework for Family Therapy,* 2nd ed. New York: Gardner Press.

Rooke, Patricia T., and R.L. Schnell
1983 *Discarding the Asylum: From Child Rescue to the Welfare State in English-Canada (1800–1950).* Lanham, MD: University Press of America.

Roscoe, Bruce, Lauri E. Cavanaugh, and Donna R. Kennedy
1988 "Dating Infidelity: Behaviors, Reasons, and Consequences," *Adolescence,* 23: 35–43.

Rosenthal, Carolyn J.
1987 "Aging and Intergenerational Relations in Canada." In Victor W. Marshall, ed., *Aging in Canada: Social Perspectives,* 2nd ed. Markham, Ont.: Fitzhenry & Whiteside.

Ross, David
1992 "Current and Proposed Measures of Poverty, 1992," *Perception,* 15(4)/16(1): 60–63.

Ross, David P., and E. Richard Shillington
1989 *The Canadian Fact Book on Poverty – 1989.* Ottawa: Canadian Council on Social Development.

Rothman, Ellen K.
1987 *Hands and Hearts: A History of Courtship in America.* Cambridge, MA: Harvard University Press.

Rothman, Sheila M., and Emily Menlo Marks
1987 "Adjusting Work and Family Life: Flexible Work Schedules and Family Policy." In Naomi Gerstel and Harriet Engel Gross, eds., *Families and Work.* Philadelphia: Temple University Press.

Roy, N. Dianne
1989 "They Also Served ..." *Perception,* 13(4): 26–28.

Royal Bank
1989 *Reporter,* Winter.

Rutter, Michael
1972 *Maternal Deprivation Reassessed.* Markham, Ont.: Penguin Books Canada.

Ryser, Rudolph C.
1984 "Nation-States, Indigenous Nations, and the Great Lie." In Leroy Little Bear, Menno Boldt, and J. Anthony Long, eds., *Pathways to Self-Determination: Canadian Indians and the Canadian State.* Toronto: University of Toronto Press.

Sachdev, Paul
1989 *Unlocking the Adoption Files.* Lexington, MA: Lexington Books.

Samuel, T. John
1990 *Immigration of Children as an Element of Immigration Policy.* Paper presented at the joint session of Canadian Population Society and Canadian Sociology and Anthropology Association, Victoria, B.C., May 30–June 1.

Sanders, William B.
1974 *The Sociologist as Detective: An Introduction to Research Methods.* New York: Praeger.

Sandness, Grace
1983 "The Miracle of Molly." In Linda Dunn, ed., *Adopting Children With Special Needs: A Sequel.* Washington, DC: North American Council on Adoptable Children.

Santrock, John W.
1992 *Life-Span Development,* 4th ed. Dubuque, Iowa: Wm. C. Brown.

Sarsby, Jacqueline
1983 *Romantic Love and Society: Its Place in the Modern World.* Harmondsworth, Middlesex: Penguin.

Saxton, Marsha
1988 "Prenatal Screening and Discriminatory Attitudes About Disability." In Elaine Hoffman Baruch, Amadeo F. D'Adamo, Jr., & Joni Seager (eds.), *Embryos, Ethics, and Women's Rights: Exploring the New Reproductive Technologies.* New York: Harrington Press.

Schlesinger, Benjamin
1990 *The One-Parent Family.* Paper presented to 2nd International Rural Mental Health and Addictions Conference, North Bay, Ontario, April.

1989 "The 'Sandwich Generation': Middle-aged Families Under Stress," *Canada's Mental Health,* 37(3): 11–14.

Schlesinger, Benjamin, and Shirley Tenhouse Giblon
1984 *Lasting Marriages.* Toronto: Faculty of Education, University of Toronto.

Schulman, Gerda

1972 "Myths That Intrude on the Adaptation of the Stepfamily," *Social Casework,* 53: 131–39.

Schulz, Patricia Vandebelt

1978 "Day Care in Canada: 1850–1962." In Kathleen Gallagher Ross, *Good Day Care: Fighting for It, Getting It, Keeping It.* Toronto: The Women's Press.

Segalen, Martine

1986 *Historical Anthropology of the Family.* Translated by J.C. Whitehouse and Sarah Matthews. Cambridge: Cambridge University Press.

Sekaran, Uma

1986 *Dual-Career Families.* San Francisco: Jossey-Bass.

Senate Committee on Youth

1986 *Youth: A Plan of Action.* Ottawa: Special Senate Committee on Youth.

Senn, Charlene Y.

1988 *Vulnerable: Sexual Abuse and People with an Intellectual Handicap.* Toronto: G. Allan Roeher Institute.

Seward, Shirley

1987 "Greying Population Generates New Policy Concerns," *Perception,* 10(5): 14–17.

Shapiro, Constance Hoenk

1986 "Is Pregnancy After Infertility A Dubious Joy?" *Social Casework,* 67: 306–11.

Shell, Donna J.

n.d. "Elder Abuse: Summary of Results — Manitoba." In Benjamin Schlesinger and Rachel Schlesinger, eds., *Abuse of the Elderly: Issues and Annotated Bibliography.* Toronto: University of Toronto Press.

Sieburg, Evelyn

1985 *Family Communication: An Integrated Systems Approach.* New York: Gardner.

Skinner, Denise A.

1983 "Dual-Career Families: Strains of Sharing." In Hamilton I. McCubbin and Charles R. Figley, eds., *Stress and the Family. Volume I: Coping with Normative Transitions.* New York: Brunner/Mazel.

Skipper, James K., and Gilbert Nass

1966 "Dating Behavior: A Framework for Analysis and an Illustration," *Journal of Marriage and the Family,* 28: 412–20.

Smith, Nancy Frasure, and Mary Kirby Grenier
1975 "English- and French-Canadian Children's Views of Parents," *Canadian Journal of Behavioural Science*, 7: 40–53.

Smyth, Mitchell
1991 "She's an Anti-surrogacy Activist," *The Toronto Star,* 28 July: A24.

Solomon, Dorothy
1979 "A Very Different Kind of Family," *Good Housekeeping,* April: 141, 246–50.

Spears, George, and Kasia Seydegart
1985 *The Portrayal of Sex Roles in Canadian Television Advertising.* Ottawa: CRTC, Catalogue no. BC 92-36/1986.

Statistics Canada
1986 "Canada in the 21st Century," *Canadian Social Trends,* Summer: 3–5.

1989 *The Family in Canada: Selected Highlights.* Ottawa: Queen's Printer.

1992 *The Labour Force: November 1992.* Ottawa: Statistics Canada (No. 71-001, Vol. 48, No. 11), December.

Steinberg, Laurence
1987 "Single Parents, Stepparents, and the Susceptibility of Adolescents to Antisocial Peer Pressure," *Child Development,* 58: 269–75.

Steinhauer, Paul D.
1991 *The Least Detrimental Alternative: A Systematic Guide to Case Planning and Decision Making for Children in Care.* Toronto: University of Toronto Press.

Stone, Elizabeth
1988 *Black Sheep and Kissing Cousins: How Our Family Stories Shape Us.* New York: Penguin.

Strong-Boag, Victoria
1982 "Intruders in the Nursery: Childcare Professionals Reshape the Years One to Five, 1920–1940." In Joy Parr, ed., *Childhood and Family in Canadian History.* Toronto: McClelland and Stewart.

Swan, Carol
1990 "Why Millions of Canadians Can't Read This Article," *Perception,* 14(3): 8–10.

Sweet, Lois
1989 "20 Years of Legal Birth Control," *The Toronto Star,* 28 May, B1, B4.

Taylor, Donald M., Nancy Frasure-Smith, and Wallace E. Lambert
1978 "Psychological Development of French and English Canadian Children: Child-Rearing Attitudes and Ethnic Identity." In Leo Driedger, ed., *The Canadian Ethnic Mosaic: A Quest for Identity.* Toronto: McClelland and Stewart.

Taylor, Georgina

1993 "Custody, Access and Abuse," *Vis-à-vis* (Canadian Council on Social Development), 10(3): 4.

Tesson, Geoffrey

1987 "Socialization and Parenting." In *Family Matters: Sociology and Contemporary Canadian Families.* Toronto: Methuen.

Thacker, Charlene

1989 "Gender Role Socialization." In K. Ishwaran, ed., *Family and Marriage: Cross-Cultural Perspectives.* Toronto: Wall & Thompson.

Toman, Walter

1993 *Family Constellation: Its Effects on Personality and Behavior,* 4th ed. New York: Springer Publishing.

Torjman, Sherri

1989 "Income Insecurity: The Disability Income System in Canada," *Perception,* 13(4): 36–39.

Torjman, Sherri, and Ken Battle

1989 "The Shrinking Safety Net: Welfare Reform Takes Aim at the Undeserving," *Perception,* 13(2): 7–10.

Tower, Cynthia Crosson

1989 *Understanding Child Abuse and Neglect.* Boston: Allyn & Bacon.

Ujimoto, K. Victor

1987 "The Ethnic Dimension of Aging in Canada." In Victor W. Marshall, ed., *Aging in Canada: Social Perspectives,* 2nd ed. Markham, Ont.: Fitzhenry & Whiteside.

United Church of Canada

1989a "A Definition of Family," *All Kinds of Families,* Fall: 14.

1989b "Contraception and Abortion: Recommendations." Toronto: Author.

United Church of Canada

1992 "Compromise on Same-Gender Covenants," *The Observer,* October, pp. 16–17.

Vadasy, Patricia F., Rebecca R. Fewell, and Donald J. Meyer

1986 "Grandparents of Children with Special Needs: Insights Into Their Experiences and Concerns," *Journal of the Division for Early Childhood,* 10(1): 36–44.

Vanderburgh, Rosamond M.

1987 "Modernization and Aging in the Anicinabe Context." In Victor W. Marshall, ed., *Aging in Canada: Social Perspectives,* 2nd ed. Markham, Ont.: Fitzhenry & Whiteside.

Veevers, J.E.
1976 "The Lifestyle of the Voluntarily Childless." In Lyle E. Larson, ed., *The Canadian Family in Contemporary Perspective.* Scarborough, Ont.: Prentice-Hall Canada.

Visher, Emily S., and John S. Visher
1979 *Stepfamilies: A Guide to Working with Stepparents and Stepchildren.* New York: Brunner-Mazel.

Voydanoff, Patricia
1983 "Unemployment: Family Strategies for Adaptation." In Charles R. Figley and Hamilton I. McCubbin, eds., *Stress and the Family. Volume 2: Coping With Catastrophe.* New York: Brunner/Mazel.

Wachtel, Andy
1989 *Discussion Paper: Child Abuse.* Ottawa: Health and Welfare Canada.

Walker, Christopher
1977 "Some Variations in Marital Satisfaction." In Robert Chester and John Peel, eds., *Equalities and Inequalities in Family Life.* London: Academic Press.

Walker, Kenneth N., and Lillian Messinger
1979 "Remarriage After Divorce: Dissolution and Reconstitution of Family Boundaries," *Family Process,* 18: 185–92.

Wallerstein, Judith S., and Sandra Blakeslee
1989 *Second Chances: Men, Women, and Children a Decade After Divorce.* New York: Ticknor & Fields.

Walsh, Froma
1988 "The Family in Later Life." In Betty Carter and Monica McGoldrick, eds., *The Changing Family Life Cycle: A Framework for Family Therapy,* 2nd ed. New York: Gardner Press.

Wannell, Ted
1991 "Losing Ground: Wages of Young People, 1981–1986." In Craig McKie and Keith Thompson, eds., *Canadian Social Trends.* Toronto: Thompson Publishing.

Ward, J.A.
1988 "Approaches to Native Mental Health Care." Paper presented to Atlantic Provinces Psychiatric Association, June 10.

Ward, Jim
1989 *Organizing for the Homeless.* Ottawa: Canadian Council on Social Development.

Ward, Margaret
1979 "The Relationship Between Parents and Caseworker in Adoption," *Social Casework,* 60: 96–103.

1980 "Children Who Change Families," *School & Parent Digest,* 6(1): 1–4.

1984a *The Adoption of Native Canadian Children.* Cobalt, Ont.: Highway Book Shop.

1984b "Step-Sibling Rivalry," *Single Parent,* June: 22–25.

Ward, Margaret, and Barbara Tremitiere
1991 "How Marriage and Special-Needs Adoption Coexist." Paper presented to the 16th North American Conference on Adoptable Children, Atlanta, Georgia, August.

Waterman, Jill
1986 "Family Dynamics of Incest with Young Children." In Kee MacFarlane, Jill Waterman with Shawn Conerly, Linda Damon, Michael Durfee, and Suzanne Long, *Sexual Abuse of Young Children: Evaluation and Treatment.* New York: Guilford.

Watson, Marguerite
1986 *Children of Domestic Violence: Programs and Treatment.* Edmonton: Alberta Social Services.

Weiler, Richard
1989 "The National Crisis in Literacy," *Perception,* 13(2): 29–31.

Weston, Kath
1991 *Families We Choose: Lesbians, Gays, Kinship.* New York: Columbia University Press.

Wexler, Judie Gaffin, and Deana Dorman Logan
1983 "Sources of Stress Among Women Police Officers," *Journal of Police Science and Administration,* 11: 46–53.

White, James M.
1989 "Marriage: A Developing Process." In K. Ishwaran, ed., *Family and Marriage: Cross-Cultural Perspectives.* Toronto: Wall & Thompson.

Wiehe, Vernon R., with Teresa Herring
1991 *Perilous Rivalry: When Siblings Become Abusive.* Lexington, MA: Lexington Books.

Wilson, Susannah J.
1990 "Alternatives to Traditional Marriage." In Maureen Baker (ed.), *Families Changing Trends in Canada,* 2nd ed. Toronto: McGraw-Hill Ryerson.

Wolfson, Lorne H.
1987 *The New Family Law.* Toronto: Random House.

Youniss, James
1980 *Parents and Peers in Social Development.* Chicago: University of Chicago Press.

Yoxen, Edward
1986 *Unnatural Selection? Coming to Terms with the New Genetics*. London: Heineman.

Zarzour, Kim
1987 "The Decline of Dating," *The Toronto Star,* 24 September: L1, L4.

Zelizer, Viviana A.
1985 *Pricing the Priceless Child: The Changing Social Value of Children*. New York: Basic Books.

INDEX

C

D

E

To the owner of this book

We hope that you have enjoyed *The Family Dynamic*, and we would like to know as much about your experiences as you would care to offer. Only through your comments and those of others can we learn how to make this a better text for future readers.

School ____________________ Your instructor's name ________________________

Course __________________ Was the text required? _____ Recommended? _____

1. What did you like the most about *The Family Dynamic?*

---

2. How useful was this text for your course?

---

3. Do you have any recommendations for ways to improve the next edition of this text?

---

4. In the space below or in a separate letter, please write any other comments you have about the book. (For example, please feel free to comment on reading level, writing style, terminology, design features, and learning aids.)

Optional

Your name _______________________________________ Date __________________

May Nelson Canada quote you, either in promotion for *The Family Dynamic* or in future publishing ventures?

Yes _____ No _____

Thanks!

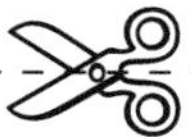

FOLD HERE

Canada Post Corporation / Société canadienne des postes

Postage paid
if mailed in Canada

Port payé
si posté au Canada

Business Reply

Réponse d'affaires

0107077099 01

TAPE SHUT

0107077099-M1K5G4-BR01

TAPE SHUT

Nelson Canada
College Editorial Department
1120 Birchmount Rd.
Scarborough, ON M1K 9Z9

PLEASE TAPE SHUT. DO NOT STAPLE.